EPICS OF DISAFFECTION:
THE DISSENTING HISTORIES OF TOLKIEN,
TOLSTOY AND E. P. THOMPSON

Epics of Disaffection is an exploration of the epic imagination. It brings a historian's sensibility and expertise to bear on four eccentric works of literary genius, each of a different genre, which underwent a metamorphosis in the course of composition, emerging as an account of a historical crisis – actual or fictional – set in a broader temporal context. Each acquired an epic theme, tone, and structure, becoming a narrative that contemplates human experience in the light not just of history but of eternity. The book links this thematic and formal convergence to the authors' personal encounter with history and politics, which in each case included frontline military service. The books are *dissenting histories*, and *epics of disaffection*, because the epic transformation was triggered in each case by a prophetic urge arising from the author's profound alienation from modernity and sense of being at the mercy of history.

Epics of Disaffection

The Dissenting Histories
of Tolkien, Tolstoy,
and E. P. Thompson

PAUL ROMNEY

Baltimore, MD

For Sharon and Dave

© 2022 by PAUL ROMNEY

All rights reserved. Copyright under Berne Convention, Universal Copyright Convention, and Pan-American Copyright Convention. No part of this book may be reproduced, stored in a retrieval system, and transmitted in any form, or by any means, electronic, mechanical, photocopying, recording or otherwise, without prior permission of the author.

ISBN 979-8-218-02223-5 (paper)

CONTENTS

PREFACE

My wife, Sharon Kingsland, suggested that I consider writing about three authors whose work had meant so much to me. She didn't expect this book, and neither did I. I thank Sharon, Jill Lake and David Aylward for reading the work in progress and giving me their advice, and Sharon for encouraging me to publish it.

Material first published in my article "'Great Chords': Politics and Romance in Tolstoy's *War and Peace*," *University of Toronto Quarterly*, 80(1), 2011, doi: 10.3138/UTQ.80.1.049, is © University of Toronto Press Incorporated 2010 and is reprinted by permission from University of Toronto Press (https://utpjournals.press).

Chapters 2 and 3 include material first published in my article "'A Particular Phase of History': Time Travel, Temporal Ambiguity, and the Pattern of History in *The Lord of the Rings*," *Lembas*, nr. 176, (Oct. 2016).

1

Introduction: Epics of Disaffection, Prophets of Alienation

My work is *not* a "novel" ...
J. R. R. Tolkien

What is "War and Peace"? It is not a novel ...
L. N. Tolstoy

The Making of the English Working Class can be read as a great historical novel ...
Michael Merrill

I'm not exactly sure that [*The Sykaos Papers*] is, in any recognised sense, a novel.
E. P. Thompson

E. M. Forster wrote: "Many novelists have the feeling for place ... Very few have the sense of space, and the possession of it ranks high in Tolstoy's divine equipment. Space is the lord of *War and Peace*, not time."[1] This understates the importance of time to *War and Peace*, perhaps because Forster was thinking about Tolstoy's masterpiece as a novel, but what he identified as an exceptional feeling for space is a key to the story's epic essence.

J. R. R. Tolkien gave equal billing to both dimensions when he described *The Lord of the Rings* as "a Frameless Picture: a search-

---

[1] E. M. Forster, *Aspects of the Novel* (Harmondsworth, UK: Penguin Books, 1962), 46-47.

light, as it were, on a brief episode in History, and on a small part of our Middle-earth, surrounded by the glimmer of limitless extensions in time and space."[2] He did not call his story an epic, but he may well have thought of it as one, since he compared it to Homer's *Iliad* (as Tolstoy did *War and Peace*).[3] He also complained of being burdened with "the epic temperament" — apparently more a curse than a blessing, since it was constantly thwarting his wish to bring the story to a speedy conclusion.[4] This was no joke, since he was meant to be writing a sequel to his children's novel *The Hobbit* and it had grown much longer than a children's story could reasonably be. It was in fact changing into something else, and how that happened is a primary topic of this book. All the works discussed here became epics despite their authors' first intention, and the ultimate question — the question that unites this book — is why that happened. We are about to study the epic temperament at work.

According to the political scientist Benedict Anderson, "within the limits of plausible argument, the most instructive comparisons … are those that surprise."[5] The four narratives discussed here belong to quite different genres. *War and Peace* is generally acclaimed as a classic novel, a pinnacle of the genre. Tolkien's story is a fantasy, remarkably elaborate by any standards but especially so for what began as a children's novel. It too is fiction, but in big bookstores it is more likely to be found in the Fantasy section than with Tolstoy's works on the shelves devoted to Literature; in fact, its popularity and influence are largely responsible for the fact that bookstores nowadays have a Fantasy section. My third writer, E. P. Thompson, achieved fame as a historian, not a novelist, and *The Making of the English Working Class* is not fiction but a deeply researched, thickly footnoted account of a moment in British history; yet it has been compared to *The Lord of the Rings* and *Moby Dick*. Ultimately, however, Thompson turned to fiction in order to frame what has authoritatively been called the "most complete single statement of his thought."[6] His fantasy, *The Sykaos*

---

[2] *The Letters of J. R. R. Tolkien* (ed. Humphrey Carpenter, Boston and New York: Houghton Mifflin, 2000: hereafter, *Letters*), 412.
[3] See below, 191 n2.
[4] *Letters*, 90.
[5] "Frameworks of Comparison," *London Review of Books*, 21 Jan. 2016, 18.
[6] Perry Anderson, "Diary," *London Review of Books*, 21 Oct. 1993, 24.

Papers, is quite different from Tolkien's, being a blend of political satire, science fiction and apocalyptic tragedy.

Different as they are, the four narratives are clearly alike in one respect: each is an outlier in its genre. It was Tolstoy's consciousness of transgressing generic norms that prompted him to deny that *War and Peace* was a novel, and the others are similarly deviant. My thesis is that each owes its singularity to its treatment of the elements mentioned by Tolkien: space and time, history and geography. Each story recounts a grand conflict with a scope and imaginative completeness that reaches beyond the personal and the mundane — the traditional terrain of the novel and of modern historical writing — to contemplate human experience in the light, not just of history, but of eternity. I call them *epics of disaffection*, and *dissenting histories*, because I contend that the metamorphosis was driven in each case by an urge to prophesy arising from the author's alienation from modernity.

What is an epic, and what gives it its distinctive breadth and depth? In *Tolstoy or Dostoevsky*, George Steiner contends that, "far more precisely than Joyce's *Ulysses*, *War and Peace* and *Anna Karenina* embody the resurgence of the epic mode, the re-entry into literature of tonalities, narrative practices, and forms of articulation that had declined from western poetics after the age of Milton." He defines the epic as "that form of poetic apprehension in which a moment of history *or* a body of religious myth is centrally engaged."[7]

Steiner makes a distinction between empirically grounded understanding of the past ("history") and the mythic accounts of human origins and ends that are the foundation of religion. Northrop Frye, however, sets the epic is set in a frame that unites the two — a frame he calls *secular scripture*, or "national stories, which as a rule shade insensibly from the legendary to the historical."[8] The Homeric heroes are glorious not just for their feats but for their association with both the gods and a critical moment in history, the conquest of Troy. Virgil's *Aeneid* traces the present glory of the *patria* to the divine favour visited on its mythic founder, the fugitive Trojan Aeneas.

---

[7] George Steiner, *Tolstoy or Dostoevsky: An Essay in the Old Criticism* (New York: Vintage Books, 1961), 9, 5 (my italics).
[8] Northrop Frye, *The Secular Scripture: A Study of the Structure of Romance* (Cambridge, MA: Harvard UP, 1976), 8.

Modern scholarship identifies a sub-genre of *dynastic epics*, which emulate the *Aeneid* by applying ancient myths to the glorification of modern rulers.[9] Virgil and his imitators celebrate the historical outcome more explicitly than the *Iliad* does, but they follow Homer in ascribing their heroes' prowess and destiny to divine favour. Even where divinities are thickest on the ground (or in the air), the narrative is focused on human destinies: thus *Paradise Lost*, which has only two mortal characters, recounts the origin of the tale of woe that is human history. These narratives, as poetic renderings of traditional oral accounts of the divinely-mediated origins of a people or polity, all engage a body of religious myth rather than a moment in history in its modern meaning.

But even if Steiner's distinction does not exactly fit the pre-modern epic, by offering a moment of history as a secular substitute for a body of religious myth it helps us bring modern texts within the ambit of the epic. Religious myth assumes the existence of divinity, which is not a matter of common consent. Committed as he was to the accurate description and interpretation of observable reality, Tolstoy could depict characters who believe in God, but he could not bring the divine into his narratives like the authors of the *Iliad* or *Paradise Lost*, epic poems in which deities are placed front and centre in the action. This problem applies equally to Thompson, and especially to his historical treatise; but even Tolkien, who had no inhibitions about depicting the supernatural and privately confided that *The Lord of the Rings* was "fundamentally religious and Catholic" in essence, tried to adapt his narrative to the predominantly secular sensibilities of modernity.[10] Engaging a moment of history poses no such challenge to modern inhibitions. Both *War and Peace*, as a historical novel, and Thompson's scholarly narrative engage a moment in history by definition. *The Sykaos Papers*, as a prophetic fantasy, recounts an imaginary history, but one grounded in contemporary reality.

What is remarkable is to find Tolkien, as quoted above, applying the term to a story full of monsters, magicians and fairy-tale creatures, which bears obvious traces of its birth as a children's novel. This is not a unique reference; and although he usually qualifies it as "feigned" or "imaginary" history, he also qualifies the qualifier by stating that his story relates an imaginary episode in

---

[9] Andrew Fichter, *Poets Historical: Dynastic Epic in the Renaissance* (New Haven and London: Yale UP, 1982).
[10] *Letters*, 172.

the history of our world, not an imaginary world.[11] Obviously, we will have to consider how far "history" means the same to him as to Tolstoy and Thompson. Taking his usage at face value, however, it suggests that all four narratives treat human experience in historical perspective. I have ascribed their epic transformation to their authors' urge to prophesy against modernity, but why did prophecy take that particular form? We need to establish how each narrative expresses not only its author's sense of history but also his engagement with the present.

To this end, I relate each narrative to the historical context of its production. This is relatively straightforward for Tolstoy, since *War and Peace* originated in his intention to write a novel addressing a contemporary crisis: Russia's predicament after its defeat in the Crimean War. In Thompson's case, his life-story and copious political writings make it easy to detect the impact of personal experience on his books. Tolkien's fantasy requires more thorough contextualization, because it is set at a greater distance from contemporary reality. However, there is one striking resemblance between all three writers. Their encounter with history in the making included front-line warfare: in Tolstoy's case the siege of Sevastopol, in Tolkien's the battle of the Somme, and in Thompson's the Italian campaign of 1943-45. I will consider how these experiences, and the broader alienation they nourished, captured each author's imagination and drove it towards epic expression.

However, this book is not just about the process that I have called epic transformation and its origins in the personality and experience of three writers. It is also about the outcome of that process: what one might call the epic effect. I will argue that all four narratives engage what Steiner calls a moment of history — in fact, the same sort of moment, a world-historical crisis — and that this is essential to their nature as epics of disaffection. But another marker, as I mentioned, is that the narrative reaches beyond history to contemplate human experience in the light of eternity. This aspect is manifest in the intrusion of themes and devices more typical of the epic than of modern genres. Strikingly, notwithstanding the constraints of modern positivism, with its privileging of empirical knowledge over intuitive understanding, these include the depiction or suggestion of phenomena beyond everyday cognition.

---

[11] See below, 69.

My investigation of this phenomenon will be guided by E. M. Forster's quirky but illuminating inquiry, in *Aspects of the Novel*, into the intrusion into that genre of what he calls *prophecy*. Exploring this topic, we must remember that, just as the transformative process is unique in each case, the sources of the epic effect can be expected to differ from one work to another. What it takes to produce an epic resonance in a work of empirical history is not necessarily what is required to produce it in a children's fairy-story.

Accordingly, my analysis is adapted to each individual case. For *The Lord of the Rings*, the first challenge is to show how a story crammed with fairy-tale characters and magical effects acquired characteristics that warrant taking it seriously as a comment on human destiny. This requires a close historical analysis of the process of composition, including the use of Tolkien's drafts, notes and correspondence to relate the transformation of the narrative to the advent and progress of the Second World War. It seems likely that the story would have taken a very different course without that stimulus, if Tolkien had managed to finish it at all. I establish the broader context of its composition by relating Tolkien's world-view to the anti-modernist strain of British social thought exemplified in the later nineteenth century by the artist and poet William Morris, whose hatred of capitalism and imperialism influenced Thompson too, and I discuss Tolkien's theory of art in order to explain the relevance of his fictional history to human experience.

War and Peace poses a different set of problems, since its status as a monument of nineteenth-century realism has obscured the ways in which the narrative transgresses the bounds of realism. I analyse its structure, characterization and style in order to expose the techniques of Tolstoyan realism as those of the conjuror or confidence trickster, employed to mislead as much as to inform. I then show how Tolstoy, using those techniques, flirts with fantasy and plants a quest romance at the heart of his narrative. Comparison of the published text with an interim version reveals the deep deliberation with which Tolstoy employed those devices.

I approach Thompson primarily via structural and thematic analysis. Like Tolkien's story, *The Making of the English Working Class* emerged from a publisher's commission to write a very different book; but here no close analysis is needed to demonstrate the epic transformation. I concentrate instead on the elements, so exceptional in scholarly discourse, which might warrant comparison to *The Lord of the Rings* and *Moby Dick*.

A similar approach suits *The Sykaos Papers*, which transforms from Swiftian satire to comic novel to apocalyptic tragedy before the reader's eyes. Thompson's fantasy has not been dismissed with disdain as Tolkien's has; but on casual reading it does not fit well with the rest of Thompson's work, and its peculiarities have caused embarrassment. However, its apparent gaucheries have counterparts in the other narratives and are arguably a feature of the epic transformation. I will contend that, in the end, Thompson's satirical fantasy owes less to Swift than to Milton.

The epic vision

My project does not require me to attempt a definition of "the epic," still less "genre." I need only reveal substantial affinities between my four subject narratives and a set of poems traditionally known as epics. Typically, such poems recount the deeds of divinely favoured heroes at a critical moment in the past — one that is important, and possibly flattering, to the poet's audience. As conquerors of Troy, the heroes of the *Iliad* and the *Odyssey* are the founding heroes of Greece's glory, and so the Homeric epics shed a vicarious lustre on audiences who saw themselves as those heroes' posterity. The *Aeneid* combines the heroic wandering theme of the *Odyssey* with the epic battle theme of the *Iliad* in recounting the adventures of the Trojan prince Aeneas, beginning with his escape from the wreck of his city and culminating in his arrival in Italy, defeat of the native ruler in battle, and marriage to the native princess Lavinia. Aeneas and Lavinia were mythic forebears of the early kings of Rome, and so Virgil's epic bore on the rise of its author's fatherland; but Virgil composed his poem not just to celebrate Rome's heroic origins but to glorify its current ruler, the emperor Augustus, who had restored political stability after decades of civil strife.

These features became typical of the dynastic epic. Some sixteen hundred years later, Edmund Spenser acknowledged the example of earlier "poets historicall" — he mentions Homer, Virgil, and the Italians Ariosto and Tasso — when he glorified the similarly restorative reign of Queen Elizabeth I of England. *The Faerie Queene* celebrated the descent of "Gloriana," through the heroes of King Arthur's Britain, from rulers dating back to Brutus, a supposed grandson of Aeneas and mythic founder of the British nation.[12] This conscious imitation across the centuries engendered a set of "epic conventions", including the poet's preliminary invocation of divine aid in his grand enterprise; the opening of the narrative *in medias res* ("in the midst of the action" — in Spenser's words, the epic poet "thrusteth into the middest, euen where it most concerneth him"[13]); the elaborate similes (aids to memory which also slowed down the narrative, making it easier for listeners to follow an oral performance); and the Catalogue (for instance, Homer's detailed tally of the forces that sailed against Troy, or Spenser's capsule history of the long line of kings founded by Brutus), which imparted amplitude and historical solidity to the tale.

Writing in the 1890s, the Scottish scholar W. P. Ker distinguished between the Homeric epics and literary imitations such as the *Aeneid* in terms of their perspective on the past. The former, as genuine folk epics distilled from oral folk poems, projected the spirit and values of a heroic age. They were not meant to impart a particular view of history, and the great historic moment served mainly as a backdrop that added lustre to the heroes whose deeds they depicted. The latter, which we have called dynastic epics but Ker called "artificial" or "manufactured" epics, reached back to a bygone heroic age to glorify, by association or analogy, a ruler of the author's own time and place. In them historical interpretation was of prime importance, because the hero was not just an object of admiration and emulation but a man or woman of destiny.[14] Ker's distinction has obvious relevance to the *Odyssey*, where the Trojan War is indeed no more than a background to the travails of the hero and his family, but arguably the *Iliad*, set amid the siege of Troy and very deliberately rooted in the past by the Catalogue, is different. In view of its antiquity, we cannot say whether or not it was originally composed to glorify some ruler, or if it was applied to that purpose at any point in its history, but it certainly spoke to its audience of the supposed origins of their glory.

---

[12] Edmund Spenser, *The Faerie Queene*, ed. Thomas P. Roche, Jr., with the assistance of C. Patrick O'Donnell, Jr. (London: Penguin Books, 1978), 15.
[13] Spenser, *Faerie Queene*, 16-17.
[14] W. P. Ker, *Epic and Romance* (London: MacMillan, 1897), 20-32. Ariosto's *Orlando Furioso* features a warrior-maiden whose progeny is catalogued at the appropriate point in the story. Of Trojan descent herself, she will give rise to several lines of rulers including, the princely house to which Ariosto's patron belonged.

As we noted, though, the historicity of the epic differs significantly from modern ideas of the historical. The ascendancy of positivism is reflected in our sharp distinction between *history*, a record of past events based on factual evidence, and *myth*, a story with little or no basis in proven fact. But both are stories that purport to illuminate the human condition: how we and our world came into being, why things are as they are, and why we are who we are, as individuals and as members of a community. Modern secular culture has engendered scholarly disciplines devoted to ascertaining the truth of the past by unearthing and interpreting evidence bearing on the validity of commonly accepted stories and beliefs, but the further back you go the less evidence you will find. The oldest, most fundamental stories — stories that tell of the creation of the world and of mankind and explain its purpose — are myths, whose acceptance depends on faith and on the authority imparted by hundreds and thousands of years of tradition. And since the history of our kind and our world must be continuous from whatever you imagine to have been the Beginning, accounts of that event have traditionally appeared at the head of the sequences of stories that constitute the histories of the peoples of the world: the "national stories" discussed by Northrop Frye, which "as a rule shade insensibly from the legendary to the historical." Two of my authors spoke to this connection. According to Tolkien, "History often resembles 'Myth', because they are both ultimately of the same stuff." Tolstoy observes in *War and Peace* that "in historical events ... the primeval conception of a cause was the will of the gods, succeeded later on by the will of those who stand in the historical foreground — the heroes of history."[15]

Tolstoy's remark is particularly germane, since the classical epic occupies a place in the story sequence where gods and heroes rub shoulders. Frye notes a characteristic staging in space and time that matches that location: the spatial site of the action is typically "a mediterranean known world in the midst of a boundlessness ... and between the upper and lower gods." By *mediterranean*, Frye means what in Old English is called *Middangeard* and in Old Norse *Midgard*: that is, the imagined location of the human world in relation to those inhabited by the beings that ultimately regulate human destiny. As to time, the action has a distinctive

---

15 J. R. R. Tolkien, "On Fairy-Stories," in Tolkien, *Tree and Leaf* (London: Unwin Books, 1964), 31; WP IV.ii.1.

location which flows from its inherently dual and cyclical time-scheme. "The cycle has two main rhythms: the life and death of the individual, and the slower social rhythm which, in the course of years ... brings cities and empires to their rise and fall. The steady vision of the latter movement is possible only to gods."[16]

The epic contemplates human destiny in historical perspective, then; but not as a historical chronicle does. Aristotle commended Homer for focusing in the *Iliad* on a crucial episode in the struggle against Troy rather than recounting the entire history of the war. This made the epic as much as possible like tragedy, the dramatic form that was Aristotle's poetic ideal.[17] In accordance with Aristotle's precepts, the epic typically takes the form of a story that forms part of a larger story — or, in Tolkien's words quoted earlier, "a brief episode in history ... surrounded by the glimmer of limitless extensions." It relates a critical moment in a larger history or "total action" that is cyclical in nature. The *Iliad* takes place at Troy, but it is part of a total action that begins and ends in Greece; the *Odyssey* is also set within that larger story. Likewise, the total action of the *Aeneid* begins with the fall of Troy and ends with the ascendancy of a new Troy, the city and empire of Rome, and the total action of which *Paradise Lost* recounts a part begins and ends in heaven. Frye sees the epic as a type of "encyclopaedic form" — a wide-ranging or composite work, touched with prophecy, which presents a broad or total vision of the human condition. It tells of a moment in history, but it also hints at a broader pattern of history which that moment establishes or epitomizes.

Frye's conception of the epic as a mirror of human experience and a vessel of prophecy is in harmony with the notion that my three authors were swept towards the epic by the urge to prophesy, but the relevance of the epic to the human condition was not to be taken for granted at the time they were writing. In the nineteenth century the ascendancy of literary realism, and of the novel as a means of representing the human condition, consigned older narrative modes to what E. P. Thompson called (in a different context) the condescension of posterity.[18] In the 1850s, Nathaniel Hawthorne felt constrained to call his stories romances rather

---

[16] Northrop Frye, *Anatomy of Criticism: Four Essays* (Princeton: Princeton UP, 1957), 55-61, 315-24 (quotations, 318-19).
[17] Aristotle, *Poetics*, trans. Malcolm Heath (London: Penguin, 1996) 10:1-5.
[18] See below, 203.

than novels on account of their fanciful elements. In his Foreword to *The House of the Seven Gables*, he declared that the novel aimed at "a very minute fidelity, not merely to the possible, but to the probable and ordinary course of man's experience," but the romance offered more latitude. It must, as a work of art, be true to human nature, but it could "present that truth under circumstances, to a great extent, of the writer's own choosing or creation." The romancer might "so manage his atmospherical medium as to bring out or mellow the lights and deepen and enrich the shadows of the picture," although he would be wise "to make a very moderate use of the privileges here stated, and, especially, to mingle the Marvellous rather as a slight, delicate, and evanescent flavor, than as any portion of the actual substance of the dish offered to the Public."

Obviously, the epic, with its population of gods, monsters and sorcerers, could not be judged by the standards of the modern novel, but it might meet Hawthorne's criterion. Accordingly, in the 1890s we find W. P. Ker distinguishing between the realism of Homer or Shakespeare and what he derides as "the premeditated and self-assertive realism of the authors who take viciously to common life by way of protest against the romantic extreme." The former is rooted, "not in a critical theory about the proper matter of literature, but in dramatic imagination," and above all in vividly imagined characters.[19] As long as the characters are lifelike — as Macbeth and Macduff, Achilles and Hector, surely are — the circumstances must necessarily be a faithful depiction of the human condition; thus the Three Witches do not compromise the realism of *Macbeth*, nor the intervention of competing deities that of the *Iliad*. The poet and scholar Lascelles Abercrombie, later Tolkien's colleague at the universities of Leeds and Oxford, seconded Ker's argument for a "broad" understanding of realism:

> It means that the story must be founded deep in the general experience of men. A decisive campaign is not, for the epic poet, any more real than a legend full of human truth. All that the name of Caesar suggests is extremely important for mankind; so is all that the name of Satan suggests: Satan, in this sense, is as real as Caesar.[20]

---

[19] Ker, *Epic and Romance*, 19.
[20] Lascelles Abercrombie; *The Epic* (London: Martin Secker, 1914), quoted in *The Epic: Developments in Criticism. A Casebook*, ed. R. P. Draper (Basingstoke: MacMillan, 1990), 110. See also James Bridges, "Lascelles

To Ker and Abercrombie, then, realism resides, not in minute reproduction of the details of daily life, but in fidelity to human nature. Fantasy is not the antithesis of reality but a special way of imagining it.

Mention of Satan brings *Paradise Lost* to mind, and Milton's poem epitomizes this idea. First published in 1667, it is an extraordinary attempt to put flesh on the bones of a Biblical story that purports to explain the human predicament: the story of the Garden of Eden and the Fall of Man. Milton sets out to imagine not only the motives of the various characters — divine, angelic and human — but also their relations and even their conversations. The narrative begins with the rebel angels sprawling defeated in a fiery lake in Hell, their newly created prison, and the action springs from Satan's plan to wreak revenge upon their conqueror by corrupting his newly created human pets. Milton's story *humanizes* its deities, and in doing so *naturalizes* the supernatural — although Milton has a tough time with God, whose omnipotence and omniscience are hard to humanize. Homer had an easier job with his all-too-human deities, but we can think of the Homeric poems too as "naturalizing" dramatizations of myth — attempts to render a people's defining stories in terms that make sense to the author's contemporaries. *Paradise Lost* imagines the very moment when human history supposedly begins, and the Homeric epics, as I have noted, are set against a crucial moment in the history of the ancient Greeks.

In order to set up a contrast between Tolstoy and Dostoyevsky as epic and tragic poets, George Steiner pairs his definition of the epic with a contrasting conception of tragedy as "a vision of life which derives its principles of meaning from the infirmity of man's estate, from what Henry James called the 'imagination of disaster.'"[21] To E. M. W. Tillyard, however, the epic is no less concerned than tragedy with "man's estate." In Tillyard's view, the essential difference is that tragedy is inherently timeless, whereas the epic depicts the human condition in historical perspective: "It is when the tragic intensity is included in the group-consciousness of an age that the epic attains its full growth." Tillyard conceives of the

---

Abercrombie". *The Literary Encyclopedia.* [www.litencyc.com/php/-speople.php?rec=true&UID=4981, accessed 19 August 2011]; Humphrey Carpenter, *J. R. R. Tolkien: A Biography* (Boston: Houghton Mifflin, 2000), 114.

[21] Steiner, *Tolstoy or Dostoevsky,* 5.

epic poet as the mouthpiece of his age, a role that requires a comprehensive grasp of reality: the poet "must express the feelings of a large group of people living in or near his own time" and "must seem to know everything ... he must also span a corresponding width of emotions, if possible one embracing the simplest sensualities at one end and a sense of the numinous at the other." This formula emphasizes the comprehensive range of epic, embracing the natural and the supernatural, the real and the fantastic — in short, the human condition in the widest perspective. Across two generations, it echoes Ker's affirmation of the inclusiveness of epic poetry: "*tragical, comical, historical, pastoral* are not terms sufficiently various to denote the variety of the *Iliad* and the *Odyssey*."[22]

Tillyard's definition of the epic serves our purpose in several ways. His insistence on both the historicity of the epic and the importance of a sense of the numinous affirms that history and religious myth belong together in this context. Secondly, his use of the term *numinous* rather than *religious* is useful in adapting the concept of the epic to more modern narratives. Coming from the Latin *numen*, meaning a lesser, place-bound deity, it suggests the supernatural without implying the existence of an all-controlling divinity or privileging any special body of dogma. As I mentioned, even Tolkien, a devout Christian, purposely excluded overt religious associations from a story that is crammed with evocations of the numinous. Instead of looking for what Steiner calls "religious myth" in the other three narratives — a masterpiece of realist fiction, a work of academic history, and a thoroughly secular political satire — we will be alert to hints of things not dreamt of in Horatio's philosophy.

Modern prose narratives are bound to differ in many ways from poetic narratives issuing from earlier and very different states of civilization and society, but to Tillyard the epic was ultimately a matter of spirit as much as form.[23] Accordingly, he found what he called "the epic strain" not only in Joseph Conrad's *Nostromo*, a story of heroism and revolution set in South America, but in Arnold Bennett's *The Old Wives' Tale*, a chronicle of the lives of two middle-class Victorian sisters set mainly in the English Midlands. James Joyce's *Ulysses*, on the other hand, although ingeniously

---

[22] E. M. W. Tillyard, *The Epic Strain in the English Novel* (London: Chatto & Windus, 1958), 15-16; Ker, *Epic and Romance*, 18 (italics in original).

[23] E. M. W. Tillyard, *The English Epic and its Background* (London: Chatto & Windus, 1954), 4-13; Tillyard, *Epic Strain*, 14-17.

modelled on the *Odyssey*, lacked the epic spirit. In Tillyard's view, its Homeric parallels were academic rather than fundamental; they did not mean anything to "the intelligent, unprejudiced, unacademic reader."[24] In contrast to *Ulysses*, the four narratives considered here are stories of heroic resistance to evil, which depict the human condition in historical perspective while hinting at a total vision of history.

Teleology and Contingency

A total vision of history implies a foretelling of the future, and I have suggested that in all four cases the epic transformation was driven by an urge to prophesy. It is no coincidence that each of my writers came to exert a remarkable influence over public opinion. Tolstoy and Tolkien each became the object of an international cult. Thompson, already a cult figure in intellectual circles, achieved wider fame in the 1980s as a campaigner for nuclear disarmament in Europe. Each in his own way exemplifies Tillyard's conception of the epic poet as the mouthpiece of his age. But what did these prophets have to say?

Andrew Fichter defines the dynastic epic as a poem whose author, imitating Virgil, "speaks of the past as if it were a future — a future to which he and his heroes are granted access only in extraordinary moments of prophetic vision during which the scroll of fate is unrolled and the divine plan is for an instant revealed." The narrative future (the poet's own time) is presented as a Golden Age, its seeds sown in the heroic struggles the poem recounts.[25] I am talking of something different — a prophetic intimation of decline, in which the Golden Age is assigned to a past that may be irretrievable.

Prophecy, after all, is typically an expression of alienation from the present, a call to repent lest the worst befall or because it has befallen. Even if the prophet foresees a better or even glorious future, that future is not the poet's own time and may not be imminent. In *Paradise Lost*, composed when Milton's hopes of a glorious new political order had been dashed by the downfall of the English Commonwealth and the restoration of the Stuart monarchy, the future is foretold from the perspective of Adam and Eve. The whole grim tale of human history must be endured before the

---

24 Tillyard, *Epic Strain*, 126-67, 171-98 (quotation, 192).
25 Fichter, *Poets Historical*, 1.

Day of Judgment brings relief to the righteous, and Milton offers no hope that the Day is nigh. Fichter's poets assume a prophetic pose in order to shed lustre on the present; Milton assumes a prophetic pose to offer consolation for a blighted present.

There is little or no Christian consolation on offer in any of the stories discussed here — even Tolkien dispenses, rather, the consolation of imagining a world in which individuals can make a difference. I might call that escapist were it not also true of *War and Peace* and *The Making of the English Working Class*. (Thompson's other story is less optimistic.) But all three writers are prophets of alienation. Like *Paradise Lost*, their narratives, rooted in a profound disenchantment with modernity, are epics of disaffection.

Comparing *War and Peace* and *The Lord of the Rings* with *Paradise Lost* may seem perverse, since Milton's poem is a response to defeat while Tolstoy's and Tolkien's stories climax in victory. The apparent paradox is clarified by David Quint's study of what he calls the politicization of the epic. Quint identifies two epic traditions: epics of the victors, a category that would include Fichter's class of dynastic epics, and epics of the defeated. The former, dominant tradition is characterized by a linear, teleological plot, which presents the triumph of the hero and the ascendancy of his illustrious progeny as predestined and permanent, and thus in two distinct senses as the End of History. The latter tends to ascribe the lamented defeat to historical contingencies, *ipso facto* precluding any presumption of predestination in the outcome.

Quint's prototype of such epics is Lucan's *Pharsalia*, an account of recent Roman history which ascribes the Caesarian ascendancy not to the divine favour that Virgil shows at work in the *Aeneid* but to accidents of fortune. Quint sees this world-view reflected in a digressive, repetitious, narrative structure, typical of the romance genre, which fits the idea of history as just one damn thing after another, not as patterned or directed. Significantly, though, Quint also includes *Paradise Lost* among his "losers' epics", although it is hardly digressive in the manner of the romance and is imbued with a Christian teleology. Milton dwells on mankind's present suffering, however, and defers the end of history to the indefinite future.[26]

---

[26] David Quint, *Epic and Empire: Politics and Generic Form from Virgil to Milton* (Princeton, N.J.: Princeton UP), 1993.

My project is different from Quint's. I am not studying epic poems, or the epic as a genre, let alone tracing a tradition where one epic poet imitates and invokes earlier epics to invest his subject-matter with similar meaning; rather, I am studying works of different genres in order to reveal affinities arising from the authors' epic temperament, which I relate to each author's world-view. However, the terms in which Quint characterizes his two types of epic serve my purpose in two respects. Firstly, they alert us to the ways in which Tolstoy and Tolkien — and Thompson too, in *The Making of the English Working Class* — subvert the apparent triumphalism of their narrative. (*The Sykaos Papers* does not project even a delusive triumphalism.) More broadly, in each of the works discussed here, the epic transformation manifests the author's historical sensibility. Each work turned into an epic because the author's sense of history inspired him to cast his prophecy as a narrative not just about individuals but about the world they inhabit — a world, moreover, which each author intended his readers to recognize as their own. Accordingly, I emphasize the character of each narrative as a response to history and politics. Quint's linkage between a political outlook and a view of history — his opposition of triumphal teleology and historical contingency — is relevant to that discussion.

We have, then, four essentially historical narratives, each projecting its author's alienation from modernity — we may think of them as dissenting, or oppositional, histories. Tolkien's story is the capstone of a "total action" or "national story" in Northrop Frye's sense, albeit a made-up one. *The Making of the English Working Class* is an academic history of revolutionary design: it treats a well-known set of events from a completely novel perspective, asserting the cardinal importance of facts which other historians scarcely registered and of people they disdained. *The Sykaos Papers* is speculative history, which takes the author's own time and place as its starting point and imagines how its history might unfold, but it is fictional in being about imaginary characters and partly about an imaginary world in a distant galaxy which some of them call home. *War and Peace* starts off as a novel, but halfway through it begins to sprout didactic essays challenging the conventional view of its historical setting. By the time that happens, it has already acquired flecks of the numinous which might have constrained Nathaniel Hawthorne to deny that it was a novel — as indeed Tolstoy did.

My discussion begins with *The Lord of the Rings* for two reasons. Firstly, it is packed with the stock character-types and situations of epic and therefore constitutes a useful model against which to measure the other three. It fulfils Aristotle's ideal of a unified plot set in a larger action; the site of the action is close enough to Frye's "mediterranean known world" that Tolkien called it Middle-earth after the eponymous *Middangeard;* [27] and it presents us with heroes and monsters galore, as well as occasional hints at higher powers who, if not pulling the strings, are certainly jogging the pinball machine. Secondly, Tolkien applied his expertise as a literary scholar to the vindication of his own art, frequently using the terms *myth* and *history* in doing so. Tolkien on Tolkien provides a useful entry to some of the themes discussed here.

A heroic romance. An anti-heroic novel. A history book. A political satire. How is it that they touch the same place in the soul? The question arises, not from a theory, but from an intuition of affinity between very different narratives. After discussion of the individual texts and their contexts, a final chapter contemplates the prophetic urge that forced my authors onto the terrain of the epic and traces it to their sense of powerlessness in the face of history.

---

[27] *Letters*, 220.

2

The Lord of the Rings: A Journey in Space and Time

The Lord of the Rings is now so embedded in our culture that it is hard to imagine the sensation it made when it first appeared.[1] Tolkien had conceived it as a sequel to a children's adventure story called *The Hobbit, or There and Back Again*, which he had published many years earlier, and it was presented to the public in this light. A sequel to *The Hobbit* was naturally expected to be like *The Hobbit*, and so it was, up to a point; but it was so long that it had to be published serially in three large volumes, each costing more than a typical adult novel. As such, it evoked strong responses from the start. Reviewing the third volume in the *New York Times*, W. H. Auden could remember few books about which he had had such violent arguments. "Nobody seems to have a moderate opinion: either, like myself, people find it a masterpiece of its genre or they cannot abide it."[2]

The Hobbit is a brilliantly inventive and captivating fairy-story peopled with an assortment of magical — or at least non-human — beings, including wicked goblins (or orcs) and trolls, benign elves, talking eagles, a bear-man, giant spiders (who also talk), and a

---

[1] Unless otherwise indicated, all citations of *The Lord of the Rings* refer to the 2nd edition (3 vols., Boston: Houghton Mifflin, 1965). Citations refer to *The Fellowship of the Ring* as FR, *The Two Towers* as TT and *The Return of the King* as RK.

[2] W. H. Auden, "At the End of the Quest, Victory," *New York Times*, 22 Jan. 1956 (http://www.nytimes.com/1956/01/22/books/tolkien-king.html).

dragon, as well as hobbits, a small humanoid people of the author's invention. There are human beings (called *men*) too, and the wizard Gandalf. The hero, Bilbo Baggins, goes on a quest with Gandalf and thirteen dwarves (not *dwarfs*, the orthodox plural form of *dwarf*) to recover a kingdom and treasure which the dwarves had lost many years earlier to a marauding dragon. The quest succeeds, and Bilbo returns home rich (not that he was hard-up to start with). He also has a magic ring, which he found on his travels under curious circumstances. He prizes it highly because it makes its wearer invisible.

The sequel begins in the same jocular vein as its forerunner, like an adult talking to small but precocious children. Soon, however, it acquires a thematic breadth and bleakness of mood that force a change in tone. The plot takes off from the discovery that Bilbo's ring has other powers, useful only for evil: it is indeed a talisman of evil, forged long ago by Sauron, the Dark Lord, as a means to world dominion. It was taken from him in a great battle, but now his power has revived and he is seeking it. To foil him, it must be destroyed by throwing it into the volcano in the heart of Sauron's realm of Mordor where it was made. As the quest proceeds, it appears that even success must entail the eternal loss of much that is good and beautiful.

This transformation gave the story a hybrid nature that made it difficult to pigeon-hole. As the themes of universal peril and loss emerge, the narrative takes on an antiquated grandiloquence reminiscent of the late nineteenth-century, knights-in-shining-armour type of novel for youngsters that originated, perhaps, in the medieval romances of Sir Walter Scott. On top of this, it is encased in a metafictional paraphernalia that seemed to some early readers to reek of an Oxford professor's self-indulgent whimsy. It is prefaced by a gazetteer-like sketch — complete with map — of the history, geography, economy and institutions of the Shire, the hobbits' bucolic homeland, purportedly based on books of lore dating from the time of the story. It ends with five Appendices, covering more than a hundred pages, which summarize the fictional history of Tolkien's imaginary world and discuss some of the languages and calendars used by its denizens. Each volume had a fold-out map tipped in at the back, illustrating that world in abundant detail.

There comes a point, some three-quarters of the way through the story, when Sauron's army starts bombarding the city of Minas Tirith with the severed heads of its slain defenders, some crushed and shapeless, others cruelly disfigured, but many of them all too familiar to their demoralized comrades and all of them branded with Sauron's token of the Lidless Eye. By this time, it might seem, *The Lord of the Rings* has long ceased to be a children's story. However, a generation that had lived through two world wars and the Great Depression, and was schooled to judge prose fiction by the standards of the realist novel, found it hard to take seriously any story peopled by fairy-tale creatures or talking animals except as a satire like George Orwell's *Animal Farm*. Tolkien's story was not such a book. By adult standards it displayed an authorial sensibility that seemed distinctly old-fashioned in its moral simplicity, lack of irony, and hints at a guiding Providence. Instead of locating evil in the human soul or human institutions, it externalized it in the form of Sauron and his Ring of Power. The characters were stock types, the heroes being very, very good, the villains horrid, and (with one major exception) only Denethor and Boromir, two secondary characters, revealing any hint of moral ambiguity. Add nostalgic ruralism and a happy ending, and you had a book whose bulk and pretentiousness seemed grotesquely at odds with its intellectual emptiness.

Auden discerned an ideological aspect to these objections. Some people, he thought, disapproved of Heroic Quests and Imaginary Worlds on principle, feeling that they could only be light, escapist reading. He maintained that Tolkien had outdone any previous writer in reconciling his fantasy with contemporary perceptions of historical and social reality. This was partly owing to the loving care with which Tolkien had delineated the geography, history and cultures of his imaginary world: it was not our world, but it was "a world of intelligible law, not mere wish," in which the reader's sense of the credible was never violated. It was, furthermore, a politically rational world, in which the characters' actions were governed by a comprehensible logic.

For Auden, then, the story passed W. P. Ker's test of realism, but the American critic Edmund Wilson denounced it as juvenile trash. Other commentators over the decades, including E. P. Thompson, have favoured the term *infantile*.[3] Michael Moorcock, a writer of

---

[3] Edmund Wilson, "Oo, Those Awful Orcs!" *The Nation*, 182 (14 Apr. 1956) <http://www.jrrvf.com/sda/critiques/The_Nation.html> (accessed Oct. 23, 2002); Robert M. Adams, "The Hobbit Habit," *New York Review of Books*, 24 Nov. 1977 <www.nybooks.com/articles/8321>, reprinted in Neil D. Isaacs and Rose Zimbardo, ed., *Tolkien: New Critical Perspectives* (Lexington, KY: UP of Kentucky, 1981); Pullman quoted in Laura Miller, "Far from Narnia: Philip Pullman's Secular Fantasy for Children," *New Yorker*, 26 Dec. 2005

pointedly un-Tolkienian fantasy, harmonizes these nuances: "*The Lord of the Rings* is much more deep-rooted in its infantilism than a good many of the more obviously juvenile books it influenced. It is *Winnie-the-Pooh* posing as an epic." From different angles, all these remarks target the "escapist" quality of *The Lord of the Rings*: its supposed avoidance of moral ambiguity and complexity, and its apparent purpose of affording consolation in the face of despair. Thus Moorcock mocks the book for its "consolatory orthodoxy," which asks no questions of the "white men in grey clothing who somehow have a handle on what is best for us."[4]

As the year 2000 approached, several opinion polls dismayed the literary establishment by placing *The Lord of the Rings* first among twentieth-century novels in readers' affection or esteem. One commentator blamed "hard-core Tolkien addicts who've elevated his books to the status of a cult." Another, the cultural critic Germaine Greer, remarked: "It has been my nightmare that Tolkien would turn out to be the most influential writer of the twentieth century. The bad dream has materialized."[5]

By now, however, the chorus of disparagement was evoking an increasingly resolute pushback from a "Tolkien industry" of growing size and sophistication. A sympathetic study of Tolkien, published in response to the polls, grouped him with Orwell, Kurt Vonnegut and William Golding as war veterans who had resorted to fantasy in order to grapple with the great public and personal traumas of an era of world war and totalitarian dictatorship. Another Tolkien specialist paired him with James Joyce as "fellow mythmakers" and asserted that the disarray in which his heroes

---

<www.newyorker.com/archive/2005/12/26/051226fa_fact?current-Page-=all>; Matthew Hodgart, "Kicking the Hobbit," *New York Review of Books*, 4 May 1967 <www.nybooks.com/articles/12093>; E. P. Thompson, "America's Europe: A Hobbit Among Gandalfs," *The Nation*, 24 Jan. 1981, 69-70; Jenny Turner, "Reasons for Liking Tolkien," *London Review of Books*, 15 Nov. 2001 (All web pages viewed 23 Oct. 2012.)

4 Michael Moorcock, "Epic Pooh". This essay has appeared in print and online in different versions. I consulted <www.znaksagite.com/-diskusije//viewtopic.php?t=3469&highlight=> (accessed 23 Oct. 2012).

5 Andrew Rissik, "Middle Earth, Middlebrow," *The Guardian*, Sept. 2, 2000 (www.guardian.co.uk/books/2000/sep/02/jrrtolkien.classics> (viewed 22 Aug. 2012); Greer quoted in Julian Dibbell, "Lord of the Geeks," *Village Voice*, 5 June 2001 <www.villagevoice.com/2001-06-05/news/lord-of-the-geeks/> (viewed 20 Aug. 2012).

find the Shire on returning from their adventure represents "a dystopian mini-state worthy of Orwell or [Anthony] Burgess."[6]

Neither set of comparisons is really convincing. Tolkien's status as a veteran of the First World War is a fact of cardinal importance, although I am going to argue that it was his experience of the Second World War that was crucial to the shaping of *The Lord of the Rings*. However, the emotions his story evokes are surely very different from those aroused by the dystopian fantasies of Orwell, Golding and Vonnegut: their theme is the crushing of hope, Tolkien's is its survival. The other comparisons lack proportion: one likens what is "academic" (to quote E. M. W. Tillyard) in Joyce with what is crucial in Tolkien, while to compare Tolkien's account of "The Scouring of the Shire" with *Nineteen Eighty-Four* or *A Clockwork Orange* is to liken a molehill to a mountain. *The Lord of the Rings* can be fully appreciated only in the light of its author's personality, beliefs and purposes; and insisting on the modernity of writings that are profoundly anti-modern is not the way to go.

This chapter describes how Tolkien's epic narrative emerged out of his initial intention to write a children's novel. It takes a historical approach, tracing the course of composition from start to finish and relating it to the advent, course and aftermath of the Second World War, which unfolded as Tolkien wrote. Having shown how the war helped to infuse Tolkien's fantasy with a scope and verisimilitude that are essential to its epic character as a narrative of a historical moment which epitomizes the pattern of history, it concludes by discussing the story as an expression of Tolkien's world-view, with special attention to the Elves as a vessel of numinous effect and religious ideology.

Tolkien's legendarium

The Lord of the Rings was composed between 1937 and 1949, and its themes and shape were strongly influenced by the great events of those years. It did not originate as a response to those events, though, but as something much more mundane. *The Hobbit* was a commercial success, and its publisher, Stanley Unwin, wanted a sequel. Tolkien was reluctant to write one. He had exhausted his ideas about hobbits and, besides, *The Hobbit* ends with Bilbo living

---

[6] Tom Shippey, *J. R. R. Tolkien: Author of the Century* (Boston and New York: Houghton Mifflin, 2000), viii, xxx; Verlyn Flieger, *A Question of Time: J. R. R. Tolkien's Road to Faërie* (Kent, OH, and London: Kent State UP, 1997), 7, 25.

happily ever after in the home he had precipitately abandoned to go treasure-hunting with the dwarves. What Tolkien really wanted to publish was a corpus of curious, elegiac tales of a quasi-mythological nature, some in a spare prose and others in lusher verse, which he had been writing and re-writing for twenty years. He sent a bundle to Unwin.[7]

Tolkien's tales *were* a response to great events, but an oddly oblique one. He had begun them while recovering from trench fever contracted on the Western Front during the First World War. Full of war and battle, they are dominated by a sense of loss and tragic destiny arising from the hubris of *homo faber* (man the creator), and by a solemn celebration of human stoicism in the face of destiny. These were themes and a mood which the war might well evoke, but the tales themselves, far from being *about* the War, told of mythic beings in an imaginary universe. Some echoed the Biblical book of Genesis or the Old Norse *Völuspá* in recounting the Creation of the Universe and the doings of its Creator or Creators. Tolkien's Creation included elves and dwarves as well as men, and his stories dealt mainly with the elves, virtually immortal beings endowed with transcendent gifts who lived in harmony with nature and delighted in creating beauty both natural and artificial — a task to which some of them, unfortunately, brought a lethal egoism. Their chief creations were the three Silmarils, jewels containing the light of the two trees of Valinor, home of the gods. The universe included a principle of active evil in the form of Melkor, or Morgoth, a former henchman of the Supreme Being like Satan in *Paradise Lost*. Morgoth exploited the elves' frailties to capture the Silmarils, which he set in his iron crown.

Tolkien began these tales after trying to address the trauma of the trenches more directly. He recalled: "I tried a diary with portraits ... of events and persons seen; but I found it was not my line. So I took to 'escapism': or really transforming experience into another form and symbol."[8] Thus he gave his mythology the very label that critics were to attach to *The Lord of the Rings* — but to him, apparently, "escapism" meant not a wilful or besotted blind-

---

[7] This section is based on Humphrey Carpenter, *J. R. R. Tolkien: A Biography* (London: George Allen and Unwin, 1977).

[8] *The Letters of J. R. R. Tolkien* (ed. Humphrey Carpenter, Boston and New York: Houghton Mifflin, 2000), 85. (Hereafter *Letters*).

ness to reality but a way of coping obliquely with reality too searing to be confronted directly.

One feels that the experience thus transformed was not only the Western Front but his whole life to date. He had lost his father at the age of four and his mother eight years later, and had spent his teens as the ward of a Roman Catholic priest, his mother having converted to that faith at the cost of estranging their family. At the age of sixteen he had fallen in love with a girl three years his elder, but his guardian had required him to break off the relationship and not see her until he reached the age of 21. Tolkien obeyed, but he resumed the relationship as soon as he could and they were married. And then came the Battle of the Somme, which wiped out two of his three closest friends and left scars of memory on Tolkien himself. All these experiences and conditions of loss, exile, and emotional privation and fulfilment resound in his *legendarium* (as he called it).

Tolkien's choice of form testifies to his idiosyncratic intelligence and sensibility. It reflects a childhood liking for fairy tales, an intense emotional and aesthetic affinity for the defunct or marginalized languages of northern Europe, and a creative impulse that first found an outlet in inventing languages but was then compelled to imagine both the peoples that spoke those languages and the histories that his invented words expressed. Throughout nineteenth-century Europe, especially in lands that were provinces of foreign-ruled empires, scholars inspired by nationalist or populist sympathies had collected, collated and published a folklore previously propagated only, or chiefly, by word of mouth. This had happened in the two countries whose languages Tolkien found especially appealing: Finland, where Elias Lönnrot had compiled the folklore into an epic poem called the *Kalevala*, and Wales, where Charlotte Guest had collated, and published in English translation, a collection called the *Mabinogion*. Tolkien's major invented languages were based on Finnish and Welsh respectively, and one of the early tales of what became *The Silmarillion* was based on a Finnish folk tale,[9] just as the legendarium as a whole was modelled on compilations such as the *Kalevala* and the *Mabinogion*.

Tolkien's subjects of study, first as an undergraduate at Oxford and then as a professional scholar, included Old English and Old Norse, languages with Germanic roots. The two differed greatly in the abundance of their extant literature. Old Norse survived in many

---

[9] Tolkien's story of Túrin is based on that of Kullervo.

sagas, preserved chiefly in Iceland, which together told the story of the cosmos from its creation to its predicted end. Old English literature was sparse in comparison, largely because the Norman Conquest of 1066 had overlaid Anglo-Saxon England with a French-speaking aristocracy that was indifferent, if not hostile, to the culture of the conquered people. Yet the smothered culture still haunted the landscape in the form of scores of burial sites and ruins and thousands of place names.

Tolkien's response to these relics was distinctively emotional, above all in his insistence on understanding the texts as works of art to be cherished for their beauty and meaning and not merely as ciphers to be decoded.[10] His keen responsiveness to the lost and the marginalized seems to chime with his formative experiences. But even if his devotion to Old English language and literature was inspired by the example of the folklorists who had revived so many vernacular cultures in the nineteenth century, the Norman Conquest had expunged any folk traditions that could be collated into a specifically English national epic like Lönnrot's *Kalevala*. In an often-quoted statement of 1951, he cited England's lack of an indigenous mythology (as distinct from the French and Celtic legends of King Arthur) as an inspiration for his attempt to compose a comprehensive mythology of his own.[11]

In terms of what Stanley Unwin wanted, Tolkien's tales might as well have been a telephone directory, and they were quickly sent back. They would appear only forty years later, by which time one could almost have published a phone book under Tolkien's name and made money. Meanwhile, Tolkien promised to "give thought" to a *Hobbit*-sequel. That story is dotted with fleeting allusions to his legendarium, inserted to give it temporal depth, and he had already speculated that his mythology might supply some theme he could adapt to Unwin's requirements. Now he repeated the idea more emphatically and in words which, if not a positive statement of purpose, were certainly prophetic of the outcome.

> I am sure you will sympathize when I say that the construction of elaborate and consistent mythology (and two languages) rather occupies the mind, and the Silmarils are in my heart. So that goodness

---

[10] Tom Shippey, *The Road to Middle-earth: How J. R. R. Tolkien Invented a New Mythology* (rev. ed., Boston and New York: Houghton Mifflin, 2003), cap. 2.

[11] *Letters*, 144.

knows what will happen. Mr. Baggins began as a comic tale among conventional and inconsistent Grimm's fairy-tale dwarves [*sic*], and got drawn into the edge of it — so that even Sauron the terrible peeped over the edge. But what more can hobbits do? They can be comic, but their comedy is suburban unless it is set against things more elemental. But the real fun about orcs and dragons (to my mind) was before their time. Perhaps a new (if similar) line? Do you think Tom Bombadil, the spirit of the (vanishing) Oxford and Berkshire countryside, could be made into the hero of a story?[12]

Either by design, or owing to the irresistible tug of Tolkien's life-work on his imagination, the "suburban" children's-story world of *The Hobbit* was set to collide with the darker ancient universe of his Apocalypse.

"Ancient History"

Almost certainly the collision was deliberate. Tolkien longed to escape, at least in imagination, from the "suburban" present into his own ancient history, and to pass beyond that to discover, if only in fantasy, a reality that might have engendered those stories about fairy realms existing in an ambiguous relationship to mortal reality which figured in the ancient literature he studied professionally. But he did not wish to travel alone. Only a year previously, he had begun writing a story that was clearly intended to frame his legendarium for publication. His recollections of its genesis vary in detail, but the gist is this. He and his friend C. S. Lewis regretted that so little new fiction was to their taste, so Lewis proposed that they write stories of their own: "thrillers" about space-travel and time-travel, "each discovering Myth" (as Tolkien put it at the time). A coin-toss assigned space travel to Lewis, who swiftly completed *Out of the Silent Planet*, the first novel of a trilogy infused with Christian myth. Tolkien drafted four short chapters of an adventure entitled "The Lost Road" but then dropped it to finish *The Hobbit*, which he suddenly had a chance to publish.[13] The mythic focus of the unfinished story is Númenor, the island abode of those men whose forebears aided the Immortals in their struggle against Morgoth. Just as in *The Lord of the Rings* and *The Silmarillion*, the Númenóreans (Men of the West), deluded by Sauron, try to attain immortality by conquering

---

[12] *Letters*, 26. Tom Bombadil was the hero of a whimsical poem that Tolkien had published in a magazine three years earlier: Carpenter, *J. R. R. Tolkien*, 165.

[13] Letters, 29, 209, 342, 347, 378; Carpenter, *J. R. R. Tolkien*, 172-74.

Valinor, the Undying Lands, but the Gods thwart them by bending the cosmos so that the Earth is made round and Valinor removed to a different dimension. Númenor is engulfed, and its inhabitants all perish except a remnant of the righteous, led by Elendil ("Elf-friend") and his sons, who flee to Middle-earth (which the Númenóreans have colonized) and found kingdoms there.

"The Lost Road" supposes the reincarnation throughout history of Elendil and his son. Two short opening chapters set in modern England introduce a teenage boy who is prone to extra-sensory perceptions both visual and linguistic, the latter being intimations of dead languages that have left no historical record. The youth is the reincarnation of Elendil, and when older he feels himself summoned back in time with his son. The other two chapters, set in Númenor, deal mainly with the plight of the righteous in a country where the state and public opinion are militantly hostile to old values. Authorial notes suggest that the Númenor episode was to be dreamt by the Elendil avatar, perhaps as some sort of inherited memory, and that there were to be several chronologically intermediate episodes in historical and mythical settings that were close to Tolkien's scholarly interests. Elendil's modern avatar expressly rejects the idea of a Wellsian Time Machine as unsuitable for travel into the past, and it seems that Tolkien intended instead to follow his hero back in time through several incarnations in historical periods increasingly remote and finally merging into myth.[14]

More than thirty years later, he recalled that he abandoned the project because "it was too long a way around to what I really wanted to make, a new version of the Atlantis legend."[15] It is easy to see why he thought so. His imaginative destination was not the historical past but a fantasy world, a world *outside* human history. The device of gradual regression through history into myth was ingenious, especially in view of the parallel between his story of Númenor and the Atlantis legend, but the need to invent all those intermediate episodes made the reincarnation contrivance cumbersome. No doubt his enthusiasm only waned further when his publisher rejected the idea along with his legendarium.

---

14 J. R. R. Tolkien, *The Lost Road and Other Writings: Language and Legend before The Lord of the Rings*, ed. Christopher Tolkien (New York: Ballantyne Books, 1996), 7-116.
15 *Letters*, 378.

Since a *Hobbit*-sequel was what his publisher wanted, it was perhaps natural that Tolkien, obsessed genius that he was, should start considering it as a means of framing the legendarium for publication. This approach was not obviously easier: there was no essential connection between his two imaginary worlds, and their prevailing moods were quite dissimilar. However, his hobbit-world turned out to afford crucial advantages as a launching-pad into the universe of the legendarium. The allusions to his mythology in *The Hobbit* had the effect of positioning the one world as the "ancient history" of the other. This allowed him to project the heroes of his sequel from the fantasy-present of the Shire into the fantasy-past of his mythology without having to transport them between incommensurate dimensions of reality and fantasy.

They still needed transporting, of course, but *The Hobbit* offered a neat solution to this problem too. Any children's story needs one or more heroes with whom a child can easily identify; often such characters are youngsters about the age of the intended reader or a little older. In *The Hobbit*, Bilbo's diminutive size, childish needs (food, warmth, security) and constant need to be looked after make it easy for children to identify with him. But because he is himself a fantasy-creature, there is no need of some expedient like Lewis Carroll's Alice dreaming her way down a rabbit-hole and through a looking-glass, or C. S. Lewis's wardrobe and assorted other clumsy contrivances that he frankly called "magic." The fantasy world can snare Bilbo in his own home and carry him off into adventure. And the same thing happens in *The Lord of the Rings*, but this time what intrudes is the past.

Both *The Hobbit* and *The Lord of the Rings* recount journeys into "the Wild," a world that is archaic compared to the Shire. According to Tom Shippey, in both stories "Tolkien found the transit from familiar Shire to archaic Wilderland an inhibiting one,"[16] so the narrative in both stories takes time to acquire momentum and a strong continuity. I agree with Shippey about *The Lord of the Rings*, but not about *The Hobbit*. The earlier story starts briskly and keeps up a smart pace throughout, but the sequel does indeed take a while to get going. Consequently, much of Book One is uneven in a way that *The Hobbit* is not.

One reason is simply that Tolkien started writing the sequel without much idea of a story, or even a hero. At first Bilbo himself

---

[16] Shippey, *Road to Middle-earth*, 105.

was to be the hero and was to leave home on another treasure quest, having exhausted the proceeds of the first. Then Frodo Baggins, his nephew and heir (at first called Bingo), became the hero, but his departure too was initially ascribed to poverty and wanderlust. At first the uncanny black-clad horseman that pursues Frodo through the Shire was the wizard Gandalf trying to catch up with him. Even after Tolkien decided that the horseman was an enemy — one of nine Black Riders, or Ringwraiths, who turn out to be Sauron's chief minions — Frodo first hid from him by putting on his ring (not yet capitalized). Then Tolkien decided that the pursuers were seeking the ring and were better evaded by *not* putting it on, and the story took off from there. But even in the final version, the early chapters (except chapter 2, "The Shadow of the Past," which Tolkien inserted once he had begun to figure out the plot and repeatedly revised as the story expanded) project the author's original lack of urgency and direction.[17]

But there is another, more interesting reason that *The Lord of the Rings* takes longer to get going, and this has to do with the fact that the sequel's Wilderland is "archaic" in a way that its precursor's is not. In *The Hobbit* there is a borderland, represented on the end-paper map by a double ruled red line labelled "Edge of the Wild." Once you have crossed it (or perhaps as you approach it), people begin speaking strangely and singing unfamiliar songs; inns and roads get worse, and sinister castles appear on the hilltops. You might almost be passing from the English West Midlands of Tolkien's childhood into the mountains of Wales (although a better analogy might be the passage from the more advanced parts of imperial India into the provinces of the North-West Frontier en route to Afghanistan — that is, into a world which is *contemporary* but clearly less *modern*). Then Bilbo and his companions are into their first adventure, which consists of being captured and nearly eaten by trolls, and chapter 3 has them stopping at Rivendell, abode of Elrond the elf-lord, for "A Brief Rest." But nothing in the whole book is much odder than what happened in the first chapter, when Bilbo found his home invaded by a small horde of exotic strangers who mistakenly supposed that he wanted to join their treasure quest. There is little "magic" except the ring, and what there is,

---

[17] J. R. R. Tolkien, *The Return of the Shadow: The History of The Lord of the Rings, Part One*, ed. Christopher Tolkien (Boston and New York: Houghton Mifflin, 1988), 1-109.

including the ring, the narrative takes in its stride. There is nothing really uncanny, like the Black Riders — nothing that needs *explaining*. In *The Lord of the Rings*, by contrast, Frodo and his friends do not reach Rivendell until the end of Book One, which is twelve chapters long. This is partly because more happens en route, but also because in *The Lord of the Rings* almost everything needs explaining (although not everything gets explained: Tolkien was well aware of the narrative value of mystification).

What needs explaining, in a nutshell, is "the shadow of the past"; but the chapter's original title, "Ancient History," expresses it even better. Tolkien had dotted *The Hobbit* with allusions to his legendarium, but they are decorative, not essential to the plot. The only historical event essential to the plot is Smaug the dragon's seizure of the Lonely Mountain, and that is scarcely *ancient* history: the dwarves' leader, Thorin Oakenshield, was there when it happened. In *The Lord of the Rings*, however, especially in Book One, the world of the earlier story gets *historicized*. Bilbo's ring swiftly becomes The Ring, a not-quite-inanimate object with a past and a purpose, and the capacity to wreak baleful effects on its custodians. Its previous owner, Gollum, acquires a terrible history of which *The Hobbit* (as originally published) gives no hint. And their histories are only part of a deeper and wider history, which comes disturbingly into focus when the Elf Gildor Inglorion, rebutting Frodo's unthinking assumption that the Shire belongs to the Hobbits, declares: "But it is not your own Shire ... Others dwelt here before hobbits were; and others will dwell here again when hobbits are no more" (FR 93). The Hobbits' homeland, apparently so tranquil and stable, is afloat on the tide of history; and the Wild, which has penetrated to the very heart of their homeland in the form of the Ring, symbolizes that history.

There are, then, two key differences between the Wild in *The Hobbit* and in *The Lord of the Rings*. First of all, in *The Hobbit* it is archaic merely in being less modern, whereas in the sequel it is archaic because it actually represents the past. The second difference is its turbulence. In the earlier story, the Edge of the Wild is as absolute as that doubled-ruled line on the map: on one side lies civilization, on the other a wilderness which map-makers have not penetrated and policemen never visit — a place where "they have seldom even heard of the king".[18] In the sequel, the Wild is not just "out there" — it is something that must actively be *kept* out there. Even the Shirefolk realize this well enough to maintain a high hedge to keep the Old Forest at bay. As the story progresses, we learn that, unknown to the Shirefolk, there is indeed a police force "out there" working to keep them safe: the Rangers led by Strider.

The features of the Wild that are peculiar to *The Lord of the Rings* — its baleful historicity and propensity to encroach — lend themselves to an analysis of the relationship between past and present in terms of the past impinging on the present. The fact that the confrontation begins and ends in the Shire fits that pattern. But Tolkien's story is not mainly about the invasion and occupation of the Shire — the story's fantasy-present — by an encroaching past; it is about a journey *into* the past as represented by the historicized Wild. In other words, Frodo's journey into the Wild is a journey into history. What is on its face a journey over land becomes the journey in time that Tolkien had first attempted in "The Lost Road."

A journey in time

But how can this idea be reconciled with Tolkien's elaborate maps and detailed chronology? As the hobbits ride or trudge over mapped terrain, one day appears to follow another in the usual way. A letter to his son Christopher records his discovery that Frodo and Sam, off on their own, have got out of sync with the other characters — a problem he fixed by making small map alterations and adding days here and there.[19] This is just one instance of a constant pre-occupation with chronological precision. With the entire action so meticulously plotted in time and space, and explicitly taking place on a single temporal plane, what room is there for time travel?

The question sounds reasonable but is based on a false premise: namely, that the maps and chronology are not only "true" but tell the whole truth. Think about this: if the Shire is "modern" and the Wild "archaic," what is Bree, the village (or cluster of villages) populated by both Hobbits and Men where Frodo and his companions stop after their adventures with Tom Bombadil? With its large inn, historically a tourist destination for adventurous Shirefolk, it seems like an outpost or enclave of modernity on, or just over, the edge of

---

[18] *The Annotated Hobbit*, rev. ed. by Douglas A. Anderson (Boston: Houghton Mifflin, 2002), 69.
[19] *Letters*, 97.

the Wild. Fair enough; but who are those men at the inn, refugees from "trouble away in the South," who have just come up the Greenway? We have been told that no men other than those of Bree "had settled dwellings so far west, or within a hundred leagues [about 300 miles] of the Shire." The relevant map includes a handy mileage scale, and 300 miles in the right direction brings us to Dunland, whose inhabitants, we will learn later, are in thrall to the renegade wizard Saruman. Near the end of the story we will also learn that some at least of the supposed refugees were actually Saruman's agents, so it may seem reasonable to assume that the refugees are from Dunland. The problem is that there is no cultural resemblance between the refugees at Bree, who are "strangers" to the Bree-folk but are not presented as foreign in speech or manners — certainly not as less "modern" — and the "wild hillmen and herd-folk of Dunland" who will shortly invade Rohan as part of Saruman's army.[20]

There is, it seems, an invisible time-warp running across the deceptively flat surface of Tolkien's map, and it reflects a time-flux that runs through his narrative. I use the word *flux* advisedly. Frodo's journey in time expresses an ingenious narrative strategy that is clearly designed to achieve what Tolkien had first attempted in "The Lost Road." In that story, however, time functions as a *dimension*, across or through which one can travel from point to point. In *The Lord of the Rings*, it is more like a *medium*. Tolkien's hobbit heroes venture into the past as one might wade into the sea, suddenly start bobbing in the waves, and then be lifted off one's feet — and in this case swept away by a rip-current. As they follow the path that will bring their "suburban" world into conjunction with that of Tolkien's legendarium, the story progressively becomes saturated with history and their eyes are relentlessly opened to that history, of which until now they have been blissfully ignorant.[21] Tolkien does not need to dream up a time-travel mechanism any more than he needed to dream up a "looking-glass moment." The

---

[20] Quotations in FR 168, 161, and TT 132.

[21] Cf. Barton R. Friedman, "Fabricating History: Narrative Strategy in *The Lord of the Rings*," *Clio* 2:2 (1973), 137 ("The recurrence of flood both as image and event in Tolkien's narrative reflects the apocalyptic sweep of the history he is unfolding"), and Lionel Basney, "Myth, History and Time in *The Lord of the Rings*," in Isaacs and Zimbardo, ed., *Tolkien: New Critical Perspectives*, 12 ("Frodo's quest is a birth into knowledge for the hobbits who accompany him").

time travel is worked into the very structure of the plot in such a way that Tolkien's chronology, for all its detail, does not reveal it.

The process is driven by a series of encounters between the hobbits and the past, each consisting of a history lesson followed by a physical confrontation with the past. Each confrontation is more direct and terrible than the last. The first encounter commences in Frodo's own home, as Gandalf reveals the presence of the past in the form of the Ring. It is from Gandalf that we first learn, very briefly and allusively, of the forging of the Rings of Power, of which Sauron's One Ring is the greatest; of Sauron's overthrow by Gil-galad the elven-king and Elendil of Westernesse (Númenor); of the fate of Elendil's son Isildur, who took the Ring from Sauron and was betrayed by it; and of the finding of the Ring long afterwards by two hobbit-creatures, one of whom, Gollum, murdered his companion to possess it, only to lose it, providentially as it might seem, just when Bilbo Baggins, fleeing in a tunnel beneath the Misty Mountains from goblins who had captured him and his dwarf companions, happened upon Gollum's lair. Forced to flee his home, Frodo is pursued through the Shire by the Black Riders — ancient kings of men transformed by Sauron's rings into his undead slaves — and has his providential but unsettling meeting with the elf Gildor Inglorion.

Fear of the Riders drives Frodo and his companions into the Old Forest, where the mysterious Tom Bombadil, master but not ruler of the unquiet spirits of forest and downs, rescues them from the toils of an oddly animated and inscrutably vengeful tree, Old Man Willow. Detained by bad weather at the house where Tom dwells in ideal domesticity with Goldberry, daughter of the River, the hobbits listen spellbound as he yarns about the Old Forest and the adjoining Barrow-downs, and then about the peoples that fought upon the downs and built the barrows. Mention of the haunted mounds distracts them from his discourse, and they recover it to find that he has "wandered into strange regions beyond their memory and beyond their waking thought, into times when the world was wider, and the seas flowed straight back to the western Shore; and still on and back Tom went singing out into ancient starlight, when only the Elf-sires were awake." Tom's winding discourse has borne them back through time almost to the First Dawn. The physical confrontation with the past occurs next day, when the hobbits are captured by a barrow-wight and Tom has to rescue them again. Roused from enchanted sleep, Merry fleetingly channels a man of ancient days slain in a night-raid by the forces of Angmar. That realm was ruled (we later learn) by the chief of the Black Riders, whom Merry will one day help to kill in the great battle before Minas Tirith with the weapon he now takes from the barrow hoard.

The next history lesson is given on Weathertop, a hill where the Black Riders have cornered them, by a man called Strider, a mysterious friend of Gandalf's who is guiding them to Rivendell. As they await the Riders' attack, he tells them the story of Lúthien and Beren from the First Age of Middle-earth. Its substance reaches us more concretely than that of Tom Bombadil's yarn, because it is given in direct speech rather than vague summary. Like Tom's, however, it is shrouded in a penumbra of mystery, because Strider begins by chanting in haunting lyrical verse and his explanation, full of names but void of dates, sounds less like history than myth. (Strider's word for it is *lore*.) This time the physical confrontation with the past is instantaneous: Strider has scarcely finished when the Black Riders attack and their leader wounds Frodo with a bewitched blade.

We have now reached a very different imaginative terrain from our starting-point, but we did not get there via some "looking-glass moment" when our heroes passed unexpectedly into a strange alternative universe. There was no need of some jejune contrivance like the characters falling into a dream-world, no rabbit-hole, wardrobe, or "preposterous and incredible Time Machine" (as Tolkien called H. G. Wells's invention in his essay "On Fairy-Stories"),[22] because the narrative has told of a fantasy world all along. Instead there has been a steady deepening of the temporal perspective as Tolkien manoeuvres the world of hobbits into a historical relationship with the universe of his legendarium, accompanied by a marked transition in mood and style, which is manifest in the account of the adventure on the Barrow-downs. Gone is the chatty dialogue of the hobbits' earlier travels; instead we see them at a distance, from above as it were, as they ride across a high country "silent except for the whisper of the air over the edges of the land, and high lonely cries of strange birds." Forty miles east of the Shire, the birds are already unfamiliar. Henceforth the landscape will typically be alien and intimidating, fraught with ominous relics of an encroaching past. In this chapter the gravitas of the main narrative is nearly achieved.

---

[22] J. R. R. Tolkien, *Tree and Leaf* (London: Unwin Books, 1964), 18.

Looking only at the plot, you might think that the three Tom Bombadil chapters prolong the lack of urgency and direction that marks the account of Frodo's passage through the Shire. They are a digression from the main story of the Ring. The adventures of the Old Forest and the Barrow-downs, though nicely atmospheric, are apparently inconsequential and quickly resolved by Tom as *deus ex machina*, much as Gandalf in *The Hobbit* rescues Bilbo and the dwarves first from the trolls and then from the goblins. But in the context of a journey back in time, bringing the world of hobbits into conjunction with that of its ancient but still balefully active history, they form a zone of transition, propelling hobbits and reader alike from the "suburban" present into the Wilderland of the past.[23]

Central to this passage is the fantastic lyrical intermezzo of the sojourn at Tom's house — significantly, the only place on Frodo's quest, other than the elf-havens of Rivendell and Lothlórien, where he spends more than one night. Tom himself dances and prances rather than walks, his diction strongly metric even when rendered as prose but constantly breaking into verse. In speech and movement Goldberry ripples like the river whence she sprang. The mere sight of her, seated amid wide earthenware vessels filled with floating water-lilies, sets Frodo speaking in lyric verse, and the water they drink at table goes to the hobbits' heads so that they suddenly find themselves singing merrily as if it were easier and more natural than talking. When Tom yarns to them the next day, his sing-song discourse is a seer's revelation, received subliminally rather than through conscious apperception. "Who are you, Master?" asks Frodo when it is over. "Eldest, that's what I am," Tom replies.

Bree, with its inn and its hobbits, feels almost like a return to hobbit normality but soon proves to be just a flood-prone eyot in the rushing stream of history. The journey into the past continues under the guidance of Strider, whom they meet on the day they finally part from Tom just as they met Tom on the day they left the Shire. Strider turns out to have a very personal link to thousands of years of history, since he is descended from the ancient rulers of Númenor and through them from Lúthien and Beren. With his recitation on Weathertop, eleven chapters into the story, the world of *The Hobbit* finally converges with that of Tolkien's legendarium, of which the tale of Lúthien and Beren is the keystone. At Rivendell, Frodo hears the story of Sauron's defeat by Gil-galad and Elendil

---

[23] For "suburban", see *Letters*, 26.

told by Elrond the elf-lord — also a descendant of Lúthien and Beren — *who was there*. In Fangorn Forest, Merry and Pippin get a new angle on the history of their world from Treebeard the Ent, "the oldest living thing that still walks beneath the Sun on this Middle-earth." In a secret cavern behind a waterfall, Faramir, son of the ruling Steward of Gondor, gives Frodo and Sam a sketch of the history of the Númenóreans in Middle-earth. At Edoras, the four hobbits see the burial of King Théoden of Rohan in a grave-mound like that from which the past reached out to snare them on the Barrow-downs. In this world the people of the grave-mounds are not even "ancient": they rank as newcomers next to the more ancient people of Gondor, whose kingdom was founded by Elendil of Númenor and his sons, and all men are newcomers beside the primal beings and cultures, elvish and entish, that final victory over Sauron has by a bitter irony condemned to eternal exile or to extinction.

Tolkien's time-travel story is epiphenomenal: that is, the time travel is not explicit but is, rather, an effect of his invention of a quest story in order to link the fictional present — the characters' own time — to its ancient history. I have no reason to suppose that he consciously conceived the story as a time-travel narrative, or that he thought of it in those terms at any point during its composition. If anything, he may have thought of it as something different from time travel — a different and better way of bridging the gap between his myth-world and the "suburban" present than the cumbersome strategy of "The Lost Road." But the essential difference lies in his substitution of the fictional present of his fictional hobbit-world for his own contemporary reality as a starting-point, enabling him to transmute a journey back in time into a journey into the Wild. Both are journeys into the past: the destination is unchanged.

War and the shaping of Middle-earth

The switch made the journey possible, but it did not make it easy. As I noted earlier, there is virtually no point of contact between Tolkien's two fantasy-worlds. To bring them together required inventing the millennia of history that link the downfall of Nùmenor, Sauron's forging of the Ring, and Bilbo's finding of it. It also meant inventing the vast geography that connects the Shire, the Lonely Mountain of Bilbo's adventure, and the volcanic fire where Sauron forged the Ring. After that, Tolkien still needed to link that geography with the different terrain of his legendarium. A crucial aid to achieving all this was the Second World War.

The difficulty of the challenge that Tolkien faced is evident in the early drafts. These show "history" bubbling close to the surface of his imagination from the start, but generally it enters the story not as first thought but as early second thought. The first elements of "The Shadow of the Past" emerged only after he decided that the Black Riders were Ringwraiths. Frodo and his companions were originally to spend only one night at Tom Bombadil's, and Tom's "guru" discourse was added later. On Weathertop Strider, in his initial incarnation as a hobbit called Trotter, was to tell stories about animals, not about the past.[24] All in all, Tolkien's early struggles to devise a plot are not what you might expect to find if he had set out to make his *Hobbit*-sequel a frame for his legendarium. Without his hints to his publisher and the evidence of "The Lost Road," one might well infer that his new hobbit-story and his myth-world converged without conscious intent, purely by the tug of his mythology on his imagination as he struggled to conjure a story out of thin air.[25]

Fusing the disparate moods of the two worlds was even harder, and there are hints that Tolkien feared that things were getting out of hand. In October 1938 he worried that his story was getting too "terrifying" and "adult" for a children's story: "The darkness of the present days has had some effect on it," he wrote. Just three days earlier, Nazi Germany had annexed the Sudetenland of Czechoslovakia under the infamous Munich Agreement between Germany, Italy, Britain and France. Nine months later, with war threatening, he wrote a memo questioning the results of nearly two years' work on Book One, during which he had two or three times brought Frodo and his companions to Rivendell without apparently having a strong idea of what should happen next. The memo toys with the idea of restoring Bilbo as hero, or else making Frodo as hero a more comic character. It sounds very much as though Tolkien feared that the hobbits' progressive immersion in history, coloured by the gloom of "the present days," had given his story a tone unbefitting a sequel to *The Hobbit*.[26]

---

[24] Tolkien, *Return of the Shadow*, 73-87, 117-24, 250, 288.

[25] Cf. Paul Edmund Thomas, "Towards Quite Unforeseen Goals," in *The Lord of the Rings 1954-2004: Scholarship in honor of Richard E. Blackwelder*, ed. Wayne G. Hammond and Christina Scull, Milwaukee: Marquette UP, 2006), 62-63.

[26] *Letters*, 41; Tolkien, *Return of the Shadow*, 369ff.

Then the war began. Nightly air raids and the mass evacuation of children from cities might well alter one's notion of what belonged in a children's story. Beneath the whine and growl of war planes, Tolkien ditched his doubts about the temper of his *Hobbit*-sequel. *The Lord of the Rings* definitively became a tale that mirrored the anguish of the human condition.

Oddly enough, in his Foreword to the second edition, Tolkien took pains to discount the war's influence on *The Lord of the Rings*. "As the story grew," he wrote,

> it put down roots (into the past) and threw out unexpected branches; but its main theme was settled from the outset by the inevitable choice of the Ring as the link between it and *The Hobbit*. The crucial chapter, "The Shadow of the Past", is one of the oldest parts of the tale. It was written long before the foreshadow of 1939 had yet become a threat of inevitable disaster, and from that point the story would have developed along essentially the same lines, if that disaster had been averted.

Tolkien granted that "an author of course cannot remain wholly unaffected by his experience," but he pointed out that his experience embraced the First World War as well as the Second.

This statement presents no problems. Although Tolkien expressed himself in general terms, he did so with a specific purpose: to scotch the notion that *The Lord of the Rings* was an *allegory* of the Second World War — that the story was contrived to mirror the salient events of the war as Orwell's *Animal Farm* mirrors those of the Bolshevik Revolution and its aftermath. This is fair enough: Tolkien's purpose was to invent a story, not to devise an allegory, and his notes and drafts reveal no hint of the didactic intent that is inherent in allegory. This does not mean that the war, which dominated the years in which he was writing the story, did not influence its development. If the Sudetenland crisis left its mark, it is likely that the war left a larger one.

Looking for signs of that influence, we are more likely to understate it than otherwise, for the simple reason that Tolkien experienced the war day by day and must have been affected by all sorts of things that elude us in hindsight. A man who loved the *Kalevala* and hated communism may well have been moved by the Winter War of 1939-40 between Finland and the USSR in ways that are not obvious to us. Perhaps we hear echoes of that conflict in the resistance of the outnumbered horsemen of Rohan to the forces of the renegade wizard Saruman at the battle of Helm's Deep, or in their heroic charge at the battle of the Pelennor Fields, but we cannot tell.

Even so, *The Lord of the Rings* is full of features and episodes that call to mind the war and its genesis. Some are fairly plain, such as the arrival in Bree-land of refugees from troubles down south, the evacuation of non-combatants ahead of expected attack in Rohan and Gondor, and the Ringwraiths — now mounted on fell flying beasts — buzzing the defenders of Minas Tirith like dive-bombers. The very idea of Sauron's resurgence mirrors the revival of German military power under Hitler, and the pervasive mood of last-ditch resistance evokes the period of Axis military ascendancy from the spring of 1940 to the end of 1942. The chapter title "The Siege of Gondor" echoes "the Battle of Britain", and one can see Tolkien's account of the battle for Minas Tirith as a whole, with its early shocking collapse and demoralization and subsequent vicissitudes culminating in hard-won victory, as a reflection of the entire emotional trajectory of the war as he experienced it. Other echoes of the war are less obvious, or did not make it into the final text; yet these too suggest its influence on Tolkien's imagination. The idea that Gondor had ceded the land of Rohan to the Rohirrim hundreds of years earlier, after the latter had come to Gondor's aid in a desperate battle, looks like an imaginative refraction of the belated yet decisive entry of the United States into the war after Pearl Harbor. The idea, briefly entertained by Tolkien, that Aragorn (Strider's real name) was descended from a king of Gondor who had been exiled by an insurrection fomented by Sauron recalls the flight of the King of Norway and the Queen of the Netherlands ahead of Hitler's armies in the spring of 1940.

Several of these elements have parallels in the First World War, of course, but the key is the timing: repeatedly, these parallels surface in Tolkien's drafts soon after the analogous event in the war of 1939-45. The mass flight of non-combatants from war zones occurred in both wars, but the refugees at Bree entered Tolkien's story in the summer of 1940, shortly after Germany had conquered much of north-west Europe.[27] European sovereigns had lost their

---

[27] The arrival of strangers from the south entered the text late in 1938: Tolkien, *Return of the Shadow*, 142, 309, 334. The notion that they, or some of them, are refugees, emerges in August 1940: J. R. R. Tolkien, *The Treason of Isengard: The History of The Lord of the Rings, Part Two*, ed. Christopher Tolkien (Boston and New York: Houghton Mifflin, 1989), 71, 74. However,

thrones to defeat and revolution in 1917 and 1918, but the idea about Aragorn's ancestry cropped up soon after the Dutch and Norwegian monarchs had fled into exile.[28] American military involvement actually had more of a "Seventh Cavalry" aspect in 1917 than in the first half of 1942, when the U.S. was suffering a series of reverses in the Pacific and had yet to make itself felt in theatres where the British were engaged, but the idea about the Rohirrim riding to the aid of Gondor crops up in Tolkien's notes shortly after Pearl Harbor.[29]

Clearly the war left traces in Tolkien's story. But what is the evidence for the major influence that I ascribe to it? Here too the key is chronology: in this case the chronology of the whole composition as reconstructed by Tolkien's son Christopher in *The History of Middle-earth*. By August 1939 Tolkien had drafted three or four versions of what became Book One, which takes the hobbits and the Ring as far as Rivendell, but there he had bogged down for months. What he called the "main theme" of the story was certainly settled by then, in that he knew that Sauron could be overthrown only by casting the Ring into the fires of Mount Doom where it was forged. It is clear, however, that he had only the foggiest notion of how the Ring was to get there from Rivendell, and indeed of where Mount Doom lay in relation to Rivendell. When Frodo and his companions first trekked south from Elrond's haven, Tolkien had no idea that the ruined subterranean dwarf-kingdom of Moria and the paradisal elf-realm of Lothlórien lay across their path. He knew that somewhere Frodo must get separated from his companions and head (originally alone) for the Cracks of Doom, but he supposed that the others would go straight to Minas Tirith, not that they would reach it only via circuitous paths leading them far to the west through Rohan and Fangorn to Saruman's fastness at Isengard. He thought that Gandalf had been held captive by "Giant Treebeard," not the traitorous Saruman, and that Treebeard (not yet an Ent) would meet Frodo, not his kinsmen Merry and Pippin newly escaped from Saruman's orcs, and as an enemy, not a friend. He had no inkling that Frodo would not

---

the idea of refugees may have been very much in Tolkien's mind late in 1938, when refugee scholars from Austria, recently annexed by Nazi Germany, added their numbers to the German savants already haunting the precincts of Tolkien's university: *Ark of Civilisation: Refugee Scholars and Oxford University, 1930-1945*, ed. Sally Crawford, Katharina Ulmschneider and Jaś Elsner (Oxford UP, 2017).

[28] Tolkien, *Treason of Isengard*, 116, 120.

[29] Tolkien, *Treason of Isengard*, 443, 444.

live happily ever after as Bilbo had. Everything after the Council of Elrond was written during or after the war. Both that crucial episode and "The Shadow of the Past," comprising Gandalf's initial revelations to Frodo, were revised repeatedly as Tolkien's conception broadened. An expansive history, of which the providential advent of the Rohirrim is just one element, was devised as a backcloth. This expansiveness — this sense of vast forces moving on a vast stage, of a universal destiny unfolding — was the war's essential contribution to *The Lord of the Rings*.

We see this effect in the growing geographical concreteness, both topographical and political, that suffuses the story from Book Three onwards. As I have shown, the first two Books are dominated by history. Tolkien's initial exposition of the problem of the Ring, in "The Shadow of the Past," is almost purely historical. It imparts a vague sense that Gandalf's story covers a wide expanse of space as well as time, but the only specific geographical element is Gandalf's statement that the solution is to cast the Ring into the depths of Orodruin (Mount Doom). To this, at the beginning of the next chapter, he adds his advice that Frodo should head for Rivendell — a proposition of little geographical complexity since Frodo, unlike most hobbits, knows that the Great East Road through the Shire leads there.

At the Council of Elrond the Big Picture is still predominantly historical, although the history gets more geographical as Elrond embellishes the story of the Last Alliance of Elves and Men with a brief account of the two kingdoms founded by Elendil and his sons. Current affairs also acquire greater geographic specificity: we hear of Saruman's fastness at Isengard, of the kingdom of Rohan and its horsemen, of Dunland, the Dead Marshes, the Morgul Vale, and half a dozen other places far from Rivendell and each other, all of which we will have visited before the story is finished. Significantly, little of this geography appears in the first sketches of the Council, which Tolkien was drafting when war broke out, or in his contemporary plot projections, and there is little notion of the spatial relationship between the places that he does mention. Christopher Tolkien suggests that at this stage the geography of the lands south and east of the Misty Mountains was still fairly sketchy. He notes the absence of Lothlórien and Rohan in this phase of composition.[30]

---

[30] Tolkien, *Return of the Shadow*, 409. The larger argument is based on a close reading of Christopher Tolkien's reconstruction in its entirety, com-

In terms of geographic texture, however, the most significant omission is Isengard. The advent of Saruman, and his installation on Rohan's western border at the edge of the forest of Fangorn, in a strategic location commanding the Gap of Rohan between the White Mountains and the southern foothills of the Misty Mountains, was crucial to the development of Tolkien's story. His establishment as a second expansionist Power (Gandalf's word) greatly widens the strategic field and calls into play two other geopolitical entities, which emerge as Merry and Pippin and their would-be rescuers pass from the Great River to the Fangorn Forest: these are the kingdom of Rohan (known to its own people as the Mark or Riddermark) and the reclusive Ents of Fangorn. It gives us a Rohan that is distracted by danger on its western border and further troubled by the subversive machinations of Gríma Wormtongue, the king's chief counsellor and Saruman's tool, even as its ally Gondor fears annihilating assault from the east. Saruman's brittle alliance with the Dark Lord, mirroring both Mussolini's alliance with Hitler and the German-Soviet pact of August 1939, complicates the strategic picture by distracting Sauron, who must fear the duplicity of his supposed ally.

This expansion of the field of action unfolds during Book Three and is fully revealed when Gandalf, having met Aragorn, Legolas the elf and Gimli the dwarf searching for Merry and Pippin in the forest of Fangorn, outlines the strategic situation from the perspective of Sauron and Saruman in turn. Sauron, thinking that Frodo and his companions are taking the Ring to Gondor to use it against him, is preparing a pre-emptive assault on Minas Tirith while Saruman distracts Rohan, threatening Gondor's hope of aid from its ally. But Saruman's treachery in carrying Merry and Pippin off to Isengard obliges Sauron to fear that Saruman may acquire the Ring, and with it the power to challenge him for mastery. Saruman, for his part, owing to the complete destruction of his raiding party by the Rohirrim, has no idea whether it captured the Ring or what else it achieved. Fearing that the talisman may have fallen into King Théoden's hands, he is hurrying to attack the Rohirrim before they discover its power. He cannot know that all his designs are futile, since the Ring, which Frodo and Sam are now carrying towards Mordor, has passed beyond his reach for ever. Meanwhile, equally unknown to him, Nemesis in the form of the ents is poised to

---

prising this volume, *The Treason of Isengard*, *The War of the Ring* and *Sauron Defeated*.

descend on Isengard and obliterate it as a strategic factor. However, the strategic and tactical themes that first emerge around him echo until the Ring is destroyed. The enduring strategic importance of Isengard itself is affirmed when Sauron's spokesman, at the parley before the Black Gate of Mordor, names it as the base from which his master will govern the subjugated West.

It so happens that we can pin down Tolkien's conception of Saruman to a day near the end of August 1940.[31] In the spring Hitler had overrun much of northwest Europe and driven the British from the continent. July had seen the start of the Battle of Britain, the prolonged German bombing assault on the United Kingdom. Perhaps in Saruman's suave assertions of the wisdom and necessity of joining Sauron rather than fighting him, reported by Gandalf to the Council of Elrond, we hear the echo of some colleague of Tolkien's musing on the desirability of making peace with Hitler and joining him to fight the Soviet Union. The idea gains force when we realize that both Saruman and Gandalf are in fact academics, although of different sorts. Saruman is an academic heavyweight: learned, ambitious, and a jealous guardian of his expertise. As Gandalf notes in explaining his own delay in identifying Bilbo's ring as the One Ring,

> he is great among the Wise. He is the chief of my order and the head of the [White] Council. His knowledge is deep, but his pride has grown with it and he takes ill any meddling. The lore of the Elven-rings, great and small, is his province. He has long studied it, seeking the lost secrets of their making; but when the Rings were debated in the Council, all that he would reveal to us told against my fears.

Nowadays Saruman might be a "public intellectual," even a media star, enlightening the public from his study (or studio) in Orthanc. Yet even before his outright treachery he was, perhaps, at least in retrospect, an enigmatic figure and maybe a bit of a phoney, more cunning than wise. His leading role in the expulsion of Sauron, alias the Necromancer, from his fastness in the forest of Mirkwood confirmed his stature in Gandalf's eyes. But Saruman had long opposed confronting the Necromancer, and besides, it is now known that Sauron had only feigned defeat while retreating as planned to his old base in Mordor.

Gandalf, at least on the surface, is a more unassuming and eclectic sort of scholar. Apart from his skill in pyrotechnics, he

---

[31] Tolkien, *Treason of Isengard*, 67, 70-72.

cultivates a side-line in arcane branches of scholarship such as Hobbit Studies (one suspects a parallel with Tolkien's own esoteric field of study). But his academic habit of mind comes to the fore in the inconspicuously hilarious moment when he and his companions must utter a password in order to open the gate to Moria. After conjuring up a glittering outline of the gate on the blank rock face, including an antique elvish inscription demanding the password, Gandalf launches into a fluent discourse on dwarf-gates and ways of opening them, calling on Gimli for corroboration. The dwarf duly provides this, along with the crucial detail that the passwords to gates of this sort have long been forgotten. But don't *you* know it, Boromir asks Gandalf, and the wizard, answering in the negative, is quite nettled by his companions' dismay. Then they wait and wait as he desperately dumps a cornucopia of arcane knowledge on what turns out to be an "absurdly simple" problem.

The professorial essence of wizards confirms the significance of Saruman, springing to life in Tolkien's mind in August 1940, as a figure of the moment. The complex of political and strategic argument and action that surrounds him, greatly expanding and enriching the story, points up the contribution of the Second World War to making Tolkien's *Hobbit*-sequel into the story of what its author called "the War of the Ring." At the outbreak of war, the epic character of Tolkien's story was still latent. His idea of hitching his *Hobbit*-sequel to his legendarium afforded scope for epic development in both time and space, but he did not yet "know everything," to borrow E. M. W. Tillyard's phrase: he had brought the present into contact with the past, but he did not fully see the future and knew remarkably little about the geography in which that future was to unfold. It was the imaginative stimulus supplied by the war that enabled him to formulate the grand themes of his story, articulate its spatial development, and work out the plot.

But the war did something else too: as I suggested earlier, it confirmed Tolkien in the use of a tone that had worried him by its unsuitability for juvenile fare. In May 1944, we find him writing that "the whole thing has grown so large in significance that sketches of concluding chapters (written ages ago) are quite inadequate, being on a more 'juvenile' level." In retrospect he decided that the prime focus of his story was not even Power and Domination, the theme symbolized by the Ring. The real theme was "something much more permanent and difficult: Death and Immortality."[32]

"Death and immortality"

The Ring is destroyed and Sauron with it. Aragorn is crowned king of Gondor, and a golden age of peace and prosperity descends on Middle-earth. Yet the abiding mood of *The Lord of the Rings* is not triumphal but elegiac, the final feeling one of irreparable loss. Such a feeling is not inappropriate to a war's ending, even in victory: after the initial feelings of triumph and relief have faded, one is left picking up the pieces and counting the cost. What is strange about *The Lord of the Rings* is the fact that the loss is largely a consequence, not of the war, but of the victory.

This outcome is foreshadowed early in the story. During Gandalf's long absence from the Shire, as Frodo restlessly roams the countryside gathering ominous rumours from "strange dwarves of far countries, seeking refuge in the West," he also encounters elves who are heading west to the Grey Havens, intent on leaving Middleearth and its troubles. Readers of *The Hobbit* will already have some idea of elves as creatures of glamour and magic, but in *The Lord of the Rings* their image is embellished. Through the hobbits' halfcomprehending eyes we gain an impression of them as joyous adepts of the natural world, which they study, not to gain riches and power, but to cultivate arts that can capture and magnify the beauty and power of nature, thereby fortifying good against everencroaching evil. Their power to do good is greatly enhanced by three rings forged with Sauron's aid before they were aware of his wickedness. Because of this taint, the destruction of the One Ring must entail the waning of their power too. They must leave Middleearth or "fade" into a shadowy folk of legend.

In the subtly dual time-scheme of Tolkien's story, in fact, elves are at once legendary and real; but this is not obvious, since Tolkien presents them as occupying the same plane of reality as the other characters. The duality of elves is, though, another manifestation of the effect whereby the hobbits journey into the past while appearing to remain on a single temporal plane: that is, it is conveyed implicitly, not by positive assertion. Thus, after reporting Frodo's encounters with wandering dwarves and elves, and thereby establishing the reality of elves as we already know them from *The*

---

[32] *Letters*, 80-81, 246, 262, 267, 284.

Hobbit, Tolkien turns to a scene at a local inn where Sam Gamgee and his drinking pals are discussing these portents not as fact but as rumour. A gardener of poetic temperament, Sam believes that elves exist and even that he glimpsed one once in the woods, but it quickly becomes clear that most hobbits are far more sceptical: when he cites Bilbo's authority for their reality, Ted Sandyman, the miller's son, dismisses it as evidence that Bilbo was "cracked". It is no surprise that Frodo and his friends return to the Shire at the end of the story to find Ted a zealous partisan of the tree-murdering New Order imposed by Saruman's henchmen.

Tolkien only hints at it, but elves are elusive to mortals even in their "real" aspect. You will not see them if they do not mean you to see them, or unless it serves some mysterious "purpose". This is true even of Frodo, who consorts with them as an elf-friend. When he asks how Gildor Inglorion's companions know his name, they tell him "We have often seen you before with Bilbo, though you may not have seen us" (FR 89). A remark of Gildor to Frodo encapsulates these hints of elusiveness, separate destinies and higher purpose:

> The elves have their own labours and their own sorrows, and they are little concerned with the ways of hobbits, or of any other creatures upon earth. Our paths cross theirs seldom, by chance or purpose. In this meeting there may be more than chance; but the purpose is not clear to me ... (FR 94)

Likewise, apart from Frodo and his friends, the only mortals who arrive at Rivendell for the Council of Elrond are Aragorn, who is Elrond's kinsman and grew up there; the dwarf Glóin, who had been there before with Bilbo; his son Gimli; and the man Boromir, who was guided from Gondor by a dream. Indeed, Elrond declares outright that all those assembled have been "called" to Rivendell "to find counsel for the peril of the world" (FR 255). No one is there by chance. It was not Elrond who put out the call, but he recognizes the signs.

Why couldn't Gildor and his companions just turn round and escort the hobbits to Rivendell, saving them all the trouble that dogs them on the road? The question simply does not arise, and the two parties continue on their separate ways. Later it will appear that the elves had sent messages to Rivendell (FR 222). This is typical in that, when the elves do act, the action is auxiliary and performed out of sight. In the War of the Ring they do not fight Sauron as allies of men, as in the days of the Last Alliance, but remain offstage as co-belligerents.

Even on stage, moreover, the elves are in mufti. Gandalf tells Frodo that in Rivendell there still live lords of the elves "from beyond the furthest seas, [who] do not fear the Ringwraiths because those who have dwelt in the Blessed Realm live at once in both worlds, and against both the Seen and the Unseen they have great power" (FR 235). Thinking back to the fracas at the ford below Rivendell, where the elf Glorfindel helped Aragorn fend off the Black Riders, Frodo recalls a white figure that shone and did not grow faint like the others, and Gandalf says "Yes, you saw him for a moment as he is upon the other side: one of the mighty of the Firstborn." And late in the story, when the Ring has been destroyed and Frodo and his friends are returning northward with Gandalf, Elrond, Galadriel and Celeborn and their retinues, the four great ones sit together communing under the stars and we are told: "If any wanderer had chanced to pass, little would he have seen or heard, and it would have seemed to him only that he saw grey figures carved in stone, memorials of forgotten things now lost in unpeopled lands" (RK 263). They converse telepathically, and only their shining eyes stir and kindle as they do so.

There and not there; in Middle-earth but not of it; prone to hinting at mysterious providences; available only to the faithful: in a story full of monsters and magic, it is the elves above all who are vessels of the numinous. Their confrontation with Sauron and his Ringwraiths is crucial to establishing the battleground as what Northrop Frye calls "a mediterranean known world ... between the upper and lower gods."[33] And as the nearest we get to the "upper gods," they are the principal bearers of the story's underlying ideology. That ideology is Christian — Tolkien described the story as "a fundamentally religious and Catholic work; unconsciously so at first, but consciously in the revision"[34] — but his point of view has often been misunderstood. This is not surprising, since he deliberately misleads us.

A frequent focus of ideological discussion is Lothlórien — the heart of Elvendom on earth (as Aragorn calls it) — where the elf-queen Galadriel, wielding one of the elven-rings, rules with her consort, Celeborn. It is even harder than Rivendell for mortals to enter. The very name is an omen: Boromir balks at the idea of going there, and mere mention of Galadriel prompts Éomer of Rohan to

---

[33] See above, 9.
[34] *Letters*, 172.

superstitious aspersions. Hearing that Merry and Pippin have passed through the Golden Wood, Treebeard declares himself surprised that they got out, but much more so that they ever got in: "that has not happened to strangers for many a year." Even Faramir, Boromir's wiser brother, deems it "perilous now for mortal man wilfully to seek out the Elder People."[35] Elves are estranged and withdrawn from mortals, even those of Gondor, descended from the elf-friends of old. To the knowing reader, however, Lothlórien is particularly rich with religious associations, all of them consonant with Frodo's impression that "on the land of Lórien there was no stain."[36] One early reader discerned in Galadriel the lineaments of the Virgin Mary,[37] and her parting gift to Frodo, a phial containing the light of Eärendil's star, later (at Minas Morgul and in Shelob's lair) functions as a symbol of religious faith very like a crucifix. But Frodo is mistaken: there is a stain on Lórien, and its emblem is the very ring that he spies on Galadriel's finger.

The uniqueness of Lothlórien is made manifest in a temporal effect. The Ring-quest may be a journey back in time, but Lórien seems to abide outside time, or in its own time. Even in Rivendell, Bilbo told Frodo, "Time doesn't seem to pass here; it just is." But entering Lórien, Frodo feels that he has stepped over a bridge of time into a corner of the Elder Days and is walking in a world that is no more. "In Rivendell there was memory of ancient things; in Lórien the ancient things still lived on in the waking world." It is a looking-glass episode inside the looking-glass. At one visionary moment, observing Aragorn, Frodo sees the younger Aragorn that had once stood on that same spot and realizes that Aragorn too is experiencing the past as present: "the grim years were removed from the face of Aragorn and he seemed clothed in white, a young lord, tall and fair; and he spoke words in the Elvish tongue to one whom Frodo could not see." At the parting picnic, Galadriel already seems to Frodo "as by men of later days Elves still at times are seen:

---

[35] FR 367, 352; TT 35, 70, 288.
[36] FR 365; and see, *e.g.*, Michael W. Maher, S.J., "A Land Without Stain: Medieval images of Mary and their use in the characterization of Galadriel," in *Tolkien the Medievalist*, ed. Jane Chance (London and New York: Routledge, 2003), 225-36; Joseph Pearce, *Tolkien: Man and myth* (London: HarperCollins, 1998).
[37] *Letters*, 172.

present and yet remote, a living vision of that which has already been left far behind by the flowing streams of Time."[38]

And so, when the companions resume their journey, now in boats on Anduin, the Great River, it seems to them as though Lórien is slipping away from them "like a bright ship … sailing on to forgotten shores" — i.e., into the past — while they sit "helpless upon the margin of the grey and leafless world." (FR 393). If ever the hobbits tried to find their way back without the proper guidance or auspices, would it even be there? If some unblest mortal lighted on the spot, would he even notice the magical kingdom that occupied it? And what would happen to him if he did? Some days later, Sam is perplexed to see by the moon that they had stayed there at least a month, although it felt like much less. Interpreting Sam's observation in terms of his own subjective impressions, Frodo suggests that in Lothlórien they were in a time gone by. Legolas contradicts him, declaring that time never tarries, "but change and growth is not in all things and places alike" (FR 404); then he describes how elves experience time. Aragorn, a mortal who has visited Lothlórien before, has the last word: while there they experienced time as the elves do, and so Sam lost count.

There is a puzzle here. Tolkien did not need an explicit looking-glass moment to launch Frodo and his friends on their journey into the past, but now he gives us one which is specifically time-related — to what end? The key is that the temporal ambiguity that the characters experience is a false sensation, since time is not actually standing still or even retarded. The relevance to death and immortality is obvious — death is the reality, immortality an illusion — and it was, in fact, around the idea of Lothlórien that Tolkien's conception of his story finally crystallized. His deliberations focused on two related questions.

One concerned the origin and importance of the elven-rings. Had they been forged by Sauron or by the elves, and how would the destruction of the One Ring affect them? No draft of the story suggests anything but the downbeat notion that the power of the elven-rings would fail, but a "small, isolated scrap of paper" among Tolkien's notes sketches an alternative outcome, in which the three rings are "*freed*, not destroyed by the destruction of the One," and the high-elven communities of Lothlórien, Rivendell and the Grey Havens are saved until such time as their members "grow weary,

---

[38] FR 243, 364, 367, 389.

and until Men ... 'eat up the world'." Frodo and Sam remain in the Shire until old age, when they sail together into the West and the Elves adopt them.[39] Even this is hardly the happiest of endings, since here too the elves are ultimately ousted by human encroachment, but it lacks that bitterness of bereavement with which Tolkien finally freighted his story.

The second question concerned the timelessness: was it real or illusory? Tolkien started by leaning towards reality and ended by opting for illusion.[40] His reasoning at the time focused on the problem of fitting the Lothlórien episode into the chronology of the broader story, but certain comments made shortly after the story was finished shed a different light, which illuminates the relationship between the temporal ambiguity and the elven-rings.

In a synopsis of his mythology, written to persuade the publisher Collins to issue his legendarium along with *The Lord of the Rings*, Tolkien declares that "there cannot be any 'story' without a fall — all stories are ultimately about the fall."[41] He is talking here about the mythology as a whole, which describes a world of several "speaking races", each with its own fall-driven history. The action of *The Lord of the Rings* is set in the context of this broader mythology, but it is also the climax of a miniature version of that story — one which begins with the forging of the Rings: not just the One but the Three, the Seven and the Nine. Tolkien's decision that the Three must be of elven craft, but fatally compromised by Sauron's sorcery,[42] sets the Elves apart from Men and Dwarves. The latter are mortal (that is, corrupt) kindreds whom Sauron ensnared by their lust for power and treasure respectively. In the Elves' case, he found their Achilles heel in their nostalgia for the pristine beauty of the elven-home beyond the Sea, and their rings, accordingly, are "operative in preserving the memory of the beauty of old, maintaining enchanted enclaves of peace where time seems to stand still and decay is restrained, a semblance of the bliss of the True West."[43] Rivendell and Lothlórien are two such enclaves. Nevertheless, the forging of the Three was "a sort of second fall or at least 'error' of the Elves."[44]

---

[39] Tolkien, *Treason of Isengard*, 286-87.
[40] *Ibid.*, 283-84, 285-86, 354-55, 358, 363-69.
[41] *Letters*, 147.
[42] Tolkien, *Treason of Isengard*, 254-56.
[43] *Letters*, 157.
[44] *Letters*, 151.

Tom Shippey sees Tolkien as torn between "the urge to escape mortality by some way other than Christian consolation" and the "conviction that that urge was impossible, even forbidden."[45] If so, in Tolkien's mythology the elves stand for that urge. However innocent it may seem, and however admirable its results, their desire to stem the tide of history is unlawful and doomed to failure. In Tolkien's explanation, therefore, the crucial words are *seems* and *semblance*. The elf-realms are not quite what they seem, and the temporal ambiguity that surfaces in Lothlórien expresses the discrepancy between perception and reality. A site of resistance to history, Galadriel's realm affords Frodo and his companions a brief respite from the churning flood on which they are fated to travel; but it is not really outside history, and its fate is tied to that of Sauron's Ring. The destruction of the Ring will deprive the Elves of all their power, not just the benefits that accrued from his collaboration; it will mean that they "must depart into the West, or dwindle to a rustic folk of dell and cave, slowly to forget and to be forgotten" (FR 380).

Tolkien had set out to bring his hobbit-world and his hobby-world into conjunction, and narrative convergence had brought emotional convergence in its wake. His *Hobbit*-sequel had become fused with a bleak larger story — his personal version of what he called the Christian myth. This was above all a story of decline: the relentless deterioration of the world from its pristine perfection, owing to the fatal responsiveness of human nature to the prompting of evil. Galadriel says of herself and Celeborn: "Together through ages of the world we have fought the long defeat." Tolkien elaborated on this in a letter to an early reader: "I am a Christian, and indeed a Roman Catholic, so I do not expect 'history' to be anything but a 'long defeat' — though it contains (and in a legend may contain more clearly and movingly) some samples or glimpses of final victory."[46] The pious reservation is not unusual when Tolkien is speaking in his own voice, but his fiction gives us the sadness unvarnished. Indeed, there can be no final victory in a tale that is itself suspended in the story of the long defeat.

The closing chapters fill with this sense of defeat in victory as Frodo and his friends ride back from their time-journey into the present that Ted Sandyman epitomizes. Steadily the world contracts

---

[45] Shippey, *Road to Middle-earth*, 327.
[46] *Letters*, 255.

until that rainy October day when Gandalf turns aside to visit Tom Bombadil.

> "Well here we are, just the four of us that started out together," said Merry. "We have left all the rest behind, one after another. It seems almost like a dream that has slowly faded."
>
> "Not to me," said Frodo. "To me it feels more like falling asleep again" (RK 276).

This exchange is one of several portents that herald the final bereavement when Sam, Merry and Pippin, doomed to remain in Middle-earth, will part for ever at the Grey Havens from Bilbo, Frodo, Gandalf, Elrond, Galadriel and "many Elves of the High Kindred who would no longer stay in Middle-earth" (RK 309). Sam's loss of Frodo mirrors Elrond's bitter parting from his daughter Arwen, who has renounced her immortality to wed Aragorn, and Celeborn's separation from Galadriel, which occurs offstage but is foreshadowed at the final meeting with Treebeard. Treebeard himself speaks for a race doomed, not by the loss of some mystic power, but by the spread of men, the main beneficiaries of Sauron's downfall.

Why should the ascendancy of man be so dire? Because of the nature of the beast. Modelled as it is on the "secular scripture" described by Northrop Frye, Tolkien's mythos is a fictive myth-history which emulates the Old Testament in telling a story that begins with the Creation.[47] Its theme is the tragedy of fallen Man as epitomized in the ineluctable fact of mortality, but the Fall brings not only death but change; the expulsion from timeless bliss brings the onset of history, which is the bane of elves as death is the bane of mortals. This explains the theme of estrangement between Elves and Men which runs through the narrative. The rift is mainly the fault of Men, whose fear of death drives them to disrupt the order that the elves cherish — makes them, in short, agents of history.[48]

Indeed, the estrangement is a correlative of the decline of men — especially the Númenóreans, or Men of the West, whose forebears received a special grace as reward for their alliance with the elves against Morgoth in the First Age only to fall from grace through fear of mortality, until at last Sauron duped them into invading the Undying Lands to wrest the gift of immortality from

---

[47] Northrop Frye, *The Secular Scripture: A Study of the Structure of Romance* (Cambridge, MA: Harvard UP, 1976), 3-31.
[48] *Letters*, 145-46.

the Valar, or gods. This idea first figured in Tolkien's time-travel fragment "The Lost Road," and in *The Lord of the Rings* the story of Númenor is told only in the Appendices. In the body of the narrative, we learn only of the escape of Elendil and his sons and of what they and their line did in Middle-earth: the creation of the kingdoms of Arnor and Gondor; the defeat of Sauron by the Last Alliance; the dwindling and vanishing of Arnor, the North-kingdom; the long-lived glory of Gondor and its slow waning as "the blood of the Númenóreans became mingled with that of lesser men" and the power of Sauron revived (FR 257-58). But Faramir of Gondor, meeting Frodo and Sam in Ithilien, links this decline to the persistence of the old obsession with mortality: "Childless lords sat in aged halls musing on heraldry; in secret chambers withered men compounded strong elixirs, or in high cold towers asked questions of the stars." Their decline obliged them to form alliances with lesser peoples, above all the Rohirrim, leading in time to assimilation of blood and culture. "As the Rohirrim do, we now love war and valour as things good in themselves, both a sport and an end; and though we still hold that a warrior should have more skills and knowledge than only the craft of weapons and slaying, we esteem a warrior, nonetheless, above men of other crafts." And like the Rohirrim, they now fear and mistrust the elves, though knowing little of them (TT 286-87).

"We are a failing people," says Faramir, "a springless autumn." But won't the final overthrow of Sauron, and the ascent of Aragorn to the thrones of Gondor and the revived North-kingdom, usher in a glorious renaissance? In the short run no doubt it will, but in the end that glory must fail. Men will dominate the earth, but they will be lesser men, lacking the grace that endows Aragorn and Faramir with a touch of the superhuman. This goes without saying: it is inherent in Tolkien's positioning of *The Lord of the Rings* and his legendarium as earlier phases of the history of our own fallen world, in which there are no more elf-friends and even elves are not what they were. As a part of that mythos, *The Lord of the Rings* is a narrative of a turning-point in history, a tale suspended in a larger history and reflective of what its author sees as the pattern of history.

3

Tolkien: History, Myth, Prophecy

Tolkien's decision to plunge his hobbit heroes into a rip-tide of history set his *Hobbit*-sequel in a potentially epic frame, and the Second World War provided the imaginative stimulus he needed to design and fill the canvas. Under the influence of a global crisis, his story acquired epic scope in time and space and became the capstone of what Northrop Frye calls a total history. By framing the victory over Sauron as a mere respite in the long defeat that is human history, Tolkien gave the story distinctively gloomy cast, closer in mood to David Quint's epic of the defeated than to the triumphal teleology of Quint's victors' epic.

Whence came this melancholy, this mood of loss? The war may have helped Tolkien express it in *The Lord of the Rings*, but the war did not beget it — it is, after all, the dominant temper of his legendarium. But the First World War did not engender it either, although his traumatic engagement with that orgy of suffering and folly certainly coloured it. In fact, Tolkien's cosmic melancholy pre-dated both cataclysms; it was the reason that his response to the First World War took such an idiosyncratic form as the legendarium to start with. It permeates his scholarly as well as his imaginative writing, since even his chosen career was an expression of it.[1]

This chapter addresses the sources of Tolkien's alienation by exploring the elements of thought and temperament that fuelled the creative process. It begins by situating his world-view in the context

---

[1] Cf. Hugh Brogan, "Tolkien's Great War," in *Children and Their Books: A celebration of the work of Iona and Peter Opie*, ed. Gillian Avery and Julia Briggs (Oxford: Clarendon Press, 1989), 356-57.

of the anti-modernist response to the Industrial Revolution. William Morris, whose art and social criticism epitomized this strain of social thought in the later nineteenth century, strongly influenced Tolkien. I use E. P. Thompson's biography of Morris to explore the paradox that Tolkien's reactionary pessimism expresses similar values to those which made Morris a utopian socialist. That discussion establishes the context for considering what Tolkien meant by calling his fiction *history* and *myth*, and I show how this idea is reflected in the shape of his story — especially in the metafictional apparatus comprising the Introductions to the first and second editions, the Prologue, and the Appendices. Having connected his conception of myth and history to his belief in Christian revelation, with its hope of everlasting life, and to his insatiable hunger for personal epiphanies, I argue that *The Lord of the Rings* is the expression of a spiritual wanderlust which tugged Tolkien's mind constantly towards the edges of the knowable. Indeed, the story can be seen as an attempt to conjure up the sensation of such epiphanies.

The process of setting the story in the context of Tolkien's ideas and personality raises broader questions relating to the realization of the supernatural in fiction. One is the phenomenon of *prophecy*, the inspired discourse by which revelation is imparted. Tolkien never wrote about prophecy *per se* but was finally obliged to acknowledge it as a possible effect of his own writing, and his essay on fairy-stories asserts the value of fantasy in terms that echo E. M. Forster's discussion of prophecy as a rare and anomalous aspect of the novel. I examine this convergence between the romancer and the novelist with the help of a pathbreaking psychological treatise, William James's *The Varieties of Religious Experience*; then I explore Tolkien's theoretical vindication of fantasy as "escape" and discuss its applicability to his own fiction. Finally, I consider how far, if at all, Tolkien's desire to reach a wide audience detracts from the power of *The Lord of the Rings* as a comment on the human predicament.

Tolkien's anti-modernism

Tolkien's outlook was founded on a deep aversion to modernity — meaning, first of all, industrialism and its consequences both material and cultural. Wartime letters to Christopher Tolkien record his distaste for the mechanization of warfare, awful enough in the First World War but now made worse by aerial warfare and the bombing of civilians. On hearing of the atomic bomb, he declared it "so horrifying one is stunned" and denounced "the physicists" for "calmly plotting the destruction of the world." But his dislike of industrial technology was not confined to its military use: he lamented its defacement of the English countryside, and particularly the destructive effects of highway-building. He also deplored its propensity to homogenize culture. "Americo-cosmopolitanism" went along with American sanitation, and in 1943 he doubted whether its victory would be "so much the better for the world as a whole and in the long run than the victory of — ". (He left the alternative blank, he explained, lest his letter to Christopher, then serving in the Royal Air Force, be censored.)[2]

However, Tolkien abhorred industrialism not only for its destructive effects on mankind and the natural environment but also for promoting large-scale social organization. A letter of 1943 reports his growing attraction to "Anarchy (philosophically understood, meaning abolition of control not whiskered men with bombs) — or to 'unconstitutional' Monarchy." He deplores the overbearing impersonality of modern government:

> If we were to get back to personal names, it would do a lot of good ... If people were in the habit of referring to "King George's council, Winston [Churchill] and his gang", it would go a long way to clearing thought, and reducing the frightful landslide into Theyocracy [*sic*].

The "quarrelsome, conceited Greeks" had combined to beat back the invading Persian king Xerxes, but nowadays "the abominable chemists and engineers have put such a power into Xerxes' hands, and all ant communities, that decent folk don't seem to have a chance." Here Tolkien suddenly reaches for the whiskers shunned earlier in his letter: "There is only one bright spot and that is the growing habit of disgruntled men of dynamiting factories and power-stations ... But it won't do any good, if it is not universal."[3]

Tolkien's pairing of anarchy and "unconstitutional" monarchy may seem eccentric, and one commentator describes it as simultaneously asserting "his preference for complete absence of government, and for the complete centralization thereof in one person's whim."[4] There is no inconsistency, though: charismatic leadership is the natural outcome in small groups lacking formal

---

[2] *Letters*, 63-66, 88, 105, 111, 116; Carpenter, *J. R. R. Tolkien*, 129-30, 162.
[3] *Letters*, 63-64.
[4] Chester N. Scoville, "Pastoralia and Perfectability in William Morris and J. R. R. Tolkien," in *Tolkien's Modern Middle Ages*, ed. Jane Chance and Alfred K. Siewers (New York: Palgrave Macmillan, 2005), 95.

institutions of governance, be they biker gangs, Robin Hood and his Merry Men, or the stranded schoolboys of William Golding's *Lord of the Flies*. Tolkien continues:

> The proper study of Man is anything but Man; and the most improper job of any man ... is bossing other men. Not one in a million is fit for it, and least of all those who seek the opportunity. And at least it is done only to a small group of men who know *who* their master is.

The last sentence is a bit obscure as it stands, but if we insert the word *properly* before *done*, the statement combines an acute critique of the will to power with nostalgia for an idealized antiquity of intimate communities ruled by charismatic, "unconstitutional" monarchs — communities like the Anglo-Saxon kingdoms and the clan communities of early Iceland, counterparts of the Greek city states. Versions of this ideal abound in *The Lord of the Rings*: the charismatic monarchies of the elves; the virtual anarchy of Fangorn; the collegial hierarchy of the Shire, with its largely nominal offices, hereditary or elective; even the human kingdoms of Rohan and Gondor. Tolkien's biographer quotes him as saying that "Touching your cap to the Squire may be damn bad for the Squire but it's damn good for you."[5] *The Lord of the Rings* is about many things, but one of them is the importance of knowing your place and doing your duty.

The obvious contrast to these images of communal harmony is the bureaucracy and destruction the hobbits find on returning to the Shire, now under Saruman's sway. This chapter has been construed as an allegory of the regime of rationing and austerity that prevailed in Britain under the Labour government of 1945-51, but that is too narrow a frame of reference. Tolkien himself declared that his vision referred to broader trends in modern life, and his wartime letters show that his hostility to "big government" was well set before Labour came to power. Dismissing the identification with post-war "socialism", a letter of 1956 notes that "the present design of destroying Oxford in order to accommodate motor-cars" is being pushed by a Conservative government.[6] Indeed, the Conservative Party could hardly have thrived as the party of big business in twentieth-century Britain if it had been opposed to modernity. Ted Sandyman and his father may build an ugly steam-driven mill and

---

[5] Carpenter, *J. R. R. Tolkien*, 133.
[6] Shippey, *J. R. R. Tolkien*, 167-71; *Letters*, 235

cut down trees to feed it, but the chief wrecker is Frodo's cousin Lotho, a grabby capitalist who opens the door to Saruman.

Fundamentally, as Tom Shippey remarks, Tolkien's thought is anti-modern rather than politically specific. Tolkien himself remarked that in reality there were "orcs" on both sides; and, even before the atom bomb was unveiled, he opined that "we are attempting to conquer Sauron with the Ring."[7] While he loathed Nazi and Soviet totalitarianism, his phrase *ant communities*, quoted above, refers to industrialized mass society in general. "I am *not* a 'democrat'," he declared, "only because 'humility' and equality are spiritual principles corrupted by the attempt to mechanize and formalize them, with the result that we get not universal smallness and humility, but universal greatness and pride, till some Orc gets hold of a ring of power — and then we get and are getting slavery."[8]

This rejection of modernity was not new in British thought. Revolutions generally provoke resistance, and the Industrial Revolution was no exception, as will appear when we get to *The Making of the English Working Class*. Starting in the later eighteenth century, the introduction in Britain of new techniques and systems of industrial production, powered first by water and then by coal, dramatically increased industrial productivity, but only at the cost of impoverishing much of the population. Communities of craft workers were ruined; towns mushroomed into filthy cities featuring industrial slums crowded with economic refugees, some of whom found work in the sweatshop factories that housed the new machinery. After the final defeat of Napoleon in 1815, mass movements arose aimed at reforming a parliamentary system largely unchanged since the Middle Ages in order to make it more representative of the nation. Another sort of protest aimed at establishing workers' rights: these years saw the birth of British trade unionism. We will run into these movements in discussing Thompson's epic history.

The new industrial order was attacked from two angles. One was reactionary, the other reformist and even revolutionary, but both critiques lamented its destruction of the community life that had supposedly flourished previously. An intricate network of personal relationships, based on ties of mutual obligation that spanned the social hierarchy, had given way to a world in which relationships were economic and impersonal. "Cash-payment is not the sole

---

[7] *Letters*, 78, 82.
[8] *Letters*, 107, 215, 246.

nexus of man with man," insisted the conservative historian and social commentator Thomas Carlyle, denouncing "the brutish godforgetting Profit-and-Loss Philosophy" that valued a man purely at the market rate for his labour. Five years later, in 1848, two young German observers of British society, Karl Marx and Friedrich Engels, adapted the idea of the cash nexus in *The Communist Manifesto* to epitomize the difference between industrial capitalism and older ways of life.[9]

In *Past and Present*, Carlyle contrasted modern conditions with an idealized picture of life on the lands of a twelfth-century English monastery; and at its extreme, the conservative critique of industrialism found expression in the nostalgic fantasies of Young England, a ginger-group of young Tory aristocrats of the 1840s who dreamed of restoring a mythical golden age in which a benevolent aristocracy had ruled over a happy and deferential peasantry. However, the Middle Ages also inspired progressive commentators such as John Ruskin, a highly influential art critic turned social critic. Marx and Engels, self-styled scientific socialists, mocked this nostalgia as self-serving sentimentalism, and the lower classes themselves preferred to dream of a countryside without landlords. One offshoot of the democratic mass movement known as Chartism was a Land Plan that envisaged buying landed estates by popular subscription and splitting them into smallholdings to be farmed by the poor.[10]

After 1848, a year of widespread revolution in Europe and the final, futile climax of Chartism in Britain, things quieted down for a couple of decades; but the progress and consequences of industrialism continued to inspire resistance, or at least dissent. A leading dissident was the writer and artist William Morris, whose work reflects a lifelong devotion to medieval themes and aesthetic values. As an undergraduate at Oxford, Morris was attracted to the High Church movement in the Church of England, which exalted Catholic ritual. After graduating, he and a college friend, Edward Burne-Jones, fell in with a group of young artists whose devotion to early Renaissance painting earned them the nickname "the Pre-Raphaelite Brotherhood." Morris successively took up architecture, painting

---

[9] Thomas Carlyle, *Past and Present*, ed. Richard D. Altick (Boston: Houghton Mifflin, 1965), 187, 188. On *The Communist Manifesto*, see below, 203-4.

[10] Richard Faber, *Young England* (London: Faber and Faber, 1987); Joy MacAskill, "The Chartist Land Plan," in Asa Briggs, ed., *Chartist Studies* (London: Macmillan, 1959).

and poetry before starting to cultivate what he called the minor arts. He and some friends set up a firm which produced a variety of decorative handicrafts, including furniture, wallpaper, tapestry, stained glass, and ultimately books. In the process he became the chief progenitor of the Arts and Crafts Movement.

Following Carlyle and Ruskin, Morris and his friends idealized the Middle Ages as a golden age of community and craftsmanship — a stark contrast to the modern industrialism that robbed work of all creativity and dignity and turned human beings into automata. Morris in particular was fascinated by medieval myth, extending from the legends of King Arthur to the Icelandic sagas. At first he saw little difference between them, but then he learned the language of the sagas and translated several of them with the help of an Icelander. As he studied them more deeply, he perceived their uniqueness as projections of human fortitude in a bleak, unforgiving land. The society they portrayed seemed to him to embody the communal ideal he cherished, and modern Icelandic life (he visited the island twice) exhibited an equality and brotherhood which seemed to perpetuate that ideal. He hailed the *Volsunga Saga* as "the Great Story of the North, which should be to all our race what the Tale of Troy was to the Greeks," and composed his own verse treatment of it. Late in life he wrote prose romances in a similar vein, which were published with illustrations by Burne-Jones.[11]

In his forties, Morris plunged into political controversy. In 1876-78, he agitated against Britain's support of the Ottoman Empire at a time when its Turkish rulers were brutally suppressing their Christian subjects in Serbia and Bulgaria. At the same time, his concern to preserve the fabric and environment of an older England prompted him to found the Society for the Protection of Ancient Buildings. Deploring the damage that industrialism and urban growth wrought on the countryside, he also became active in rural conservation. Finally, after decades of vain resistance to the baleful consequences of industrialism on many fronts, his engagement with the enemy impelled him to embrace a comprehensive solution to the crisis of the age. In the 1880s he espoused socialism and set up his own political organization, the Socialist League, to fight the tyranny of Private Property.

---

[11] Quoted in E. P. Thompson, *William Morris: Romantic to Revolutionary* (London: Lawrence & Wishart, 1955), 217. For Morris's life in general, see Fiona McCarthy, *William Morris: A Life for Our Time* (London: Faber & Faber, 1994).

"Out of due time": Tolkien and William Morris

Between Morris and Tolkien, affinities abound: the hatred of industrialism and love of countryside and craft; the shared taste for heroic romance and a distinctively Northern pastoralism; the visual aesthetic expressed in Tolkien's case by the pre-Raphaelite flavour of the water-colour frontispiece to *The Hobbit*, with its bright colours, clear lines and slightly flattened perspective, and in the flowing lines and ornate detail, reminiscent of the Art Nouveau style, of his pen-and-ink drawings in the same book. I suspect that a similar kinship of taste links Morris's early attraction to High Church Anglicanism and Tolkien's devotion to the Church of Rome. Tolkien's aesthetic inclinations owed much to the influence of his mother, who taught him the calligraphic skill that adorns *The Lord of the Rings*. It was something of an heirloom, passed down from forebears who had been engravers by profession.[12]

A taste for Morris's work was one of the things that drew Tolkien and C. S. Lewis together, and there is abundant evidence of its influence on Tolkien. His published letters mention Morris only twice, but they hint at a virtually lifelong affinity. In 1914 he writes that he is trying to turn one of the stories of the *Kalevala* "into a short story somewhat on the lines of Morris's romances with chunks of poetry in between"; in 1960 he mentions the influence of the romances on a particular scene in *The Lord of the Rings*.[13] *The House of the Wolfings*, mentioned in the later letter, contains a forest called Mirkwood and a country called (like Theoden's realm) the Mark; the Wolfings share with Theoden's people a Germanic appearance and nomenclature (their chief is named Thiodolf); the action begins with the advent of a messenger bearing the arrow of war, a symbolic summons to battle against an invader which also figures in Tolkien's story. Tom Shippey notes affinities between Tolkien's work and other romances by Morris; Tolkien's biographer suggests that the structure of one of Tolkien's early "legends" resembles that of *The Earthly Paradise*, a multi-volume narrative poem that Morris published in the years 1868-70; and Chester Scoville cites a letter in which Tolkien quotes the poem. This last

---

[12] Carpenter, *J. R. R. Tolkien*, 26, 29.
[13] *Letters*, 7, 303.

connection is especially significant because it is very the letter, discussed above, that expresses his sympathy with anarchism.[14]

I mentioned in chapter 1 that E. P. Thompson too was influenced by Morris's critique of industrial capitalism; but he was not influenced to quite the same effect. I cited him among the writers who associated *The Lord of the Rings* with infantilism; and in a study of Morris which appeared about the same time as Tolkien's story, he labels *The Earthly Paradise* as "the poetry of despair" and disparages it in terms that would soon be applied to Tolkien's book.

> Consistently the vocabulary is limited so as to prevent the intrusion of the humdrum, the sharp realistic detail, the unpleasant or shocking fact. If scenes of labour are presented, they are seen by the observer as picturesque — the sickle, the bare-footed damsels, the mellowing grapes. If scenes of battle, they are decorative, as seen through a dim heroic mist. If scenes of love, they are sensuous but featureless, presented as a mood of luxury rather than as a human relationship. The characters are the simplest shadows of folk types ... They are brought into relationship, not through the pressures of character, but through the incidents of the story. From the very opening of the poem ... we are transported to a "shadowy isle of bliss", a land of "romance" insulated from the real world, in which we are not invited to judge either the events or the characters according to our own experience of life.[15]

And yet, Thompson remarks, "Morris did not think that he was writing fairy stories for children, but adult poetry." Why, he asks, did Morris choose "tales of magic and dragons" as the subject of his most sustained poetic work?

In Thompson's view, the poem is deliberate escapism, rooted in despair but attempting to evade or contain rather than confront it. He ascribes Morris's despondency partly to the failure of his marriage but emphasizes two other sources: fear of mortality, and alienation from a modernity that Morris felt powerless to change. Both emotions are expressed in the poem's opening lines, which announce its author's escapist intent in words that frankly proclaim his sense of impotence:

> Of Heaven and Hell I have no power to sing,
> I cannot ease the burden of your fears,

---

[14] Scoville, "Pastoralia and Perfectability"; Theresa Freda Nicolay, *Tolkien and the Modernists: Literary Responses to the Dark New Days of the Twentieth Century* (Jefferson, NC: McFarland, 2014), 121-22; Carpenter, *J. R. R. Tolkien*, 80-81, 98, 100; Shippey, *Road to Middle-earth*, 351.

[15] Thompson, *William Morris*, 147; and see, in general, pp. 140-54.

Or make quick-coming death a little thing,
Or bring again the pleasure of past years,
Nor for my words shall ye forget your tears ...
* * *
The heavy trouble, the bewildering care
That weighs us down who live and earn our bread,
These idle verses have no power to bear ...
* * *
Dreamer of dreams, born out of my due time,
Why should I strive to set the crooked straight?
Let it suffice me that my murmuring rhyme
Beats with a light wing against the ivory gate,
Telling a tale not too importunate ...

After characterizing himself as "The idle singer of an empty day," the bard mentions a wizard of northern legend who conjured up at the winter solstice a tableau whereby

> through one window men beheld the spring,
> And through another saw the summer glow,
> And through a third the fruited vines a-row ...

He presents himself as striving to build a similar earthly paradise,

> a shadowy isle of bliss
> Mid-most the beating of the steely sea,
> Where tossed about all hearts of men must be;
> Whose ravening monsters mighty men shall slay,
> Not the poor singer of an empty day.

Thompson amplified this confession of impotence with Morris's own recollections, nearly thirty years later, of his state of mind at the time:

Apart from the desire to produce beautiful things, the leading passion of my life has been and is hatred of modern civilisation ...What shall I say concerning its mastery of and its waste of mechanical power, its commonwealth so poor, its enemies of the commonwealth so rich, its stupendous organisation — for the misery of life! Its contempt of simple pleasures which everyone could enjoy but for its folly? Its eyeless vulgarity which has destroyed art, the one certain solace of labour? All this I felt then as now, but I did not know why it was so. The hope of the past times was gone, the struggles of mankind for many ages had produced nothing but this sordid, aimless, ugly confusion; the immediate future seemed to me likely to intensify all the present evils by sweeping away the last survivals of the days before the dull squalor of civilisation had settled down on the world.[16]

Borne down by a sense of futility, the Morris of *The Earthly Paradise* could attempt nothing better than "idle verses" with "light wings" and a "murmuring rhyme", but no subject matter that might unduly "importune" his readers.

Tolkien's "anarchist" letter of 1943 contains echoes of both texts. His lament at the power that modern technology has put into the hands of "Xerxes" chimes with Morris's horror at the "stupendous organisation" of industrial capitalism "for the misery of life": both writers see the enemy as a Leviathan, not just terrible but irresistible — or in Morris's case, not to be resisted by the author of *The Earthly Paradise* at any rate. And so Tolkien winds up the letter by quoting Morris's poem. "We were born in a dark age out of due time (for us)," he tells Christopher. "But there is this comfort: otherwise we should not *know*, or so much love, what we do love. I imagine the fish out of water is the only fish to have an inkling of water."[17]

As Thompson tells it, however, the despair that Morris sought to stave off by writing *The Earthly Paradise* was a phase, a long dark night of the soul from which he finally emerged to glory. The young Morris had displayed some sparks of the spirit of revolt that had inspired the Romantic movement before its collapse into escapism and sentimentality. After long wallowing in that slough, the middle-aged Morris shook off his despair and escaped across "the River of Fire" (Morris's own words) to socialism: the "Romantic in Revolt" (Thompson's words) became "a realist and a revolutionary." Tolkien did not. His letter professed to find hope — or at least consolation — in "the growing habit of disgruntled men of dynamiting factories and power-stations," but he did not himself take up arms against "Americo-cosmopolitanism" and the burial of the past beneath concrete and steel. Instead he remained in his closet, polishing and revising versions of his own Earthly Paradise, a zone of fantasy where a doomed beauty still glowed amid tragedy and, for a moment, prevailed.

Why didn't Tolkien follow Morris into active rebellion? Chester Scoville dwells on the influence of Tolkien's religion, and the doctrine of Original Sin in particular, which precluded the belief in the perfectibility of human nature that underlay Morris's socialist

---

[16] Thompson, *William Morris*, 153-54.
[17] *Letters*, 63-64.

idealism. Tolkien's Shire may resemble the socialist utopia limned in Morris's political fantasy *News from Nowhere*, observes Scoville, but hobbits are far from perfect and Saruman has apt material to hand in the likes of Ted Sandyman.[18] This is likely enough, but it is not the whole story. Tolkien's religion may have estranged him from even the Christian-tinted socialism, primarily low-church and "chapel" in hue, that predominated in Britain in his day, yet many Catholics have managed to reconcile their religious beliefs with socialism in different times and places, and socialism has taken forms that relied less on the perfectibility of human nature than Morris's utopian creed.

The obstacles to Tolkien's acceptance of socialism were not only doctrinal: they were historical and political. Half a century on, there was simply less scope for optimism. Industrialism was even more strongly entrenched, and its impact on the environment was becoming still harsher with the advent of the automobile and the paving of the countryside. It was harder to feel optimistic about human nature after the First World War, and harder to be rosy-eyed about socialism after the rise of a tyrannical variant in Russia and the atrocities perpetrated against the Catholic Church during the Spanish Civil War. Tolkien loathed Nazism, but the Second World War saw his own country aligned with the United States and the Soviet Union against Finland and the powers that had intervened on the "Christian" side in Spain. He might well conclude that there were orcs on both sides.[19]

Besides, even if Tolkien's religion affected his attitude to socialism, it cannot account for his extreme anti-modernism. For a century after the French Revolution, the Catholic Church was indeed a bastion of political reaction. About the time of Tolkien's birth, however, under Pope Leo XIII, it achieved a partial reconciliation with modernity. There was, then, no necessary correlation between Catholicism and anti-modernism, and we may understand their relationship in Tolkien's world-view as reciprocal rather than causal. His religion was one component of his outlook, not necessarily more significant than others in intellectual terms and certainly not determinative. He was not just a Catholic, but a Catholic of emphatically anti-modern cast.

---

18 Scoville, "Pastoralia and Perfectability," 96-102.
19 *Letters*, 37-38, 55-56, 93.

I suggested earlier that his sympathy for anarchism and "unconstitutional monarchy," as declared in a letter to Christopher, expresses nostalgia for bygone forms of small-scale government, such as the petty kingdoms of Anglo-Saxon England. Other remarks in the same set of letters point the same way. "I love England (not Great Britain and certainly not the British Commonwealth (grr!))" he writes. Responding to an observation by Christopher, who was training in South Africa, he deplores colonial attitudes to black Africans. Contemplating the continuing war against Japan after Germany's surrender in May 1945, he declares: "as I know nothing about British and American imperialism in the Far East that does not fill me with regret and disgust, I am afraid I am not even supported by a glimmer of patriotism in this remaining war."[20] These declarations suggest that he identified, not with the capitalist and imperialist entity known as the *United Kingdom of Great Britain and Northern Ireland*, but with *England* — and not the England of his own day, but one so old that his allegiance to it did not translate into allegiance to the upstart Church of England, founded in 1534 when the English state, in the person of King Henry VIII, repudiated the spiritual supremacy of Rome. The apparent discrepancy between his faith and his patriotism only reinforces the idea that both were expressions of anti-modernism.

No doubt Tolkien's espousal of Catholic teaching as Truth owed something, not just to the substance of the doctrine, but to personal temperament, filial piety, and the aesthetics of Catholic worship. But the peculiar mixture of Roman Catholicism and English — not British — patriotism in his world-view points to something that is more important for our present purposes: the historical component of his faith. He was not just a Catholic but an English Catholic. Catholicism was the Christianity of Anglo-Saxon and medieval England; it suffused the texts he studied as a scholar of Old and Middle English. The England he loved was the land of words, place-names and ruins that preserved echoes of that vanished past — a past first obliterated by the Norman Conquest of 1066 and then further sundered from the present by England's breach with Rome. Tolkien could cherish Catholic teaching as a surviving gleam of pristine truth and glory, and repudiate his country's Protestant modernity by embracing the claim of the Roman Church to stand for original Christianity. Such fatalistic cherishing of a doomed beauty

---

[20] *Letters*, 65, 73, 115.

is the keynote of *The Lord of the Rings*: the response of a "fish out of water," to quote Tolkien's letter of November 1943, or perhaps of a fish inside the Whale.

Born out of his due time, Tolkien conjured up in his fiction an alternative time to dream in, amplifying in his imagination the ancient world of courage, grace and charisma — and magic and dragons — that he could faintly discern through the prism of a few, sometimes fragmentary, ancient texts. Was this escapism? Long before his critics posed the charge, Tolkien framed his answer in words I have already quoted: "I took to 'escapism': or really transforming experience into another form and symbol."[21] Unable to stare the trauma of the trenches in the face, he fashioned a mirror of fantasy in which to scrutinize the human condition as Perseus had the Gorgon. Like the shield of Perseus, Tolkien's mirror was meant to reflect reality, not obscure it, and what he saw in it was far too melancholy to count as escapism in the sense that E. P. Thompson applies the term to *The Earthly Paradise*. That is why he frequently called his story *history* and took pains to present it as such. It was a narrative of the long defeat.

History, myth and allegory

By describing his fiction as history, Tolkien meant two things, or perhaps one complicated thing. Though his story was fantasy, it was an imaginative depiction of the real world. It was not, however, an allegorical figuring of reality. When he denied that *The Lord of the Rings* was an allegory of the Second World War, he first sketched the very different story he would have told if he had meant to write such an allegory; then he disparaged allegory in general:

> I much prefer history, true or feigned, with its varied applicability to the thought and experience of readers. I think that many confuse "applicability" with "allegory"; but the one resides in the freedom of the reader, and the other in the purposed domination of the author (FR, 7).

His story was not written to impose a particular world-view on its readers: it was history, albeit "feigned" — that is, fictitious or invented — history.

Tolkien had to admit, however, that any fantasy with a strong tincture of reality ran the risk of allegorical interpretation. Even *The*

---

[21] See above, 23.

Hobbit had evoked that response,[22] and when he wrote his synopsis for the publisher Collins he found himself resorting to similar language: "I dislike Allegory — the conscious and intentional allegory," he admitted, "yet any attempt to explain the purport of myth or fairytale [*sic*] must use allegorical language." What he disliked most was readers' propensity to assume that their own interpretation was what he, as author, "meant". When the very first reader of *The Lord of the Rings*, his publisher's son Rayner Unwin, detected a "struggle between darkness and light (sometimes one suspects leaving the story proper to become pure allegory)," Tolkien remarked:

> Of course, Allegory and Story converge, meeting somewhere in Truth ... but the two start from opposite ends. You can make the Ring into an allegory of our own time, if you like: an allegory of the inevitable fate that waits for all attempts to defeat evil power by power. But that is only because all power magical or mechanical does always so work. You cannot write a story about an apparently simple magic ring without that bursting in, if you really take the ring seriously, and make things happen that would happen, if such a thing existed.[23]

Readers could interpret the story as they wished, but they were not entitled to impose their interpretation on him as author, since his intention was not to propagate a particular world-view but simply to write the best story he could.

Still, he admitted that his story carried a cargo of values. George Orwell wrote: "Every writer, especially every novelist, has a 'message', whether he admits it or not ... All art is propaganda." Tolkien said something similar of himself. He told one reader:

> As for "message": I have none really, if by that is meant the conscious purpose ... of preaching, or of delivering myself of a vision of truth specially revealed to me! I was primarily writing an exciting story in an atmosphere and background such as I find personally attractive. But in such a process inevitably one's own taste, ideas, and beliefs get taken up.

Even while rebutting Rayner Unwin's perception of allegory, he granted that "There is a 'moral', I suppose, in any tale worth telling."[24] *The Lord of the Rings*, however, was not a tale told in order to impart a moral.

---

[22] *Letters*, 41.

[23] *Letters*, 121; other quotations pp. 120, 145.

[24] George Orwell, "Charles Dickens," in *The Collected Essays, Journalism and Letters of George Orwell. Volume 1: An Age Like This, 1920-1940*, ed. Sonia

The invocation of history is a recurring theme in Tolkien's exegesis of his mythology. What Rayner Unwin saw as allegory is to Tolkien "just a particular phase of history, one example of its pattern, perhaps, but not The Pattern." The foreword to the first edition presents the story as a chapter of "almost forgotten history … not yet universally recognized as an important branch of study." Commenting on W. H. Auden's reference to "imaginary worlds" in the *New York Times*, Tolkien remarks "I am historically minded. Middle-earth is not an imaginary world", and "Mine is not an 'imaginary' world, but an imaginary historical moment on 'Middle-earth' — which is our habitation."[25] The history is imaginary, but it is an imaginary part of the history of our world.

In chapter 1, I quoted Tolkien on the essential similarity of history and myth, and we have seen that his mythos is modelled on Northrop Frye's secular scripture, which commences with the mythic origin of the people or even the Creation. Accordingly, we sometimes find Tolkien counterposing to allegory not *history* but *myth* and its cognates. The Collins synopsis records his youthful passion "for myth (not allegory!) and for fairy-story, and above all for heroic legend on the brink of fairy-tale and history"; it refers to the entry of Men into his legendarium at the point "where the stories become less mythical, and more like stories [*sic*: histories?] and romances."[26] The sundering of Middle-earth from the Undying Lands is, from this standpoint, a step in the transition from myth to history: "The new situation … leads on eventually and inevitably to ordinary History … Gone was the 'mythological time' when [the Undying Lands] existed physically in the Uttermost West … Only the Eldar (or High Elves) could still sail thither, forsaking time and mortality, but never returning." *The Lord of the Rings* is a further phase in that transition: it "exhibits 'myth' passing into History or the Dominion of Men."[27]

This helps to explain the apparently quirky frame of scholarly exegesis in which Tolkien set his tale: the introductory gazetteer of

---

Orwell and Ian Angus (Penguin Books: Harmondsworth, Middx., 1970), 491-92; *Letters*, 267, 121.

[25] *Letters*, 121, 174, 244.

[26] *Letters*, 144, 149.

[27] *Letters*, 186, 207. Friedman, "Fabricating History," presents a complementary perspective on the relationship of myth and history in *The Lord of the Rings*.

the Shire and appendices on history and philology, all supposedly derived from books of lore in a long-dead language. Much of this was material that Tolkien had generated in writing the story but deemed surplus to the requirements of the narrative; thus, reporting the unexpected advent of Faramir in the spring of 1944, Tolkien mentions that his new character is holding up the story by relating

> a lot of stuff about the history of Gondor and Rohan (with some very sound reflections no doubt on martial glory and true glory): but if he goes on much more a lot of him will have to be removed to the appendices — where already some fascinating material on the hobbit Tobacco industry and the Languages of the West have gone.[28]

This remark obviously refers to material that Tolkien had had to invent *in order to write the story*, including a historical overview of the long interval between the narrative present and the time of his legendarium. It paid a huge bonus in enriching the *mise en scène*. However, as a whole, the scholarly apparatus does more than provide colour and context: it serves an important thematic function by tying Tolkien's mythology to human history.

As we saw in the last chapter, Tolkien had originally, in "The Lost Road," planned to forge this link by regressing from contemporary England via a complicated mechanism of inherited memory made manifest in dreams. In *The Lord of the Rings* a direct narrative link to human history was impossible, because his launching-pad into the past was the fantasy-present of *The Hobbit*. This may explain why, even with the sequel two-thirds written, he began work on a second abortive story recounting the travel of an Englishman of his own sort back in time to his myth-world.[29] In the end, though, he contrived to make the appendices his means of connecting *The Lord of the Rings* to his own time — a more effective means, perhaps, since the link is to human history in general rather than that of a specific people.

While the historical appendices help to cement the fictive present to its past, others forge a similar link between us, the readers, and the hobbits who are our guides to Middle-earth and its history — for instance, by telling us that the hobbits did not actually speak English and that the names by which we, the readers, know

---

[28] *Letters*, 79.

[29] J. R. R. Tolkien, *Sauron Defeated: The End of the Third Age (The History of The Lord of the Rings, Part One)*, ed. Christopher Tolkien (Boston and New York: Houghton Mifflin, 1992), 145-327.

them are only linguistic transpositions of their actual names. A startling last-minute estrangement from characters with whom we have all along been encouraged to identify, this revelation reinforces a theme first sounded in the Foreword to the first edition, which tells us that the story is derived from annals set down by Bilbo, Frodo and Sam, and in the Prologue, which makes it clear that the heyday of Hobbits is long gone. Thus the fictional present of the Shire is set up as the distant past of the reader. *The Lord of the Rings* is positioned as a nostalgic evocation of a world *we* have lost and, in addition, as part of the tragic story of our losing it.[30]

Myth, legend, fairy-tale, romance and history together formed a single grand narrative, which told of the Fall and of the travails of the fallen. What, then, distinguished the "mythic" from the "historical" parts of the tale? A letter to Christopher contains a revealing juxtaposition. Responding to a comment about the story the Garden of Eden, Tolkien opines that most educated Christians

> have been rather bustled and hustled now for some generations by the self-styled scientists, and they've sort of tucked Genesis into a lumber-room of their mind as not very fashionable furniture, a bit ashamed to have it around the house, don't you know, when the bright clever young people called ... In consequence they have indeed, as you say, forgotten the beauty of the matter even "as a story."

Affirming his own belief in the story, he remarks, in a poignant testimony to his alienation from modernity:

> It has not, of course, historicity of the same kind as the N[ew] T[estament], which are virtually contemporary documents, while Genesis is separated by we do not know how many sad exiled generations from the Fall, but certainly there was an Eden on this very unhappy earth. We all long for it, and we are constantly glimpsing it: our whole nature at its best and least corrupted, its gentlest and most humane, is still soaked with the sense of "exile" ... As far as we can go back, the nobler part of the human mind is filled with the thoughts of *sibb* [kinship], peace and goodwill, and with the thought of its *loss*.[31]

Thus Tolkien nods to the modern distinction between myth and history but sees no reason to doubt the myth. He bases his belief on

---

30 Paul Romney, "'A Particular Phase of History': Time Travel, Temporal Ambiguity, and the Pattern of History in *The Lord of the Rings*," *Lembas*, nr. 176 (Oct. 2016), 111-12. See also Vladimir Brljak, "The Books of Lost Tales: Tolkien as Metafictionist," *Tolkien Studies*, 7 (2010).
31 *Letters*, 109-10. Italics in original.

another sort of authority: the very generality of the myth and of the emotions it expresses. As he put it in the Collins synopsis: "I believe that legends and myths are largely made of 'truth', and indeed present aspects of it that can only be received in this mode; and long ago certain truths and modes of this kind were discovered and must always reappear."[32]

Tolkien's scholarship alerted him to the human propensity to explain the mysteries of life and death by telling stories about them. He realized that human apprehension of those mysteries varied according to local circumstances and experience: thus the idea of deities of an extremely local nature, such as nymphs and dryads, would naturally crop up in sedentary rustic communities.[33] But though experience was local, human nature was universal, so ultimately there was just the one Story, universal in essence though exhibiting countless local variants. Myths, fairy-stories and history were all aspects of this one Story because they were all attempts to make sense of human existence and experience by telling stories. History was an account of human experience based on external evidence; myths and fairy-stories were symbolic depictions of human experience whose truth was affirmed by their cross-cultural provenance and centuries of survival.

In outward appearance, "the Christian myth" conformed to this pattern. To Tolkien, as a Christian, however, the story of Jesus was at once fiction and history. In his essay "On Fairy-Stories", he suggested that "The Gospels contain a fairy-story, or a story of a larger kind which embraces all the essence of fairy-stories ... There is no tale ever told that men would rather find was true, and none which so many sceptical men have accepted as true on its own merits."[34] They possessed this character, and commanded such belief, because they contained, both in the birth of Christ and the Resurrection, that essential element of fairy-story which Tolkien calls *eucatastrophe*, or "the Consolation of the Happy Ending." This consolation

> is not essentially "escapist", nor "fugitive" ... It does not deny the existence of *dyscatastrophe*, of sorrow or failure; it denies (in the face of much evidence, if you will) universal final defeat and in so far is

---

[32] *Letters*, 147.

[33] See C. S. Lewis's summary of Tolkien's ideas quoted in Meredith Veldman, *Fantasy, the Bomb, and the Greening of Britain: Romantic Protest, 1945-1980* (Cambridge, Eng.: Cambridge UP, 1994), 57.

[34] Tolkien, *Tree and Leaf*, 62-63.

evangelium [gospel, good news], giving a fleeting glimpse of Joy, Joy beyond the walls of the world, poignant as grief.[35]

Tolkien explains this Joy as "a sudden glimpse of underlying reality or truth."

How could the gospels be both fairy-story and history? Note that Tolkien does not say that the Gospels *are* a fairy-story but that they *contain* one ("or rather a story of a larger kind which embraces all the essence of fairy-stories"). In a letter to his son summarizing his argument, he describes the Gospels as *telling* a fairy-story and explains that "Man the story-teller would have to be redeemed in a manner consonant with his nature: by a moving story." *Eucatastrophe* might be a defining feature of fairy-stories, or at any rate of a "good fairy-story", but it was not limited to fairy-stories — it could be achieved in any act of story-telling, oral or written. Tolkien thought that he himself had achieved such a moment in *The Hobbit*, so the feat was hardly beyond "the supreme Artist and Author of Reality." Unlike merely human stories, though, which were confined to the "secondary world" of imaginative "sub-creation," the Christian myth had "entered History and the primary world." The Gospels were not myth dressed up as history but history dressed up as myth.[36]

Tolkien was a subtle and exact thinker, but he was also a very feeling man. Thinking apprised him of the limits of reason, and feeling imbued him with a need for knowledge beyond reason; hence his ultimate criterion of truth was intuitive rather than intellectual. Deepest truth was to be found in stories whose authenticity was affirmed by their broad acceptance across cultures and across time, stories expressing a truth that was informed by reason though not apprehensible by it. This idea, of truth that is accessible to intuition but not to reason, is the underlying theme — the ground bass — of *The Lord of the Rings*.

Intuition and inspiration

The idea appears in Tolkien's scholarly discourse even before he gave it artistic expression. In lectures dating from 1936 and 1938 — the time he began writing "The Lost Road," finished *The Hobbit*, and started work on *The Lord of the Rings* — he applies it first to myth

---

[35] Tolkien, *Tree and Leaf*, 60.
[36] *Letters*, 100-1; Tolkien, *Tree and Leaf*, 62.

and then to fairy-stories. In his lecture on the Old English poem *Beowulf,* he warns that myth is inherently resistant to analysis:

> The significance of a myth is not easily to be pinned on paper by analytical reasoning. It is at its best when it is presented by a poet who feels rather than makes explicit what his theme portends; who presents it incarnate in the world of history and geography, as our poet has done. Its defender is thus at a disadvantage: unless he is careful, and speaks in parables, he will kill what he is studying by vivisection ... For myth is alive at once and in all its parts, and dies before it can be dissected.[37]

In his essay on fantasy he ascribes a similar quality to fairy-stories, which he defines as tales of encounters between human beings and visitors, sometimes called *elves,* from the magic land of Faërie. The magic land lies beyond the "Primary World" of everyday reality, and its magic is not an end in itself but a means to satisfy certain primordial human desires, such as surveying the depths of space and time and holding communion with other living things — desires which Tolkien himself felt intensely, as we shall see. It "cannot be caught in a net of words; for it is one of its qualities to be indescribable, though not imperceptible." Evidently the magic land, like myth, requires the deft touch of intuition to be properly apprehended; but this is no surprise, since fantasy — a name for mankind's efforts to apprehend that realm — comprehends both myth and fairy-story (or *folk-tale,* as Tolkien calls the latter in the *Beowulf* lecture).

Fantasy "does not destroy or even insult Reason; and it does not blunt the appetite for, or obscure the perception of, scientific verity."[38] It is simply a mode of inquiry applicable to a sphere which reason and science cannot reach. Its value lies in affording *Recovery,* meaning the capacity to experience the world anew with childlike freshness; *Escape,* signifying imaginative release from the constraints and miseries of daily life, the greatest being Death; and *Consolation* — above all, *eucatastrophe.* Fantasy, or at least good fantasy, can trigger *eucatastrophe* precisely because it is not a denial of reality — not "escapist" — but an intuitive apprehension of a reality that is not amenable to analysis.

Tolkien's letter to Christopher on *eucatastrophe* illuminates the roots of this notion in his own psychology. It relates an account he had recently heard of a miraculous cure at Lourdes, and cites the

---

[37] J. R. R. Tolkien, "Beowulf: The Monsters and the Critics," *Proceedings of the British Academy,* 22 (1936), 256-57.
[38] Tolkien, *Tree and Leaf,* 50.

emotion this story ignited in him as an example of *eucatastrophe*. After summarizing his then-unpublished argument on the subject, Tolkien recounts his recent experience of

> one of those sudden clarities which sometimes come in dreams (even anaesthetic-produced ones). I remember saying aloud with absolute conviction: "But of course! Of course that's how things really do work". But I could not reproduce any argument that had led to this, though the sensation was the same as having been convinced by *reason* (if without reasoning). And I have since thought that one of the reasons why one can't recapture the wonderful argument or secret when one wakes up is simply because there was not one: but there was (often maybe) a direct appreciation by the mind (sc. reason) but without the chain of argument that we know in our time-serial life.[39]

Tolkien does not mention the substance of the revelation — it is presented simply as a sort of feeling — but the same letter tells how, meditating in church one day, he

> perceived or thought of the Light of God, and in it suspended one small mote (or millions of motes to only one of which was my small mind directed), glittering white because of the individual ray from the Light which both held and lit it ... And the ray was the Guardian Angel of the mote: not a thing interposed between God and the creature, but God's very attention itself, personalized.

Tolkien recalls "the great sense of joy that accompanied it and the realization that the shining poised mote was myself (or any other human person that I might think of with love)."[40]

One can see *The Lord of the Rings* in its entirety as an attempt to capture in art this sort of transcendent experience, which we may imagine as a fleeting glimpse of the Infinite. The hobbits' journey into the past is a journey towards the beginning of Time; it is adumbrated in Tom Bombadil's yarn linking the here-and-now with the First Dawn, and is mediated for the hobbits and for us by the elves, who — in the persons of Elrond and Galadriel especially — are a direct link with the Infinite. Our leader in the quest is Gandalf the professor. Here he is, explaining the *palantír* (an ancient telecommunications device through which Sauron has trapped and dominated both Saruman and Denethor, Steward of Gondor) and

---

[39] *Letters*, 101.
[40] *Letters*, 99.

talking about the temptation it posed to his fellow-scholar Saruman and poses to himself:

> "Alone it could do nothing but see small images of things far off and days remote. Very useful, no doubt, that was to Saruman; yet it seems that he was not content. Further and further abroad he gazed, until he cast his gaze upon Barad-dûr. Then he was caught!
>
> "... And how it draws one to itself! Have I not felt it? Even now my heart desires to test my will upon it, to see if I could not wrench it from him [Sauron] and turn it where I would — to look across the wide seas of water and of time to Tirion the Fair, and perceive the unimaginable hand and mind of Fëanor at their work, while both the White Tree and the Golden were in flower!" He sighed and fell silent (TT 203, 204).

Gandalf is wise enough to know that, while the Infinite may reveal itself to us, it cannot be coerced. If we seek to know it on equal terms, if we actively pursue the mastery of Knowledge as Saruman so rashly did, the fate of Adam and Eve, or perhaps of Faust, awaits us.

It is ironic and revealing, then, that one of the flaws of *The Lord of the Rings* is Tolkien's penchant for forcing moments of revelation into the narrative. Other commentators have noticed this,[41] but it is worth mentioning the almost embarrassing frequency with which Aragorn is "revealed" as more than he seems. This starts when the hobbits first meet him ("He stood up, and suddenly seemed to grow taller. In his eyes gleamed a light, keen and commanding"), but it is most obtrusive in Books 2 and 3 and tends to involve some histrionic gesture with his sword.[42] It is no coincidence that Aragorn was Tolkien's most problematic character, who had started out as a hobbit called Trotter and only gradually revealed himself to Tolkien as a central character as the story unfolded. More on that shortly: at the moment, suffice it to say that Tolkien sometimes comes across as a "revelation junkie" — someone with a craving for such sensations. Diana Wynne Jones suggested that it is "symptomatic ... that he at all times overworks the word 'suddenly.'" To my mind the adjective "clear", relentlessly applied to the voices and visages of Goldberry and assorted elves, is no less hackneyed.[43] I suggest that

---

[41] See, e.g., Shippey, *Road to Middle-Earth*, 212-13.

[42] FR 183, 366-67, 391, 409; TT, 36, 115; Janet Menzies, "Middle-earth and the Adolescent," in Robert Giddings, ed., *J. R. R. Tolkien: This Far Land*, 61-62; Shippey, *Road to Middle-earth*, 212-13.

[43] Diana Wynne Jones, "The Shape of the Narrative in *The Lord of the Rings*," in Giddings, ed., *J. R. R. Tolkien*, 88-9; FR 88, 133, 134, 146, 222, 225, 235, 239, 250, 252, 255, 356, 370, 381.

his fondness for both words, *suddenly* and *clear*, reflects an addictive thirst for "sudden clarities" like those mentioned in his letter on *eucatastrophe*.

This idea gains force from a remark in the letter on the Eden myth written just a couple of months later. It responds to something Christopher had written, and therefore is somewhat allusive, but its basic meaning is plain enough.

> There are two quit[e] diff. emotions: one that moves me supremely and I find small difficulty in evoking: the heart-racking sense of the vanished past (best expressed by Gandalf's words about the Palantir); and the other the more "ordinary" emotion, triumph, pathos, tragedy of the characters. That I am learning to do, as I get to know my people, but it is not really so near my heart, and is forced on me by the fundamental literary dilemma. A story must be told or there'll be no story, yet it is the untold stories that are the most moving. I think you are moved by *Celebrimbor* because it conveys a sudden sense of endless *untold* stories ...[44]

"Gandalf's words about the Palantir" are the passage quoted above. It eloquently projects that longing for the lost past which attracted Tolkien to myth and the study of a vanished culture and which accounts, I have suggested, for the "time-travel" aspect of his masterpiece. The allusion to Celebrimbor is obscure but explicable: as the maker of the three elven-rings in the Second Age of Middle-earth, he plays a crucial part in Tolkien's mythos; but he is mentioned only in passing, giving him an intriguing obscurity. The main point, however, lies in what Tolkien says about untold stories. It suggests that he craved the possibility of revelation even more than the reality.[45]

This insight illuminates his insistence that his big ideas had their genesis in inspiration rather than conscious invention. The stories of the legendarium "arose in my mind as 'given' things, and as they came, separately, so too the links grew ... [A]lways I had the sense of recording what was already 'there', somewhere: not of 'inventing'," he wrote in the Collins synopsis. To W. H. Auden he claimed not to have consciously invented either the ents ("The chapter called

---

[44] *Letters*, 110.

[45] Cf. Shippey, *Road to Middle-Earth*, 53-54: "We can say that the quality he evidently valued in literature was that shimmer of suggestion which never quite becomes clear sight but always hints at something deeper further on."

'Treebeard', from Treebeard's first remark ... was written off more or less as it stands, with an effect on my self ... almost like reading some one else's work") or the *palantíri*. Even more striking are the contemporary testimonies. There is the sudden advent of Faramir, mentioned earlier: "A new character has come on the scene (I am sure I did not invent him, I did not even want him, though I like him, but there he came walking into the woods of Ithilien)."[46] And most extraordinary of all, perhaps, there is the long gestation and sudden metamorphosis of Aragorn, which had Tolkien repeatedly asking himself in his notes: "Who is Trotter?"[47]

As regards *The Lord of the Rings*, each of these inspirations is associated with a major broadening of the *mise en scène*. Aragorn, initially such an enigma to his author, ends up as a central character: the King whose Return is signalled by the title of Volume III. As the descendant of Eärendil and Elendil, he personifies the thousands of years of history that separate *The Lord of the Rings* from the legendarium; and, fittingly, it is his verse-chant on Weathertop that cements the connection between the two milieux. Treebeard broadens our field of vision by offering a completely new perspective on the concerns of the story. Apart from hobbits, the ents are the only "race" of Tolkien's own invention, and like hobbits they mirror the Common Man; but whereas hobbits exhibit him in his everyday aspect, ents embody the People, normally quiescent, and therefore exploited or neglected by the mighty, but capable of turning the world upside down when goaded beyond endurance. They are the apotheosis of the incendiary anarchists (beards and all) of Tolkien's letter of November 1943. Faramir's account of his people gives historical and political reality to Gondor, hitherto little more than a name, by sketching in the three thousand years from Elendil's day to the time of the story. As for the *palantíri*, Tolkien's elaboration of this idea, seemingly so inconsequential at its inception (like the Ring itself), is a masterpiece of inspired story-telling.

The ents, Faramir, Aragorn, the *palantíri*: these are four of the seven great pillars of Tolkien's story, the others being the Ring itself, Saruman and his fortress, and Lothlórien, which all show signs of similar inspired birth. In general, although Tolkien worked hard to fit everything together once inspiration had done its work, the main elements of *The Lord of the Rings* came to him in a flash (or series of

---

[46] *Letters*, 53, 211-12n, 217, 231, 334.
[47] Tolkien, *Return of the Shadow*, 210, 214, 374.

flashes). "I have long since ceased to *invent*," he wrote in 1956, "(though even patronizing or sneering critics on the side praise my 'invention'): I wait till I seem to know what really happened. Or till it writes itself."[48]

Fantasy and prophecy

One term for discourse arising from inspired revelation is *prophecy*. In a letter written less than two years before his death, Tolkien mentions his work in terms that echo E. M. W. Tillyard's conception of the epic poet as a prophet, the mouthpiece of his age. It tells of a visitor who

> had been much struck by the curious way in which many old pictures seemed to him to have been designed to illustrate *The Lord of the Rings* long before its time ... When it became obvious that ... I had never seen the pictures before and was not well acquainted with pictorial Art, he fell silent. I became aware that he was looking fixedly at me. Suddenly he said: "Of course you don't suppose, do you, that you wrote all that book yourself?"
>
> Pure Gandalf! I was too well acquainted with G. to expose myself rashly, or to ask what he meant. I think I said: "No, I don't suppose so any longer." I have never since been able to suppose so. An alarming conclusion for an old philologist to draw concerning his private amusement. But not one that should puff any one up who considers the imperfections of "chosen instruments", and what sometimes seems their lamentable unfitness for the purpose.

Noting his correspondent's allusion to the book's pervasive "sanity and sanctity," and another reader's remark that he had created "a world in which some sort of faith seems to be everywhere without a visible source, like light from an invisible lamp," Tolkien comments that "if sanctity inhabits [a writer's] work or as a pervading light illumines it then it does not come from him but through him." Unless filled with the same light, his readers "would see and feel nothing, or (if some other spirit was present) you would be filled with contempt, nausea, hatred." In any case, *The Lord of the Rings* "has been brought forth and must now go its appointed way in the world." He is "comforted to know that it has good friends to defend it against the malice of its enemies. (But not all the fools are in the other camp.)" Pure Tolkien, you might say, both in his quirky

---

[48] *Letters*, 231.

recognition that there are fools, like orcs, on both sides, and in the shrewd realization that prophecy exists in the eye of the beholder.[49]

Tolkien often referred to his work as fantasy and never as prophecy, which might have seemed to him too preachy, too much like allegory. However, despite his unease with the prophet's mantle, his conception of fantasy as a vessel of inspired revelation is strikingly congruent with an idea emanating from a very different place on the critical spectrum: E. M. Forster's notion of prophecy as an aspect of the novel. Forster speaks of a "fantastic-prophetical axis" and describes fantasy and prophecy as variants of one thing: a note or accent that subverts the essential realism of the novel as a literary form. They are "alike in having gods, but unlike in the gods they have," and they each project "the sense of mythology which differentiates them from other aspects of [the novel]."[50] Prophecy, specifically, is alien to the mundane world of the novel — the world of tables and chairs, "the furniture of common sense." It manifests itself not in plain words but in "an accent in the novelist's voice ... His theme is the universe, or something universal, but he is not necessarily going to 'say' anything about the universe; he proposes to sing ..."[51]

The Lord of the Rings bears several of the hallmarks of prophecy as Forster sketches it. His efforts to define it evoke Tolkien's idea of *eucatastrophe*, his premises and examples resemble the narrative strategies that Tolkien employed in trying to find a way back from a fictional present into the past of his legendarium, and his emphasis on the medium rather than the message, helpfully avoiding any suggestion of preachiness, harmonizes with Tolkien's disavowal of any intention to preach. He also recognizes the determining role of the audience: unless we listen with humility, "we shall not hear the voice of the prophet, and our eyes will behold a figure of fun instead of his glory."[52] A more apt comment on the range of Tolkien criticism is hard to imagine.

To illustrate his idea, Forster compares passages from *Adam Bede* and *The Brothers Karamazov*. In George Eliot's novel, Hetty is to be hanged for murdering her baby, and Dinah the Methodist is urging her to repent and seek God's grace. Through prayer and exhortation, she softens Hetty's heart and gets her for the first time

---

[49] *Letters*, 412-13.

[50] E. M. Forster, *Aspects of the Novel* (Harmondsworth, UK: Penguin Books, 1962), 113, 115.

[51] Forster, *Aspects*, 129.

[52] Forster, *Aspects*, 130.

to confess. Hetty bursts into tears and asks if God will assuage her agony of guilt. In Dostoyevsky's novel, Mitya Karamazov has been arrested for his father's murder and the examining magistrate has been reviewing the evidence. Mitya lies down on a wooden chest, falls asleep and has an incongruous dream, in which he is driving across the steppe in bad weather and passes a group of homeless women, one holding a starving baby. He is seized by a feeling of compassion for the beggars and is overcome with ecstatic gratitude when he wakes to find that someone has put a pillow under his head. When asked, he declares himself ready to sign anything they want. "'I've had a good dream, gentlemen,' he said in strange voice, with a new light, as of joy, in his face."

What makes Eliot a preacher and Dostoyevsky a prophet? "Eliot talks about God but never alters her focus; God and the tables and chairs are all in the same plane, and in consequence we have not for a moment the feeling that the whole universe needs pity and love — they are only needed in Hetty's cell." The scene has a single narrow focus: Hetty, her self-pity and her concern with her own salvation. Mitya's dream, by contrast, is a vision of the suffering of others, and the pity it induces in him is not self-centred but outward-reaching and potentially universal in scope.

> In Dostoyevsky the characters and situations stand for more than themselves; infinity attends them, [and] though they remain individuals they expand to embrace it and summon it to embrace them; one can apply to them the saying of St Catherine of Siena that God is in the soul and the soul is in God as the sea is in the fish and the fish is in the sea.

We cannot understand Mitya, Forster concludes, "until we see that he extends, and that the part of him on which Dostoyevsky focused did not lie on that wooden chest or even in dreamland but in a region where it could be joined by the rest of humanity."[53]

Forster recognizes the Christian inspiration of Dostoyevskian prophecy, but for him the religious tincture is secondary. Prophetic fiction "reaches back," sometimes to pity and love but not always: Herman Melville, for instance, "reaches straight back into the universal, to a blackness and sadness so transcending our own that they are undistinguishable from glory." Both strains, however, sound like Tolkien's account of *eucatastrophe*. The remark about Melville recalls Tolkien's unassuageable sense of cosmic bereave-

---

[53] *Aspects*, 131-37 (quotations, 136, 137).

ment and yearning back towards Eden or the First Dawn; it suggests an emotional response much like what Tolkien, as quoted above, calls "that essential emotion: Christian joy which produces tears because it is qualitatively so like sorrow, because it comes from those places where Joy and Sorrow are at one, reconciled, as selfishness and altruism." Likewise, when Forster speaks of the place where Mitya mentions his dream, "with a new light, as of joy, in his face," as "releasing floods of our emotion," one recalls Tolkien's definition of *eucatastrophe* as "*evangelium*, giving a fleeting glimpse of Joy, Joy beyond the walls of the world, poignant as grief."[54]

Song. Reaching back into the universal. Floods of emotion. Not preaching, which brings everything together in a single plane. Prophecy in this sense signifies less the fact of revelation than the suggestion of it, the sense of something behind the cracked or clouded glass. It is manifest not on the surface, as fantasy is, but rather as a kind of harmonic overtone vibrating suggestively behind the melody. It is the sudden intimation that the universe is much vaster than you had thought, that something is going on — has always been going on — behind the scenes. It is the abrupt recognition that there is more — or horribly less — in heaven and earth than is dreamt of in your philosophy. It is the light that blinded Paul, not what he did afterwards. Tillyard would recognize it as a sense of the numinous. It is epitomized in Tolkien's vision of a mote gleaming in the Light of God, and *The Lord of the Rings* is drenched in it. One might perhaps quibble that it is better called epiphany or revelation, that what Paul did afterwards is also an aspect of prophecy, and that there may be a valid distinction between prophetic preaching, which is inspired by direct revelation, and what Forster calls preaching, which is inspired — or at least authorized — by texts.

The key to this convergence between Forster and Tolkien can be found in William James's pioneering work of psychology, *The Varieties of Religious Experience*. The personal revelations that Tolkien recounts in his letters resemble those recorded in James's chapter on mystical experience, but no less significant is James's exploration of what he calls "the reality of the unseen":

> It is as if there were in the human consciousness *a sense of reality, a feeling of objective presence, a perception* of what we may call "*something there*," more deep and more general than any of the special and

---

54 *Letters*, 100; Tolkien, *Tree and Leaf*, 60.

peculiar "senses" by which the current psychology supposes existent realities to be originally revealed.

"Why," asks James, "may the world not be so complex as to consist of many interpenetrating spheres of reality ...?" The congruence of this notion with Forster's idea of prophecy is less surprising when we find that James's short-list of pantheist mystics includes a friend of both Forster and William Morris: the socialist poet Edward Carpenter, known as "the English Tolstoi" on account of his devotion to Tolstoyan ethics.[55] Tolkien – Morris – Carpenter – Forster: the distance between the great romancer and the great novelist turns out to be not so great. Forster was, after all, the author of a prescient anti-technological dystopia, "The Machine Stops," several short stories tinged with the supernatural, and a character (Helen Schlegel in *Howard's End*) who imagines goblins stalking the staves of Beethoven's Fifth Symphony.[56]

Yearning for consolation, Tolkien reached back towards the Beginning, and his yearning found expression in his legendarium. First in "The Lost Road," and then in *The Lord of the Rings*, he attempted to build a bridge between the pre-history of his legendarium and the present. Forster's examples of prophecy suggest a reason for his initial failure and ultimate success. The role of dream as the medium of prophetic intimation in *The Brothers Karamazov* recalls its use as the means of time travel in "The Lost Road" and suggests its unsuitability for that purpose. Forsterian prophecy may strike from the blue as a sudden flash into mundane consciousness from another plane or dimension of perception, as in Dostoyevsky's novel, and a dream will do well enough to convey that idea. It will also afford rapid transit from one world into another. What it cannot easily do is sustain the kind of long voyage into and beyond history that Tolkien had in view. The successful narrative strategy of *The Lord of the Rings* is closer to that of *Moby Dick*, a story in which no character receives a revelation like Mitya's dream. Both stories carry us off on a quest, and in both there comes a point when we realize that the story has entered a plane of consciousness very

---

[55] William James, *The Varieties of Religious Experience: A Study in Human Nature* (New York: Longmans, Green, 1916), 58, 122-23, 425; T. H. Bell, *Edward Carpenter: The English Tolstoi* (Los Angeles: The Libertarian Group, 1932).
[56] This affinity may help to explain why Tolkien nominated Forster for the Nobel Prize: Dennis Wilson Wise, "J. R. R. Tolkien and the 1954 Nomination of E. M. Forster for the Nobel Prize in Literature," *Mythlore*, 36 (2017).

different from its starting-point and that the starting-point may not readily be regained. Applying Forster's notions of a "fantastic-prophetical axis" and of prophecy as involving multiple planes of perception, we may view *The Lord of the Rings* as prophecy set in a frame of fantasy. The prophetic aspect first manifests itself with the intrusion of the past upon the fantasy-present of the Shire.

Where *Karamazov* may resemble Tolkien's story is in the way Mitya's dream projects his mind — and the reader's with it — into a vast open space, in strong contrast to the cramped scene of the current action and of most of the novel. Although Forster maintained that prophecy was a genuine aspect of the novel as a genre, he could think of only four writers whose work illustrated it: Dostoyevsky, Melville, Emily Brontë and D. H. Lawrence (citing *Women in Love*).[57] It is a curious quartet, and Forster was worse than vague in defining the medium of revelation. Thus: "the essential in *Moby Dick*, its prophetic song, flows athwart the action and the surface morality like an undercurrent. It lies outside words." With Brontë too, "what is implied is more important ... than what is said." And in the scene in *Women in Love* where Rupert Birkin throws stones into a pool, shattering the moon's reflection, "Why he throws, what the scene symbolizes, is unimportant." However, a clue to their common property may lie in an observation by William James, who noted that many of the most striking intimations of the Divine presence had been experienced out of doors and suggested that certain aspects of nature seemed to have "a peculiar power of awakening such mystical moods."[58] Accordingly, in each of Forster's cases, the effect he calls prophetic may spring from the contrast between close quarters and boundless nature. It is certainly so in *The Lord of the Rings*, where the journey into the Wild from the "suburban" confines of the Shire is also a journey back in time, and I will be pointing out similar effects in *War and Peace* and in Thompson's books. I will also consider why Forster, who is so sensitive to the representation of space in *War and Peace*, did not include it in his examples of prophecy.

------

[57] He might, however, have noted the Marabar Caves episode in his own *A Passage to India* as an example.
[58] James, *Varieties*, 394.

Tolkien's romance

Forster treated prophecy as an anomaly, an intrusion of the numinous into a realist genre; but to Tolkien, as we have seen, evoking the numinous — or "discovering Myth," as he put it — was the main point of the exercise. Accordingly, he declared that his story was not a novel but a heroic romance, by which he meant the medieval narrative genre, not the hearts-flowers-and-cleavage genre of modern pulp fiction that is its distant offspring. In doing so, he was aligning himself with the protest of his confrère W. P. Ker against the "self-assertive realism" of the contemporary novel.[59] His fullest statement of his position is to be found in his essay on fairy-stories, which elaborates the idea, propounded by Ker and Lascelles Abercrombie, of a realism applicable to the epic and extends that idea to fantasy in general. It also develops Ker's disparagement of realism as an approach to reality.[60]

In chapter 1, I mentioned this quarrel in connection with Nathaniel Hawthorne's sense of a distinction between the novel and the romance. That distinction was no new topic even in Hawthorne's day. As early as 1750, we find Samuel Johnson commenting on the modern rejection of heroic romance in favour of fiction which exhibits "life in its true state, diversified only by the accidents that daily happen in the world." Authors of such fiction face the challenge of retaining the reader's interest "without the help of wonder" — that is, without recourse to such staples of heroic romance as "giants to snatch away a lady from the nuptial rites, nor knights to bring her back from captivity."[61] In 1764, Horace Walpole describes *The Castle of Otranto*, his prototypal Gothic romance, as "an attempt to blend the two kinds of romance, the ancient and the modern. In the former, all was imagination and improbability: in the latter, nature is always intended to be, and sometimes has been, copied with success. Invention has not been wanting, but the great resources of fantasy have been dammed up, by a strict adherence to common life." In 1811, Sir Walter Scott notes Walpole's intention in that story "to unite the marvellous turn of incident and imposing tone of chivalry, exhibited in the ancient romance, with that

---

[59] *Letters*, 413-14; and see above, 26, 11-12.
[60] Tolkien, *Tree and Leaf*, 11-70.
[61] *The Rambler* (London, England), no. 4, 31 March 1750.

accurate display of human character and contrast of feelings and passions which is, or ought to be, delineated in the modern novel."[62]

In Hawthorne's day, then, commentators had already been distinguishing for a century or more between two sorts of narrative: one sort dealing in marvellous or fantastic events and adventures, the other defined by its truth to life. But that framework of analysis harboured changing standards of fidelity to the real. In the mid-nineteenth century, the historical content of Walter Scott's novels imparted a tincture of realism even in the eyes of such a sophisticated reader as George Eliot; but a young Russian nobleman, Lev Tolstoy, was shortly to compose fiction so revolutionary in its approach to the depiction of human experience that he hesitated to call it a novel. Sixty years after its publication, E. M. Forster would hail *War and Peace* as the way ahead for the novel while disparaging Scott as a mere story-teller.[63]

An essay published while Tolkien was finishing *The Lord of the Rings* epitomizes the modernist consensus against which Tolkien was reacting. In it George Orwell distinguishes two meanings of the term *novel*. Broadly speaking, it means almost any fiction longer than a short story, but more narrowly it signifies stories that attempt "to describe human beings and ... show them acting on everyday motives and not merely undergoing strings of improbable adventures." To fit this narrower definition, a story needs "at least two characters, probably more, who are described from the inside and on the same level of probability."[64] When Orwell remarks that the novel in this sense had hardly existed before the nineteenth century, and had flourished chiefly in Russia and France, we can be sure that *War and Peace* is among the novels he had in mind.

In arrogating the term *novel* as a title of honour to a subset of narrative fiction that is meritorious precisely for eschewing the marvellous and fantastic in favour of the depiction of human nature and everyday life, Orwell was expressing the ideological bias which Hawthorne hinted at, Ker derided, and W. H. Auden blamed for the animosity aroused by *The Lord of the Rings*. Northrop Frye disparaged this bias in *Anatomy of Criticism*, his attempt to devise a non-

---

[62] Scott's words are in his introduction to an edition of *The Castle of Otranto*; Walpole's are from his preface to the second edition of the story.
[63] Forster, *Aspects of the Novel*, 38-45, 170.
[64] George Orwell, "George Gissing," in *The Collected Essays, Journalism and Letters of George Orwell*, ed. Sonia Orwell and Ian Angus (4 vols., Harmondsworth, Middx.: Penguin Books, 1970), IV: 490-1.

ideological approach to literary criticism. Because the romance was older than the novel, he asserted, the unhistorical habit had developed of dismissing it as a juvenile and undeveloped form, something to be outgrown; but a great romancer should not be scorned as escapist and marginalized merely because critics had not learned to take the romance seriously. In singling out William Morris and Walter Scott as victims of such malpractice, Frye was responding to the disparagement of Scott by Forster and others, and perhaps to E. P. Thompson's new study of Morris. He may even have been influenced by the fuss over Tolkien's newly published romance.[65]

Besides vindicating the romance as a literary form, Frye denied any absolute distinction between it and the novel. The essential difference lay in the treatment of character: the novelist aimed to create "real people," whereas the romancer dealt in stock characters, or archetypes. The distinction between the two forms was real enough that one could talk of a "typical novel" with characteristics distinct from those of romance, but in reality "pure" examples of neither form were to be found.

> There is hardly any modern romance that could not be made out to be a novel, and vice versa ... In fact the popular demand in fiction is always for a mixed form, a romantic novel just romantic enough for the reader to project his libido on the hero and his anima on the heroine, and just novel enough to keep these projections in a familiar world.[66]

Later he elaborated this idea by calling realistic fiction of the eighteenth and nineteenth centuries "essentially parody-romance" in that they "use much the same general structure as romance, but adapt that structure to a demand for greater conformity to ordinary experience."[67] These remarks, and much else that Frye wrote about romance, will turn out to be just as relevant to *War and Peace* as to *The Lord of the Rings*.

Tolkien's own riposte to the modernists occupies a slightly different space from these discussions. He is clearly talking about the same thing: for instance, where Samuel Johnson declares that

---

[65] Northrop Frye, *Anatomy of Criticism: Four Essays* (Princeton and Oxford: Princeton UP, 1957), 303-7; *Northrop Frye's Notebooks on Romance*, ed. Michael Dolzani (Toronto: University of Toronto Press, 2004), 191. Frye's personal annotated copies of *The Lord of the Rings*, held by the Victoria University Library at the University of Toronto, are 1955 and 1956 imprints.
[66] Frye, *Anatomy of Criticism*, 305.
[67] Frye, *Secular Scripture*, 38-39.

the depiction of everyday reality is more difficult than heroic romance because everyone has the knowledge to judge the performance, Tolkien takes the opposite position, rating fantasy as the higher form of art because the artist must make his audience believe in things not to be found — or "generally believed not to be found" — in the Primary World. However, except for his passing private remark that his story is a heroic romance and not a novel, his discussion is not pitched on the level of genre but on the broader ground of an antithesis between fantasy and realism as modes of approaching reality. This has the surprising result that, in his lecture on *Beowulf,* his chief target is W. P. Ker.

Tolkien subtitled his lecture "The Monsters and the Critics" because he meant to defend the poem against the common complaint that it was magnificently written but marred by a "cheap" or "preposterous" plot (both terms are Ker's), a plot which involved the hero in fantastic battles against a succession of monsters rather than in more plausible encounters with human foes.[68] The critics, Ker among them, looked longingly at the poem's allusion to apparently historical episodes and regretted that its author had not taken one or more of these as his main subject. In a riposte that is striking for its sense of history, Tolkien contended that these objections were fundamentally misconceived. *Beowulf* should be read as the sole survivor of an abundant literature in which those other subjects had already been treated. The author was a Christian looking back nostalgically on his people's defunct pagan traditions, to which that literature gave expression. His subject was the "northern theory of courage," which, lacking any doctrine of resurrection, accepted that death was final and celebrated the heroism of those who met it bravely, cleaving to their duty in the face of "defeat inevitable yet unacknowledged." The ogres that Beowulf overcomes in the first part of the poem, and the dragon that is his downfall in old age, represent death with a universality that a named human foe could not. Brimming with a sense of history, *Beowulf* "must have succeeded admirably in creating in the minds of the poet's contemporaries the illusion of surveying a past, pagan but noble and fraught with a deep significance — a past that itself had depth and reached backward into a dark antiquity of sorrow."[69] But its subject is the pagan past of the poet's people, not the history of Denmark

---

[68] Tolkien, "Beowulf", 251.
[69] Tolkien, "Beowulf", 270

and its neighbour kingdoms about 500 A.D. While it invokes that history for artistic effect, the very allusions that so have so tantalized the historians and critics are themselves the product of art.

Perhaps because he was arguing, not with some unregenerate modern, but with his own revered forerunner in asserting the dignity of ancient texts, Tolkien tried to understand Ker's point of view, and his interpretation reveals the same strong historical sense as his primary argument. He suggested that Ker's very excellence as a scholar was one source of his error:

> stories and plots must sometimes have seemed triter to him, the much-read, than they did to the old poets and their audiences. The dwarf on the spot sometimes sees things missed by the travelling giant ranging many countries. In considering a period when literature was narrower in range and men possessed a less diversified stock of ideas and themes, one must seek to recapture and esteem the deep pondering and profound feeling that they gave to such as they possessed.[70]

In substance, though not in tone, this argument resembles Frye's mockery of modern critics for their condescension towards pre-modern genres.

Tolkien's riposte to the moderns, in his essay on fairy-stories, was much more combative in tone. First aired as a lecture in 1938, when he had just started writing *The Lord of the Rings*, it was published in 1947, when he was in the final stages of composition, and revised after *The Lord of the Rings* had been published and reviewed. It defines fairy-stories in terms very applicable to his own work, as we have seen, and one could fairly take it as an apologia for his own epic fairy-story even if he had not said it was.[71]

According to Tolkien, art is the skill of giving imagined forms "the inner consistency of reality." Because it attempts to depict the paranormal, fantasy when done well is the most potent form of art; but because it is difficult it is often done badly: "It is and has been used frivolously, or only half-seriously, or merely for decoration: it remains merely 'fanciful'." Such abuse gives colour to the sneers of those who stupidly or maliciously confound fantasy with dreaming and mental disorder. Tolkien in turn mocks critics who identify reality with the transient accoutrements of industrial modernity while condemning art that concerns itself with the permanent and

---

[70] Tolkien, "Beowulf," 250-51.

[71] Colin Manlove, *Modern Fantasy: Five Studies* (Cambridge: Cambridge UP, 1975), 158.

truly real, such as lightning, as escapist. "I cannot convince myself that the roof of Bletchley station is more 'real' than the clouds."[72] Likewise, *Escape* nowadays signifies retreat from the ephemeral modernity typified by "electric street-lamps of mass-produced pattern" and "self-obstructive mechanical traffic" back towards the ancient and eternal.

In all ages, however, fairy-story has helped us escape from the world of toil and tears to an imagined transcendent realm where death has no dominion.[73] Rooted in intuitive understanding, Faith and Fantasy alike help us escape from everyday reality by means of the suspension of disbelief, and the realism that sneers at "escapism," equating fantasy with mental disorder and banishing the Eden myth to the lumber-room, is a sort of treason: the treason of the quisling, whose mantra is realism.

> Just so a Party-spokesman might have labelled departure from the Führer's or any other Reich and even criticism of it as treachery ... Not only do they confound the escape of the prisoner with the flight of the deserter; but they would seem to prefer the acquiescence of the 'quisling' to the resistance of the patriot. To such thinking you have only to say 'the land you loved is doomed' to excuse any treachery, indeed to glorify it.[74]

In this instance "the land you loved" seems to be a spiritual domain, the world of faith that has been doomed by science, technology and secular humanism: that is, by the modernity whose spokesman in *The Lord of the Rings*, so suavely counselling accommodation to the new order, is Saruman. So much for Michael Moorcock's complaint that the story poses no challenge to the "white men in grey clothing who somehow have a handle on what is best for us."[75]

Tolkien's manifesto demonstrates why his story could no more have been a novel than an allegory. We may think of the novel, in Orwell's sense of it, as an inquiry into the human condition (or some aspect of it) with special attention to human nature, which it explores through the temperaments, motives and interactions of the characters. Tolkien was interested in the human condition, but less so in human nature — which, as we have seen, he found less engag-

---

[72] Tolkien, *Tree and Leaf*, 43-45, 55-56. Bletchley was where you changed trains when travelling between Oxford and Cambridge.
[73] Tolkien, *Tree and Leaf*, 16, 18, 43ff.
[74] Tolkien, *Tree and Leaf*, 54.
[75] See above, 21.

ing than what he called the heart-racking sense of the vanished past. He could "do" character well enough and could probably have done it better if he had cared. His ethnic types and individuals are effectively differentiated; they have interesting things to say, and each has a distinctive outlook and style of discourse. In a word, they have personality. If they are not well-developed, it is not because Tolkien was simple-minded but because the foibles of human nature, all too obvious in daily life, did not appeal to him as a subject of fiction. He was moved less by "character" — the motives and emotions of individuals — or even by "story" than by the tragedy of fallen (and possibly not to be redeemed) man as reflected in the entirety of human history. To him, therefore, the highest purpose of literature was not to portray the sordid quotidian reality of the human condition but to exemplify and extol the sort of devotion to duty that might, against all odds, momentarily stem the "long defeat," and to console and inspire those embroiled in the struggle. Likewise, the highest form of literature was that which most closely resembled in character and purpose the Gospels, the greatest fairy-story ever told. The goal of art was not to discover fresh truth but to freshly depict revealed truth.

Tolkien's "novel"

Still, Tolkien had deliberately disguised his heroic romance as a novel in order to reach a wide public, and its fantasy-world was developed with a naturalism and density of detail that seemed to license precisely what Frye condemns: treating it as a novel in order to disparage it. Thus a typical critique dating from 1975 quotes Tolkien as saying that his story "was a deliberate attempt to write a large-scale adult fairy-story," but then postulates as a "simple fact" that, in choosing a "little man" as hero, he was also undertaking to write a novel ("a story of ordinary lives faced with extraordinary demands"). It then proceeds to detail the story's shortcomings as such. According to this commentary, it fails to convey its hero's "inner conflict" as a novel should, a weakness ascribed to its "absolute distinctions between good and evil."[76] As a whole, this critique consists of a series of easily rebuttable assertions, but it has one extraordinary feature (apart from misidentifying the hero of Tolkien's "novel"): it completely misses the place in Tolkien's story that comes closest to justifying its criticism.

---

[76] Manlove, *Modern Fantasy*, 171, 174-80.

Unquestionably, in reading Tolkien's tale one has to make allowances for its odd conception and development. Having begun life as a children's story, it was never wholly purged of that original tincture of juvenility. One problem is the essential childishness of hobbits. Pippin is truly juvenile, still four years short of the hobbits' somewhat retarded age of majority (thirty-three), and behaves accordingly. Sam, somewhat older, exhibits a mental simplicity that is scarcely penetrable by experience. When Gandalf conscripts him as Frodo's companion, he responds by bursting into tears. They are tears of joy, as it happens, but it is not an adult response either way. Merry and Frodo are a cut above this, but even at fifty years of age Frodo hardly figures as more than a bright undergraduate, even at his most fully realized: for instance, in his long discussion with Gandalf in "The Shadow of the Past." In the first volume the hobbits show a distinct tendency to fall asleep when the going gets tough (in the Old Forest, and crossing the Misty Mountains), or even before it gets tough (the Barrow-downs).

Stories about children need not be juvenile, let alone infantile: *Lord of the Flies* and Joyce Cary's *Charley is My Darling* present completely different cases to the contrary, and it will appear that *War and Peace* is a third. The problem with Tolkien's story is not that hobbits are essentially children but that they retain substantial vestiges of Bilbo's function in *The Hobbit* as a child-surrogate — a character with whom children can identify. We see the world of *War and Peace* largely through the eyes of Tolstoy's children, just as we see Middle-earth for the most part through the hobbits' eyes. But Tolstoy's world is one in which children must make their way without the protection of elves and wizards — protection that aids even Frodo and Sam on their trek to Mount Doom. Indeed, it is a world in which elves and wizards turn out to be disappointing delusions — a world in which children have to grow up or perish. And it is not a world presented *for* children: it is one in which a child can be jailbait, and in which dazzling adult femininity takes the form not of Galadriel but of the depraved Hélène Kuragina. Adult sexuality is not completely absent from the world of *The Lord of the Rings*, but it is never allowed to shape the plot. There is a whiff of carnality in the hint that Wormtongue, Théoden's false counsellor, has been lusting after the willowy Éowyn, but this is a sign of Wormtongue's corruption. That Aragorn should take advantage of Éowyn's crush on him, or she express it by throwing herself into his arms, is unthinkable. Of course, Tolkien did not set out to imitate *War and Peace*, and to blame him for not doing so would be to do what Frye condemns and Tolkien himself derides. However, I will point out a place where I think the story goes off the rails precisely by taking a turn that is false to Tolkien's world-view and artistic purpose.

On the whole, the juvenility of Tolkien's hobbits can be tolerated as a scar left by the emergence of his epic from the matrix of a children's novel. There is, however, one serious blemish that can neither be explained away as a rough surface left by the creative process that produced Tolkien's imaginative universe nor justified by appealing from the canons of the novel to those of the romance. Significantly, it occurs at the very point where the story comes closest to being a novel. It is the only place where Tolkien has only a single character to work with, and we witness that character's struggle with a moral dilemma. With Frodo apparently dead from Shelob's poison, Sam Gamgee must work out on his own what to do next. His solitary struggle entails a fullness of development that makes him, as Tolkien put it at the time, "the most closely drawn character" in the story, "the successor to Bilbo ... the genuine hobbit. Frodo is not so interesting, because he has to be highminded [*sic*], and has (as it were) a vocation."[77] But Tolkien's elaboration of Sam strains the fragile fabric of illusion by raising questions too heavy for it to bear, and here the author's hand really does bear too heavily on the outcome.

Sam was not one of Frodo's original hobbit companions, and one suspects he was brought in to add a little clumsy humour along the lines of Sam Weller in *The Pickwick Papers*. Indeed, Tolkien hinted as much in a retrospective comment, which acknowledged the difficulty that some readers have with Sam but without quite getting it (although evidently he thought he did). "Sam is meant to be lovable and laughable," he wrote.

> Some readers he irritates and infuriates. I can well understand it. All hobbits at times affect me in the same way, though I remain very fond of them. But Sam can be very "trying". He is a more representative hobbit than any others that we have to see much of: and he consequently has a stronger ingredient of that quality which even some hobbits found at times hard to bear: a vulgarity ... a mental myopia which is proud of itself, a smugness (in varying degrees) and cocksureness, and

---

[77] *Letters*, 105.

> a readiness to measure and sum up all things from a limited experience, largely enshrined in sententious traditional "wisdom".[78]

According to Tolkien, all the hobbits we get to know well are exceptional in possessing "a vision of beauty, and a reverence for things nobler than themselves, at war with their rustic self-satisfaction" — even Sam has been elevated somewhat by Bilbo's teaching him to read and to love the elves. But Sam is not quite as elevated as his companions, and herein lies a problem.

Despite his rise to hero status ("the chief hero," Tolkien called him in the Collins essay),[79] Sam remains the archetypal country bumpkin that Tolkien originally imagined — remains, that is, a cultural stereotype — and what is so peculiarly irritating is not the traits he may share with "all hobbits" but those that distinguish him among "hobbits we get to know well". All the others belong to the hobbit gentry, and forelock-tugging, "laughable" Sam stands apart as a mixture of Harriet Beecher Stowe's Uncle Tom and Jar Jar Binks, the bumbling *Star Wars* character with unfortunate echoes of the blackface stereotype. This might matter less if Sam's handicaps were limited to the narrow-mindedness that Tolkien mentions — but no: his inferiority is comprehensive. He is the most childish and stupid of the hobbits, and — as Tolkien remarks — smug in his stupidity. On the path to Cirith Ungol, when he and Frodo are buoying their spirits with the thought that they are playing a part in a tale that reaches back to Beren and the Silmarils, Sam's response to the notion that sooner or later their part will be over is:

> "And then we can have some rest and some sleep" ... He smiled grimly. "And I mean just that, Mr. Frodo. I mean plain ordinary rest, and sleep, and waking up to a morning's work in the garden. I'm afraid that's all I'm hoping for all the time. All the big important plans are not for my sort" (TT 321).

Indeed, he and Frodo have almost reached Mount Doom before it occurs to him to wonder just what they must do when they get there, by which time Frodo is beyond explaining.

The crisis of Frodo's apparent death at Cirith Ungol fully exposes Sam's limitations. Suddenly this inveterate follower has no one to follow, and he dithers like the ninny he is wont to call himself.

---

[78] *Letters*, 329.
[79] *Letters*, 161.

> "Why am I left all alone to make up my mind? I'm sure to go wrong. And it's not for me to go taking the Ring, putting myself forward."
>
> "But you haven't put yourself forward; you've been put forward. And as for not being the right and proper person, why, Mr. Frodo wasn't, as you might say, nor Mr. Bilbo ..."
>
> "Ah well, I must make up my own mind. I will make it up. But I'll be sure to go wrong: that'd be Sam Gamgee all over" (TT 341).

And sure enough he does go wrong. Abandoning Frodo, even dead Frodo, is "altogether against the grain of his nature." Even after facing up to the obvious and taking the Ring, he hesitates, and the moment the enemy patrol finds Frodo lying on the path he abandons his resolve.

> He sprang up. He flung the Quest and all his decisions away, and fear and doubt with them. He now knew where his place was and had been: at his master's side, though what he could do there was not clear (TT 344).

Note that this is *before* he hears that Frodo is still alive; and when he does hear it, he laments: "You fool, he isn't dead and your heart knew it. Don't trust your head, Samwise, it is not the best part of you."

Does the discovery that Frodo is alive justify Sam's choice, then? You might think that his duty was to push on regardless, leaving Frodo to his fate. But that is not the point. What matters is that Sam is willing to sacrifice himself to defend not just the living Frodo but even his corpse, even though the Ring will inevitably be found, leading to the destruction of the world as he knows it. And why? "I can't help it. My place is by Mr. Frodo. They must understand that — Elrond and the Council, and the great Lords and Ladies with all their wisdom. Their plans have gone wrong. I can't be their Ring-bearer. Not without Mr. Frodo." This might do for a pet dog, but it is a complete collapse of moral fibre in a thinking being.

Tolkien was writing at a high level of inspiration throughout Book 4, and these climactic chapters are no let-down considered as narrative. We see further into Sam's character than before, and what we see — the mental limitations, the crippling lack of self-esteem — is not out of character. Nor can it be said that the character is implausible in itself.[80] It is jarring, though, because it raises issues which have no place in the world of the romance. I cannot

---

[80] Discussing two books that focus on "ordinary people" in Britain in the 1940s, Nicholas Spice remarks that similar attitudes to Sam's are reported on almost every page: Spice, "Don't Look Down," *London Review of Books*, vol. 32, no. 7 (8 April 2010), 14.

contemplate Sam's dog-like devotion to his "master", inability to think things through and radical lack of autonomy without reflecting that in the real world such servility is a product of nurture as well as nature. If Sam's upbringing had placed a bit more emphasis on intelligence and initiative, Frodo might have had to plant and dig his own potatoes. It is as though Tolkien were suddenly to start talking about who empties the privies at Rivendell. But far from recognizing Sam's unthinking subservience as an outcome of oppression, Tolkien evidently sees it as a sort of grace. Thus when Sam puts on the Ring he is beset by grandiose fantasies, but they can gain no purchase on his mind.

> In that hour of trial it was the love of his master that helped most to hold him firm; but also deep down in him lived still unconquered his plain hobbit-sense: he knew in the core of his heart that he was not large enough to bear such a burden ... The one small realm of a free gardener was all his need and due, not a garden swollen to a realm; his own hands to use, not the hands of others to command (RK 177).

Tolkien has apparently forgotten that Sam's "own hands" were in fact others' to command and were used in a garden that was not his own.

But it is the subsequent development of the episode that really disappoints. *The Lord of the Rings* is pre-eminently a story in which actions have fitting consequences. Denethor and his son Boromir, Saruman and his minion Wormtongue, pay with their lives for their dereliction of duty — even Frodo's last-minute lapse at the Crack of Doom costs him his ring-finger. But here Sam wantonly "flings away the Quest", not from heroism but from something close to despair. Making due allowance for the awfulness of his predicament, so momentous a lapse should still have consequences. They should not be unduly punitive, perhaps, since Sam is doing his best (albeit a poor, country-bumpkin best), and his delinquency is not prompted by lust for the Ring. Still, he should have to earn his redemption — the very logic of the story, which is all about keeping the Ring from the Enemy by the only means possible, demands it. But Tolkien lets him off scot-free.

The story is one in which providential deliverances abound — one has only to think of the three victories in battle snatched from the jaws of defeat — but as a rule they are well prepared by the author and earned by the courage and resource of rescuers and rescued alike. In the present instance, however, the deliverance is just too easy. It is plausible enough that the two companies of orcs that have captured Frodo should quarrel over the booty, since we saw similar animosity among the captors of Merry and Pippin (though in that case the factions served different masters). However, it fatally strains credulity that the two units, each numbering several score, should kill each other almost to a man. It is as though Tolkien's conception of Sam is so patronizing and derogatory that he cannot think of any plausible way in which Sam could handle the predicament "on his own".

This is not the whole story, of course. Sam may be a bumpkin, but he is also "the chief hero". It speaks to how far the story diverged from Tolkien's initial conception in the course of writing that, from being a figure of fun in a *Hobbit*-sequel, he has developed into a portrait of a type of individual that Tolkien had encountered in the trenches of the Somme and deeply admired.[81] He has just fearlessly fought off the loathsome Shelob, and even his failure of nerve is expressed in a way that manifests high physical courage. His bumbling is existential: he has no intellectual frame of reference to guide him in the predicament in which he finds himself. He cannot see his way. He is Everyman, who hasn't much of a clue when it comes to the big issues and can only be saved by grace. But while this may mitigate the condescending depiction of Sam, it hardly redeems it. In a novel the story is subordinate to the characterization, while in a romance the reverse is true, and Tolkien excused the sketchiness of his characters with the plea that he had written a romance, not a novel. But when he calls Sam the chief hero, and declares that he is a more interesting character than Frodo because the latter has a "vocation" (that is, because Frodo's role is that of hero of a quest), he is invoking the conventions of the novel against those of the romance and the character can fairly be judged by novelistic standards.

What went wrong here? The passage of time may be important. Tolkien composed the incandescent scenes of the fight with Shelob and the capture of Frodo in 1944, but he did not pick up the thread until 1947. He was no longer writing under the immediate inspiration of the Second World War, and perhaps he was in a post-war frame of mind, more closely attuned to elegy than adventure. It was in these final stages of composition that the theme of death and immortality became more fundamental to his story than the battle between Good and Evil — it was only now, for instance, that he conceived the character of Arwen, Elrond's daughter, who sacrifices her

---

[81] Carpenter, *J. R. R. Tolkien*, 89.

immortality to marry Aragorn.[82] The chapters that take Frodo and Sam from Cirith Ungol to Mount Doom are competently done on the whole, but they are about suffering rather than adventure. Indeed, between those two points on the map the hobbits have only one direct confrontation with the enemy, and it is another narrative nonsense. Disguised as orc soldiers, they are swept up unrecognized by a passing company of orcs on the march and then, just as Frodo can march no further, another absurd incident allows them to escape. This is not adventure but the avoidance of adventure. One feels that Tolkien was looking ahead to the challenge of the narrative climax at the mountain, and to the joy and mourning that lay beyond.

A frameless picture, a tuneless song

In the last analysis, to criticize *The Lord of the Rings* as a novel is to miss the point; but if not a novel, what exactly did Tolkien mean to foist on an unsuspecting public disguised as one? The obvious answer is a heroic romance, as he himself said — the logical, if unforeseeable, outcome of his bid to use his *Hobbit*-sequel as a means of introducing his fictional myth-world to a modern audience. But it is a heroic romance of distinctive timbre, and its special tone is best understood by recalling the commanding influence on his imagination of *Beowulf*. A Christian author reflecting with nostalgic admiration on the ancient traditions of his people; an ostensibly heroic narrative which is really a lament for the transitory nature of all earthly glory; a poem, not overtly Christian but expressing a profoundly Christian sensibility, enriched by "the illusion of surveying ... a past that itself had depth and reached backward into a dark antiquity of sorrow,"[83] but belittled by critics who misunderstood it — if Tolkien had composed his lecture on *Beowulf* after *The Lord of the Rings* instead of before it, one would have to suspect him of special pleading; but the lecture came first.

Discussing W. P. Ker's strictures on the plot of *Beowulf*, Tolkien insisted that the poem should not be classed as a narrative poem, an exciting story. No: it should be seen as a *static* structure, a pictorial composition rather than a piece of music — "a great scene, hung with tapestries woven of ancient tales of ruin." It comprised, he

---

[82] The late emergence of Arwen (originally Finduilas) and her previous absence are traceable in Christopher Tolkien's history of the story's composition: *see esp.* Tolkien, *Sauron Defeated*, 66.
[83] See above, 88.

thought, two tableaux: a picture of the hero at the moment of his rise to heroic stature, and another of him in old age, facing death with the same undaunted valour. In this second tableau, "Disaster is foreboded. Defeat is the theme. Triumph over the foes of man's precarious fortress is over, and we approach slowly and reluctantly the inevitable victory of death." Despite certain similarities to Virgil's *Aeneid*, which some critics had ascribed to deliberate imitation of the Latin epic, *Beowulf* itself was not an epic but a heroic elegy, its first 3,136 lines (out of 3,182) but the prelude to a dirge.[84]

The Lord of the Rings was meant to be an exciting story, of course. Tolkien himself said so, and by calling it a heroic romance he endowed it with the epic implications that he denied were applicable to *Beowulf*. In this respect, then, one might think of it as the music that he said *Beowulf* was not; and in fact Diana Wynne Jones, whom I quoted earlier regarding Tolkien's overuse of the word *suddenly*, characterizes the story as a series of symphonic movements.[85] Still, we have seen that, in the final Book, the narrative drive starts to dissipate and the elegiac tone, with its focus on death and immortality, becomes more and more insistent. Except for the brief revival of conflict when the hobbits return to the Shire, the final chapters are predominantly in this vein, preparing the ground for the poignant finale. This is the impression that the story leaves, and the Appendices reinforce it by zooming out into a chronological widescreen, flattening the picture even as they broaden it. What finally emerges is silent, far-off and irrecoverable — not a tale of triumph but a long-forgotten episode in the long defeat.

Music can do this too, as it happens. An apt example is the symphonic poem *En Saga* ("A Saga") by Sibelius — a Finn who shared Tolkien's feeling for the *Kalevala* — in which the hurly-burly of heroic action ends with a quiet, poignant coda that fades into silence. However, considering *The Lord of the Rings* pictorially, I think first, not of the "frameless" panorama, vast yet distant, that Tolkien himself suggested, but of one of Turner's paintings of the Grand Canal, Venice.[86] It is not Turner's teeming urban scene that brings it to mind, nor the brilliant colour, nor even the big sky. The

---

[84] Tolkien, "Beowulf," (quotations pp. 259, 270, 260, 274).
[85] Jones, "The Shape of the Narrative."
[86] Above, 1; http://commons.wikimedia.org/wiki/Image:Turner,_J._M._W._The_Grand_Canal_-_Scene_-_A_Street_In_Venice.jpg (viewed Oct 23, 2012). I speak of my experience when viewing the actual painting.

picture, moreover, is solidly framed and not especially large — especially not wide, being in portrait rather than landscape format. That, however, is essential to the resemblance, because it is not a matter of breadth but one of depth. As you sit before Turner's painting, your eye is at first held at bay by a glittering surface of apparently inchoate colour, but then, as you focus and begin to decode the pattern, your gaze is sucked in by the deep perspective and your mind finds itself *inside* the scene. This effect resembles the way in which Tolkien's story suddenly opens up into something much grander than is promised by the opening pages — the effect which I likened to being seized and swept away by a rip current.

But there is also a second parallel, intellectual rather than sensational. In the bottom right-hand corner of the painting, tiny and hardly noticeable, stands a familiar figure: Shakespeare's Shylock, from *The Merchant of Venice*, demanding his pound of flesh. That brief allusion to individuality, to character, only highlights the fact that the painting is about something else entirely. It is a variant of a common theme in Turner's landscapes and seascapes, in which tiny figures, or human artifacts such as ships, are dwarfed by some immense or stormy scene, suggesting the fragility or insignificance of mankind in the face of vast universal processes.

Tolkien notes how, at certain points in *Beowulf* and above all at the end, "we look down as if from a visionary height upon the house of man in the valley of the world. A light starts ... and there is the sound of music; but the outer darkness and its hostile offspring lie ever in wait for the torches to fail and the voices to cease."[87] I am suggesting that Tolkien's art and Turner's art present mankind in much the same relationship to the universe. The enduring image in *The Lord of the Rings* is of tiny figures crawling on a vast landscape: hobbits seen from above, as it were, traversing the Barrow-downs; the Fellowship of the Ring, already diminished by one, floating in tiny boats on the Great River; Frodo and Sam, sometimes with Gollum, creeping across a hostile terrain towards Mount Doom. It is a Ringwraith's or eagle's-eye view, and at the end the fleeting glorious hubbub fades into the silence of long ago, lost in "the glimmer of limitless extensions in time and space" even as the ship carrying the Ring-bearers and elven-ring wearers slips into the night down the long grey firth, disappearing from Sam's gaze.

---

87 Tolkien, "Beowulf," 277.

> And the ship went out into the High Sea and passed on into the West,
> until at last on a night of rain Frodo smelled a sweet fragrance on the
> air and heard the sound of singing that came over the water.[88]

Tolkien recognized the importance of consolation, the value of
Escape, but the escape he clung to was less the sure and certain
hope of the resurrection to eternal life than a hope against hope that
the tragedy of the human condition — of "man at war with the
hostile world, and his inevitable overthrow in Time," as he
summarized the subject of *Beowulf* — might not be the end of the
story. And so, towards the end of his life, he characterized his own
masterpiece with a pictorial metaphor similar to that which, thirty-
five years earlier, he had applied to *Beowulf*.

The same elegiac mood is expressed in one of the most unusual,
yet most characteristic, passages of *The Lord of the Rings* — the
poignant exchanges between Aragorn and Arwen when the king
takes to his deathbed and his queen at last confronts the meaning
of her choice of mortality. "Let us not be overthrown at the final
test," he adjures her, and offers the consoling thought that "we are
not bound for ever to the circles of the world, and beyond them is
more than memory." It is only a hope, though, and the story ends
with Arwen leaving her home and her children and trekking up-
river to faded Lothlórien, there to meet a silent and solitary death
on the very spot where long ago, in a time out of time, she had first
met her love (RK 344). Tolkien called this passage "a part of the
essential story" but tucked it into the appendices because, he
explained, he could not see how to fit it into the "hobbito-centric"
main narrative.[89] This expedient seems to epitomize the whole
crazy scheme of trying to conjoin the world of hobbits with that of
the legendarium.

The story of the death of Aragorn and Arwen is, in fact, not just a
part of the essential story; it is the capstone of an epic structure that
is remarkably complete. Together with the legendarium, *The Lord
of the Rings* forms part of four nested narratives. The main narrative
tells of a critical moment in the history of Middle-earth. It begins
with Bilbo's and Frodo's birthday party and ends with Sam's arrival
home from the Grey Havens after Bilbo's and Frodo's departure
from Middle-earth. This rests within another, also wholly contained
within *The Lord of the Rings*: the entire saga of the Rings of Power

---

[88] *Return of the King*, 310; and see above, 1.
[89] *Letters*, 237, 246.

beginning with the forging of the One, the Three, the Seven and the Nine and ending with the last event in Tolkien's imagined history: the departure of Celeborn from the Grey Havens, "and with him ... the last living memory of the Elder Days in Middle-earth" (FR 25). Climaxing as it does with the destruction of the surviving Rings, and the departure of the last of the Wise from Middle-earth, this second narrative validates Tolkien's conception of *The Lord of the Rings* as comprising not just a *moment* but a *phase* of history. As such, it nestles in turn within a third narrative which is History as a whole: an imaginary national story, or secular scripture (Northrop Frye's terms), reaching back to an imaginary Beginning but also reaching forward to connect with the reader's history. This third, encyclopaedic narrative comprises the totality of *The Lord of the Rings* — Foreword, Prologue, main narrative and appendices — and much of the legendarium. It is the story of the long defeat and is necessarily unfinished.

However, the metaphysical cast of Tolkien's idea of history demands still more. Accordingly, the three narratives that I have so far defined are nested within a fourth: that of History temporally extended into Myth. This largest narrative is extended back to the Beginning by the Ainulindalë, Tolkien's account of the Creation in *The Silmarillion*; but how can it be extended into a future which is our future too? This is the work of the story of Aragorn and Arwen. Aragorn's dying assurance to his wife is a mythic invocation of the end of human history, the fictional counterpart of those "glimpses of final victory" which for Tolkien helped to alleviate the long defeat. Thus the story of the death of Aragorn and Arwen, the last desperate step in Tolkien's quest to integrate the worlds of *The Hobbit* and the legendarium, reveals the full meaning of his statement that the "real theme" of *The Lord of the Rings* is Death and Immortality even as it completes the narrative arc of his mythology as a whole.

4

War and Peace: Tolstoy's "Novel"

Tolkien did not set out to write an epic, but he did embark on a scheme that was potentially epic and his epic temperament enforced the outcome. It drove him to infuse his story with the requisite temporal depth and to conjure up a fantasy world of convincing breadth and substance — by which I mean convincing geography, mythology, history and politics. That world came into being, moreover, not through an act of abstract or academic whimsy, but as a response to history in the making. Would Tolkien ever have finished his story without the imaginative stimulus of the Second World War? If he had finished it, would it have attained epic scope? The very spectacle of current events being put to such use highlights the epic's responsiveness to epochal events in the present, an aspect that helps to imbue it with a sense of history.

In a fantasy set in an imaginary past, these features required extensive demonstration, but *War and Peace* is the opposite: a masterpiece of literary realism set in the relatively recent, well-documented past. To the critical consensus that Northrop Frye chided for disparaging the romance, it was the Everest of narrative fiction. E. M. Forster hailed it as the novel's way forward and noted widespread agreement that it was the greatest in the Western literary canon. George Orwell recalled his regret, on first reading it as a young man, that it did not go on longer. To cite the Russian novel as a peak of achievement in the genre, as Orwell did, was to invoke Tolstoy above all. These were only two voices in a chorus of British and American authorities that exalted Tolstoy and his masterpiece.

Even C. S. Lewis declared it pre-eminent among novels.[1] *War and Peace* hardly needs justifying as an artistic imagining of human experience, then; and since Tolstoy is known to have conceived it as a response to Russia's humiliating defeat in the Crimean War (1853-56) and ensuing domestic crisis, it should not be difficult to demonstrate the influence of current events on his imagination.

Yet these matters require consideration even so. Discussing the relationship of the novel to the romance, Frye proposes that most so-called historical novels are in fact romances (presumably owing to the nostalgic appeal of the historical setting to the author), and that "a novel becomes more romantic in its appeal when the life it reflects has passed away" (presumably owing to the setting's nostalgic appeal to the reader).[2] Both observations apply to *War and Peace*, which was written in the 1860s and is set half a century earlier, and it also happens that one of Tolstoy's favourite techniques of plot construction is to take a stock sentimental trope and give it a subversive twist. Add a gallery of aristocratic heroes and heroines — handsome young men in uniform and bejewelled beauties in low-cut gowns — and it is no surprise to find an online customer review that acclaims the novel as "one of the greatest love stories of all times — a true soap opera of epic proportions."[3]

How can a narrative commend itself to one reader as a realist masterpiece and to another as a soap opera, albeit of epic proportions? The proportions may be part of the answer. *War and Peace* is distant from us in time, and from most of us in place as well. Besides that, its very length and amplitude make it hard to apprehend in its entirety, inducing readers to define the whole in terms of the aspect that most impresses itself upon them. Its status as a masterpiece of literary realism is well founded, but since it portrays a cast of glamorous folk behaving as such folk commonly did, readers attuned to

---

[1] Forster, *Aspects of the Novel*, 46-47, 170; "As I Please," in *Collected Essays, Journalism and Letters of George Orwell*, III: 129; Roger Lancelyn Green and Walter Hooper, *C. S. Lewis: A Biography* (London: Souvenir Press 1988), 152. This view of *War and Peace* is enshrined in that compendium of twentieth-century modernist orthodoxy, *Encyclopedia Britannica*: "*War and Peace* in particular seems virtually to define this form for many readers and critics." Gerald S. Hawkins, "Tolstoy, Leo," *Britannica 2003 Ultimate Reference Suite DVD*.

[2] Frye, *Anatomy of Criticism*, 307.

[3] www.amazon.co.uk/review/R1F1GR94514R10 (viewed 2/8/2016).

the glamour and sentiment can easily slight the nuances and receive the story as a soap opera.

However, one can celebrate it as a masterpiece of literary realism and still overlook much of importance. This is partly due to the vanishing of the world portrayed in the novel, but also because much of the novel's political meaning is symbolically expressed in a quest romance of which the love story is but the visible outcrop, and that quest romance is where Tolstoy invokes the numinous. Tolstoy's story has been viewed through the same ideological filter as *The Lord of the Rings* — namely, the dogmatic realism disparaged by W. P. Ker and Northrop Frye — but to the opposite effect. Applied to Tolkien's elaborate fantasy, the filter has tended to distract critics from the story's bearing on the human condition; applied to Tolstoy's minutely observed portraits of human manners and idiosyncrasy, it has blinded them to the places where he forsakes the strait path of realism to conjure the numinous. Even if one is on the lookout for the politics in *War and Peace*, it is easy to assume that it is confined to the novel's copious satirical passages and overlook the symbolism of the quest romance.

This brings us to Tolstoy's denial that *War and Peace* was a novel. As it was appearing, he published an article which stated: "What is 'War and Peace'? It is not a novel, still less a poem, still less a historical chronicle. 'War and Peace' is that which the author wished and was able to express in the form in which it has been expressed."[4] This rather odd statement was a challenge to the critical norms of the day. The "everyday" was recognized as the distinctive sphere of the novel, but subject to certain formal rules of art. Among other things, the action was expected to culminate in a climax to which every character and incident contributed.

War and Peace defied these expectations. In a bid to achieve even greater fidelity to real life, and to create an imaginative universe commensurate with the grandeur of his theme, Tolstoy packed his narrative with incidents and characters whose sole function is to evoke the extraordinary breadth and complexity of the context. He prolonged the story far beyond its emotional climax and ended it

---

4 L. N. Tolstoy, "*Neskol'ko slov po povodu knigi 'Voina i mir'*," in Tolstoy, *Polnoe sobranie sochinenii*, vol. 16 (Moscow: Gosudarstvennoe Izdatel'stvo Khudozhestvennoi Literaturiy 1955), 7-16 (transl. as "A Few Words About the Book 'War and Peace'" in A. V. Knowles, ed., *Tolstoy: The Critical Heritage*. London: Routledge and Kegan Paul, 1978, 124-33).

with a boy dreaming about the future, his thoughts fading into an ellipsis. The narrative was inconsistent in style, tone and perspective, sometimes presenting the characters from within and sometimes from without, and sometimes forsaking the narrative voice to tell the story through the characters' letters or diaries. The plot interwove historical and fictional events, involving historical figures in fictional situations. The second half of the narrative was interlarded with an increasingly intrusive historiographical polemic which mocked everything that had ever been published about Napoleon's invasion of Russia in 1812 and insisted at great length that historians simply did not understand what history was — that, like novelists, they habitually imposed a false pattern on reality. The book ended, not with the dénouement I have just described, but with a lengthy exposition of Tolstoy's philosophy of history.

So it was that, although Tolstoy had set out to write a novel, from quite an early stage he was drafting prefaces that declared his inability to adapt his narrative to the traditional form and content of the genre. He became so committed to this view of his masterpiece that he seems to have forgotten that it had started out as a novel. Several years later, when he began writing *Anna Karenina*, he called the new project "this novel, the first I have attempted."[5]

Contemplating the puzzlement and repulsion that surrounded *War and Peace* for decades after it appeared, the critic Gary Morson contends that English-speaking commentators of the mid-twentieth century, in celebrating it as the acme of realistic fiction, simply ignored the novelties and eccentricities that made it "not a novel" to Tolstoy and a very odd novel to his contemporaries.[6] Morson's allegation is unfair at least to Forster, who celebrated Tolstoy's story precisely on account of its formal peculiarities: "Expansion. Not completion. Not rounding off but opening out ... Such an untidy book. Yet, as we read it, do not great chords begin to sound behind us ... ?" Forster ascribed the "great chords" to Tolstoy's extraordinary feeling for space, which he recognized as a feature that distinguished *War and Peace* from the common run of novels.[7] But even he did not get beyond the sense of space to the quest romance that it defines. He did not hear in the great chords the "song" of prophecy.

---

[5] John Bayley, *Tolstoy and the Novel* (New York: Viking Press, 1967), 30.
[6] Gary Saul Morson, *Hidden in Plain View: Narrative and Creative Potentials in "War and Peace"* (Stanford, CA: Stanford UP, 1987), 76–80.
[7] Forster, *Aspects of the Novel*, 170.

On what basis, then, do I assert the existence of a feature of Tolstoy's narrative that has eluded generations of distinguished commentary? First of all, on a comparison that I hope Benedict Anderson would applaud: contemplating *War and Peace* in the light of *The Lord of the Rings* alerted me to an apparent discrepancy between Tolstoy's realism and his repeated allusion in a certain context to *volshebnoye tsarstvo* (variously translated as *fairyland*, *the enchanted realm*, and *a magical kingdom*). This perception brought other features of the quest romance into view. Then another comparison came into play: that between Tolstoy's published text and a fairly complete, but much more conventional, interim version. This revealed that every key feature of the quest romance, and virtually every other aspect of the narrative that I will identify as epic, are either missing in the interim text or, still more significantly, arise from major revision of it.

All this is explained in the next chapter. To fully grasp the ways in which Tolstoy's masterpiece is "not a novel" we must first consider those in which it is one. For one thing, as noted earlier, a hallmark of the epic as defined by W. P. Ker and E. M. W. Tillyard is its inclusive or multigeneric character. Although not just a novel, *War and Peace* is still more a novel than anything else; but, even considered as such, it contains elements or suggestions of different types of novel,[8] and this very plenitude contributes to the epic effect. Secondly, the quest romance is a sort of epiphenomenon, inseparable from the story as a whole — much as, in *The Lord of the Rings*, the time-travel aspect only appears in relation to the overland journey. It is so embedded in Tolstoy's realist novel that we can only get at it by pinpointing the places where the narrative hints at something that is not "real," and it is achieved by the very narrative techniques of implication and indirection that he uses to capture so much of the "real" world in so comparatively small a span. In this chapter, therefore, after sketching the origins of Tolstoy's project, I focus on the techniques of characterization and plot-construction by which he attempts to establish the reality of his fictional world in the reader's mind. In the next I discuss the epic treatment of time and space, of which the quest romance is but one example, and compare the published and interim versions in order to show how — and how purposefully — he changed his novel-in-progress in order to achieve this.

---

[8] Cf. Bayley, *Tolstoy and the Novel*, 75.

Politics and romance

The accession of Tsar Nicholas I in December 1825 triggered an abortive uprising by a secret society of army officers (hence known as Decembrists), some of whom had acquired liberal ideas while serving in western Europe during the fight against Napoleon. From then until the outbreak of the Crimean War, Russia's government was one of unrelieved autocracy. This matched the country's posture in international affairs. Russia's military might and leading role in the defeat of Napoleon made it the chief arbiter of the reactionary post-Napoleonic order in Europe, and in 1848 and 1849 it intervened to suppress revolutions in Germany and the Austro-Hungarian Empire. Defeat in the Crimea, which coincided with the death of Nicholas and the accession of Alexander II, discredited the Tsarist autocracy and released a pent-up demand for reform. This resulted in the introduction of institutions such as local government and a French-style judicial code, and in the abolition of serfdom, a system under which most peasants were bound in servitude to the land.

During the war, Tolstoy spent nearly a year as an artillery officer in the garrison of the besieged port of Sevastopol. Amid the fighting, he began to publish semi-fictional "sketches" of the siege. The first, full of patriotic idealism, won the new tsar's approval; the second, reflecting the horror and disillusionment of six months of battle, was mutilated by the censor and earned the disapproving attention of the police. Tolstoy emerged with respect for the rank-and-file soldier and a lasting hatred of war and scorn for bureaucracy, both civil and military. These attitudes would find eloquent expression in *War and Peace*.

As a proud country nobleman, however, Tolstoy found little to like in the westernized intelligentsia that came to the fore during the post-war political ferment. He approved of abolishing serfdom and educating the peasantry, but his efforts to do so on his own estate aroused suspicion both in his peasants and the government. This persuaded him that reform-minded bureaucrats influenced by urban intellectuals, all of them ignorant of the realities of the countryside, were undermining the landowners' position and setting the peasants against them. For their part, the secret police saw him as some sort of social revolutionary. They raided his home, scrutinized his private papers, and dragged the pond in search of the illegal printing press they thought he must own.[9] These events engendered an alienation *so* complete that, in the words of the Russian Formalist critic Boris Eichenbaum, it left him at odds "with history itself, with the very fact of the historical process." So estranged was he from all currents of opinion that throughout the 1860s, the decade in which he wrote *War and Peace*, "people of the most varied persuasions kept referring to Tolstoi as a crank and an eccentric." Eichenbaum depicts him in these years as a reactionary whose extreme antipathy to modernity found expression in an anarchism which rejected all need for government.[10] Tolstoy, writes a modern scholar, "rejected as illegitimate those personality traits that make human beings political." Politics was bad because it threatened the independence and integrity of the individual.[11]

War and Peace originated in Tolstoy's impulse to thrash out these issues in fiction. The first fruits of his inquiry were three chapters describing the return to Moscow of an old Decembrist after thirty years' exile in Siberia. But his musings on contemporary affairs took him back, first to the rising itself and then to the war against Napoleon — that is, to an earlier time when western ideas had stirred the Russian intelligentsia and military defeat had goaded the government to ponder social and administrative reform. For a long time, he clung to his intention to "lead not one but many heroes and heroines of mine through the historical events of 1805, 1807, 1812, 1825 and 1856."[12] But as he worked out his complex plot, he came to realize that he could say most of what he wanted about politics, war and the human condition without going beyond 1812, except for a short epilogue set some years later. In the process, his initial political concerns became subsumed in a grand saga of human destiny, but they did not vanish. In the final tale they find expression in Count Pierre Bezukhov's initial infatuation with revolutionary ideals, embrace of Freemasonry, and efforts to improve

---

[9] Kathryn B. Feuer, *Tolstoy and the Genesis of 'War and Peace'*, ed. Robin Feuer Miller and Donna Tussing Orwin (Ithaca, NY: Cornell UP, 1996), 135-67; A. N. Wilson, *Tolstoy* (London: Hamish Hamilton, 1988), 137-39, 150-54, 163-71, 189-90.

[10] Boris Eikhenbaum, *Tolstoi in the Sixties*, trans. Duffield White (Ann Arbor, MI: Ardis, 1982) 7-9, 150-51, 208-13.

[11] Donna Tussing Orwin, *Tolstoy's Art and Thought, 1847-1880* (Princeton, NJ: Princeton UP, 1993), 8.

[12] Quoted in R. F. Christian, *Tolstoy's 'War and Peace': A Study* (Oxford: Clarendon Press, 1962), 22.

his peasants' lot, and in his friend Prince Andrei Bolkonsky's more successful improving endeavours and brief participation in the modernizing administration (1809-1812) of Mikhail Speransky.

Tolstoy's attitude is massively sceptical. Speransky and his circle are portrayed as shallow hypocrites, with whom Andrei is briefly infatuated but soon disillusioned. But reactionary bureaucrats are even more harshly portrayed, in particular the obtuse Count Rostopchin, governor of Moscow, who kicks Pierre out of the city in 1812 as a suspected French sympathizer and evades a lynch-mob by focusing their anger on a hapless liberal whom he tars as a French agent. Besides the unsympathetic portrayal of historical figures, Tolstoy's bleak outlook is manifest in his satirical treatment of the courtiers and careerists who are in their element at the soirées of Anna Scherer, herself a courtier, in Saint Petersburg, the imperial capital. Scherer's guests are supposedly the cream of the capital's intelligentsia, but none of them says anything that rises above shallow wit. At his first sight of them, Pierre is like a child in a toyshop. The rise of Hélène, his corrupt and promiscuous wife, to pre-eminence among these chatterboxes and at court is a sure sign of Tolstoy's contempt.

So far, I have dwelt on the differences between Tolstoy and Tolkien, but similarities are starting to appear. Both men emerged from warfare with deep respect for the rank-and-file soldier. Both were profoundly alienated from the politics and society of their day. Each, intent on transmuting troubling experiences into art, found it necessary to transpose his experience to a different milieu: Tolkien to a mythic past of his own imagining, Tolstoy to a historical past that was still within living memory. We shall see that the master-fantasist and the arch-realist were surprisingly close in their social ideals, a similarity that is reflected in their art. In *War and Peace*, Tolstoy the realist ventures into the realm of the ideal; and it is when he does so that his story assumes the lineaments of a quest romance. It is a quest romance of a somewhat different sort from Tolkien's, however. Frodo Baggins knowingly undertakes his quest to save the world, but the heroes of Tolstoy's romance are in quest of personal redemption, although that goal is never explicitly articulated. Secondly, the quest of Tolstoy's heroes is expressed through the symbolism of sexual relations — their attraction to a woman. In our quest for Tolstoy's quest romance, therefore, we must consider the question of *romance* without the definite article.

For all Tolstoy's commitment to realism, *War and Peace* is full of "romance", along with other stock attributes of soap opera. The leading characters are all members of the nobility: Prince Andrei Bolkonsky and his sister Princess Marya, Count Nikolai Rostov and his sister Countess Natasha, and Count Pierre Bezukhov. Andrei is gravely wounded at the battle of Austerlitz (1805) and fatally wounded at the battle of Borodino (1812). In the interim his wife dies and he becomes betrothed to Natasha, but he breaks off the engagement when Natasha tries to elope with another suitor, the brother of Pierre's wife Hélène. The lovers are later reunited in what proves to be a deathbed reconciliation. Then Hélène dies and Natasha marries Pierre, who has always loved her. Nikolai is engaged to his cousin Sonya for most of the story but ends up marrying Princess Marya after rescuing her under romantic circumstances.[13]

Amorous relationships, separation and longing, adultery, a duel, a thwarted elopement, and the poignant reunion of estranged lovers, not to mention some blatant coincidences, all involving families belonging to the more or less idle rich — these sound like staple ingredients of soap opera. In addition to these stereotyped plot elements, there is a touch of fairy-tale glamour to Tolstoy's characters, with their opulent lifestyles, vast estates, and armies of servants at their beck and call. In these respects, *War and Peace* epitomizes Northrop Frye's comments on the relationship between the novel and the romance. In denying that it is a novel, Tolstoy is in a sense denying that it is a romance, since he is addressing its failure to conform to the structural norms that prompt Frye to characterize the realistic novel in general as "parody-romance." In fact, though, creative deployment of romance elements is a prominent feature of the narrative.

To start with, all its marvellously developed main characters have an archetypal core. When Prince Andrei appears in Anna

---

[13]Two points about names. Firstly, the Russian court nobility commonly used French. Tolstoy often presents them as doing so and Frenchifying each other's names in the process: thus Vasili becomes *Basile*, Andrei *André*, and Lisa *Lise*. But he always refers to Pierre and Hélène in this way, rather than by the Russian form of their names, even when using the Russian Cyrillic alphabet. Secondly, Russian names are inflected, so the surnames have different gender forms: e.g., Rostov-Rostova, Drubetskoy-Drubetskaya. Foreign names, even when belonging to Russians, are not inflected: e.g., Scherer.

Scherer's salon in Saint Petersburg at the beginning of the novel, he is introduced as

> an extremely handsome young man of medium height with clear-cut impassive features. Everything about him, from his weary, jaded aspect to his slow, measured step, was in the sharpest contrast to his vivacious little wife. It was obvious that he not only knew everyone in the drawing-room but was so thoroughly bored with them that he found it tedious either to look at them or listen to them (I.i.3).[14]

A Russian counterpart of Jane Austen's Mr. Darcy, no less — and while his married state may preclude his being a cynosure of husband-seeking eyes, this no longer applies when he returns to the seat of government four years later.

> The feminine world, *society*, welcomed him with delight because he was rich, distinguished, a good match, and almost a newcomer, with an aureole of romance on account of his supposed death [at Austerlitz] and the tragic loss of his wife. Moreover, the general opinion of all who had known him previously was that he had greatly changed for the better ... that he had softened and matured, and lost his former pride, affectation, and disdainful irony, and had acquired the serenity that comes with years (II.iii.5).

And when, at a grand New Year's Eve ball, Pierre urges him to dance with Natasha, a debutante who is feeling overwhelmed by the occasion, he is gallantry itself and turns out to be one of the best dancers of the day into the bargain.

And so we are set up to see him with Natasha's eyes when, after vicissitudes proper to a tale of true love, she beholds the mortally wounded hero for the first time since he so rashly went abroad for a year at his father's behest in order to test the strength of their engagement.

> He was the same as ever, but the feverish flush on his face, his glittering eyes rapturously gazing at her, and especially his neck, delicate as a child's and showing above the turned-down collar of his nightshirt, gave him a singularly innocent, childlike look, such as she had never seen in him before. She went up to him and with a swift, supple, youthful movement, fell to her knees.
>
> He smiled and held out his hand to her (III.iii.31).

---

[14] Since *War and Peace* consists of mainly brief chapters and has been published in many languages and editions, I cite it by Book, Part and chapter. Except where indicated, I quote from Leo Tolstoy, *War and Peace*, transl. Ann Dunnigan, introd. by John Bayley (New York: Signet Classic, 1968).

Such passages project Prince Andrei as the archetypal Prince Charming.[15]

While Andrei, as the tragic hero of Tolstoy's quest romance, is the most obvious example, his female foil is no less archetypal in essence. Natasha embodies the Eternal-Feminine: an element varying in its manifestation from good fairy to enchantress to jailbait, according to the male who is exposed to it. But Natasha's is a complex case, since she is at the centre of the plot and is the only principal character who has sustained interactions with all the others. A clearer instance is Andrei's sister, Princess Marya, who goes through the novel as the myopic, ungainly, submissive butt of her father's tyrannical whims and her brother's sarcasm until fate presents her with a glimpse of the happiness she has always longed for. On her second meeting with Nikolai Rostov, some weeks after he rescued her from refractory peasants under circumstances that struck them both as romantic, she is suddenly revealed as the Ugly Duckling.

> When Rostov entered the room the Princess lowered her head for an instant, as if to give her visitor time to greet her aunt, and then, just as Nikolai turned to her, she raised her head and met his gaze with shining eyes. She half rose, her movements full of grace and dignity, and with a smile of pleasure held out her slender, delicate hand to him, and began speaking in a voice that for the first time vibrated with a new, deep, womanly note. Mademoiselle Bourienne ... looked at Princess Marya in bewildered surprise. Herself an accomplished coquette, she could not have maneuvered better on meeting a man she wished to attract.
>
> 'Either black is particularly becoming to her or she has actually grown better-looking without my noticing it. And above all — what grace and tact!' thought Mademoiselle Bourienne.
>
> Had Princess Marya been capable of reflection at that moment she would have been even more astonished than Mademoiselle Bourienne ... (IV.i.6)

The Ugly Duckling does not choose to become a swan, it is fated to become one.

The archetypal essence is more muted in the other two principals, but in Pierre at least its manifestation is as startling as it is brief. A mild-mannered giant, he turns into an avenging Golem

---

[15] Cf. Edward Wasiolek, *Tolstoy's Major Fiction* (Chicago: University of Chicago Press, 1978), 105.

figure when roused,[16] but there are only three or four fleeting moments of transformation. One occurs when, goaded beyond endurance by his wife, he brandishes a massive marble table at her in a paroxysm of rage; another is when he runs her brother, Natasha's would-be ravisher, out of Saint Petersburg by grabbing his collar and shaking him until he gets the message. There are also a couple of brief tussles with French soldiers in 1812 (III.ii.32, III.iii.33). As for Nikolai, he is to all appearances a dashing young hussar.

Did Tolstoy manage to write, then, over six years and with great effort, precisely the sort of fiction he was striving to avoid? Not really: Northrop Frye distinguishes the novel from the romance by its "greater conformity to ordinary experience," and for every archetypal moment Tolstoy supplies a dozen that defeat conventional expectations. Love, longing, coincidence, elopement — all are features of human life, and in Tolstoy's day duels were too: during his childhood two leading Russian writers, Aleksandr Pushkin and Mikhail Lermontov, died in duels. As for the aristocrats who throng the story — well, Tolstoy himself was that sort of person, and he wrote about the life and people he knew. He even wrote (but in the end did not publish) a mock apology for doing so. To write about aristocrats as though they represented the whole of Russian life was, he admitted, "untrue and illiberal, and I can give only one answer, an irrefutable one. The lives of officials, merchants, theological students and peasants do not interest me and are only half comprehensible to me; the lives of the aristocrats of that time ... are comprehensible, interesting and dear to me."[17]

Even if *War and Peace* resembles soap opera in its characters and circumstances, then, it does not in the way Tolstoy treats his material. Soap opera characters are stereotyped and superficial, lacking inwardness, and the situations are essentially melodramatic and sentimental. Tolstoy's leading characters, by contrast, are fully engaged with the world and exhibit a full range of emotions: some of them ponder the meaning of life at almost tedious length, and along with their elation, fear and lust we witness their boredom, depression and self-loathing. And Tolstoy purges his story of sentimentality and melodrama by immersing its dramatic elements in his sceptical view of the reality of daily life. His quest romance is embedded in a historical novel of uncommon realism. As will

---

[16] Cf. Lydia Ginzburg, *On Psychological Prose*, trans. Judson Rosengrant (Princeton, NJ, Princeton UP, 1991), 252-53.

[17] Quoted in Christian, *Tolstoy's* War and Peace, 22.

appear when we come to the quest romance, however, the techniques by which he achieves that realism also allow him to subvert it.

Realism and romance: Tolstoy's characters

One thing that makes *War and Peace* so much more than a soap opera is the way its archetypes are embedded in thoroughly rounded characters. Our love-hate relationship with the arrogant hero depends on seeing the arrogance from without, as with Mr. Darcy, but after our first glimpse of Prince Andrei we spend the next few hundred pages observing him almost entirely from within, with only a rare glimpse of a crisp uniform and an easy posture astride a horse in some glamorous retinue to keep the heart a-flutter until something happens to expose his archetypal core. And so it is with the other leading characters. Natasha first appears as a skinny, lively, wilful child and Pierre as a moon-faced fatty: in both cases the archetypal essence is buried deep. Marya certainly comes across as ugly, but with no hint of the eventual transformation that defines her archetype. And Nikolai's archetypal essence will turn out to be quite surprising.

One of Tolstoy's most potent tricks of characterization, which he also uses to set up his quest romance, is to hint at things that are never stated outright. Pierre's first meeting with the Freemason Osip Bazdeyev is recounted in a way which makes it obvious that he is in search of a father-figure. This is a key to his character, which explains most of we have read about him so far and much that is to happen to him subsequently. It illuminates Andrei's affectionate but condescending attitude towards him, like that of an elder brother. It explains why his scheming father-in-law, Prince Vasili Kuragin, so successfully manipulates him; why he clings to Freemasonry even though it fails to provide a satisfying world-view and most of its adepts are social-climbing hypocrites; and why, when imprisoned by the French in Moscow, he embraces the peasant Platon Karatayev as a guru. Not that his craving for a mentor is the only explanation of his response to Karatayev: his old mentor Bazdeyev has just died, and he is ripe for re-programming, having just undergone a soul-shattering experience when he thought he was about to be executed by a firing-squad. All these things are left for the reader to infer, to the confusion of some early commentators who complained about the apparent arbitrariness of the characters' behaviour. They illustrate what the critic John Bayley calls Tolstoy's ability to lead the reader to "kinds of realisation which seem to come not from Tolstoy but from our own experience of life."[18]

This technique is particularly evident in the way that Tolstoy's characters are deepened by their family context. Pierre's essential fatherlessness fully explains his craving for paternal guidance, and we hear nothing about his mother. His mild, ingratiating nature suggests a person who, while not maltreated, and perhaps even treated affectionately by those responsible for his care and upbringing, has always felt that he needed to earn that affection. Prince Andrei and his sister are likewise convincing products of their family. Their father is a great man of the last century now in embittered retirement. Some of the traits that Andrei shares with him are masterfulness, pride, ambition, energy, acute intelligence, and misogyny. Andrei's gifts have enabled him to excel in all the skills, from thinking to dancing, that his father-defined destiny requires of him, but he has somehow managed to encumber himself with a wife, now pregnant, whom he despises. He is thoroughly at home in that sphere, so alluring to the ambitious but impecunious Prince Boris Drubetskoy, where young staff officers can lord it over field commanders, and when we first meet him he is callow enough to enjoy being there; thus he is not above bragging to Boris about touring the Austro-Russian positions before the battle of Austerlitz in the suite of the allied chief-of-staff, the Austrian General Weyrother. He also dreams of achieving some brilliant military stroke like that which had set his hero Napoleon on the road to glory a dozen years earlier. But he is not just a pretty face. Kutuzov, the Russian commander-in-chief, favours him not only out of respect for his father but because he has inherited his father's intelligence and dedication and is one of the few staff officers who takes a serious interest in the general progress of the campaign.

Princess Marya is at first sight the very opposite of Andrei: submissive instead of masterful, devout instead of sceptical, masochistic instead of unfeeling, plain and ungainly instead of handsome and graceful. All this is quite consistent with her place in a household dominated by misogynistic males: like Andrei, she has willed herself to be what she was expected to be. And she shares some traits with her male kin. One is family pride, the Bolkonsky arrogance that is so quick to assume a stranger's inferiority. When Natasha, as Andrei's betrothed, first meets her, there is none of the instant bonding we

---

[18] Bayley, *Tolstoy and the Novel*, 110; Morson, *Hidden in Plain View*, 56-57.

might expect. Far from it: like her father, Marya looks down on Natasha as unworthy of Andrei, and later she shares her father's joy when the elopement scandal ends the engagement. We may recall that the two women's brothers had felt a similar antipathy for each other five years earlier when they met on campaign.

Another family trait is the tactical intelligence that enables Marya to recognize and seize an opportunity. Like her brother, she has her dreams: not callow male dreams of military glory but womanly dreams of "earthly love," of a masterful man who will rescue her from her daily travail. And when at last the chance comes (not of rescue from her father, who has died, but of earthly love), plain, clumsy Marya instinctively seizes it, and the swashbuckling hussar, who fancies himself as a ladies' man, is hooked — but hooked, after all, by a general's daughter. Tolstoy's use of the word "manoeuvre" (*manevrirovat'*) is exact.

As it happens, hooked is not landed. First there is the obstacle of Nikolai's engagement to his cousin Sonya, and as soon as that vanishes another crops up: the Rostov estate has been ruined by the war and his father's extravagance, and in his poverty he is too proud to court an heiress, even one he loves (he was never willing to court one he despised, for all his mother's entreaties). When Marya nerves herself to call on him and his mother in their little house in a bad corner of Moscow, she realizes that she has made a bad move; and when, some time later, he returns the call, it is apparently only to fulfil the demands of etiquette. But as he is about to leave, Marya's evident, though muted, misery causes him to drop his guard slightly; and although he quickly resumes it, she divines his weakness and exploits it with a tactical flair her father might appreciate and her brother envy — not by dissembling, but by expressing her true feelings.

> "For some reason you wish to deprive me of our former friendship. And it hurts me." There were tears in her eyes and in her voice. "I have had so little happiness in my life that every loss is hard for me — Excuse me, good-bye." She suddenly burst into tears and hurriedly started toward the door (Ep.i.6).

The general's daughter has reproduced the circumstances of their first meeting, when she was in dire need of rescue, and Nikolai is only too happy to repeat the favour. This time, though, it is really she who is rescuing him.

As with Pierre, there is no mention of Marya's and Andrei's mother, but she is perhaps to be divined in those large, luminous eyes which can so transform Marya's face, and which Andrei passes on to his son, Nikolenka. In Marya and Nikolenka those eyes express devotion to an ideal, or at least the capacity for such devotion. In Marya that capacity finds fulfilment in the Christian stoicism that empowers her to endure her long martyrdom to the whims of her increasingly senile father; in Nikolenka its potential is implicit in his fondness for his father's old friend Pierre (of which more later). Andrei's nature is more complex, because the challenge of making himself what he was expected to be has impaired his ability to *feel*, and his eyes, like his father's, are more apt to glitter than shine. Like his father he is agnostic and mocks his sister's piety. Yet his whole career reveals that, despite himself, he shares her feeling that one cannot save one's soul by conforming to conventional mores. His prolonged sojourn in the countryside after Austerlitz is due less to his wound than to guilt-feelings about his wife's death in childbirth and to disenchantment with the world of ambition as he experienced it on campaign. His second foray into that world — his government service under Speransky — is also short-lived.

In the end, both Marya and Andrei find within themselves traits characteristic of the other. There is a martyr-like connection between Andrei's physical suffering on his deathbed and the epiphany of universal love that comes upon him in his agony: it is as though pain is the price of his ascent to that plane of spiritual grace where Marya has dwelt all along. Marya, for her part, released by her father's death from her long martyrdom to his whims, finds within herself both the physical grace that had made Andrei one of the best dancers of the day and a new power to shape her own destiny. Marya, however, pays no spiritual price for this temporary accession of physical grace. Our last glimpse of her is through Nikolai's eyes at the end of their bedtime conversation in the Epilogue.

> Countess Marya's spirit was ever aspiring to the infinite, the eternal, the absolute, and could therefore never be at peace. An austere expression of the lofty, secret suffering of a soul burdened with a body appeared on her face. Nikolai looked at her.
>
> "My God! What would become of us if she were to die, as I always fear when she looks like that!" he thought ... (Ep.i.15).

"Spirit burdened by the flesh": the image calls to mind, across eight years and hundreds of pages, the dying Andrei. Nikolai senses in his wife the egoism of the martyr, just as we see it in her brother.

The Rostov family too (except the eldest sibling, the possibly autistic Vera) are clearly of a kind. This quality accounts for a striking feature of the episode that culminates in the death of Petya, the youngest. He has been hovering — or, rather, rushing about — on the fringes of the Rostov family since we first met them, but in the second half of the novel his individuality begins to emerge and he undergoes a gradual metamorphosis from accessory to object of concern. As Napoleon's invasion advances, he schemes with a friend to join the army and, in the patriotic furore of the moment, overcomes his parents' objections. He adores Natasha, and after the elopement fiasco is the one member of the family with whom she feels at ease. As the family belatedly packs to flee Moscow, the house resounds with his and Natasha's running footsteps, shouts and laughter: "They were exuberant and mirthful, not because there was any cause for laughter, but because there was laughter and gaiety in their hearts ..." (III.iii.12). And then, as we are watching a guerrilla band led by Vasska Denisov — Nikolai's old friend and fleetingly Natasha's suitor — tracking a prisoner convoy that happens to include Pierre, Petya turns up with a message which, hungry for glory, he had insistently volunteered to carry, and suddenly we are seeing through his eyes as if he were one of the major characters. Yet there is no feeling of strangeness, because he is a Rostov. Unfortunately, he is Natasha with testosterone — a lethal combination. We are shocked but not surprised when, in the attack on the convoy, he charges ahead in defiance of Denisov's strict orders and is shot dead.

Realism and romance: Tolstoy's subversion of sentimentality

Neither Petya's death nor Andrei's occurs in the interim version of the novel. Clearly a work in progress rather than the "original version" touted by its publisher,[19] it is a conventional affair compared to the published text — remarkably so, in view of Tolstoy's early protestations that he could not achieve his intentions in the form of a novel. As far as the beginning of the great battle of Borodino, its plot is much the same as the final version, though with many

---

[19] Leo Tolstoy, *War and Peace: Original Version* (trans. Andrew Bromfield, New York: Harper, 2007). It is somewhat less than a complete and homogeneous text, even though the last page ends with "The End". Its history and problems are discussed in Hugh McLean, "Review Article: *War and Peace*, Original Version," *Tolstoy Studies Journal*, XX (2008): 82-87.

important variations in detail, but then it trails off into a cursory and distressingly trite conclusion featuring a happy ending. Andrei recovers from his wound but nobly renounces his claim on Natasha because he recognizes that she and Pierre are meant for each other. Sonya cedes Nikolai to Princess Marya with equal grace, allowing the story to close with a double helping of what E. M. Forster calls, in reference to Scott's *Antiquary*, "that idiotic use of marriage as a finale."[20] Tolstoy thought of calling it *All's Well That Ends Well*.

The *dénouement* is plausible up to a point, since (as John Bayley remarks[21]) it really is quite difficult to imagine Natasha and Andrei in the sort of settled domesticity that we see her sharing with Pierre at the end of the story. However, it is a soap-opera ending and, worse still, it is repetition instead of development. Andrei has already had a near-death experience at Austerlitz, and Tolstoy could hardly reprieve him again without diminishing both the carnage of 1812 and Andrei's epiphany in the field hospital. Besides, Pierre too survives two near-death experiences on his road to enlightenment — his duel with Dolokhov, the story's evil genius, and his firing-squad trauma. Tolstoy must have realized that he could not let them both off, so he upgraded Andrei's self-sacrifice to full-fledged martyrdom and reinforced the logic of his vision by bumping off young Petya into the bargain. Nothing less tragic could have done justice to the hard-won victory of 1812.

Both deaths shock the reader — Petya's because Tolstoy has placed us inside the character's head, immersing us for several chapters in his youthful zest and Rostovian essence, and Andrei's because Tolstoy contrives to make us hope for the hero's survival in defiance of all likelihood. Tolstoy sets up the drama of Andrei's death by a brazen coincidence, attaching him anonymously to the wagon-train of wounded soldiers which Natasha and her family are conducting from Moscow. Once the estranged lovers have discovered each other, with all the emotion to be expected on both sides, Tolstoy reports the doctor's conviction that Andrei's resulting physical improvement is only temporary; but he shapes the situation so deftly that we hope for the best all the same. When Princess Marya arrives to learn from Natasha that Andrei has just taken a critical turn, we feel it as a personal blow.

---

[20] Forster, *Aspects of the Novel*, 45.
[21] Bayley, *Tolstoy and the Novel*, 78.

Tolstoy then caps this twist by defeating Marya's (and our) expectations of the dying man.

> She understood ... that he had suddenly become gentle and resigned, and that this sweet humility could only be the precursor of death. As she approached the door she already saw in her imagination Andrei's face as she remembered it in childhood — tender, diffident, full of feeling. She was sure he would speak soft, loving words to her such as her father had uttered before his death, and that she would not be able to bear it and would break into sobs in his presence (IV.i.15).

We too expect this, since we have already seen Andrei through Natasha's eyes looking just like that and have witnessed his new loving gentleness. But no: Marya enters the room to find him withdrawn, indifferent, almost hostile, as though she were an unwelcome intruder. "Had he uttered a shriek of despair, the cry would have struck less horror in into Princess Maria's heart than the tone of his voice." Now she truly understands Natasha's words: Andrei has suddenly moved towards death and lost all empathy for the living. She, Marya, might as well not have come. He tries to be gracious but his mind is elsewhere, even when his son is brought in. When at last Marya does burst into tears, he quietly reproves her.

This episode illustrates Tolstoy's basic narrative strategy. The Russian literary theorist Viktor Shklovsky coined the term *ostraneniye*, variously translated as *defamiliarization*, *estrangement*, *alienation*, or *making it strange*, to denote Tolstoy's technique of revealing the familiar in a fresh light by portraying it as bizarre, as in the famous scene where the opera appears through Natasha's eyes as a ridiculous spectacle. In *War and Peace* a somewhat different distortion of the familiar, often through a character's perception, is not just a bravura effect but a basic method of plot construction. Tolstoy repeatedly sets up a potentially trite situation in order to deflate the expectations it evokes by making the characters respond in a manner which, though it disappoints or disconcerts us, is recognizably true to character. We expect (and want) Marya and Natasha to hit it off at their first meeting, but they don't because Marya, fatally honest, cannot dissimulate her ambivalence and Natasha, with her usual quickness of perception, instantly senses this and turns off the charm (II.v.7). We expect and want Andrei to receive Pierre cordially when the latter visits him on the battlefield on the eve of Borodino — but no: quite apart from the distractions of the impending battle, Andrei is still smarting from his humiliation at the hands of Natasha. Pierre, their mutual friend, is the last person he wants to see (III.ii.24). Even more disconcerting is the way Pierre shuns the weakening peasant Platon Karatayev on their forced march from Moscow instead of rallying to him as we might wish (IV.iii.12-14). This lamentable lapse of brotherly love does not haunt Pierre later on: as far as we know, he never gives it a thought, though he often talks of Karatayev and what the man meant to him. Tolstoy is rarely so forgiving, but it was, after all, a death march. Without dwelling on the horror, Tolstoy hints at its desperate reality by trampling our sentimental expectations.

Andrei's death represents the variant whereby Tolstoy reinforces the reader's expectations by ascribing them to a character too (in this case Marya) and then disabuses reader and character together. Marya approaches her brother's sickroom with *sentimental* expectations — she imagines herself shedding tears of sympathy for Andrei, herself, and everyone else involved — only to be confounded by Andrei's unexpected aloofness. When she finally bursts out crying, it is less from pity than from shock and frustration. Likewise, young Nikolai Rostov, unhorsed in his first cavalry charge, stands rooted to the spot, his agreeable expectations of slaughter suddenly dispelled, grappling with the realization that these advancing strangers are trying to kill *him! Nikolai! whom everyone loves!* before hurling his pistol at the nearest enemy soldier and running for his life (I.11.19). Pierre stalks through burning Moscow, bent on assassinating Napoleon, only to find himself "rescuing" a sickly, scrofulous-looking child, unattractively like her mother, who is in no actual danger but has become separated from her parents. The latter have disappeared when he returns, leaving him holding the baby (III.iii.33).

A distinct subset of these disorienting situations involves characters that are oddly Tolkienian in aspect. Each of the three heroes encounters at least one of these and is fundamentally changed by the experience. While the accounts of these incidents vary markedly in perspective and tone, their similarity is no accident. The characters are what one might call heuristic archetypes, whose narrative function is to teach the hero a life-changing lesson.

The artillery officer Captain Tushin, whom Andrei meets at the battle of Schoengrabern in 1805, personifies the "little man" whose fortitude so impressed Tolkien in the trenches and whom Tolkien's hobbit heroes are meant to epitomize.[22] A kindly, diminutive pipe-smoker, he displays a Bilbo-like sentimentality and even talks like Bilbo (at least in English translation). As his forgotten battery fires away at the wrong target, because no one ever told him what to aim at, he puffs madly at his pipe and fantasizes that the enemy guns pounding his position are tobacco-pipes sending up puffs of smoke. His bravery and persistence under fire is crucial to the Russian success; but afterwards, instead of applauding his heroism, staff officers desperate to cover their backsides blame him for the mistakes that made victory possible (I.ii.15-21). This spectacle is the first episode in Andrei's progressive disillusionment with the life of military service and personal ambition to which he has been raised.

Tushin illustrates a point common to both writers: that history is not made by the mighty but by humble folk who elude their attention. However, whereas Tolkien makes heroes of his humble folk, in the guise of Frodo and his companions, Tolstoy introduces Tushin simply for the enlightenment of Prince Andrei, and through him the reader, and he reinforces his point for the latter's benefit by screwing his "hobbit" up and throwing him away. Two or three years later, we encounter Tushin again at a field hospital in Poland where Nikolai is visiting Vasska Denisov. He is still smoking his pipe but has only one arm left to do it with (II.ii.18). The little man may make history, but he remains a little man and, if a hero, generally an unsung one. This one will be lucky to leave hospital without contracting a lethal infection.[23]

Nikolai has nothing to learn from a hobbit archetype, for reasons that will appear in the next chapter, and Tushin makes no particular impact on him when they meet. His life-changing encounter is with an elf-prince, or more exactly elf-queen: the young Tsar Alexander I.

> He was entirely absorbed by happiness at the nearness of the Emperor ... Not daring to look down the line, and not glancing round, he was conscious by an ecstatic instinct of *his* approach ... Nearer and nearer moved this sun ... shedding around him rays of blissful and majestic light, until Rostov felt himself enfolded in that radiance and heard *his* voice, caressing, serene, regal and yet so simple.
>
> ... Casually glancing up and down the squadron, the Sovereign's eyes met Rostov's and for upwards of two seconds rested on them. Whether or no the Tsar realized what was going on in Rostov's soul (it seemed

---

[22] Carpenter, *J. R. R. Tolkien*, 89; Shippey, *Road to Middle-earth*, 154-60.
[23] Frodo, of course, is unsung on his return to the Shire.

> to Rostov that he saw everything), at any rate for the space of two seconds his blue eyes gazed into Rostov's face. A soft, mild light poured from them ... (I.iii.10).[24]

This could be Galadriel, a champion soul-reader, as apprehended by Sam and Frodo at Lothlórien, and the androgynous aspect implied by this resemblance appears to be intentional. When Nikolai sees the Tsar again, during the battle itself, his idol appears as the epitome of feminine vulnerability, attended only by a single officer as he vainly urges his horse across a ditch: "The Tsar's cheeks were sunken, he was pale and hollow-eyed, but the charm and gentleness of his face was all the more striking." Nikolai is too bashful to approach.

> As an enamored youth is benumbed, trembles, and dares not utter what he has spent nights dreaming of, and timorously looks about seeking help, some chance of delay, or flight, as soon as the longed-for moment has arrived when he alone with her, so Rostov ... did not know how to approach the Tsar, and thousands of reasons why it would be inexpedient, improper, and impossible, came to his mind (I.iii.18).

He watches enviously from afar as a bolder officer rides up, helps the Tsar across the ditch on foot, and offers words of consolation as Alexander, unwell and needing to rest, sits beneath an apple tree, weeping and gratefully pressing his new companion's hand. Nikolai's infatuation survives this spectacle unabated, only to sustain a harder fall two years later when he sees Alexander consorting with Napoleon at Tilsit on the occasion of their signing the peace treaty. Galadriel fraternizing with Sauron! Nikolai's world is turned upside down. He responds by getting plastered and brainwashing himself into a lifelong refusal to question authority (11.ii.21).

Pierre encounters two "Tolkienian" characters. With his aura of power veiled by an appearance of age, severe expression that breaks into an unexpected fatherly smile, and occult wisdom, the freemason Bazdeyev is distinctly Gandalfian. He appears at a moment when Pierre's life is in ruins, and his guidance is a tonic to his despondent protégé, but its effect is short-lived and his "wisdom" proves to be sheer charlatanry. Tolstoy pokes fun at Pierre's earnest efforts to achieve enlightenment by immersing himself in Masonic mysticism, especially the numerological hanky-panky whereby he persuades himself that he is destined to save Russia by assassinating Napoleon. The Masonic Order turns out to

---

[24] This is taken from Rosemary Edmonds's translation for Penguin Classics.

be a nest of social-climbing hypocrites, and Pierre's devotion to it does him no good beyond diverting him from the emptiness of his life. Bazdeyev himself is a man of probity, and at first sight a wholesome contrast to the Francophile phoneys who have blighted Pierre's life; but he is ultimately revealed as a false prophet, the oracle of a chimerical, European faith.

The peasant Karatayev, who appears providentially to salve Pierre's spiritual wounds after his traumatic experience at the hands of the French firing-squad, is the real thing. Critics have commonly noted that Karatayev is less realistic than other secondary characters in *War and Peace*; and, indeed, it would only take a little more of what Nathaniel Hawthorne called managing one's atmospherical medium to turn him into a figment of Pierre's imagination.[25] With his gnomic utterance, sing-song voice, "young-old" appearance, and slightly apparitional quality, he is a *numen*, or nature spirit — in this respect, a counterpart of Tom Bombadil (IV.i.13). Real thing or not, though, Tolstoy disposes of him with even less ceremony than Tushin.

How do these Tolkienian apparitions fit into the world of Tolstoyan realism? I have discussed Tolstoy's leading characters as romance archetypes clothed in an integument of personal idiosyncrasy. Here he seems to be creating characters with an archetypal core as life-lessons for his heroes. Considered as an archetype, Gandalf is a father-figure, and so is Bazdeyev. But what about Galadriel? Tolkien's elves project a fey quality that might appeal to adolescent male homoeroticism, but the clue to Galadriel's essence lies in the fact that the character reminded some of the Virgin Mary.[26] Like Galadriel to the mortals who encounter her, Tsar Alexander projects to the adolescent Nikolai the charisma of royalty. It is no coincidence that Nikolai ends up falling for a pious virgin named Marya, who exudes a powerful spiritual authority. Like Sam Gamgee, Nikolai is an Everyman archetype.[27]

Bazdeyev-as-Gandalf and Alexander-as-Galadriel represent what the observing character needs to be true, and the chimerical nature of the ideal is profoundly important to the character's development. Tushin and Karatayev are authentic rather than delusive apparitions, in that what the observing character sees in them is true

---

[25] See above, 11.

[26] Tolkien, *Letters*, 172, 288, 407.

[27] See below, 163.

rather than false. All four are phenomena that speak to the observing character's state of mind, however; thus Tushin has no impact on Nikolai when their paths cross, and the Tsar casts no spell on Andrei, who rejects his patronage in 1812 by choosing to serve in a field regiment rather than at court. As such they illuminate the nature of *War and Peace* as a *Bildungsroman*, a novel that recounts the formative experiences of its youthful protagonist.

In fact, as I said in the last chapter, *War and Peace* is largely a story about children. Natasha is a child when we first meet her and never quite loses her childish self-absorption. Both Nikolai and Petya are children when they go off to war. Pierre is essentially childish in his naivety and craving for a father-figure, and the book celebrates such naivety even when seeming to mock it. Pierre's guide to wisdom — or at least to serenity — in the end is not the father-figure Bazdeyev but the childlike Karatayev. Andrei is not quite a child, and that is precisely what is wrong with him; but he is, like the others, an innocent, in that he is capable of redemption. And what of his sister? It might sound glib to say that Princess Marya possesses a childlike faith were it not that that same faith is Andrei's spiritual terminus.

Sentiment and Satire

As Gary Morson points out, Tolstoy's technique of repeatedly defeating the reader's expectations enhances the impact of those occasions when he allows the scene to attain a conventional consummation.[28] The technique is so pervasive, however, that one is tempted to think of it as a matter less of choice than necessity, as though Tolstoy could only advance the plot on such a large scale by setting up the obvious cliché and then subverting it. That is, after all, the story of the composition of *War and Peace* as a whole: a process whereby he imagined a conventional novel and then transformed it into something unique. However, he could hardly have applied this technique so obsessively and effectively had it not been an authentic expression of his world-view. The novelist Thomas Mann, a noted ironist, is reported to have identified the absence of irony as a fatal flaw in Tolstoy's writing.[29] That is simply not true of *War and Peace*.

---

[28] Morson, *Hidden in Plain View*, 149.

[29] Frederic Prokosch, *Voices: A Memoir* (New York: Farrar, Straus & Giroux, 1983), 12.

To set up a cliché in order to subvert it is an inherently ironic gesture, and Tolstoy's life-lessons are laden with irony.

But if Mann's judgment is off the mark, George Steiner's characterization of Tolstoy as an ironist but not a satirist is no more accurate.[30] The account of Andrei's death is a specimen of tragic irony, but even here there is a *frisson* of something not quite tragic in the upending of sentimental expectations — the reader's, if not Marya's. As an expression of his alienation, Tolstoy's irony tends towards satire, which Northrop Frye defines as "militant irony,"[31] and satire, as a means of attacking through ridicule, is comic rather than tragic. This is in fact the first surprise that *War and Peace* offers the modern reader: the title signals an epic narrative of heroism and romance, but you find yourself reading a satirical comedy. The satire, which strikes several different notes to the modern ear, contributes to the generic plurality that W. P. Ker and E. M. W. Tillyard identify as a feature of the epic.

Tolstoy's belief in the delusiveness of intention and the futility of command betokens a deeply ironic view of human affairs, and much of the satire is aimed at official pretensions and follies, as we have seen. A leading theme is scorn for the Hegelian belief in Great Men as moving spirits of human history, and so the fictional account of Napoleon's invasion is interspersed with a historical polemic which ridicules not just the image of Napoleon as a great man but the idea that the course of events owed anything at all to the designs of the generals and statesmen who fondly supposed that they were directing it. The first half of the book is imbued with the same idea, though it is left implicit. Our first sight of the Russian army in 1805 is at a regimental inspection ordered by the commander-in-chief, Kutuzov, to show his Austrian allies that the newly arrived troops are too fatigued and disorganized to go into action as the Austrians wish. Kutuzov's design is nearly thwarted by the zeal of the regimental commander, who keeps the men up all night putting themselves and their gear in parade-ground order. The error is corrected in the nick of time, and no doubt the men are well and truly fatigued when the generals arrive to inspect them (I.ii.1). Likewise, when Nikolai gets his first taste of action, in the rearguard at a river crossing, his unit keeps perfect order under fire and withdraws without casualties,

---

[30] Steiner, *Tolstoy or Dostoevsky*, 98.
[31] Frye, *Anatomy of Criticism*, 224-25.

but owing to a misunderstanding they only prepare the bridge for burning instead of setting fire to it themselves as ordered. Military order dissolves in a mad scramble to rectify the mistake, and men are hit by grapeshot — but not to worry: the losses are not worth mentioning (I.ii.8). In the same vein, the Russians succeed at Schoengrabern because the misdirected fire of Tushin's forgotten battery deceives the French.

Tolstoy's targeting of military folly presages the anti-war satires of Jaroslav Hašek and Joseph Heller; but the very technique of undermining sentimental clichés strikes at another, no less important, target: the Romantic view of human nature as essentially benevolent. This attack strikes two distinct notes. The milder is epitomized by Boris Drubetskoy's mercenary courtship of Julie Karagina, the heiress whom Countess Rostova had picked out for Nikolai only to be foiled by his devotion to the penniless Sonya. This is reminiscent of Jane Austen at her least forgiving: thus Boris's thought, as he steels himself to propose to Julie, that he "can always arrange so as not to see her often," echoes Charlotte Lucas's remark in *Pride and Prejudice*, after marrying the odious Mr. Collins for similar reasons, that she so manages things that she often has to spend only a few minutes a day in his company.

This at least is funny — although, as Frye observes, one wonders how long Mr. Collins would continue to be funny if the married life of Mr. and Mrs. Collins was the main theme of Austen's novel.[32] In *War and Peace* the main focus of the satirical comedy is the married life of Pierre, and the humour is so mordant that one scarcely laughs. Pierre (a name so close to Pierrot) is in fact a comic character, a hapless innocent like the protagonists of Voltaire's *Candide* or the marquis de Sade's *Justine,* who endure a succession of chastening or degrading experiences without quite waking up to the world's injustice. The resemblance is no accident. Just as Tolstoy uses the clichés of sentimental fiction to create false expectations in the reader and then dash them, here he satirizes the genre's underlying view of human nature: a belief in the essential benevolence of uncorrupted humanity, in the superiority of personal feeling to conventional morality as a guide to right action, and in the capacity for empathy (*sensibility*, in the cant of the age) as more virtuous than actual charity performed out of a sense of duty. Tolstoy follows Voltaire and Sade in mocking this world-view

---

[32] Frye, *Anatomy of Criticism*, 226.

when he makes Boris read Nikolai Karamzin's story "Poor Liza," a classic of Russian sentimentalism, aloud to Julie, his voice choked with emotion (II.v.5).[33]

Seen in this light, Pierre is the satirical embodiment of a stock theme of sentimental fiction: the theme of Virtue in Distress, which bemoans the travails of innocence in a corrupt world. His clueless innocence is evident in his naive behaviour at the opening soirée at Anna Scherer's salon and his utter incomprehension, at his father's deathbed, of the muted contretemps he sees unfolding between Prince Vasili and Anna Drubetskaya as the latter thwarts the Prince's conspiracy to steal and destroy the will making Pierre his father's sole heir. He is surrounded by false friends who are really in love with his money, and Prince Vasili nimbly recovers from his failure over the will by manoeuvring Pierre into marrying his daughter, the gorgeous but depraved Hélène, who is rumoured to have committed incest with her brother Anatole. Subsequently Pierre is condemned to the undignified role of cuckold, maintaining an air of benevolent eccentricity among his wife's friends while trying hard, with only partial success, to blind himself to his wife's infidelities.

The prime focus of his laborious self-deception is the fast-rising Boris, now a star of the Petersburg salons and, as the reader knows, Hélène's lover. The consolation Pierre finds in Freemasonry, with its "complex and arduous process of inner development ... revealing much to him, and giving rise to many spiritual doubts and joys" (II.iii.9), is likewise ridiculed in a chapter of musings from Pierre's diary that exposes the meretricious nature of his philosophizing, and humiliation intrudes even into this spiritual refuge when he is obliged to nominate Boris for membership in the Saint Petersburg lodge. With typical subtlety, Tolstoy makes Pierre ascribe his dislike of Boris to the latter's insincerity rather than to his own repressed suspicions about Boris's relations with Hélène.

Just as Pierre is a sort of Justine, so Hélène is a sort of Juliette, Justine's sister and moral opposite, who ruthlessly exploits conventional hypocrisy to rise to the top of her world. For Hélène, this means becoming the *grande dame* of the pro-French circle of Saint Petersburg society, and to this end nothing more ruthless is required than bestowing her favours where it will serve her best. When Pierre returns to Saint Petersburg and starts living with her

---

[33] R. F. Brissenden, *Virtue in Distress: Studies in the Novel of Sentiment from Richardson to Sade* (London: Macmillan, 1974).

again, he is surprised to find that she has gained "the reputation of 'a charming woman, as witty as she is beautiful.' ... To be received in the Countess Bezukhova's salon was regarded as a certificate of intellect" (II.iii.9). Pierre fears constantly that her stupidity will be exposed, but her reputation for wit is so secure that her most banal remarks are construed as Delphic wisdom. She is still flying high at the time of Borodino, pondering whether to marry a Russian grandee or a foreign prince without worrying overmuch that she is still married to Pierre, when she dies from an abortion. Ironically, this is the first hint that she is fertile.

A third stereotype from the reaches of sentimental literature is Anatole Kuragin's friend, the demonic outsider Dolokhov. He is the story's evil genius, who will exercise a baneful influence on the lives of all the principal characters. His dalliance with Hélène, and the resultant duel, set Pierre en route to the death march from Moscow; his fleecing of Nikolai Rostov at cards hastens the ruin of Nikolai's family; his animating role in Anatole's planned elopement with Natasha sets off a train of events that culminates in Prince Andrei's death; finally, his demonic charisma is responsible for the death of Petya, the youngest Rostov sibling. Noting Dolokhov's resemblance to a Byronic hero, John Bayley sees him as an "extreme" character, who would be at home in Dostoyevsky but is somewhat out of place in *War and Peace*.[34] Arguably, though, Dolokhov is just as much at home as Pierre: each is a satirical stereotype attached to a rounded character. In Dolokhov's case, though, mystery is part of his character, which is a peculiarly uncanny psychological type.

Essentially, the Byronic hero is a man of superb natural gifts and decent instincts who has "gone bad," perhaps because, as a youth of exceptional sensitivity, he experienced the world's cruelty and turned against it. The resulting blend of sensibility, misanthropy and diabolical charisma makes a sort of noble savage, repellent at first glance yet also mysteriously alluring. But these conflicting traits form an unstable compound: beneath the glacial surface the Byronic hero is tormented by demons, which ultimately drive him to destruction. Virtue in Distress may pine away because its embodiment is too good for this wicked world. The Byronic hero typically brings about his own death to stop himself doing wrong, or to atone for some past unforgivable wrong.[35]

---

[34] Bayley, *Tolstoy and the Novel*, 109.
[35] Mario Praz, *The Romantic Agony*, trans, Angus Davidson (Oxford: Oxford UP, 1933), cap. 2.

Dolokhov's secret suffering soul comes to light when Nikolai Rostov takes him home wounded from his duel with Pierre. The scapegrace daredevil and ruthless duellist turns out to live with most affectionately with his old mother and hunchback sister. According to his mother, complaining about Pierre's mistreatment of her son, her Fedya is "too noble and pure-souled for the corrupt society of our time. No one cares about virtue these days ... Not many people understand him. His is such a lofty, angelic soul ..." Dolokhov himself sounds the same theme:

> People consider me a bad man, I know ... Let them! I don't care about anyone but those I love; but when I love anyone, I'd give my life for him: the rest I'd strangle if they stand in my way. I have an adored, a precious mother, and two or three friends, you among them, and as for the rest, I pay attention to them only insofar as they are useful or harmful to me. And most of them are harmful, especially the women ... I have never yet found that angelic purity and devotion that I seek in a woman ... And believe me, if I still value life it is only because I still hope to meet such a divine creature, who would regenerate, purify, and elevate me (II.i.10).

We next see him falling heavily for Sonya, only to have his hopes of regeneration apparently dashed by her refusal to "elevate" him. The bad Dolokhov re-emerges to revenge itself on Nikolai (who is, of course, Sonya's reason for rejecting him), and on the Rostov household as a whole, by cheating Nikolai at cards. Then he disappears for five years, re-surfacing to inflict more pain on the Rostovs, first as the evil genius behind Anatole's elopement plot and then by his fatal influence on Petya.

Dolokhov is the most complex of the secondary characters in *War and Peace*, and his apparent inconsistencies are the more puzzling because the narrative neither lets us into his thoughts, as it does with the five primary characters, nor comments on his motives, as it often does with the secondary characters; thus the revelation of his softer side is as surprising to us as to Nikolai. However, Tolstoy as narrator tells us so much, and with such an air of candour, that one can be fooled into thinking that he is telling us everything, and that everything he tells us can be taken at face value. Nikolai's discovery is so plainly stated that we may take it at face value and only later realize that it is an illusion. But Tolstoy is no less a trickster than Dolokhov, and here his trickery goes beyond simply setting up a trite situation and subverting the expectations it arouses. Dolokhov is one of two characters that he develops by defeating the expectations engendered by his own narrative style:

that is, by using his normal tone to convey information that is either false or seriously misleading.

Tolstoy the trickster

In the case of Dolokhov, Tolstoy fools us with information calculated to deceive us while quietly furnishing all the information we need to see the character for what he really is. Thus we read that Nikolai "learned to his great surprise that Dolokhov the brawler, Dolokhov the rabid duellist, lived in Moscow with his old mother and hunchback sister and was the most affectionate son and brother" (II.i.5). This deadpan statement is so different from Tolstoy's usual "point-of-view" style that we tend to accept it as true, if surprising, when in fact it is something that we might call "reported point-of-view" and what Nikolai "learns" is quite misleading. Meanwhile, clues to Dolokhov's true nature emerge indirectly, either in the conversation of the characters or in coded language which, without being ironic, belies its ostensible meaning. The former device is manifest in the language that Dolokhov and his mother use in opening their hearts to Nikolai. "Too noble, too pure in heart for the corrupt society of our day ... No one cares about virtue anymore" (II.i.10) — these notions are the stock-in-trade of eighteenth-century sentimentalism, and the idea that an excess of sensibility can both cause and extenuate the crimes of its possessor is typical of its early nineteenth-century phase, in which the Byronic hero flourished. This idea appears in the narrative account of Dolokhov's feelings for Sonya. These are presented as a statement of fact, and only the oddly trite language hints that the narrative is actually projecting the sentimental preconceptions of the onlookers:

> He paid marked attention to Sonya and looked at her in such a way that not only could she not bear his glances without turning scarlet, but both the old Countess and Natasha blushed when they saw that look.
>
> It was clear that this strong, strange man was irresistibly attracted to this dark, graceful young girl who was in love with another (II.i.10).

This gives us no more reason to believe in the sincerity of his attachment to Sonya than in his other manifestations of feeling.

What, then, is "the truth" about Dolokhov? In essence he is a psychopathic confidence trickster, whose scam depends on exploiting contemporary sentimental axioms about human nature and society. This idea is very much in tune with the literary context in which Tolstoy was writing, since the figure of Dolokhov would have reminded Tolstoy's first readers of Aleksandr Pushkin's Eugene

Onegin, whom Pushkin exposes in a crucial passage as a poseur who apes Byronic models. But while both characters assume charismatic fictional personae, they assume different personae and for different reasons. Onegin is a moral nullity who plays the Byronic hero because he would like to be one. Dolokhov is a Byronic figure, but he does not play the Byronic hero (which would be an anachronism, since Byron published the relevant poems between 1812 and 1818). He adopts the *pose* of injured innocence, and not for its own sake but because of its appeal to others.

John Bayley's allusion to Dostoyevsky calls to mind Nikolai Stavrogin in *The Demons*,[36] Dostoyevsky's nightmarish satire on the liberalism, rooted in sentimentalism, which he believed had engendered the nihilism of his own day. Just like Dolokhov, Stavrogin is handsome, charismatic, gloomy, and given to random acts of sadistic cruelty — including senseless duels. He also commits excesses that are ostensibly, but not really, charitable, and this too is part of the Byronic repertory:

> Too high for common selfishness, he could
> At times resign his own for others' good,
> But not in pity, not because he ought,
> But in some strange perversity of thought,
> That sway'd him onward with a secret pride
> To do what few or none would do beside:
> And this same impulse would, in tempting time,
> Mislead his spirit equally to crime.[37]

Stavrogin's chief folly of this sort is his secret marriage to a half-wit, and the corresponding crime is his rape of a fourteen-year-old girl, who kills herself. He ends up hanging himself as his victim did, less from remorse than because his life is devoid of moral purpose and he finds it unbearable.

Stavrogin too has an apologist: not his mother, who has the sense to be worried by his conduct, but his former tutor, Stepan Verkhovensky, who assures her that her son's excesses, like those of Shakespeare's Prince Hal, are "only the first violent outburst of a too richly endowed nature." Just as Stavrogin is a caricature of the

---

[36] Often rendered as *The Possessed* or *The Devils.*

[37] *Lara*, canto I, stanza XVIII, quoted by Praz. It is noteworthy that Joseph Frank, *Dostoevsky: The Miraculous Years, 1865-1871* (Princeton, NJ: Princeton UP, 1996), 129, applies these lines to another of Dostoyevsky's characters: Svidrigailov in *Crime and Punishment.*

Byronic hero, so Verkhovensky is a caricature of Virtue in Distress, and it is clear that his paranoid preaching about the world's wickedness is largely responsible for his pupil's moral void. The chief "demon" in the novel is Verkhovensky's estranged son Pyotr, who is European-educated, like Pierre in *War and Peace.*

While Stavrogin and Dolokhov are similar in outline, however, their respective authors develop them quite differently. Dostoyevsky preserves the enigma of Stavrogin until the very end, when he cracks open the stereotype of the Byronic hero to expose the hollowness within. Tolstoy introduces Dolokhov in Byronic mode, but every subsequent appearance contains clues to the underlying reality. Since part of that reality is a posture of injured innocence, one is tempted at first to fall for it along with Nikolai Rostov. By the end, however, Tolstoy has stripped the character of all its romance and reduced the stock justifications for Byronic excess to a mother's self-deceiving excuses. There is no hint of a conscience.

Far from being (in Byron's words) "too high for common selfishness," Dolokhov is a shameless self-promoter and a leech, who does nothing even spuriously self-sacrificing. Indeed, the character works effectively to discredit the idea of the Byronic hero by suggesting the sordid reality that could have inspired it. Tolstoy achieves this by stripping the iconic figure of its glamour to reveal a common-or-garden psychopath. In the lead-up to the duel with Pierre, we are inside Pierre's mind as he ponders Dolokhov's sadistic proclivities and his look "in moments of cruelty, as when he had tied the policeman to the bear and dropped them in the water; or when, without provocation, he had challenged a man to a duel; or killed a sledge driver's horse with a shot from his pistol" (II.i.4). Nikolai Rostov gets the evil eye after Sonya refuses Dolokhov's marriage proposal, and soon he too feels the lash of Dolokhov's sadism. Our last glimpse of Dolokhov focuses on that same look, this time as he gazes balefully at some prisoners of war whom we know he means to slaughter. "The French, excited by all that had happened, were talking loudly among themselves, but as they passed Dolokhov, who stood lightly flicking his boots with his whip and watching them with a cold, glassy gaze that boded no good, they fell silent." (IV.iii.15). Byron had words to describe that gaze:

> And where his frown of hatred darkly fell,
> Hope withering fled, and Mercy sigh'd farewell![38]

---

38 *The Corsair*, I.ix.

But there is no hint that Dolokhov will come to a bad end like the Byronic hero.

The other character that Tolstoy develops in a deliberately misleading fashion is Sonya, Natasha's constant companion. Beautiful, desirable even though penniless, and an increasing vexation to the Countess because of her hold on Nikolai's affections, she is not Natasha's rival — they both know that she lacks the latter's flair and magnetism — but her friend and foil, always there but never front and centre, with two exceptions.

The first is a magical Yuletide evening at Otradnoye, the Rostovs' country estate, when mummers perform, and the young members of the household don fancy dress, and they rush off in troikas to carry the fun to a neighbour's house. Sonya's costume as a Circassian youth is generally agreed to be the best disguise of all (surely no coincidence), and she finds herself empowered.

> Her moustache and eyebrows were remarkably becoming to her. Everyone told her how pretty she looked, and she was in a spirited, energetic mood not usual with her. Some inner voice told her that now or never her fate would be decided, and in her masculine attire she seemed quite a different person (II.iv.10).

Racing through the frosty moonlight, Nikolai is intoxicated by the excitement of the drive and bewitched by Sonya's transformation. After an hour's fun and supper, someone raises a general dare to go alone to a haunted barn. Sonya eagerly accepts the dare and sets off with a glance at Nikolai. He sneaks out another way and meets her, and they passionately embrace. Next day he announces his intention to marry her and quarrels with his mother; then he returns to his regiment, intending to resign his commission. The Countess falls ill, and so is not on hand in Moscow to guard Natasha from Anatole's Kuragin's advances (though Sonya herself is there to prevent the worst).

Sonya's second turn at centre stage occurs in a chapter that explains the miraculous arrival, apparently in response to Nikolai's prayers, of a letter that releases him from his engagement to her and seems to clear his way to marry Princess Marya. It is very different from the first episode but is directly linked to it. Sonya's life, marred even before then by the Countess's resentment, has been very uncomfortable since that night, and her misery has been aggravated by Nikolai's romantic rescue of Princess Marya and the hopes it has aroused in the Countess. A few days before they flee Moscow, the

Countess tearfully implores her to repay the family's kindness by setting Nikolai free. Sonya responds with impassioned but vague assurances but inwardly holds back. Self-sacrifice has become second nature to her as a dependant, but hitherto it has been alleviated by the thought that her sacrifices brought her closer to Nikolai. Now she begins to resent the people who have befriended her only to torment her: even Natasha, who has never needed to sacrifice herself and, although habitually self-centred, is beloved by all. "Sonya, whose life of dependence had made her instinctively secretive, after replying to the Countess in vague general terms, avoided any further talk with her, and resolved to wait until she could see Nicolas, not with any idea of giving him his freedom, but, on the contrary, of binding him to her forever" (IV.i.8).

What changes her mind is the advent of the wounded Andrei, which she takes as Divine Providence, since she knows that he and Natasha will fall in love again and convinces herself that he will live and marry Natasha, thereby precluding, under the rules of the Russian Church, the marriage of Nikolai and Marya. It is she who tells Natasha that Andrei is travelling with them. When the Countess pathetically begs her again to write to Nikolai, Sonya is transported by this sense of Divine favour.

> Now that she knew that the renewal of Natasha's relations with Prince Andrei would prevent Nikolai from marrying Princess Marya, she rejoiced in the consciousness of a return of that habitual mood of self-sacrifice in which she loved to live. And blissfully aware of performing a magnanimous deed, she wrote the touching letter — interrupted several times by the tears that dimmed her velvety black eyes — that had so astounded Nikolai when he received it (IV.i.8).

This is devastating stuff, the more so for being so unexpected. The world has been turned upside down — Russia is reeling, Moscow burning, the Rostovs far gone on the road to ruin, Prince Andrei teetering on the verge of death — and suddenly we find ourselves confronting the hidden depths of Sonya (whom we, like the Rostovs, have pretty much taken for granted) and feeling the unsuspected pathos of her life. All along there was this other story hidden in the pages of *War and Peace*.

And what a story! The cruel comedy of the scene of her writing to Nikolai painfully resembles Tolstoy's Voltairean jests at the expense of Pierre and the young Nikolai Rostov, but there is extra cruelty here because Sonya is not a clueless innocent but a victim of circumstances that condemn her to a life of inauthenticity and self-repression. In this scene she has contrived, by a supreme act of self-delusion, to resume the role of magnanimous self-sacrifice that has become second nature to her, and we watch her enacting a stereotyped, *sentimental* drama of renunciation, like an actress so wrapped up in her part that she is moved to tears by the pathos of the invented situation. But as usual, Tolstoy sets up a trite situation only to demolish the expectations it evokes. We next see Sonya through the eyes of Princess Marya, as the Princess arrives at the Rostovs' temporary refuge to see her wounded brother and is greeted by "a rosy-faced girl with a thick black braid, smiling, as it seemed to Princess Marya in an unpleasantly affected way" (IV.i.14). We may think we understand that smile, since Sonya is at last meeting her rival for Nikolai's affections. What we don't know yet, although Sonya must, is that Prince Andrei is dying and her house of cards has collapsed.

Tolstoy's treatment of both Dolokhov and Sonya exploits sentimental preconceptions to mislead the reader, but the mode of mystification is quite different in each case. Dolokhov is an inherently mysterious figure, because he is in fact a confidence trickster who projects a deceptive image of himself; but the narrative masks his true nature by denying us access to his thoughts and by presenting him through other characters' eyes without always making it clear that it is doing so. Sonya's mind is not a closed book like Dolokhov's, since we know that she is bent on marrying Nikolai — and what else is there to know? Here the trick is in making Nikolai reciprocate her affections, a ploy which effectively disguises her plight as a story of true love until, at the critical moment, Tolstoy zooms in on her thought and lays bare the desperate calculation at the root of her passion. Hers is a predicament of authenticity: emotional honesty is a luxury she cannot afford. All her relationships are compromised by her self-interest, and finally she settles for what she can get, becoming a hanger-on in the household of Nikolai and Marya.

The revelation of Sonya's hidden depths is a shock because its timbre is subtly different from anything else in *War and Peace*. Just as the novel incorporates different sorts of satire, it turns out to encompass different sorts of tragedy. Prince Andrei is a classical tragic hero: like Hamlet and King Lear, he arrives at a state of grace through a course of suffering that is capped by his dying, and his redemption, like Lear's, is symbolized by his loving reunion with a woman he has wronged. Sonya's story is the tragedy of a woman trapped in circumstances that prevent her from living a fulfilling life or engaging in open, fulfilling relationships even with her closest friends. As a poor relation in a wealthy household who is attracted to her cousin, her situation parallels that of Fanny Price in *Mansfield Park*, and if she and Nikolai had married her story might be an Austen comedy; but she cannot achieve her desire because she is deceitful whereas Fanny is virtuous. Tolstoy was to treat the tragedy of a woman trapped between circumstances and desire extensively in *Anna Karenina*. Sonya's life of forced disingenuousness and self-repression, with its secret, abortive rebellion, smacks more of Henry James.

Epic scale

In the unpublished preface that declared his intention to lead "many heroes and heroines ... through the historical events of 1805, 1807, 1812, 1825 and 1856,"[39] Tolstoy went on to warn: "I do not foresee in any one of these periods a *dénouement* in the relations between these people. However much I tried to think up a novel-like plot and *dénouement* I was convinced that it was not within my means ..." John Bayley cites these words to show how much more of a novel *War and Peace* turned out to be than Tolstoy originally intended: "for the final version has a *dénouement*, and the relations between its characters *are* resolved. In finally deciding to seal off for himself a period of history, Tolstoy also sealed off — whether he wanted and intended to or not — a framework for a novel."[40] Bayley's observation is true up to a point. However, it illustrates the difficulty of holding the text of *War and Peace* and its complex evolution steadily in view and how that difficulty contributes to what Gary Morson identifies as the tendency of mid-twentieth-century criticism to normalize Tolstoy's masterpiece as an icon of literary realism, ignoring the eccentricities that perplexed earlier readers. Bayley knows perfectly well that *War and Peace* evolved out of Tolstoy's intention to write a novel addressing Russia's current predicament, yet here he quotes words that apply to a subsequent phase of the project as though they refer to that original intention. He also ignores the implications of Tolstoy's insistence that the published text was *not* a novel. *War and Peace* is undoubtedly more a novel than anything else, but the novel that Bayley describes, with its

---

[39] See above, 109.
[40] Bayley, *Tolstoy and the Novel*, 122. *Cf.* Forster's truer analysis, above, 106.

sealed-off timeframe and conventional plotting, sounds like the interim version rather than the published text.

At any rate, *War and Peace* is not just a very long novel like the interim version, or like *Anna Karenina*. It is an exceptionally complex structure, and the complexity is part and parcel of its epic immensity. The next chapter probes this epic quality in depth and addresses the ways in which Tolstoy altered the interim version to achieve it. Based on what we have seen already, however, we can conclude this chapter by reviewing its two main aspects: the formal and the tonal.

The most obvious manifestation of formal complexity is the interleaving of the second half of the fictional narrative with a parallel polemical and didactic discourse. Within the fictional narrative, the most salient is the sheer scope of the plot, with its abundance of characters and story-lines. The Bolkonsky and Rostov households, and the quasi-household of Pierre and his Kuragin accessories, are each developed in sufficient amplitude to sustain a novel on their own had Tolstoy been so minded. Their stories intertwine, and other characters move in and out of view as they follow their careers. It is part of the symmetry of *War and Peace* that a number of the young men in uniform whom we meet in 1805 reappear in 1812 after several years' absence. When Dolokhov and Anatole Kuragin turn up together at the Moscow Opera on the fateful occasion of Anatole's introduction to Natasha, we have not seen Dolokhov since he fleeced Nikolai, nor Anatole (except peripherally as Boris Drubetskoy's rival for the hand of Julie Karagina) since his farcical courtship of Princess Marya several years earlier. Denisov was last seen in 1807 in hospital with Tushin. Other such characters who crop up a little more frequently are Vera, the eldest Rostov sibling, Alphonse Karlovich Berg, her fiancé and later husband, and Boris.

But the formal complexity of the fictional narrative goes beyond the fusing of three household-based proto-novels into a single story: episodes within it are embryonic novels in themselves. One example is the two or three chapters which comprise Pierre's duel with Dolokhov and its antecedents. Sonya's story is another: for most of the narrative, she is simply a bit-player in the Rostov story, but the few paragraphs which expose her inmost thoughts display everything that we have learned of her over the years in a new light. The passage serves a technical purpose in plausibly releasing Nikolai from his pledge to Sonya without making him into an utter scoundrel; but the point is that the transforming touch enhances the epic complexity of the text by placing her at the centre of a distinct, though embryonic, subplot.

As for tonal variety, we have noted the various veins of tragedy and satirical comedy that run through the narrative. There is no point in pursuing this aspect further here, if only because our exploration of the quest romance, focusing on Tolstoy's treatment of the elements of time and space, will open up yet further dimensions of both formal and tonal complexity: we are about to encounter the pastoral and the numinous. But we have seen enough to appreciate how *War and Peace* can encompass the tragedy of Prince Andrei without itself being a tragedy: so much else is going on.

Andrei's death forms the emotional climax of the novel, but it does not signify the end of an epoch like the death of Hamlet or King Lear. Pierre hears the news while returning to Moscow from the battle and gives it scarcely a thought. He has other things on his mind; and, significantly, he is misinformed: Andrei still has several weeks to live. But even for those close to the event it is just part of the flow. The deluge may have flattened Sonya's house of cards, but that is Sonya's private grief. Soon afterwards, Petya's death — much more harmful to the Rostov household than Andrei's — precipitates a protracted emergency for Natasha in particular and drives Andrei's death into the background. After that, as Tolstoy records in his most detached tone, Natasha and Marya "still refrained from mentioning *him*, for fear of profaning ... the exalted feeling in their heart by words, but this reticence led them, though they would not have believed it, into gradually forgetting him" (IV.iv.3).

This is quite an idea to spring on readers so soon after they have lived with Natasha and Marya through Andrei's final days. Shakespeare does not encourage us to imagine Hamlet being forgotten quite so soon. Nor is it easy to imagine *Hamlet* without Hamlet's dying, or even without Hamlet at all; yet what we know of the composition of *War and Peace* confronts us with both possibilities in relation to Prince Andrei. In view of his importance both as tragic hero and as the chief fictional medium for Tolstoy's ideas about war and history, it is remarkable that he was one of the later characters to emerge in the early sketches for the novel and that his fate remained in doubt for a long time. As early as 1865, about the time that the first Book of *War and Peace* was published in its initial form under the title *1805*, and therefore some years before the novel was finished and Andrei's fate decided, Tolstoy wrote in a letter:

> I needed a brilliant young man to be killed at the battle of Austerlitz ...
> In the further course of the novel I only needed the old Bolkonsky and
> his daughter, but since it was awkward to describe a character not
> connected with the novel in any way, I decided to make this brilliant
> young man the son of old Bolkonsky. Then he began to interest me; I
> imagined a part for him to play in the further course of the novel and I
> took pity on him, merely wounding him seriously instead of killing
> him.[41]

First he was to die at Austerlitz, estranged from his father but leaving an infant son to reawaken his father's capacity for compassion; then, as we know, he was not to die even at Borodino.

These facts are not in themselves conclusive; but in fact, *War and Peace* does not project the sense of inevitability that is characteristic of tragedy but rather the sense that all is contingent — that things might well have turned out otherwise — and Tolstoy's protracted wavering over Andrei's fate illuminates the creative dynamic that produced that effect. If he had meant to write a tragedy, he would have known from the start that Andrei was doomed. As it is, his narrative diminishes the dramatic force of even the most tragic incidents by submerging them in the ceaseless flow of history.

Tolstoy likened his story to the *Iliad*, and this acknowledgement of the grand flux of life is one point of resemblance. The *Iliad* expresses it thus:

> As is the generation of leaves, so is that of humanity.
> The wind scatters the leaves on the ground, but the live timber
> burgeons with leaves again in the season of spring returning.
> So one generation of men will grow while another dies.[42]

The same idea of looking beyond death to regeneration echoes in Tolstoy's account — brilliantly true to the character's egoism — of Natasha's recovery from her ordeal.

> One day after hurrying upstairs she was out of breath. She immediately
> found some pretext for going downstairs and then ran up again, testing
> her strength and observing the result.
>
> Another time when she called Dunyasha her voice cracked. She
> called again — although she could hear her coming — in the chest tones
> in which she used to sing, and listened to herself.

---

[41] *Tolstoy's Letters* (vol. I, sel., ed. and trans. R. F. Christian, New York: Scribner's, 1978), 194.

[42] *The Iliad of Homer*, trans. Richmond Lattimore (Chicago and London: University of Chicago Press, 1951) book 6, lines 146-50.

She did not know and would not have believed it, but underneath what seemed to her an impenetrable layer of slime that covered her soul, tender, delicate young shoots of grass were already thrusting up, which, taking root, would so cover with their living verdure the grief that weighed her down that soon it would be unseen and forgotten (IV.iv.3).

The grass will cover Andrei's grave, and Petya's, and the Count's, but when we last see her, in 1820, Natasha will be the mother of four children.

That very feature, however, points to a crucial difference between the two stories. The *Iliad* looks forward to the epochal victory over Troy and enacts it symbolically in Achilles' triumph over Hector, but it stops short of the actual event. Tolstoy carries his narrative beyond the defeat of Napoleon into an ominous future, and so the ceaseless flow of history submerges not only the tragedies of Andrei and Petya but the historic victory itself. In this way, and by his relentless insistence on historical contingency, he stifles any notion of 1812 as a divinely ordained transition to a new order. In David Quint's terms, it is an ending redolent of the losers', not the victors', epic.

Tolstoy was, after all, writing in the wake of his country's defeat on its own soil by an alliance including a France ruled by Napoleon's nephew, Emperor Napoleon III, and his epic was the outcome of an intention to write a novel addressing Russia's condition in the aftermath of that defeat. In the next chapter, as we trace the emergence of *War and Peace*, complete with quest romance, from that initial idea, it will appear that Andrei is not in fact forgotten; but his memory is evoked in a context portentous of future travail.

5

"Not a Novel": Time and Space in Tolstoy's Epic

When Tolstoy insisted that his project could not fit the conventions of the novel, it was because his original idea of a novel addressing Russia's current predicament had ballooned into a chronicle rambling over half a century and involving successive generations. A story with a single set of characters, unfolding over seven years and having a single grand climax, could fit the form more easily; and as his narrative became focused on the national ordeal of 1812 a novel became more feasible. I have mentioned that John Bayley sees Tolstoy's published text as that novel — but why, then, did Tolstoy declare in 1868 that the published text was "not a novel"? I think it was because he had substantially completed that novel by 1866 and then decided that there was more he needed to say.

We have already noted some of the ways in which Tolstoy changed his monumental unfinished novel in order to produce a still larger structure which could express the epic vision that possessed him. He expanded his account of the campaign of 1812 (less than a quarter of the interim version) to a size almost equal to all that precedes it. By killing off Prince Andrei, he gave the story an emotional climax it had previously lacked; then he diminished that climax by extending the narrative to cover Napoleon's catastrophic retreat from Moscow, including the major fictional incidents of Pierre's encounter with Platon Karatayev, the death-march from Moscow, and the death of Petya. He revised the trite ending by deferring the two weddings to an Epilogue, which opens up his story to the future by prolonging the narrative to 1820 and concluding it in the shadow of the Decembrist uprising of 1825. He also added the mass of historical and polemical material that assimilates his fictional narrative to the grand march of human history.

The differences between the interim and published versions of *War and Peace* are the key to its epic character. As with *The Lord of the Rings*, a crucial aspect is the story's framing in time and space. The changes already mentioned serve in the main to extend the temporal scale of the narrative; but no less important are alterations that Tolstoy made in the earlier, completed chapters to produce, or suggest, a quest romance. A quest implies a journey, and the effect of these changes is to emphasize and enhance the spatial scale of the narrative. In the 1920s, the relative importance of time and space as features of *War and Peace* became a matter of dispute between E. M. Forster and another novelist and critic, Percy Lubbock. It was in response to Lubbock's declaration that "Time is all-important" in the story that Forster asserted that "space is the lord of *War and Peace*, not time."[1] In this chapter, it will appear that, while Tolstoy's treatment of space is crucial to the quest romance at the heart of the epic, his treatment of time is essential to the epic character of the narrative as a whole. Like the epiphenomenal time-travel story in *The Lord of the Rings*, in fact, the epiphenomenal quest romance depends in part on the author's symbolic treatment of space to stand for time.

These aspects of *War and Peace* are the main topic of this chapter. I describe how Tolstoy situates the battle of Borodino in an epic timescale that reduces it to a mere moment in the stream of time, and how the Epilogue does the same to the entire preceding narrative. I then outline the quest romance, emphasizing the spatial framing that establishes Otradnoye (the Rostovs' country home) and its environs as an idyllic refuge, sequestered in space and time. Citing *The Lord of the Rings* and Walter Scott's *Waverley* for comparison, I suggest that Tolstoy's evocation of "fairyland" imparts a tincture of other-worldliness to the refuge and its denizens. Then I show how he uses the narrative techniques examined in the last chapter to work the quest romance, with its numinous highlights, into a narrative justly famed for its realism, and I document the systematic manner in which he altered his novel-in-progress to do so. After pondering the failure of certain critics to grasp this aspect of

---

[1] Percy Lubbock, *The Craft of Fiction* (New York: Scribner's, 1921), 50; and see above, 1.

Tolstoy's art, I conclude my discussion of *War and Peace* as an epic by distinguishing it from *Anna Karenina* and discussing the structural and aesthetic flaws left by the epic transformation.

Epic time

As noted, the epic effect of *War and Peace* depends partly on Tolstoy's extension of the main narrative beyond its emotional climax, the death of Prince Andrei. The epilogue augments this effect by distancing the characters, and with them the reader, from the events that have engrossed them over seven years and more than a thousand pages. It begins flatly enough and could easily have been a letdown. In fact, though, it is a *tour de force*, which derives its power from two main sources. One is our familiarity with the personality and history of the characters, including our sense of them as survivors of a holocaust. The other is Tolstoy's strong feeling for his characters' future, not just eight years on from 1812 but decades beyond that. Not that he says anything about it — it is a legacy of the story's origin in a project that was to address Russia's contemporary crisis.

The opening sentence, "Seven years had passed since the year 1812," establishes the epilogue's temporal perspective, but the narrative immediately switches to the author-narrator's contemporary point of view as Tolstoy shifts into polemical mode.

> The storm-tossed sea of European history had sunk to rest upon its shores. The sea appeared to be calm, but the mysterious forces that move humanity (mysterious because the laws that govern their action are unknown to us) were still at work.
>
> Though the surface of the ocean of history seemed motionless, the movement of humanity continued as uninterrupted as the flow of time ...
>
> The ocean of history was no longer, as before, swept from shore to shore by squalls; it seethed in its depths ...
>
> This activity of the forces of history the historians call *reaction*.

Didactic disquisitions of this sort descend upon us thick and fast in Books III and IV along with the French invader. Some are a drag on the narrative, but others contribute to its epic expansion. A prime example of the latter is the account of Napoleon's Pyrrhic victory at Borodino, which did not prevent his occupying Moscow but fatally weakened his army and his resolve.

The battle is partly presented through the eyes of Pierre and Andrei, but these front-line vignettes occupy less than half of the length and are framed by a parallel narrative which tells the story from Napoleon's point of view. This parallel narrative, an ironic commentary on the destructive folly of overweening ambition, begins with a repellent description of Napoleon having a bath, from which he emerges to receive a portrait, newly arrived from Paris, of his infant son and heir, the King of Rome. This episode draws force from the fact — unstated by Tolstoy but well known to his audience — that Napoleon is on the verge of the catastrophe that will cost him his throne and his son his inheritance. After a short discussion of Napoleon's battle-plans, adorned with barbed commentary on the folly of the historians who ascribe his failure on this occasion to his having a bad cold, we see the emperor going to bed. A dozen pages ensue in which Pierre, having set out to observe the battle, finds himself in the thick of the fighting but miraculously escapes unscathed. We then observe Napoleon slowly beginning to realize that his plans are failing, a scene that is offset by a glimpse of Kutuzov, the Russian commander-in-chief, angrily rejecting his generals' assurance that the battle is lost. Then we descend on Andrei and his regiment waiting stoically in reserve under withering artillery fire. After Andrei is wounded and carried off to the field hospital, we return once more to find Napoleon responding to the ruin of his plans by commanding that the battle should continue, as though he is still in control of events. Tolstoy's point, of course, is that he never was in control.

The final chapter of this account, which ends an entire section of the book, locates this critical event in epic time. It begins by evoking the centuries of rural tranquillity that had constituted the story of this place until the moment when two vast armies descended on it:

> Several tens of thousands of men, in various uniforms and attitudes, lay dead on the fields and meadows belonging to the Davydov family and to Crown serfs — those fields and meadows where for hundreds of years the peasants of Borodino, Gorky, Shevardino and Semyonovsk had harvested their crops and pastured their cattle.

It ends by gazing ahead to the historic result of the encounter:

> The direct consequence of the battle of Borodino was Napoleon's groundless flight from Moscow, his return along the old Smolensk road by which he had come, the destruction of the invading army of five hundred thousand men, and the downfall of Napoleonic France, on which, at Borodino for the first time, the might of an opponent of stronger spirit had fallen (III.ii.39).

But there is more.

Beginning a new section of the narrative (Book 3, Part 3), Tolstoy does not at once plunge back to earth and re-engage with his characters. On the contrary, he soars even higher, starting with a disquisition on the laws of motion and the inability of the human mind to comprehend absolute continuity of motion. What is the point of this? It turns out that Tolstoy is setting up an analogy with the equally mysterious "laws of historical movement" and the inability of historians to come to grips with the problem of absolute continuity of time. From here we descend to the failure of a particular subset of historians to understand the crucial turning-point of Napoleon's transition from relentless advance (which culminated in his occupation of Moscow) to increasingly headlong retreat. Going on down, we return by stages to Pierre and the Rostov family in Moscow, pausing en route to consider Kutuzov's quandary as the commander-in-chief faces the necessity of abandoning the historic metropolis, then glancing at Rostopchin, the governor of Moscow, as he confronts the same exigency, and finally detouring to Saint Petersburg to watch Countess Bezukhova, as apparently unstoppable as Napoleon, taking further surprising steps to enhance her standing in court circles. The effect of this multi-layered narrative is to link the domestic saga, not just to the larger history in which it unfolds, but to what is called a metanarrative: an all-embracing explanation of history as a whole.

The disquisition that opens the Epilogue is less expansive but no less in harmony with the fictional narrative. Tolstoy discourses for a dozen pages or more on the ultimately unfathomable nature of the historical process and mocks, in fine reactionary fashion, those who criticize Emperor Alexander because he "had not the same conception concerning the welfare of humanity as a present-day professor who from his youth up has been engaged in study, *i.e.* in reading, listening to lectures and making notes on those books and lectures in a notebook." Then he turns to his characters and fills in the gaps between 1812 and 1820: the marriage of Natasha and Pierre; Count Rostov's death, which shows that the invasion had continued to devastate even after it had been repelled; Nikolai's purgatory, with his mother and Sonya, in the small house in Moscow as he strives to pay off his father's debts; his rescue by Princess Marya. From there we shift smoothly into an account of the married life of Nikolai and Marya and his husbandry of their estates. Tolstoy has reached the main point of the narrative epilogue: to show how his characters have changed yet remain the same, just as the ocean of history is at once calm and seething.

To do this, Tolstoy gathers the Rostov and Bezukhov families at Bald Hills together with Vasska Denisov one day in December 1820 and records their interaction. Here too a surface calm conceals a certain amount of seething. Nikolai comes in tired and cross from a busy morning on the estate. Marya handles his mood clumsily because she is pregnant again and pregnancy makes her feel ugly, and this makes her jealous and resentful of Sonya, which in turn makes her feel guilty. Natasha, who is nursing her fourth child, is cranky because Pierre has gone to Saint Petersburg and overstayed his leave by some weeks, and her mood and appearance leave Denisov aghast at the changes that time and domesticity have wrought on the bewitching sylph whom he had asked to marry him nearly fifteen years previously.

Nikolai's good humour (and consequently Marya's) is restored by a nap, and Natasha's (and consequently Denisov's) by the return of Pierre. Pierre's customary amiability pervades the household during tea, but the calm is disrupted when the men retire to the study and, covertly observed by young Nikolenka, Prince Andrei's son, start arguing about politics. Pierre has been visiting Saint Petersburg to help organize a liberal opposition to the reactionary chief minister, Count Arakcheyev. Denisov scoffs at the idea of peaceful opposition as opposed to "a pwoper wevolt" (Denisov has a speech impediment). Nikolai is increasingly upset by this subversive talk and finally loses his temper. "You are my best friend, as you know, but ... if Arakcheyev ordered me to lead a squadron against you and cut you down — I should not hesitate a second, but should do it" (Ep.i.14). Equanimity returns over supper, but Pierre and Nikolai are sufficiently disturbed by the quarrel that each brings it up in bedtime conversation with his wife.

As these transactions proceed, the characters pass before us and Tolstoy tells us how they have changed over the years; but he also equips us to draw our own conclusions. Nikolai has clearly changed a good deal from the light-hearted spendthrift who joined the army in 1805. He evidently bears the scar of two traumas: his fleecing by Dolokhov, which nipped his Rostovian profligacy in the bud, and the sight of his beloved emperor consorting with Napoleon as an equal during the treaty negotiations of 1807, which tipped him permanently towards unquestioning loyalty rather than independence of mind. His wife seems to have changed less. She retains the serenity of spirit that, even in 1805, enabled her to dismiss her brilliant brother's sophistries of reason, but she seems to have lost, at least in pregnancy, the physical grace that so charmed Nikolai in 1812. Nikolai, however, remains besotted by her beauty of spirit.

Natasha and Pierre present a subtler problem of analysis. After four pregnancies, Natasha is no longer slim and rarely vivacious. She is totally wrapped up in her family and Pierre is completely under her thumb.

> From the very first days of their married life Natasha had made known her demands. Pierre was greatly surprised by his wife's view, to him a totally novel one, that every moment of his life belonged to her and to the family. His wife's demands astonished him, but they also flattered him, and he acquiesced completely (Ep.i.10).

As well he might, having found so little peace of mind in his old life of depressive dissipation. The changes in Natasha do not reach below the subcutaneous fat layer, however: the egoism that once embraced herself alone now enfolds her family; the will to command that was once confined to the Rostov household now extends to her husband. As for Pierre, he is apparently the same old liberal idealist — and this is significant, because it suggests that, despite his sufferings in 1812, his quest is not yet complete.

And it is this — the politics — that really leaves *War and Peace* open to the future. The victory over Napoleon has receded into the past, the Decembrist uprising is just five years ahead, and Tolstoy has brought Pierre to the brink of becoming that old exile (also called Pierre, and with a wife called Natasha) who was to have been the hero of the projected novel from which *War and Peace* emerged. And he has brought someone else to the brink. It is a pregnant moment when Nikolenka — having listened to his uncle and guardian Nikolai Rostov, who is not really fond of him and whom he does not at heart respect, arguing with Pierre, whom he adores — looks at the latter with bright and luminous eyes and asks whether Papa would agree with him.

> And Pierre suddenly realized what an extraordinary, complex, powerful, and independent process of thought and feeling must have been going on in this boy during the conversation, and remembering all he had said, regretted that the youth should have heard him. He had to give him an answer, however.
>
> "Yes, I think so," he said reluctantly ... (Ep.i.14)

The dream from which the boy awakens vowing to be worthy of his father is one in which they and Pierre are menaced by his angry uncle.

Space, romance and politics: Tolstoy's epic zone

Just as Tolstoy extends his narrative forward in time, he extends it into the past; but his brief evocation of epic time in connection with the battle of Borodino is almost his only reference to past history. His main temporal recursion is more mythic than historical — although it hardly registers as such because, like Tolkien's time-travel story, it is also a journey in space. The end result of these temporal extensions is not just a historical novel but — like *The Lord of the Rings* — a story suspended in history and emblematic of the pattern of history. Its overarching symbol is the boy, present *in utero* in the opening scene, whose thoughts bring the narrative — but not the story — to an end.

Tolstoy's narrative ends with the very politics in which it originated, but the significance of the politics is easily overlooked. For one thing, Tolstoy presents the political argument in moral terms — his heroes' search for meaning in life — so the action is not overtly political. A second obstacle is the early nineteenth-century setting, which masks (especially for foreign readers) the story's political relevance to the period in which it was written. Tolstoy's characters live their lives, and we can form quite a sophisticated understanding of their interactions without even noticing the political symbolism. The predominant realism of the narrative further compounds the problem, since the politics resides in the subtle, almost surreptitious departure from realism that is Tolstoy's quest romance.

Politics and a quest romance may sound like strange bedfellows, but each lends itself to spatial representation: politics commonly has a geographical aspect, and a quest entails a journey. The journey of Tolstoy's questing heroes is essentially abstract, since it is a search for meaning rather than a pursuit of some purpose entailing actual travel like the Arthurian quest for the Holy Grail or the mission of Tolkien's heroes to destroy the Ring of Power. However, its political aspect allows Tolstoy to give it a spatial colouring which is partly geographic and partly fantastic. The war between Russia and Napoleonic France is one manifestation of a broader conflict, older than the war and persisting into the post-Napoleonic peace, between the old, "Russian", and spiritual, and the new, "European", and secular: East versus West.

We can, accordingly, divide the world of *War and Peace* into a European, or satirical, zone and a Russian, or epic, zone. The hub of the former, its status symbolized by its German name and peripheral location, is Saint Petersburg, the political capital of Russia, founded less than a century before the date of the story by the modernizing (and therefore Europeanizing) emperor Peter the Great. It is here, in Anna Scherer's salon, that the story begins, with Prince Vasili Kuragin and the hostess chatting in French at the start of one of her soirées; and it is at this soirée, amid a very select party of courtiers, that we first meet Pierre and Andrei. After a few chapters, however, the scene shifts to a very different sort of party occurring some 400 miles to the southeast — a lavish family celebration at the Rostovs' grand house in Moscow, the ancient capital that Russians call the Third Rome (Constantinople being the second). At first the Rostovs look like the quintessence of the ordinary, but they are in fact our guides to the epic zone. As the story unfolds, they will appear as the embodiment of a threatened, even doomed, ideal. It is in the light of this ideal that Tolstoy's quest romance can be glimpsed within *War and Peace* the novel.

While the denizens of the European zone prefer to speak French, the Rostovs speak it rarely and badly. They are instinctive patriots: on hearing the emperor's call to defend the motherland in 1812, the Count exclaims, to Natasha's approval, "Let him but say the word and we'll all go" (III.i.20). Who better than he, six years previously, to manage Moscow's patriotic dinner in honour of Prince Bagration after Austerlitz? "Few men knew how to plan a banquet as lavishly and as hospitably as he, and still fewer were able or willing to spend their own money, should the necessity arise" (II.i.2). Luckily the Count was flush that year, having just re-mortgaged his estates.

Nikolai is cut from the same cloth. He is a soldier from patriotism rather than careerism, and when he finds his old friend Boris Drubetskoy fraternizing with French officers during the peace conference at Tilsit in 1807, and sees his beloved emperor consorting with Napoleon, he gets drunk rather than think through the challenge to his patriotic faith. Nikolai scorns heiress-hunting as he scorns careerism; and this is truly quixotic, since he could certainly have married an heiress and had Sonya too. On campaign in Poland, he confounds his fellow-officers by sheltering a displaced Polish family in his billet. "What a cwazy bweed you Wostovs are," exclaims Denisov, with tears in his eyes no doubt evoked by thoughts of Natasha (II.ii.15). Summoned home to deal with the family's financial plight, Nikolai tears up a large IOU from Princess Drubetskaya for the price of Boris's Guards uniform, saying "I don't like Anna Mikhailovna and I don't like Boris, but they were our friends and are poor" (II.iv.2). Ironically, Boris will soon marry Julie Karagina, the heiress the Countess has picked out for Nikolai.

Natasha, for her part, is prodigal with her emotions and her talents. "Crying out for a husband, two even, needs children, love, bed," wrote Tolstoy in his notes for the novel,[2] and Prince Andrei's belief that he could absent himself for a year after arousing her passions speaks volumes about his failure to understand her (and possibly any woman). Natasha's abundant talents owe little or nothing to nurture. Her untrained voice is flawless, and so is her feeling for dance. Caught up by Denisov in a mazurka quite different in style from what she has learned in the ballroom, she instinctively matches him step for step, and later we see her perform a Russian peasant dance with a spirit and innate flair that her "European" education and training have quite failed to suppress. But is she clever? No: "She does not think it worthwhile to be clever," replies Pierre when Princess Marya asks (II.v.4). Cleverness belongs in the European zone. Like the somnolent, one-eyed Kutuzov, who presents such a conspicuous contrast to the ambitious, preening, strategizing mass of generals on display at HQ, the Rostovs favour the heart over the brain in all things — often to their cost.

With one exception: the personality of Vera, the eldest Rostov sibling, is oddly discrepant with the family norm. "Vera was pretty, well brought up, a good student, and not at all stupid; she had a pleasant voice, and what she had just said was both apt and true, yet, strange to say, everyone ... looked at her as if wondering why she had said it, and they all felt awkward" (I.i.9). Vera's husband is a dense but insinuating career army officer, and it is he who inadvertently crystallizes the issue for Natasha when her parents are quarrelling about whether to convey furniture or wounded soldiers from Moscow. Colonel Berg drops in to borrow a cart so he can transport a nice piece of furniture he has picked up for his dear Vera. It belongs to an absconded nobleman whose steward, an acquaintance of Berg's, has offered to sell it — upon what authority we are left to guess. Natasha can hardly express her outrage at the idea of favouring goods above people, but it crystallizes in the words: "Are we a lot of loathsome Germans?" (III.iii.16) The

---

[2] Quoted in Christian, *Tolstoy's* War and Peace, 12.

Countess, in challenging the Count's option for people over goods and in urging Nikolai to marry an heiress, may seem to resemble Vera as John Bayley suggests.[3] That is not true, though, since her feelings in both cases are prompted by love of her family, not herself. Her true nature, which had impelled her to reject Prince Vasili as a suitor in favour of the Count, is evident in her tears of joy when giving her old friend Anna Drubetskaya the price of Boris's Guards uniform and later when Nikolai tears up her friend's IOU.

Except Vera, then, the Rostov family embodies a symbolic contrast to the hypocrites and poseurs of the European zone, and the symbolism is bound up with the distance separating Saint Petersburg from Moscow. However, the contrast is far from obvious at first sight. When we first meet them they are not merely surrounded but penetrated by characters who will turn out to be their symbolic opposites, and there is nothing clearly different about them. Princess Drubetskaya is an old friend of the Countess, Boris has grown up as part of the household, he and Natasha are fancifully engaged to each other, and Berg is already on hand as Vera's betrothed. Julie Karagina is there too and seated next to Nikolai at dinner, much to Sonya's distress. Pierre, newly arrived from Saint Petersburg, is part of their circle. They are apparently all of the same class, social milieu, and Europeanized aristocratic culture. Nor, at the start, is there anything distinctively epic about the Rostovs, or Tolstoy's depiction of them. When we first see them, we appreciate them as a finely worked tableau of domesticity. What could be epic about a genial, loquacious middle-aged man, a teenage officer cadet, a skinny thirteen-year-old girl?

This initial obscurity testifies to Tolstoy's passionate realism, which subordinates his characters' symbolic function to their dramatic function as facsimiles of human idiosyncrasy. Their symbolic significance is not stamped on their surface but unfolds as the characters evolve; it is produced by the action. Boris, for instance, is at first somewhat embarrassed by his mother's shameless efforts to advance him — although, on campaign in 1805, he does not scornfully discard his letter of introduction to Prince Andrei as Nikolai discards his to Prince Bagration. It is only when he perceives and succumbs to the allure of headquarters life, and then discovers his flair for ingratiating himself with people who can promote his interests, that he acquires symbolic significance by virtue of the contrast

---

[3] Bayley, *Tolstoy and the Novel*, 133.

between his hypocrisy and the integrity of three other characters, all of whom were, at different times and in differing degrees, his friends. One of the three is Nikolai, whose patriotic commitment to the front line contrasts with Boris's careerism; the others are Prince Andrei, whose moral journey from HQ to battlefield impels him in the opposite direction to Boris, and Pierre, whose progress from Hélène to Natasha also inverts Boris's. These three in turn acquire symbolic significance from their changing relationship to him and each other.

These are metaphorical movements, of course, and even with the symbolic underpinning of the Saint Petersburg–Moscow antithesis they hardly suffice to make a quest romance out of (or constitute one within) what I have already called a *Bildungsroman*. After a few hundred pages, however, Tolstoy begins to extend and amplify the spatial symbolism by sending one of his heroes on an actual journey. Disillusioned by his experiences on campaign in 1805, and haunted by his wife's death in childbirth, Andrei has remained at home, shunning public service. A time comes when he must visit the province of Ryazan on business, and while there he pays a courtesy call on the local marshal of the nobility, who happens to be Count Rostov. Andrei has never met any of the family except for his brief quarrel with Nikolai on campaign some years earlier, and we are given no reason to suppose that he associates Nikolai with his hosts, even if he remembers the quarrel; still, he feels only scorn for the household in general. His brief exposure to Natasha, however, leaves him profoundly rejuvenated, although he lacks the self-awareness to connect cause and effect. He decides that his life is not over, and in August 1809 returns to Saint Petersburg and public life. It is there that he dances with Natasha at the New Year's Eve ball, resigns his government post and proposes to her, just as Denisov had done years earlier after dancing the mazurka with her.

Andrei's journey is significant not only for what happens but how and where it happens. Driving up the avenue to the Rostovs' house at Otradnoye one bright spring day, all gloomy and distracted with business, he hears merry voices and sees a group of girls running across his path. One of them runs towards him shouting something, but when she realizes that he is a stranger she runs off laughing without looking at him. He feels a sudden pang at her indifference and wonders why she is so happy. He continues to wonder as he glimpses her with her friends from time to time throughout the day. Later the vision recurs as an auditory apparition. In his room, its window open to the balmy, moon-drenched night, he overhears Natasha pouring out her feelings to Sonya. "And in his soul there suddenly arose such an unexpected turmoil of youthful thoughts and hopes, contrary to the whole tenor of his life, that, feeling incapable of explaining his condition to himself, he promptly fell asleep" (II.iii.2). He leaves early next day without seeing Natasha again.

This brief but crucial episode is not just about Andrei but about the Rostovs. Tolstoy has gradually revealed them (except Vera) as a "crazy breed" — especially Nikolai, with his odd sensitivity and quixotic gallantry, and the quicksilver Natasha, with her magical gifts and artless witchery. Now he begins to set them further apart from the satirical zone by distancing Otradnoye from the realm of everyday reality. When he packs Andrei off to fall under Natasha's spell, he emphasizes this distance by tracking him on his journey to Ryazan and back again. Critics usually mention this episode for the symbolism of the huge oak tree Andrei notices in passing, still wintry and leafless on the outward leg but bright with spring verdure on his return. Just as important, though, is the tree's effect in highlighting the sequestration of the Rostov domain from the world in which we have seen Andrei hitherto. Significantly, Ryazan province is southeast of Moscow, the exact opposite direction to Saint Petersburg. By locating Otradnoye there, Tolstoy extends the axis along which the story has unfolded hitherto and sets up the Rostov domain as the true antithesis of Saint Petersburg.

However, it is not until Andrei has gone abroad, leaving his betrothed to fret over his absence, that the uniqueness of the Rostov domain and its denizens is fully revealed. Only then do we get to observe them (minus Vera, who has married Berg) at their country home unmediated by Andrei, who was hardly equipped to appreciate what he saw although he carried away something life-changing even so. That was just an overnight visit anyway. Now we are there for a long stay and can fully appreciate the impressive scale of the family's daily life and their connection to the land and its people. This extensive passage occupies an entire Part of the narrative, the only one that is devoted to a single place and story-line.[4]

---

[4] Strictly speaking, the same is true of Book IV, Part 2. This, however, contains only four short narrative chapters, being mainly a non-fictional hiatus after the emotional climax of Prince Andrei's death.

Even now, the epic emerges only gradually from the domestic. The episode begins with Nikolai returning at his mother's summons to deal with the family's worsening financial plight, unhappily noting the discord it is generating between his parents, and thrashing the steward, Mitenka. This theme of looming financial disaster is hardly redolent of epic, and it will sound at intervals throughout the episode. But chapter 3 opens with a graphic evocation of the vast Russian countryside, which we have so far encountered only briefly in this very urban novel (even at Bald Hills we were mostly confined to the house), and a hunt gets under way. And what a hunt — it is virtually a military operation.

> Fifty-four hounds were led out by six whippers-in and grooms. Besides the members of the family and their leashes, there were more than forty borzois and eight borzoi kennel-men, so that in all about a hundred and thirty dogs and twenty horsemen were in the field.
>
> Every dog knew its master and its call. Every man in the hunt knew his business, his place, and what he had to do. As soon as they had passed the fence, they all spread out evenly and quietly, without noise or talk, along the road and field leading to the Otradnoe forest (II.iv.4).

En route they meet "Uncle" (*dyadushka*), a neighbour and distant relative, with four more horsemen and his own dogs. They "join forces," and the phrase is scarcely a metaphor. At the covert they meet the Count, who has driven out with two grooms and several more dogs but now mounts his horse, having strapped on his hunting-knives and horn. In accordance with time-honoured custom, the Count has drunk a silver goblet of mulled brandy, taken a snack and washed it down with half a bottle of his favourite Bordeaux. Another member of the household rides up. "This individual was a grey-bearded old man dressed in a woman's cloak with a tall peaked cap. He was a buffoon who went by the name of Nastasya Ivanovna" (II.iv.4).

There follows a detailed account of the day's sport, as the hunters compete to chase a wolf, a fox and a hare. Tolstoy vividly portrays the excitement of winners and losers and pays as much attention to the hounds, mentioning several by name, as to the humans. The Count goes home after the wolf-hunt, but the rest (including Natasha and Petya) press on until dusk, when they go to Uncle's house for rest and refreshment. Here is a scene very different from any we have seen the Rostovs in so far: "a little wooden house … buried in the midst of an overgrown garden"

(II.iv.7), but also a very crowded one, since several male and a score of female serfs appear to assist or stare at the party. Natasha, riding side-saddle and bearing a horn and a knife, is scrutinized as a sort of prodigy. Indoors, the house has un-plastered walls hung with wolf and fox skins and is pervaded with the smell of fresh apples, but Uncle's study, where he seats his guests, smells strongly of dogs and tobacco.

Uncle changes into Cossack dress, and Natasha feels that this garb, which she had regarded with surprise and amusement when he wore it at Otradnoye, is "the perfect costume and in no way inferior to a swallowtail or frock coat." They are served a repast of various liqueurs, herb brandy, mushrooms, rye cakes made with buttermilk, honey in the comb, still mead and sparkling mead, apples, raw and roasted nuts, and honey and nut confections. This is followed by a freshly roasted chicken, ham, and preserves made with honey and with sugar. "Natasha ate everything, and thought she had never seen or tasted such buttermilk cakes, such savory preserves, such honey and nut confections, or such chicken any-where." Mitka the coachman starts playing the balalaika — Russian peasant music — in the hunters' room, as always after a chase. Nikolai expresses his appreciation in an unconsciously condescend-ing fashion, but Natasha is enraptured and asks for more. Uncle calls for his guitar, and plays songs that captivate both Natasha and Niko-lai. (Petya is asleep throughout.) Then Uncle strikes a chord and cries "Now then, little niece!" And Natasha dances a dance that sets at defiance her "European" upbringing (II.iv.7).

This is all a far cry from the salons of Saint Petersburg and Moscow and even some way from Otradnoye, as Tolstoy makes clear. Even the Rostovs belong to that select group of families which formed the Russian aristocracy of that era; even Otradnoye is polluted by the presence of their scheming steward. Uncle is more typical of the serf-owning gentry: no French governess, no singing and dancing masters, un-plastered walls, herb and cherry brandy instead of Bordeaux. But the Rostovs are connected to this land and its people in spirit as well as blood, and in this milieu they are a kind of royalty, with the Count as Old King Cole. The style and scale of their life, and their connectedness to the land and the people, lend a mythic grandeur to their portrayal; and this affinity, and the reciprocal relations of loyalty and respect between masters and servants, make them into something more than individual symbols of Russian values. They and their milieu stand as a symbolic microcosm of the Russian land and people — or at least of the "Russia" that stands against the threat of "Europe."

Northrop Frye writes of "the perennially childlike quality of romance ... its extraordinarily persistent nostalgia, its search for some kind of imaginative golden age in time or space."[5] This observation resonates as we contemplate Otradnoye and Mikhailovka. The Rostov domain is an ideal, but it is a nostalgic ideal, an expression of the thoroughgoing alienation from modernity that impelled Tolstoy to start writing the story that became *War and Peace*. As such, it reveals an unexpected affinity between him and Tolkien, whose anti-modernism, with its corresponding attraction to anarchism and charismatic monarchy, suffuses all his writing. Otradnoye and Mikhailovka, sequestered from the satirical zone by a spatial seclusion which also hints at a temporal separation, are counterparts of Tolkien's elf-havens. Without any obvious change in tone, the prevailing realism of Tolstoy's narrative has given way for a time to the poetic evocation of a utopian realm of harmonious hierarchy. The retreat from realism is not complete, since the sequence is framed by the theme of the Rostov family's money troubles; but even in Tolkien's story Elrond and Galadriel are moving house by the end.

This frame of realism obscures the shift, which is further camouflaged by the fact that it owes less to a change in tone than in the sort of details that Tolstoy chooses to present. Military episodes apart, most of the action so far has taken place in Saint Petersburg and Moscow; yet there have been periodic visits to the Bolkonsky domain, where the sun and moon must shine as brightly and which is, presumably, no less sequestered from both cities. Tolstoy, however, does not present Bald Hills and Bogucharovo in terms of sunshine and dazzling moonlight, let alone Tillyard's "simple sensualities." We are mostly indoors there, and the emphasis is on business, not bucolic bliss — old Prince Bolkonsky's constant building and planning, Andrei's efforts to improve the life of his serfs, the fuss of military recruitment. And Bald Hills in particular is a scene of oppression, where the old prince tyrannizes over his household. The confinement of the narrative reflects the fact that for Princess Marya, and for Princess Lisa whilst she lives, the house is a prison. In the Rostov domain, by contrast, the chief huntsman scolds the Count for bungling his part in the wolf hunt, a pert serving-woman

---

[5] Frye, *Anatomy of Fiction*, 186.

at Mikhailovka asks Natasha — using the familiar (second-person singular) form of address — how she can ride side-saddle without falling off, the Otradnoye house-serfs delight in fulfilling Natasha's endless whims, and masters and servants join in festive merry-making both there and at Mikhailovka. Ultimately it is on a different plane from the realm of everyday reality that embraces Bald Hills and Bogucharovo along with the two metropolises.

Fittingly, our guides to this ideal zone are themselves childlike — not just Natasha and her brothers but their parents too. Think of the Count at the hunt, wrapped in his fur coat and looking like a child taken out for a drive and then, later, glancing round like a guilty schoolboy when berated by his chief huntsman. Who but a child would jettison the family valuables, as he does at Natasha's insistence, to save wounded soldiers? His wife may complain, but she is scarcely more worldly than he: witness her demanding several hundred roubles from him to massage her old friendship with Anna Drubetskaya, of all people. "You're just like me, an awful giggler," Natasha tells her at one point (II.iii.13). When his fairy-tale kingdom crumbles, Old King Cole can only die. By the end of the tale, his widow is somewhat prematurely into her second childhood.

Two quests, three heroes

It is in this light that Tolstoy's *Bildungsroman* stands revealed as a quest romance. Inspired by their encounters with the good fairy Natasha, Andrei and Pierre pursue their quests though a course of purgative suffering. Each character's journey involves the acquisition of self-knowledge and the identification of self with nation, but it is not a simple, linear process in either case.

When the story begins, Andrei is already disenchanted with the Scherer-Kuragin milieu (including, apparently, his wife, whose German maiden name is no coincidence), and this prejudice is reinforced by his family circle. The old prince shares Andrei's contempt for the Kuragins and later becomes a leading opponent of the pro-French, reforming tendency in the government, while Princess Marya, who has already attained spiritual enlightenment, is essentially "Russian" from the start. Pierre, by contrast, is burdened with a foreign education and entangled with the Kuragins, and his marriage only mires him more deeply in the satirical zone. In some respects, therefore, it may seem that Pierre has further to go.

But in other respects the opposite is true. Pierre retains throughout the story the humility proper to his initial, somewhat marginal position as an illegitimate son. He is less encumbered by pride, and thus more open to enlightenment, although also more easily led astray. And he is part of the Rostov milieu from the start. Andrei, brought up in the arrogance of wealth and privilege, is heir also to his father's wilfulness. He is thoughtful and intelligent enough to perceive his father's flaws — his reason for not returning to the army after Austerlitz is the duty he feels to restrain his father's despotic impulses as a general in charge of military recruiting. But when he sets off on campaign in 1805, his sister tells him: "You are good in every way, Andrei, but you have a kind of pride of intellect ... and that is a great sin" (I.i.25). It will take a long time and much suffering for him to overcome his own failings, rooted like his father's in pride.

Some key stations on Andrei's journey are his encounter with Captain Tushin, his near-death at Austerlitz, his wife's death, his first encounter with Natasha, and their subsequent betrothal and break-up. These experiences usher him towards gradual realization of the inauthenticity and ultimate insignificance of the world of "great men." But such is his lack of self-knowledge that his first response to his vision of Natasha is to return to Saint Petersburg and government service, clearly a false move in hindsight, and it takes renewed exposure to Natasha at the New Year's Eve ball to open his eyes. His trip abroad is another blunder.

Not until Napoleon's invasion do we see any clear signs of enlightenment. First he chooses a field posting in preference to service in the Tsar's entourage; but the crucial episode is his visit, made "with a characteristic desire to aggravate his own sufferings" (evidently he is quite as masochistic as his sister), to Bald Hills, his childhood home, as the Russian army retreats towards Moscow. He finds it vandalized by the retreating forces and nearly deserted. Suddenly he comes upon two little peasant girls making off with fruit from the hothouse. Alarmed at his appearance, they drop the fruit and hide.

> Prince Andrei turned away with startled haste, not wanting them to see that they had been observed. He felt sorry for the pretty, frightened little girl, and was afraid to look at her, but at the same time felt an irresistible desire to do so. A new sensation of solace and relief came over him as he became aware of the existence of other human interests, quite remote from his own and just as legitimate. Evidently these little girls desired one thing — to carry away and eat the green plums

without being caught — and Prince Andrei shared their wish for success in this enterprise (III.ii.5).

Returning to his regiment, he finds the men joyously bathing in a mill-pond and shudders as he views their naked flesh and imagines its vulnerability to shrapnel, a vision that foreshadows his own fate.

The little girls may remind us of Andrei's first sight of Natasha, romping with friends at Otradnoye, and soon, on the eve of Borodino, we witness him kicking himself (again with a characteristic desire to aggravate his own sufferings) for his cavalier disregard of her feelings. By now, as we have seen, Tolstoy has set Natasha up as an emblem of the Russian nation, but this was not yet clear when she and Andrei met. Andrei's empathy for peasant girls and common soldiers affirms that his change of heart is a matter not only of personal enlightenment but of identification with the Russian people. When Pierre meets him on the eve of the battle, Andrei fumes about the unfitness of the predominantly German-speaking army command to defend the Russian fatherland.

At this moment Andrei has come to see his whole life — even its ostensibly altruistic aspects — as one of egoism. This climax of self-perception is followed by his wounding and death. If his living was an exercise in egoism, is his dying an atonement? Probably, but — as usual in *War and Peace* — the logic of narrative exposition is artfully fogged by Tolstoy's feeling for the complexity of human motivation. At the moment when the fatal shell has landed but not exploded, why does Andrei not dive for cover like his adjutant? In that instant he realizes that he loves life and does not want to die, so his immobility is not an act of suicide. But even as he thinks these thoughts, he remembers that people are looking at him and starts to chide his adjutant. Does this response spring from some notion of setting an example, or is it just another act of vanity on the part of a man who, we know, dislikes nothing more than appearing ridiculous?

After his wound is treated and his agony relieved, Andrei is suffused by a sense of well-being such as he has not felt since childhood. Finding himself next to an anguished Anatole Kuragin, whose leg has just been amputated with the boot still on it, he recalls Natasha as he first saw her in the country and then feels a surge of sympathy for Anatole and all mankind, friend or foe. This feeling, he realizes, is "the love which God preached on earth, and which Princess Marya tried to teach me, and which I did not understand"

(III.ii.37). The journey of moral awakening foreshadowed by Princess Marya's words in 1805 is complete, and we understand Tolstoy when he later alludes to the common spirituality of brother and sister as a matter of fact: "In men Rostov could not stand to see the expression of a lofty spiritual life (that was why he did not like Prince Andrei) … but in Princess Marya, that very sadness which revealed the depth of a whole spiritual world that was alien to him, was an irresistible attraction" (IV.i.7).

Unlike Andrei, Pierre never visits Otradnoye — but why should he? We see him in the Rostovs' Moscow circle right from the start, and he may have been a little in love with Natasha even then. He certainly is by the time of the New Year's Eve ball, when Andrei's declaration of love for her plunges him back into the depression to which he is prone, and clearly he is acting under that influence when he stays in Moscow in disguise after Borodino and sets out to assassinate Napoleon. Besides, he is not an arrogant dolt like Andrei and doesn't need to be struck by lightning. He needs intellectual purgation, not a personality makeover, and he gets it through a course of suffering that culminates in his encounter with the peasant Platon Karatayev, who is neither a father-figure like the Freemason Bazdeyev nor (though brotherly) an elder brother like Andrei.

But what of the story's third hero? Like Natasha, Nikolai despises cleverness — that is why he is not interested in large questions touching the meaning of life like Pierre and Andrei. He is a man of action, with an instinctive flair that appears in a skirmish in 1812, when he spontaneously leads a charge that saves the day. He is not above flirting with other men's wives, but he has an instinctive decency which makes him instantly attracted to Princess Marya even while remaining resolutely loyal to Sonya. The callow youth who lost 43,000 roubles to Dolokhov, and whose only idea of estate management in 1810 was to beat up his father's steward, is last seen capably running the Bald Hills estate with a view to regaining Otradnoye, lost to creditors by his father's profligacy. He has paid all his father's debts although he could have repudiated them.

But for all his probity and flair for action, Nikolai is a problematic hero. He has flaws of personality that are neither tragic like those of Prince Andrei nor engaging like Pierre's. His dislike of both men, and the antipathy between him and Nikolenka that is hinted at in the epilogue, betoken unheroic limitations of mind, as does his unquestioning loyalty to a reactionary regime. Handsome dashing hussar though he is, he does not have a conventional heroic archetype. There may be something of Chaucer's Parfit Gentyl Knyght about him,[6] but at bottom he is Everyman, and his Tolkienian analogue is Sam Gamgee, another character who is emphatically indifferent to the big picture. Indeed, just as Sam is the "chief hero" of *The Lord of the Rings* considered as a novel, Nikolai may be the "chief hero" of *War and Peace* the *Bildungsroman*.

Certainly, the idea of *War and Peace* as a *Bildungsroman* is particularly applicable to Nikolai, who is still a schoolboy when it begins. The story of Andrei and Pierre, young though they are, is less one of formation than of reformation or redemption, epitomized in each case by a shift from admiring Napoleon to hating him. That is why their story is a quest romance and that of Nikolai, who hates Napoleon from the outset and encounters politics only to shun it for life, is not. As a Rostov, however, he figures in their quest romance along with his siblings (except Vera) — hence his visit to *volshebnoye tsarstvo*: the enchanted realm, fairyland.

Fairyland

In Chapter 1, I quoted E. M. W. Tillyard's prescription that the epic poet must, if possible, span a range of emotions "embracing the simplest sensualities at one end and a sense of the numinous at the other," and I asked how the latter might be achieved within the realist novel. Tolstoy's portrayal of the Rostov family is rich with the sensual, typically represented by feasts. The repast at Uncle's takes us back to the nameday banquet when we first met the family, and it has another counterpart in the juicy roast lamb and sweet raisins that Petya enjoys on the night before his death. But what of the numinous? The sequestration of the epic zone, the magical radiance of sun and moon that colours Andrei's visit to Otradnoye — these might seem to be as much as Tolstoyan realism will allow in that line, and at first glance they seem to be enough for Tolstoy's purposes. But he contrives to go further, and the question is why.

His insertion of fairyland is sparing yet systematic. Riding home from Uncle's through the dark, damp night, Natasha fantasizes that she and Nikolai might find that they have arrived not at Otradnoye but in fairyland. She feels that she will never be as happy and tranquil as she is now, and Nikolai feels that he would be happy to

---

[6] I so identified him in "'Great Chords': Politics and Romance in Tolstoy's *War and Peace*," *University of Toronto Quarterly*, 80 (2011), but I have changed my mind.

drive like this with her for ever. But fairyland can mark mortal visitors in ways that do not serve them well in the "real" world, and both of Natasha's brothers visit it to their cost.

Nikolai does so during Christmas Week. The episode begins slowly, with Natasha vexed by her fiancé's prolonged absence and bored to death, and slowly gathers energy through a couple of conversations and Natasha's singing for the company. Then it erupts with the arrival of serf mummers, some festive cross-dressing, and a high-speed troika ride in that bright Otradnoye moonlight. Nikolai feels himself transported into another realm.

> "Where's this we're going?' wondered Nikolai. "Through the sloping meadow, it should be. But no — this is something new, which I've never seen. It's not the sloping meadow and not Dyomkin Hill, but God knows what. It's something new and magical ..."
>
> Checking his horses again, Nikolai looked around him. All around was the same magical plain drenched in moonlight and strewn with stars.
>
> "Zakhar's shouting that I'm to turn left, but why left?" thought Nikolai. "Are we really going to the Melyukovs'? Is this the way to Melyukovka? We're going God knows where, and God knows what's happening to us, but whatever's happening to us is very strange and nice ..."
>
> "Look, his moustache and eyelashes are all white," said one of the strange, pretty, unfamiliar figures with fine eyebrows and moustaches sitting there.
>
> "I believe that was Natasha," thought Nikolai. "And that's Madame Schoss, but maybe not, and I don't know that Circassian with the whiskers but I love her ..."
>
> But here was some kind of magical forest with cascading black shadows and sparkling diamonds and some kind of flight of marble steps, and what looked like the silver roofs of magical buildings, and the piercing shrieks of some sort of wild animals. "And if this really is Melyukovka, then it's even stranger that we drove God knows where and arrived at Melyukovka ..."[7]

The excitement lifts Nikolai to unwonted heights of exaltation and leaves him open to the witchery of Sonya, herself liberated and energized by her disguise. The outcome is catastrophic, as we have seen.

A year or two later, Petya visits this enchanted realm with consequences even more calamitous. The ambience surrounding

---

[7] WP II.iv.10. Translated by author.

Denisov's guerrilla band is distinctly reminiscent of the hunt at Otradnoye — the weather is similar and there is even a comparable feast — but this time Petya stays awake. And after staying up all night, he lapses into a trance as a convenient Cossack whets his (Petya's) sabre.

> Petya should have known that he was in a forest, in Denisov's band, a kilometre from the road, that he was sitting on a wagon captured from the French, with horses tethered around it, that below him sat the Cossack Likhachov sharpening his, Petya's, sabre, that the big black patch to his right was a watchman's hut, that the red patch down to his left was a dying campfire, that the fellow looking for a cup was a hussar who wanted a drink; but he knew nothing of this and did not want to. He was in an enchanted kingdom, where nothing resembled reality.[8]

Is that dark shadow a hut or the entrance to a vast cavern? Is that red patch a campfire or the eye of some huge monster? Is he sitting on a wagon or on a high tower? He nods off, and his fantasy takes an extraordinary turn. The sound of sabre on whetstone conjures up

> a melodious orchestra playing some sweet, solemn hymn. Petya was as musical as Natasha, and more so than Nikolai, but he had never learnt music or thought about it and so the harmonics that suddenly filled his ears were to him absolutely new and intoxicating. The music swelled louder and louder. The air was developed and passed from one instrument to another. And what was played was a fugue — though Petya had not the slightest idea what a fugue was. Each instrument ... played its own part, and before it had played to the end of the motif melted in with another, beginning almost the same air, and then with a third and a fourth, and then they all blended into one, and again became separate and again blended, now into solemn church music, now into some brilliant and triumphant song of victory.

He lurches, realizes that he is dreaming, and embraces his dream.

> He closed his eyes. And from different directions, as though from a distance, the notes fluttered, swelled into harmonies, parted, came together and again merged into the same sweet and lovely hymn. "Oh, this is lovely! As much as I like, and as I want it!" said Petya to himself. He tried to conduct this tremendous orchestra.
> "Hush now, softly die away!" and the sounds obeyed him. "Now fuller, still livelier. More and more joyful now!" And from unknown depths rose the swelling triumphal chords. "Now the voices!"

---

[8] WP IV.iii.10: quotations from Rosemary Edmonds's Penguin Classics version.

> commanded Petya. And, at first from afar, he heard men's voices, then
> women's, steadily mounting in a slow crescendo ...

One does not expect adolescent boys engaged in military adventure to start composing hymns or choral tone poems in their heads, but Petya's extraordinary instinctive musicality brings home to the reader his nature as Natasha-plus-testosterone, so the episode is as plausible as it is functional.

At this point Tolstoy's story badly needs some twist to restore the solemnity and emotional weight that it lost with the death of Prince Andrei. It needs it to carry the story far enough beyond Andrei's death to put that massive event in perspective and make him "forgettable", and also to counterbalance the polemical treatise that at this point threatens to overwhelm the fictional narrative. Perhaps only another death will do, but it must be a death of sufficient pathos. Having no major character to spare, Tolstoy fattens up Petya for the slaughter, using the boy's Rostov nature to jump-start our sympathies. As I noted in the last chapter, Petya is close enough in kind to his siblings that we immediately feel closer to him than our previous slight acquaintance might otherwise warrant. But Tolstoy goes beyond character traits to conjure up an ambience that is peculiarly Rostovian: the ambience of the epic zone.

To evoke fairyland, Tolstoy uses the technique of narrative reticence that I noted in the last chapter: he presents information in the form of a character's perceptions, without commentary. He says nothing that endows fairyland with any sort of fictive reality, but also nothing to undermine its reality. It only crops up in relation to the Rostov siblings, and you can, if you like, assimilate it to the predominant realism by seeing it as denoting a state of mind — a susceptibility and recklessness typical of the Rostovs and perhaps also, given the Rostovs' symbolic significance, typically Russian.

By leaving it open to interpretation, however, Tolstoy invests it with a dual role, which owes as much to context as to content. It is no accident that it appears at a point where Tolstoy has eased his narrative away from the predominant realism. The resulting effect recalls Nathaniel Hawthorne's distinction between the novel and the romance. By a deft selection of circumstantial detail, Tolstoy applies a feigned realism to the evocation of a poetic ideal; by conjuring up fairyland, he "manages his atmospherical medium" to bring out certain lights and deepen certain shadows. At that point he has passed beyond even feigned realism: if anything, he is feigning fantasy. But to what end?

Petya may carry fairyland far afield, but its initial presentation in the context of the Rostov domain, and its place on Tolstoy's narrative trajectory, combine to project it as an imaginative extension of a space peculiarly identified with the Rostovs. That space is designed to project an ideal of harmonious hierarchy, but for that the hunting and feasting, the singing and dancing, and the romanticized picture of relations between masters and servants would suffice. Fairyland adds an exotic touch, but its main effect is different: it is a sort of glimmer, like a saint's halo, which invests the Rostov domain, already set apart from mundane reality, with an otherness, an out-of-this-world, timeless quality — and above all a doomed quality.

This function comes into focus when we compare Tolstoy's story with *The Lord of the Rings* and Walter Scott's *Waverley*. The critical consensus that extolled Tolstoy's realism and belittled Tolkien tended to dismiss Scott as a romancer, a mere story-teller unworthy of extended critical consideration as a novelist,[9] but in this comparison it is *Waverley* that is the exception. Scott 's remarks on *The Castle of Otranto*, quoted earlier, reveal his strong sense of a distinction between the romance and the novel, and *Waverley* actually begins with a declaration that it is a novel and not a romance because its setting, though historical, is too modern to offer any taste of romance. The story is solely focused on "the characters and passions of the actors; — those passions common to men in all stages of society." The plot and style of *Waverley* may incline one to doubt Scott's contention — it is incontestably romantic, if not a romance, and ranks far below *War and Peace* as a rendering of human personality and experience. If we compare Scott's fairy glen with Tolstoy's fairyland, however, it is clearly Scott, not Tolstoy, who is striving for realism.

Like Tolstoy's story, *Waverley* deals with historical events that took place fifty or sixty years before the time of writing.[10] The hero is a young English army officer (about Nikolai's age) whose

---

[9] Northrop Frye, *The Secular Scripture: A Study of the Structure of Romance* (Cambridge, MA: Harvard UP, 1976), 38-42. E. M. Forster is a case in point: *Aspects of the Novel*, 33-49.

[10] Sir Walter Scott, *Waverley; or, 'Tis Sixty Years Hence*. Here cited by volume and chapter in the two-volume format. In continuously paginated editions, vol. 2 begins with cap. 30.

Jacobite-influenced upbringing and juvenile immersion in romance literature predispose him to be charmed by the romance of the Highlands. Posted to Scotland on the eve of the uprising of 1745, he takes leave to visit an old Jacobite friend of his uncle. Thence he enters the adjacent Highland domain of Fergus MacIvor, laird of Glennaquoich. MacIvor and his sister, the lovely Flora, are determined to gain Waverley for the Jacobite cause, and Flora accordingly lures him to a picturesque spot beside "a romantic waterfall", where she bewitches him with her wild Highland music. The word bewitch is scarcely a metaphor:

> The sun, now stooping in the west, gave a rich and varied tinge to all the objects which surrounded Waverley, and seemed to add more than human brilliancy to the full expressive darkness of Flora's eye, exalted the richness and purity of her complexion, and enhanced the dignity and grace of her beautiful form ... The wild beauty of the retreat, bursting upon him as by magic, augmented the mingled feeling of delight and awe with which he approached her, like a fair enchantress of Boiardo or Ariosto, by whose nod the scenery around had been created, an Eden in the wilderness (I.xxii).

Waverley is won over to the cause of Prince Charles Edward, the Young Pretender, and takes part in the uprising.

Waverley's encounter with Flora in the glen has points in common with the Rostov brothers' visits to fairyland. Nikolai too is a susceptible young man, his heightened consciousness on the sleigh ride is expressed partly in terms of his response to "magical" scenery, and his mood is played on by a designing young woman, while Petya's fantasy is plainly shaped by childhood encounters with fairy-tales. There is also a similarity in the two stories' imaginative geography, since the isolation of Glennaquoich mirrors that of the Rostov domain. But there is an important and paradoxical difference between the two authors' treatment of their subject-matter. Tolstoy projects fairyland purely in terms of the character's perceptions, without any authorial commentary to guide the reader's understanding. By contrast, when Waverley heads up the glen to his tryst with Flora, Scott keeps the reader grounded in the reality of his hero's personality by citing "the fanciful and susceptible peculiarities of his character" and invoking Boiardo and Ariosto, the authors of the *Orlando* poems, to remind us of the voracious reading of romances and chivalric chronicles that shaped it. Scott's mention of the two Italian romancers tames the image of the enchantress by whose nod the scenery "seemed" to have been created, and the very word *seemed* works to the same effect by rooting the image in Waverley's perception — besides, Scott has already told us that the scenery has indeed been enhanced by trees and shrubs planted at Flora's orders. He also reports that "Flora, like every beautiful woman, was conscious of her own power and pleased with its effects." In short, while the scene plays on the imagery of enchantment that has pervaded perceptions of men's susceptibility to women from time immemorial, Scott's purpose is not to depict an enchantress ensnaring a hapless youth: it is to portray the reality underlying such imagery.

This distinction is mirrored in the broader comparison between Tolstoy's portrayal of the Rostov domain and Scott's of Glennaquoich and the Jacobite milieu in general. Glennaquoich is separated from Hanoverian London by the length of Great Britain, and its mountains isolate it even from the neighbouring Lowlands. This certainly marks off the MacIvor domain from the modernity that threatens it. However, these are facts of geography, not purely imaginative like Tolstoy's placement of the Rostov domain in Ryazan, and the mere fact of its remoteness no more imbues it with the mythic, timeless quality of Tolstoy's ideal than any other aspect of its portrayal. The basic reason for this is that it does not in fact represent an ideal. Scott was a Tory, but he was an ambitious lawyer of Lowland antecedents, a child of the Scottish Enlightenment, and he did not doubt the benefits his country had reaped from its union with England in 1707.[11] He depicts even the Lowland villages as miserable by English standards, and the Highland clans are half-savage bands of cattle thieves ruled, in the case of the *Sliochd nan Ivor*, by a pair of misguided zealots who have gained polish but little wisdom from their upbringing in France at the court of the exiled Pretender.

In *Waverley*, Scott indulges an antiquarian interest in a bygone social order. He romanticizes it by harping on the picturesque Highland landscape and the exotic glamour of Fergus and Flora MacIvor, but he distances himself from that effect by ascribing it to his hero's susceptibility. When he sheds his hero's romantic blinkers, his account is actually more sociological in its detail than Tolstoy's. Compare the lyrical catalogue of delicacies consumed at Mikhailovka with the menu of the great feast at Glennaquoich, where the *haute cuisine* at the head of the table gives way to "immense clumsy

---

[11] Graham McMaster, *Scott and Society* (Cambridge, Eng.: Cambridge UP, 1981), 59-78, 149-50.

joints of mutton and beef," while "Lower down still, the victuals seemed of yet coarser quality ...Broth, onions, cheese, and the fragments of the feast, regaled the sons of Ivor, who feasted in the open air" (I.xx). Compare, too, the grumpy crone who washes Waverley's feet beforehand with Uncle's concubine, Anisya Fyodorovna.

The same sociological eye is cast on the Jacobite army arrayed in preparation for its march from Edinburgh, in which the fine appearance of the leading clansmen is offset by the squalor of the peasant rank and file, "indifferently accoutred, and worse armed, half naked, stinted in growth, and miserable in aspect." Scott bluntly describes the latter as "Helots ... forced into the field by the arbitrary authority of the chieftains under whom they hewed wood and drew water" (II.xxi). There is no hint here of the instinctive patriotism that the Decembrists, and Tolstoy following them, ascribed to the Russian serf soldiers of 1812. Fergus and Flora are glamorous figures drawn with pathos; but while Scott glamorizes the characters, he makes no attempt to idealize the slave society over which they rule as Tolstoy idealizes Otradnoye and Mikhailovka. In this respect, a closer analogue to the Rostov domain is to be found in *The Lord of the Rings* than in *Waverley*.

When it comes to fairyland, however, all three writers are agreed on one thing: what counts is the glamour. Fairyland helps to glamorize the Rostovs, and, as in both *Waverley* and *The Lord of the Rings*, the glamorous people — the MacIvors in Scott's story and the elves in Tolkien's — are doomed: doomed because they personify a past that is vanishing or vanished beyond recall. Tolkien the scholar interpreted *Beowulf* as an elegy not just for its fallen hero but for the irrecoverable past he represents.[12] *The Lord of the Rings* is an echo of that interpretation; explicitly set in an irrecoverable past, it is ultimately a lament for the impossibility of Lothlórien. *War and Peace* is likewise a lament for the impossibility of Otradnoye, although the elegiac note is less obvious because the story seems to end on a note of recovery. By December of 1820, Nikolai is negotiating to recover Otradnoye. He can even dream of dancing with his daughter at a ball one day as his father had with Natasha. What is missing is the sense that Otradnoye can ever be the idyllic refuge that it was under his father.

Of course, Otradnoye might never have been lost had Nikolai's father taken better care of it, and Tolstoy the novelist makes no

---

[12] Tolkien, "Beowulf: The Monsters and the Critics," 31-33.

secret of the fate that threatens it, Napoleon or no Napoleon. But we will now see how Tolstoy the romancer projects his social alienation onto what the interim version of *War and Peace* depicts as a domestic sanctuary, turning it into a timeless utopia of harmonious hierarchy and spinning a tale in which history and politics are as much to blame for its demise as the old count's profligacy — or, if you like, a tale in which the old count's profligacy is a concomitant of his devotion to a social ideal which modernity has rendered untenable. In this light, fairyland is an aspect of Tolstoy's protest against history and politics, a protest embodied by the Rostovs in general but none more than Nikolai, with his inexpressible chagrin at the sight of the tsar consorting with Napoleon and his angry response to the political talk in the Epilogue. At the end the story is looking ahead; but what lies ahead is the Decembrist debacle and the crisis of Tolstoy's own day. History and politics still threaten; there will be no escape.

Tolstoy the conjuror: realism and the numinous

In terms of the quest romance, we can think of the Rostov domain as a sort of barebones Middle-earth, with the Rostovs doubling as hobbits and elves and fairyland supplying the barest hint of other worlds beyond the edge of rational knowing. A barebones Middle-earth is all Tolstoy needs, because for him, unlike Tolkien, the quest romance is not the main point of the exercise but simply a way to symbolize the political concerns that inspired him in the first place. Fairyland in particular owes its existence to just nine instances of the adjective *volshebnyi* in a text of several hundred thousand words;[13] it is a mere "management of his atmospherical medium" *á la* Hawthorne. Lightly drawn though it is, however, comparison with the interim version shows that it is no accident; it involves too many changes of several different sorts, some of them in places far from the Otradnoye episodes. Naturally, though, the chief changes are in the description of Otradnoye and its environs, and they all tend in the same direction: that is, towards expansion. They enlarge the Rostov domain itself, the space separating it from the outside world, and the space between characters. In doing so they create space for the numinous, thereby adding to the narrative a dimension that is

---

[13] The adjective occurs 12 times in all, including twice as part of the compound noun *magic lantern* and once in reference to the weather. *Volshebnitsa* ("enchantress") appears 3 times to express Denisov's perception of Natasha.

noticeably at variance with the prevailing realism. Or so one might think: after documenting the transformation as revealed by comparison of the two versions, I will consider why it is that Tolstoy's fairyland has attracted so little notice.

The account of Andrei's visit is altered in three main respects. Firstly, the earlier version is quintessentially novelistic in its emphasis on characters interacting in a social, indeed a domestic, milieu. The episode takes place in the realm of what Hawthorne called the probable and ordinary, and it is entirely "ordinary" in its conception. Andrei lodges in the nearby town, and we see him hobnobbing with the market girls before the count picks him up in his carriage to go to tea at Otradnoye. The main emphasis is on his dealings with the family — the episode is, in fact, very much a portrait of the family as seen through Andrei's eyes (except the absent Nikolai) — and he likes them all except Vera, who he realizes is sizing him up as a possible suitor. In this version, he meets Natasha in the normal course of his visit and they are instantly taken with each other. The visit takes place not in 1809 but two years earlier, and subsequently he re-visits Otradnoye occasionally, refreshing his feelings for Natasha and her family.[14] The published version focuses much more intensely on Andrei and his vision of Natasha. There is no mention of a town; he approaches the house alone (his coachman and footman are not mentioned and do not count); his encounter with the family is pared down to a short paragraph, with no mention of Vera. Natasha remains at a distance, first as a sunlit apparition, then as a disembodied voice in the moon-drenched night. Although she is the exclusive object of Andrei's interest, her name is only mentioned once in passing.

Secondly, the interim version contains no symbolic geography. The oak tree, instead of serving as a marker of Andrei's passage to and from Ryazan, appears only when he returns home, for it stands near his father's house and he will pass it from time to time and be reminded of his feelings for Natasha. But it could not have marked his journey to Ryazan in any case, because in the earlier version of this episode Otradnoye is not in Ryazan but in the province of Tver, which lies *between* Moscow and Saint Petersburg; thus the symbolism of Otradnoye as an extension of the Saint Petersburg–Moscow axis is missing.

---

[14] Tolstoy, *War and Peace: Original Version* (hereafter OV), 461-71, 495-97.

No less striking is the transformation of the ambience. The interim version contains no hint of a fairy vision, no sunlight and dazzling moonlight (it is not even certain that Andrei stays the night). However, it includes an incongruous moment when, at tea with the family on the drawing-room balcony, Andrei glances briefly at the sky and sees it "afresh once more, as at the battle of Austerlitz." This statement refers back to the occasion when, as the wounded Andrei falls to the ground, the hubbub of battle fades from his mind and he is aware of "nothing at all apart from the high sky — the high sky with the grey clouds creeping across it … 'Why did I never see this high sky before' thought Prince Andrei" (I.iii.16). The revelation remains unexplained and unmentioned until Pierre visits him at Bogucharovo two years later. As they are boarding a ferry to cross a river, Pierre affirms his belief in God and, "for the first time since Austerlitz," Andrei sees "the same high eternal sky" as he had seen it then and is amazed that he should have forgotten it.[15] This third occurrence follows very soon after, both in narrative time and in the text, which specifies that "now there were no clouds creeping across. It was blue, clear and infinite."[16]

The trope of the hero staring skyward and receiving an intimation of the ineffable is recurrent in *War and Peace*, and George Steiner cites the Austerlitz episode among others as evidence of Tolstoy's inability to convey transcendence effectively. I discuss Steiner's criticism below. Amid the domesticity of Otradnoye as portrayed in the interim version, however, the effect is clearly incongruous, and Tolstoy discarded it. Of course, its proximity to the Bogucharovo epiphany, where he retained it in the published version, was reason enough for this; but his transformation of the entire Otradnoye episode, including its transposition in time, suggests that he had more in mind. The sky as a symbol betokens mankind's relations with the celestial — it signifies revelation. Tolstoy seems to have decided that the Rostov domain is not about revelation but about wonder. The sky is still there in the published version, but not the Austerlitz sky, which belongs to the everyday world. What matters is the light: first sunshine, and then dazzling moonlight, both transforming the landscape in a possibly magical effect that can overwhelm the observing mind.

---

[15] OV, 369, 454.
[16] OV, 467.

Transformed in its ambience and stripped down to its essence, the account of Andrei's visit is more *archetypal*. It sets up a contrast that Northrop Frye calls typical of romance: one between an idyllic world graced with images of spring and summer, flowers and sunshine, and a demonic or night world of harrowing experience.[17] As such it is capable of projecting the aura of romance even to readers who do not know why it matters that Otradnoye is in the province of Ryazan. And in striking proof of the deliberation with which Tolstoy executed it, the work of transformation is not confined to the episode itself — it is complemented by alterations in events that occur three years earlier and three years later. Firstly, Tolstoy inserts into the account of Denisov's visit to the Rostovs after Austerlitz the episode of the mazurka and Denisov's proposal of marriage, thereby creating a previous instance of Natasha's bewitchment of an adult. Secondly, the account of Andrei's visit to his father's abandoned estate shortly before the battle of Borodino is revised so that Andrei's first, fleeting glimpse of Natasha is mirrored in the moment when he empathizes with the two little girls stealing plums from a greenhouse; in the earlier version they simply cross his path carrying plums, hardly noticed.[18] Thus a vision belonging to the idyllic world carries over into the night world, and the romance penetrates the novel.

In contrast to the account of Andrei's visit, the hunt and Yuletide episodes are very similar in the interim and the published version — probably because, by the time Tolstoy wrote them, his vision of the Rostov domain was already in transition. The clue to this lies in the account of the New Year's Eve ball. In a passage which belies all that we have previously been told about his relations with the Rostov family, Andrei does not recognize Natasha and remarks, when Pierre identifies her: "Ah, I know: her father is that stupid marshal of the nobility in Ryazan" — Ryazan, not Tver. Then, a few pages later, he recollects the astounding effect of his first ride up the avenue to Otradnoye, with its revelation of "a special world entirely alien to him" — a recollection quite inconsistent with the earlier narrative, in which he goes in the count's carriage and does not see

---

[17] Frye, *Secular Scripture*, 36, 53-54.

[18] OV, 777. In OV, Denisov is taken with Natasha from the start but does not go beyond flirting. In cap. XXV, the action proceeds directly from WP II.1.11 to 13 without the intervening episode of Iogel's ball, and Denisov's proposal of marriage is also missing.

Natasha until dinner.[19] These details are consistent with the final account of Prince Andrei's visit, not with that in the interim version.

But despite their similarity to the final versions, the interim versions of the hunt and Yuletide episodes still do not reflect Tolstoy's transformed conception, and the apparent similarity only makes the differences more striking.[20] The most remarkable difference is the insertion of fairyland, of which the interim version contains no hint; but two other, seemingly small, changes compound the effect of this addition. One is Tolstoy's treatment of the moon. Obviously, an account of a moonlit sleigh-ride can hardly ignore the moon; but in the interim version, except during the climactic encounter of Nikolai and Sonya, the moon is comparatively pallid. In the final version the moonlight is more transformative and disorienting, like the light by which Andrei eavesdrops on Sonya and Natasha. The second change is the shift in the terminus of the sleigh ride from Uncle's house, as it is in the interim version, to a new destination, Melyukovka. This has a twofold effect, which is complementary to that of fairyland itself. The insertion of fairyland tends to enchant the epic zone, of course; but it also tends to enlarge it, since it entails that intensified sense of space noted by E. M. Forster. Adding a third locus of action to the epic zone works to the same end.

In addition, the substitution of Melyukovka for Mikhailovka as the destination of the sleigh ride is also one of two critical modifications in the treatment of Uncle. In the interim version, he also pops up at the battle of Borodino. By confining him to the Rostov domain, Tolstoy reinforces the nature of the epic zone as a sequestered space, and by confining our exposure to Mikhailovka to a single visit, he makes it not just a "special" but a magical place, the abode of a *numen*. Natasha and Nikolai first think of the enchanted realm after encountering Uncle for the first time on his home turf — and Petya was there too.

As I said earlier, fairyland is lightly sketched. Yet it is there, and it is there because Tolstoy deliberately inserted it in the course of revising his treatment of the Rostov domain to underpin the quest romance. Thus the failure to take due account of it, as of the quest romance as a whole, suggests an inability to discern the larger structure of Tolstoy's narrative. In the last chapter I cited Gary Morson's contention that English-speaking commentators of the

---

[19] OV 549-50, 553.
[20] Compare OV 607 and 619-23 with WP II.iv.7, 10 and 12.

mid-twentieth century simply ignored the novelties which made it, to Tolstoy, "not a novel." The *reductio ad absurdum* of this approach is a translation and abridgement published in 1949 by a writer who, although the daughter of the famous Russian anarchist Peter Kropotkin, was born and raised in England. Alexandra Kropotkin avoids the problem of fairyland by simply omitting it. She cuts out the entire hunt scene and visit to Uncle's house, as well as the episode of Petya's dream. The Yuletide scene is mostly retained, but the sleigh-ride lacks Nikolai's internal monologue — that is, precisely the passages that allude to fairyland. The episode of Andrei's visit is retained in its entirety, but his journey to and from Ryazan is omitted, thus eradicating, not only the thoughts inspired by the oak-tree, but Tolstoy's extension of the Petersburg-Moscow axis and sequestration of the Rostov domain.[21] Generally speaking, she turns *War and Peace* back into a conventional novel.

Kropotkin was not a critic, of course, but critics both amateur and professional have fallen short in their brushes with the quest romance, probably because of the consensual fixation on Tolstoy's realism. It is perhaps surprising that E. M. Forster, who felt that Tolstoy's treatment of space "leaves behind an effect like music," did not sense its similarity to the sort of numinous, song-like resonance that he identified as prophecy; but Forster was insufficiently attuned to Tolstoy's intentions and technique to notice the subtle deviations from realism that constitute the quest romance. Gary Morson, although better informed than Forster, interprets the hunt and Yuletide episodes solely as instances of Tolstoy's determination to avoid a conventional linearity of plot in pursuit of enhanced realism.[22] Other commentators commit the solecism of explicating one allusion to fairyland in a way that takes no account of the others.[23]

A particularly interesting case is that of Northrop Frye, whose book on the romance cites *War and Peace* only in passing as an example of "realistic fiction", while the marginal notes on his personal copy display no recognition either of fairyland or the quest

---

[21] Leo Tolstoy, *War and Peace*, abridged translation rev. by Princess Alexandra Kropotkin (Garden City, NY: Literary Guild of America, 1949).
[22] Morson, *Hidden in Plain View*, 68, 149.
[23] *E.g.*, George R. Clay, *Tolstoy's Phoenix: From Method to Meaning in War and Peace* (Evanston, IL: Northwestern UP, 1998), 47-8; Lydia Ginzburg, *On Psychological Prose* (1971; tr. Judson Rosengrant, Princeton, NJ: Princeton UP, 1991), 248; Bayley, *Tolstoy and the Novel*, 108.

romance in general. This is the more remarkable because the quest romance is a textbook example of what Frye calls the "two forms of the upward quest" (i.e., the quest directed towards personal redemption), "one a sublimated quest ending in virginity, the other a sexual quest ending in marriage."[24] You might expect Frye, of all critics, to notice that Prince Andrei, alone among the younger male characters (the boy Petya excepted), apparently leads a celibate life throughout the story; however, the narrative says nothing on the subject, and Andrei does supposedly have a sexual history, so this is one more case where silence lets Tolstoy — or at any rate the reader — have it both ways. On one hand, it authorizes the virgin quest; on the other, it allows us to relate Natasha's resentment of his long absence to a shrewd suspicion of what male aristocrats get up to on trips abroad. Especially aristocrats who chat up market girls — but of course, Tolstoy left that out in the end.

The habits of thought underlying critical neglect of the quest romance are epitomized in George Steiner's account of Tolstoy's mind, which leaves little room for the possibility of fairyland. According to Steiner, Tolstoy "was obsessed with reason and a desire for clear understanding. The part of Voltaire in him was too prominent to accept for long shadowy intimations of the divine presence." To this unappeasable desire for certainty Steiner ascribes what he sees as the great flaw in Tolstoy's art: an inability to convey states of heightened or altered consciousness, uplifting or otherwise. Tolstoy's genius lay in his "groundedness in material fact, the intransigence of his demand for clear perceptions and empirical assurance ... [It] was inexhaustibly literal ... When he approached an episode or condition of mind not susceptible to lucid account, he inclined to evasion or abstraction." He "was omniscient at a price; the ultimate tension of unreason and the spontaneity of chaos eluded his grasp."[25]

Steiner cites three brief episodes in *War and Peace* where he holds that Tolstoy stumbles in the attempt to depict one of his characters as receiving an intimation of the ineffable. One is the moment at Austerlitz when the wounded Prince Andrei stares up at

---

[24] Frye, *Secular Scripture*, 56, 152. Frye's personal copy of *War and Peace* may be consulted at the E. J. Pratt Library of Victoria University in the University of Toronto. A revealing annotation at the end of the narrative Epilogue states: "I don't get the point of this at all."

[25] Steiner, *Tolstoy or Dostoevsky*, 265, 273-4, 277.

the immeasurably lofty sky, and the grey clouds gliding slowly across it, and realizes the insignificance and folly of the battle going on around him, with which he had been so preoccupied. The second is when Pierre, having declared his love for the disgraced Natasha, sees in the night sky a great comet which,

> after travelling in its orbit with inconceivable velocity through infinite space, seemed suddenly — like an arrow piercing the earth — to remain fast in one chosen spot in the black firmament, vigorously tossing up its tail, shining and playing with its white light amid the countless other scintillating stars. It seemed to Pierre that this comet spoke in full harmony with all that filled his own softened and uplifted soul, now blossoming into a new life.

Finally, Pierre again, at the outset of the death march from Moscow, sees the full moon hanging high in the sky amid the twinkling stars and feels one with the universe. Steiner outlines the symmetry of these three visions, in each of which the character's mind reaches out to infinity and then retracts into itself, and generalizes that "in each instance, a natural phenomenon moves the observing mind towards some form of insight or revelation." All three fail as art, however, because they exemplify a tendency on Tolstoy's part to "convey a psychological truth through a rhetorical, external statement, or by putting in the minds of his characters a train of thought which impresses one as prematurely didactic."[26]

I agree with Steiner's judgement of these episodes. The trope of a character's being moved to spiritual revelation or eloquence by some vision of natural splendour is distressingly trite, and the metaphorical equation of the comet with some playful animal, verges on tawdry. In all three cases Tolstoy seems to be trying to force the revelation, just as Tolkien sometimes does in *The Lord of the Rings*. He tells us instead of showing us.

The Austerlitz instance reveals the problem at its worst.

> Above him there was nothing but the sky, the lofty heavens, not clear, yet immeasurably lofty, with gray clouds slowly drifting across them. "How quiet, solemn, and serene, not at all as it was when I was running," thought Prince Andrei, "not like our running, shooting, fighting; not like the gunner and the Frenchman with their distraught, infuriated faces ... how differently do these clouds float over the lofty, infinite heavens.

---

[26] Steiner, *Tolstoy or Dostoevsky*, 271, 274. The episodes are in I.iii.16, II.v.22 and IV.ii.14. Steiner ignores the reappearance of the Austerlitz sky during Pierre's visit to Bogucharovo.

How is it I did not see this sky before? How happy I am to have discovered it at last! Yes! All is vanity, all is delusion, except those infinite heavens. There is nothing but that. And even that does not exist; there is nothing but stillness, peace. Thank God ..."

This passage is ploddingly didactic. Every stage of thought is spelled out, and it all leads to a trite Biblical allusion and an invocation of the deity. The later visions leave out God and the Bible but are no less explicit. The vision is described; an account of its effect on the observing character follows. As Forster remarks of the interview between Hetty and Dinah the Methodist in *Adam Bede*, everything is on the same plane.

However, the magic that besets the Rostov family is a different matter, and Steiner overlooks it. Rather than witnessing an object — a comet, the moon — the character is exposed to an influence: dazzling moonlight. Unlike the celestial apparitions, which are revelatory or cathartic, the influence is disorienting, a goad to impulsive action. It drives Andrei back to Saint Petersburg after four years' absence, Nikolai to plight his troth to Sonya, and Petya to his death. There is no explicit link between cause and effect, but the connection is palpable. And while the sky is still involved — the bright sunlight in which Andrei first sees Natasha, the brilliant moonlight of his nocturnal eavesdropping, the still more dazzling luminosity of Nikolai's visit to fairyland — attention is focused on the reflected light of the lower air.

Forster helps us understand the significance of this too. Distinguishing between fantasy and prophecy as aspects of the novel, he assigns the realm of prophecy to "the deities of India, Greece, Scandinavia, and Judea, to all that is medieval beyond the grave and to Lucifer son of the morning," and that of fantasy to "all beings who inhabit the lower air, the shallow water, and the smaller hills, all Fauns and Dryads ... and all that is medieval this side of the grave." The latter he calls "rather small gods ... I would call them fairies if the word were not consecrated to imbecility."[27] They are, of course, gods of the lower air.

Paradoxically, though, the most remarkable celestial manifestation of all occurs on a damp autumn night, unlit by moon or stars, when Petya is visited in his reverie by a choir of angels with orchestral backup. This is the exception that proves the rule. Imagine how trite such an apparition would seem in the context of any sky-

---

[27] Forster, *Aspects of the Novel*, 115-16.

focused attempt to evoke the numinous — or, for that matter, at the death-bed of Prince Andrei. It works brilliantly here because there is no didactic gloss, nothing is said about the effect of the apparition on the character's mind, and the outcome is instant and unexpected.[28]

Steiner contrasts Tolstoy with Dostoyevsky and Henry James, but without noticing that *War and Peace* encompasses significant aspects of each writer's universe.[29] Dostoyevsky and James are mystifiers. The former is supremely adept at depicting pandemonium — it is no accident that Steiner illustrates his comparison with a snatch of dialogue between Stavrogin and Pyotr Verkhovensky, the two demons at the heart of the most demoniacally headlong of all Dostoyevsky's novels. Apart from that, mysteries are central to several of his fictions. What is Stavrogin's secret? What is Versilov père up to in *A Raw Youth*? Who killed old Karamazov? In *The Demons* and *A Raw Youth*, Dostoyevsky uses the device of a naive narrator to heighten the mystery. James sometimes uses a naive observer, such as Strether in *The Ambassadors*, and sometimes just locks us up inside his characters' minds without fully revealing their thoughts. We know less than they do, and they know little enough, being in a state of bewilderment as to everyone else's motives if not in denial as to their own. This confusion is encased in prose of an elaborate opacity, which interposes itself between the reader and the subject-matter. Even when light dawns, the realization is so vaguely rendered that still we see as through a glass, darkly.

Jamesian and Dostoyevskian mystification both depend on extended passages of chaotic or disoriented action without authorial elucidation. Tolstoy's enterprise is too vast for such indirection: it demands a terse, pithy style with a muscular authorial presence. His mode is realism, and he does it by being blunt: Anna Scherer's old aunt swallows her phlegm; Prince Vasili has bad breath; old men lie paralyzed and mute on their deathbeds; Andrei's putrefying death-wound stinks. This frankness may suggest that Tolstoy is telling us everything. But for all its apparent transparency, there is often more in a Tolstoyan text than meets the eye, and we have seen that both the Dostoyevskian and the Jamesian subplot of *War and Peace* depend on mystification, albeit on the smaller scale enforced by the scope of the narrative. I have called

---

[28] This topic is discussed further below, 292-95.
[29] Steiner, *Tolstoy or Dostoevsky*, 275-77; see also *ibid.*, 124-25.

Tolstoy a conjuror, and he was quite capable of injecting a little magic into his realism.

Often in *War and Peace* we find Tolstoy scrutinizing his world with penetrating insight and minute precision but also with a certain detachment, like a spy drone with highly refined and versatile instrumentation. Not for him the humble suspension of inquiry in the face of ultimate mystery: his quest for understanding pushes him to explore his characters' minds on the very brink of death, and one might well be surprised to find fairyland as a station on the journey. At other times his perspective is closer to a more subjective sort of lens, the movie camera. In the account of Pierre's first meeting with Osip Bazdeyev, the oddly charismatic old Freemason, the narrative touches on every detail of the scene, stretching out over several paragraphs an episode that might have been dispatched in a sentence or two. We are seeing through the eyes of Pierre, a man so tormented by his thoughts that he sees and hears nothing. More through what he sees than through any articulation of his thoughts, we are made to feel his ennui, his metaphysical doubt, and finally his growing attraction to the father-figure he so desperately needs. It is a brilliant "point-of-view" effect, meant not to mystify but to illuminate: its subject is not Bazdeyev but Pierre's state of mind as revealed by his perception of Bazdeyev. Whatever the camera, though, the lens only sees what it is pointed at, and even what it sees can be modified by filters: Dolokhov and Sonya are cases in point. Tolstoy the conjuror fools us not by any evasiveness or involution of style but by what he chooses to place before his lens. He employs the illusion of clarity.

A style so subtle can certainly encompass abnormal states of mind: one has only to think of those hectic chapters in *Anna Karenina* which pursue Anna to her death. In fact, Tolstoy was quite adept at portraying heightened states of consciousness, morbid or exalted, and on one level fairyland is just that. As I said earlier, it denotes a state of mind typical of the Rostovs, which may catapult one into the clutches of a false fairy or even death itself. But by presenting fairyland strictly as something that befalls the Rostov siblings, Tolstoy imbues it with a psychic reality that installs it as a magical extension of his epic zone, edging the Rostov domain with a glimmer of otherness that separates it still further from the mundane reality of the satirical zone.

Tolstoy's epic

The quest romance entered Tolstoy's narrative as part of a broader revision and expansion of the interim version that turned his novel-in-progress into something he insisted was not a novel. That transformation had three other major aspects. One was the addition of a polemical discourse, partly historical and partly philosophical. The second was the hollowing out of the narrative by a purge of plot and character elements that are not necessarily extraneous to the novel but diminish the scope of the narrative. The third was the extension of the narrative for several years beyond the great victory of 1812 and the two marriages that form the climax of the interim version. Together, the quest romance and the narrative Epilogue in particular have the effect of setting the story that begins in Anna Scherer's salon in 1805 in a wider temporal frame that assimilates it to Northrop Frye's conception of the epic as a type of "encyclopaedic form." But while it is common enough to refer to the resultant text as an epic, it does not follow that the term is always applied with a complete or accurate understanding of the story's epic character.

For instance, it is common to speak of *War and Peace* and *Anna Karenina* in the same terms, ignoring Tolstoy's description of the latter as the first novel he had attempted. But in every respect the earlier one is grander in scale — even the title. Rumours of war resound from the start, but it is the title as a whole that proclaims the epic. The entire first half, an evocation of the universe that will be rent by war, is a but prologue to the cataclysm that dominates the second — a saga of ruin, displacement and death that leaves the survivors to pick up the pieces as at the end of *King Lear* or *Hamlet*. Old Prince Bolkonsky dead and young Prince Andrei; young Petya Rostov and his father; Anatole and Hélène. Prince Vasili is suddenly tottering on the brink of senility; old Countess Rostova, whom once he wooed, is plunged into it by the ruin of her world. *War and Peace* leaves us feeling that we have witnessed, or experienced in our imagination, an apocalypse — a fundamental and irreversible change in the universal order.

Monumental though it is, *Anna Karenina* does not. Tolstoy thought of calling it "Two Couples" or "Two Marriages," but neither title has the scope of "War and Peace" and the difference is reflected in the breadth of the plots. The novel tells the parallel stories of two married couples: Aleksei Karenin and his wife Anna, and Konstantin Levin and his eventual wife, Kitty. These couples are conjoined by a third, whose marital difficulties sound the primary theme of the novel: Stiva Oblonsky, who is Anna's brother, and Dolly, who is Kitty's sister. Early on, another major character also links the two couples: Count Vronsky, who at the start of the novel is Kitty's suitor but soon ditches her to become Anna's lover. The plot is much more closely focused on its major characters than that of *War and Peace*. None of the families is developed as amply as the Rostovs or even the Bolkonskys.

To the immense plot-structure of *War and Peace*, the temporal and spatial contexts add extra dimensions of magnitude that have no parallel in *Anna Karenina*. The story told in the latter is entirely enclosed within its pages, whereas *War and Peace* tells a story that extends beyond the final full stop. In fact, there is no final full stop to the narrative: the main narrative trails off in an ellipsis, as Natasha voices one of those characteristic fragmentary, inconclusive remarks that reflect her inability to find words for what she feels. So does the narrative epilogue, as young Nikolenka vows to himself to do something worthy of his father, a vow made ominous by the prospect of the Decembrist uprising. It is no accident that the final words of this massive chronicle, and such pregnant words, are given to a representative of a new generation. *Anna Karenina*, by contrast, reaches a definite climax with Anna's suicide, which looms much larger than the death of Prince Andrei and in effect brings the novel to a close. A final Part serves as a sort of coda to permit an emotional recoil after the incandescent chapters that culminate in Anna's death, but it is set only two months later and is devoid of dramatic tension, being more an occasion for Tolstoy to sound off on the meaning of life and on a contemporary international crisis arising from a rebellion in the Balkan provinces of the Ottoman Empire (the same crisis, by the way, that thrust William Morris into political activism). It is a thin, flat, preachy afterthought, fixed in the same temporal space as the rest of the novel. The epilogue of *War and Peace* has no equivalent in *Anna Karenina*.

As with *War and Peace*, and with the same satirical intent, Tolstoy situates the characters of *Anna Karenina* in the world of public affairs. Karenin is a prominent member of the imperial government, and Levin's interest in the reform of rural life involves him in local government. Russian politics after the Crimean War were shaped firstly by the government's efforts to modernize the country's social institutions and economy in an attempt to keep up with the other Great Powers of Europe, and secondly by the rise of revolutionary terrorism. This subject-matter offered ample material for dramatic exploitation, as we see in Dostoyevsky's *Demons* and several of Ivan Turgenyev's novels. *War and Peace* itself, of course, was inspired by contemporary politics.

Anna Karenina was not inspired by contemporary politics but by a newspaper story of a woman who threw herself under a train. That tragedy is very specific in nature, in contrast to the universal tragedy that ultimately dominates *War and Peace*. Anna defies social convention and is driven to suicide; the characters of *War and Peace* live their daily lives and are caught up in a tsunami. The politics in *War and Peace* are essential to the plot, but those in *Anna Karenina* remain extraneous and so the juxtaposition of public and private affairs in the later story does not yield the epic effect achieved in its precursor. It is a domestic saga, in which Anna's tragedy is set against the rocky path of Levin and Kitty towards such happiness as family life can offer. The epic mode incorporates such tragedies in a wider canvas, which portrays the tragedy of nations or of all humanity in historical perspective. *War and Peace* is set in history; *Anna Karenina* is trimmed with political science. There are pastoral scenes in Tolstoy's "first novel" but no equivalent to the Rostov domain, tasty meals but no counterpart to the feasts that the Rostov siblings enjoy on the perilous margins of fairyland.

The contemporary setting of *Anna Karenina* precluded Tolstoy from closing the novel in the same way as *War and Peace*, and this may help to explain the novel's lack of epic resonance. As we have seen, the traditional epic is set in a mythic past: Homeric Troy, Camelot, the multiple spheres of *Paradise Lost*. The narrative perspective of *War and Peace* is not temporally distinct from its subject-matter to this degree, but the historical treatment of world-shaking events fosters the impression, characteristic of epic, that the story treats of a time apart. Arguably, though, it is less the contemporary setting than the subject-matter that accounts for the absence of epic effect in the later work. Michael Cimino's *The Deer Hunter* is virtually contemporaneous with the Vietnam War, but it achieves epic grandeur because it creates an impression that its traumatic events happened not just to the characters but to the entire American people, as represented in microcosm by the Lemko community in Pennsylvania's steel country from which Cimino draws his characters. Anna's story is one of increasing and finally complete isolation, and her tragedy is purely personal and private. The characters gathered at the end of *War and Peace* and *The Deer*

Hunter are survivors. Those gathered at the end of *Anna Karenina* are onlookers.

Citing Aristotle, Gary Morson observes that *War and Peace* does not really begin *in medias res* in the traditional sense, since "it does not start in the middle of a story whose beginning and end are described later."[30] That is true, strictly speaking, although — as we have seen — Tolstoy sets his narrative in epic time, thus establishing it as but a moment in a grand process. Besides, we are not talking here about a tradition of narrative poetry exemplifying, or adhering to, Aristotelian structural canons. Our subject-matter is four prose narratives belonging to different genres, which are yet alike in projecting epic themes and motifs, especially in recounting a turning-point in history. Tolstoy set his story in the recent past of his own people and could count on his audience knowing how it began. He achieves an epic temporal structure in other ways: by projecting a mythic past onto his history in the form of the idyllic community figured in the Rostov domain, by leaving the ending of his story open to the future, and perhaps by harping on the absolute continuity of time. And he achieves an epic spatial structure by the sequestration and numinous edging of the Rostov domain.

Tolstoy's epic turned out quite different from the author's original conception, and consequently it shows signs of disintegration like *The Lord of the Rings*. This becomes apparent by comparing Andrei with that intriguing apparition, Trotter-Strider-Aragorn-Elessar, since each is the character at the epicentre of the creative transformation and each exhibits flaws of construction as a result. Aragorn's proto-fascist histrionics result from Tolkien's compulsion to prematurely ignite the prophetic charge that increasingly pervaded his story. We have seen that Tolstoy did this too, and Andrei's celestial vision at Austerlitz is only the most glaring example. On the whole, though, the flaws associated with Andrei appear neither in thought nor deed but in the narrative architecture founded on the character. In the Austerlitz episode, for instance, he exhibits signs of callowness that belie his moral growth in the preceding Schoengrabern episode, probably because Tolstoy went back and inserted Schoengrabern after writing about Austerlitz.[31] Likewise, the crucial chapter recounting his visit to his father's abandoned home, where he observes the two little peasant girls stealing plums and

---

[30] Morson, *Hidden in Plain View*, 162.
[31] Feuer, *Tolstoy and the Genesis of 'War and Peace'*, 20.

returns to find his men bathing in the mill pond, fits rather clumsily with the chapters leading up to it.

More pervasive, however, are certain chronological flaws. *War and Peace* is riddled with discrepancies of varying magnitude. Vera Rostova ages from 19 in 1806 to 24 in 1809, and a miscellany of errors arises from Tolstoy's confusion of the European and Russian calendars, which were ten days apart. These inconsistencies are trivial enough, but others are structural flaws, visible signs of the disintegration resulting from the progressive transformation of Tolstoy's narrative idea. The largest is a chronological fault that pervades Book Two, engendering a persistent uncertainty as to the year in which the narrative is located at certain moments. As a result, Pierre pays Andrei a visit that is said in different places to have occurred in 1807 and in 1808, Boris Drubetskoy's rise on the general staff seems phenomenally rapid, Pierre's cuckolding by Dolokhov apparently pre-dates his marriage by several months, and his resentment of Boris, which is implicitly evoked by the latter's dalliance with his wife, is expressed in a diary entry dated only four days after the date of his reconciliation with her, although it seems to reflect lengthy observation.

The narrative rupture first appears when Nikolai, returning home "early in 1806" after the battle of Austerlitz, is said to have been absent for eighteen months, although we first met him at home in September 1805. The next hint of it is the suggestion that Pierre had tolerated Dolokhov's affair with his wife for twelve months before challenging him, although the marriage in fact took place only a few months previously. It is wholly plausible that Dolokhov's relations with Hélène pre-dated the marriage, but the terms of the reference do not allow for that. Book Two, Part 2 shows us Pierre touring his estates in the spring of 1807 and visiting Andrei on his way back; but in Part 3, which has to take place in 1809 so that Andrei can join the new administration of Mikhail Speransky, we find confusion as to whether Pierre's visit to Andrei had occurred one year or two years previously, and the narrative states in one place that five years have elapsed since Andrei was last in Saint Petersburg (which we know was in 1805).[32]

Two discrepancies are particularly bizarre. One is the protracted pregnancy of Prince Andrei's wife. In the interim version Princess

---

[32] Nikolai's homecoming: WP II.i.1; Pierre's marriage: II.i.10; Visit to Andrei: II.ii.8, II.ii.10, II.iii.1, II.iii.5, II.iii.7.

Lisa is visibly pregnant on the July evening when the narrative commences, and it is expressly stated that she is expected to come to term at the end of November, but she does not go into labour until March 19th of the following year, implying a pregnancy lasting a year or more. The published version retains this bizarre time-line but does not mention the expected term of the pregnancy.[33] The second discrepancy involves the episode of Natasha's seduction, culminating in Andrei's termination of their engagement on his return to Russia. In the interim version this is unambiguously placed in the early months of 1811, but in the published version the years 1810 and 1811 are telescoped so that Prince Andrei does not return until later in the year. This temporal compression results from the fact that the episode is chronologically anchored at the start to Napoleon's annexation of the duchy of Oldenburg at the beginning of 1810 and at the end to the spectacle of the Great Comet of 1811.

The chronological ambiguity that pervades Book Two is easily excused by the difficulty of managing so vast a narrative, especially when the medium of creation was cursive handwriting. Tolkien had a typewriter. However, a different order of carelessness is involved when a plausible time-line is distorted to produce a physiological impossibility and a chronological nonsense. What these episodes share is the subordination of chronological plausibility to melodramatic effect. Tolstoy had to protract the pregnancy of Andrei's wife in order to bring her husband "back from the dead" at the very moment of her death in childbirth, and the Great Comet came in because Tolstoy felt impelled to mark the end of Book Two of his story — which covers so much time and carries his characters so far — with a suitably grand climax. It is hard to imagine that he perpetrated either absurdity on purpose, but they are undeniable lapses of execution.

Grotesque as they are, however, these lapses are oddly inconspicuous, probably because they are buried beneath so much circumstantial detail (presumably, that is why neither Tolstoy nor his wife, who made fair copies of his manuscripts, noticed them). As a result, they do not invalidate the overall conception, and it is at this level that formal criticism of *War and Peace* has generally occurred. Percy Lubbock, for instance, complained that the story is actually a mish-mash of two novels, neither of them fully achieved:

---

33 Lise's pregnancy: OV, 145, 406; Telescoping of years 1810 and 1811: OV, 632, 650, WP II.v.3, II.v.22.

it starts out as a tale of the rise and fall of successive generations, to which the grand pattern of war and peace is merely a contrastive background, but turns into a story of the clash of nations, in which the lives and deaths of the characters we have come to know so well are mere incidents. He could discover no point of view from which these two stories appear to merge into a single integrated narrative: "Neither is subordinate to the other, and there is nothing above them (what more *could* there be?) to which they are both related."[34] He also bridled at the didactic and polemical interpolations in the second half, encouraging readers to skip them if inclined.

Of course, this is precisely the sort of criticism that Tolstoy had tried to forestall by saying that his story was not a novel, and Lubbock was not the first to make it. As it happens, the charge of disintegration does not stand up, since it overlooks the symbolic relationship between Tolstoy's historical narrative and his domestic saga. As we have seen, the clash between the Russian and Napoleonic empires mirrors a conflict of values within Russia itself, a conflict which not only engages the characters but in the cases of Pierre and Andrei takes place within them. Lubbock's dismay at the didactic digressions is more justified. They are often intriguing in themselves, but they are hardly an artistic enhancement — particularly the second part of the epilogue, which is purely didactic.

In the body of the novel, the great test is Book 4, Part 2, which recounts the beginning of Napoleon's retreat from Moscow. It claims our interest because of its focus on a turning-point in history, but only four of the nineteen chapters are fictional and they are Lenten fare. Only a genius could get away with it, and it is easy to see why Tolstoy promptly ramped up the action with the episode of Petya's death. Even here, however, it can be argued that the didactic interlude serves an artistic function by affording the reader an emotional respite after the death of Prince Andrei. Perhaps, too, we may see the near-disintegration of the fictional narrative at this point as a counterpart to the disintegration of the old order with the death of the tragic hero. In Tolstoy's epic, of course, the fictional narrative resumes and life goes on

In any case, while Lubbock's approach may suit the novel that Tolstoy had set out to write, it is wrong for an epic. The epic vision does not make for tidiness. The very ugliness and intrusiveness of Tolstoy's didactic digressions betrays their importance: they are not

---

[34] Lubbock, *Craft of Fiction*, 26-58 (quotation p. 33).

there to help the narrative but because they are the point of the narrative — or, more exactly, because Tolstoy came to see them as the point of it.[35] They are not essential to the epic, but they are expressions of the idea that drove him to transform his unfinished novel into an epic. We may regret their prominence, if not their presence, but we should receive them with respect. Like the improbable pregnancy of Princess Lisa and the surreal compression of the year 1811, they are flaws of execution rather than conception. They are the deformities of epic.

----

[35] With the stated qualification, I concur with Isaiah Berlin and George Steiner: Berlin, *The Hedgehog and the Fox: An Essay on Tolstoy's View of History* (New York: Mentor Books, 1957) 18; Steiner, *Tolstoy or Dostoevsky*, 280-81.

6

An Unfinished Epic? *The Making of the English Working Class*

According to Northrop Frye, "a narrative poet ... may write any number of narratives, but an epic poet normally completes only one epic structure, the moment when he decides on his theme being the crisis of his life." Frye ascribes this to the encyclopaedic thematic range of the epic, "from heaven to the underworld, and over an enormous amount of traditional knowledge".[1] Transposing his observation to the modern prose epic, we can cite both Tolkien and Tolstoy as proof. *The Lord of the Rings* is part of a single grand narrative which is encyclopaedic precisely in Frye's sense. From its inception during the First World War, that narrative preoccupied Tolkien so completely that *The Hobbit*, an unconnected story originally quite different in tone, was retrospectively absorbed into it, while the rest of his fictional output was confined to a few short stories. *War and Peace* also fits into a broader narrative, and it treats its subject-matter so comprehensively that nothing else that Tolstoy wrote, not even *Anna Karenina*, approaches it in scale. E. P. Thompson, however, substantially achieved two epic structures, each emerging from a projected narrative of a very different nature — a history textbook and a Swiftian satire — transformed by the author's urge to prophesy his alienation from modernity. This was, perhaps, because his entire adult life was involved in war: the Second World War, the Cold War, and the class war.

---

[1] Frye, *Anatomy of Fiction*, 318.

As we turn from fictional narratives to a work of history, we should bear in mind how history pervades both Tolkien's and Tolstoy's narratives. It is more obvious in the case of *War and Peace*, since the story is set in actual human history and the fiction sometimes comes close to disappearing beneath a mass of historical polemic and philosophical disquisition: the great "novel" ends with a long essay on historical causation. As for *The Lord of the Rings*, its genre, combined with residual traces of the children's tale from which it evolved, seems to preclude any relevance to reality. Yet it too was influenced by contemporary events, and it extends and completes a fictional myth-cycle that originated in Tolkien's need to process his experience of trench warfare during the First World War. As we have seen, he described the story as *history* and shaped the elaborate front-matter and appendices to link his myth-world to human history, thus making the entire edifice a representation in fiction of his fascination with Story as an expression of the continuity of human experience from the Beginning. As sustained intrusions of expository discourse into a work of fiction, the metafictional elements in both Tolkien's and Tolstoy's narratives exemplify that multigeneric expansiveness of form which W. P. Ker and E. M. W. Tillyard saw as typical of the epic. Their counterpart in the *Iliad* is the Catalogue of participants in the Achaian expeditionary force, and in later epics it is the genealogical list.[2]

The intrusion of academic modes of discourse into narratives as different as *War and Peace* and *The Lord of the Rings* speaks to the importance of history to the epic; and as we have seen, they did more or less force their way into both stories. But the epic treats history in ways that sit uneasily with the canons of academic history. The epic has heroes and villains; it takes sides; it idealizes; it presents archetypal characters in exemplary situations. It also imagines worlds beyond that of everyday experience — even Tolstoy subtly modulates his hard-edged realism to hint at fairyland. But

---

[2] In his drafts, Tolkien compared the account of the muster of forces in defence of Minas Tirith to the Homeric Catalogue, but this parallel is inexact. The muster occurs in the narrative present, and so its description does not function as a temporal recursion like the Catalogue: i.e., it adds spatial breadth to the narrative but does not increase its temporal depth. J. R. R. Tolkien, *The War of the Ring: The History of The Lord of the Rings, Part Three*, ed. Christopher Tolkien (Boston and New York: Houghton Mifflin, 1990), 229.

academic history must be even more tightly bound to reality than the most earnestly realist fiction. If, then, as Tillyard says, the epic is marked by a breadth of vision that spans the gamut from the simplest sensualities to a sense of the numinous, where shall we seek the numinous in an empirical work of historical discovery? If, as Frye says, the site of epic action is typically a middle ground between the upper and lower gods, where are we to find the gods?

This is not a matter of "subjective" versus "objective" approaches to history so much as one of mode and tone. The academic narrative is essentially univocal, even though the narrator may quote other voices; the tone is even and dispassionate, although the lack of passion may be feigned; the mode is didactic. And the academic historian does not generally have one eye cocked towards eternity, as the epic narrator does. This may make our excursion into academic history seem challenging, if not unpromising. But *The Making of the English Working Class* has evoked comparison with both *The Lord of the Rings* and *Moby Dick*. Leaving Melville's masterpiece aside for now, here is the historian Meredith Veldman's account of her experience of reading Tolkien's story at a time when she was immersed in *The Making*:

> I began to feel like I was reading the same book. I decided that I must need a vacation. For what could Thompson have to do with Tolkien? What could a Marxist share with a supporter of Franco? On what common ground could the politically active, cause-oriented Thompson meet a man who spent much of his life in a world of his own making?

In answer, Veldman invokes romanticism, which she defines as a world-view rooted in the belief that the empirical and analytical methods of modern science cannot comprehend all of reality. Both Tolkien and Thompson were heirs of the Romantic revolt against the modernity represented by industrialism and empiricism.[3]

We noted Thompson's imputation of a Tolkien-inspired infantilism to U.S. foreign policy, and his scorn for the "escapism" of William Morris's *The Earthly Paradise* — a work that, at least in its prefatory confession of alienation, evidently meant a lot to Tolkien.[4] Nevertheless, Thompson and Tolkien were alienated by many of the same things — hence their appeal to the counter-culture of the

---

[3] Meredith Veldman, *Fantasy, the Bomb, and the Greening of Britain: Romantic Protest, 1945-1980* (Cambridge, Eng.: Cambridge UP, 1994), 1-3.
[4] See above, 21, 62-67.

1960s. They responded differently to their alienation: Tolkien retreated, while Thompson emulated Morris by becoming a communist and plunging into a life of activism. However, both men possessed (or were possessed by) the epic temperament, and in Thompson's case, as in Tolkien's, it combined with his alienation to produce a work — in fact, two works — of genius.

Like epics, works of genius are very rare in academic discourse, and for much the same reason: academic discourse operates within constraints that are inimical to genius and tend to repel it. This is not necessarily a bad thing. Tolstoy's sarcastic remarks about history professors may sound very well, but his portrait of Kutuzov is notoriously idealized and a competent academic would not make those absurd chronological errors we have just been discussing: Tolkien took scrupulous care over his chronology. Still, Tolkien the academic resorted to fiction for the full expression of his genius, and so would Thompson.

In this chapter, however, we confront a work of academic scholarship that I wish to consider as an epic and a work of genius. Like its cousin the Byronic hero, genius arises from a combination of nature and circumstances. Accordingly, I first sketch Thompson's antecedents, upbringing and early career, revealing the sources of the personality and political activism that gave his writing its special character. Then I turn to the work itself and its intellectual sources in order to reveal its epic features and explain how genius manifested itself in a work of academic history. In this phase of the discussion, I emphasize the ways in which *The Making* deviates from academic norms in structure and tone, including a temporal setting that functions in a manner corresponding to the evocation of the numinous in fiction. I also point out echoes of Thompson's personal experience in the narrative.

A libertarian communist

Edward Palmer Thompson was born in 1924, and his formative years encompassed the Great Depression and the Second World War. In fact, he ended up fighting in the war. One day, the 20-year-old lieutenant was ordered to lead his tank squadron's advance into the Italian city of Perugia. A tank troop consisted of three tanks, one commanded by an officer and the other two by non-commissioned officers. Standard procedure required that an advancing troop be led by an NCO's tank, with the officer's next in line. The leading tank was likely to be hit by gunfire, and Lt. Thompson briefly pondered taking the lead himself before ordering his sergeant to go ahead. The leading tank was hit, and Thompson was left with the consciousness of having ordered three men to their death. Of course, if he had led the advance himself, three other men might have died; and not necessarily Thompson himself, since his sergeant escaped the carnage whole. Such niceties afford little solace to a lively conscience, but they offer a powerful lesson in the importance of happenstance, or contingency.

Next day Thompson returned to the tank to find that a German soldier had dropped a hand grenade into it overnight and set it on fire. A pile of ashes, moulding the lower half of a man, remained in the driver's seat. Yet the military bureaucracy saw fit to list the victims as "Missing, believed killed," condemning the young lieutenant to an agonizing correspondence with families tortured by hopes that he knew to be groundless. It continued once hope was lost. "He was our only child." "My brother was all I had in this world." "Please did one of his friends pick some wild flowers and place [them] on his grave?"[5]

This was not the only scar the war left on his life. Frank, his brilliant older brother, was an officer in the Special Operations Executive, an organization set up to aid resistance movements in occupied Europe. Early in 1944, Frank had parachuted into Bulgaria. Shortly before Edward's Perugia ordeal, he was captured and executed: a hero who died a hero's death, and both living and dying a tough act to follow. But investigation raised the suspicion that his death was due to collusion between his captors and his country. At the time the British government was trying to bring the Bulgarian regime, a German ally, over to its side in order to forestall Soviet influence. It was also anxious to purge known communists (of whom Frank was one) from its secret organizations. Abandoning the Bulgarian communist resistance and consigning Frank to the mercies of his captors served both ends.[6]

---

[5] E. P. Thompson, *The Heavy Dancers* (London: The Merlin Press, 1985), 183-89.

[6] E. P. Thompson, *Beyond the Frontier: The Politics of a Failed Mission, Bulgaria 1944* (London: Merlin/Stanford, 1996); Freeman Dyson, *Disturbing the Universe* (New York: Harper and Row, 1979), 34-40; Peter J. Conradi, *A Very English Hero: The Making of Frank Thompson:* (London, Bloomsbury 2012).

By the time Edward Thompson recorded his Perugia experience, forty years after the event, he had become not just a leading historian but a major public figure. A recent public opinion poll had declared him the most admired man in Britain (the poll was not gender-specific, and he came fourth behind Prime Minister Margaret Thatcher, Queen Elizabeth, and the Queen Mother). His celebrity was due to his role as a leader and spokesman of the organization called European Nuclear Disarmament, and his reminiscence was inspired by the coincidence that END had just held its annual convention in Perugia. Of special interest here is his account of the objectives that had inspired the Europeans who had fought against Nazism and Fascism. The summer of 1984 was also the fortieth anniversary of the Allied invasion of Normandy, and the British media were full of nostalgic recollections of the country's last hurrah as a great power. Thompson had a few things to add.

Nowadays, he remarked, most people had no experience of war and tended to think of it in abstract terms, as a matter either for romance or disgust. Like most thoughtful and sensible people, Thompson's fellow-soldiers had felt disgust: they had just wanted to get the job done and go home with their sense of honour intact. Their main object had been personal survival; but that ambition had been qualified by a sense of the need to fulfil "certain necessary duties and loyalties," a commitment which often made survival impossible. Addressing the "good-hearted" feminism which understood war simply as an expression of male aggression, Thompson observed that he himself had seen little evidence to support that idea. The conspicuously *macho* soldier, usually an officer, was feared and hated as someone likely to involve others in futile and fatal adventures. British soldiers had fought, not from any testosterone-fuelled lust for battle, but out of a sense of obligation to resist Nazi and Fascist aggression.[7]

Thompson criticized the popular media's depiction of the War on two grounds. He condemned its tendency to focus on the actions of "a few rugged individuals ... photogenic individuals displaying cunning or heroism and thereby becoming the actors who 'won' the war." This emphasis on individual agency was deceptive, since modern warfare was the ultimate negation of human agency. "Much of the killing in World War II was done at long-distance between enemies who rarely ever saw each other. In World War III they will

---

[7] Thompson, *Heavy Dancers*, 189-92.

never see each other ..." This meant that people who wanted to be agents in the next war needed to act now, before it began. Secondly, Thompson blamed the media for projecting an image of war which left out the dimension of bereavement. "Two generations of Europeans — those of my parents and my grandparents — had to endure this monstrous thing: the knowledge that their children, scarcely out of school, faced death at any time ... I hold myself and my generation in Europe ... to be greatly fortunate that we never had to endure that kind of aching fear on behalf of our own." [8]

The leading spokesman for European Nuclear Disarmament ignored the contribution the nuclear stalemate might have made to his generation's good fortune, but he did warn against worrying only about nuclear armaments when modern conventional weapons were also horrific. The obsession with nuclear weapons simply played into the hands of the Soviet Union, which sought to exploit Western peace movements to weaken the Western nuclear threat while its own immense conventional armament still threatened the peace of Europe. Thompson noted that his broader anti-militarism, which involved him in supportive exchanges with dissidents in Soviet-occupied Europe, had recently prompted Soviet propagandists to brand END as a tool of the U.S. Central Intelligence Agency. [9]

The best, and perhaps only, solution to the crisis lay in the union of the peoples — not governments — of Europe; and this reflection brought him back to the Second World War and the objectives of the Europeans who fought against fascism — objectives which he felt gave them something in common with the modern peace movement.

> In 1944 all of Europe, from the Urals to the Atlantic, was moved by a consensual expectation of a democratic and peaceful post-war continent. We supposed that the old gangs of money, privilege and militarism would go. Most of us supposed that the nations of West and Southern Europe would conduct their anti-Fascist alliances towards some form of socialism. Most of us (including many of the communists of those countries) supposed that the nations of Eastern Europe would be governed by some sort of authentic socialist popular front. We all supposed that the people of the Soviet Union (before whose measureless sacrifices we felt humility) and the people of the rest of Europe would cohabit on the same continent agreeably as good

---

8 Thompson, *Heavy Dancers*, 192-95.
9 Thompson, *Heavy Dancers*, 195-96.

neighbours. It was brave rhetoric, and we bought it, and some bought it with their lives ...

My fellow soldiers who burnt in that tank were not ardent politicians. But they were democrats and anti-Fascists. They knew what they fought for, and it was not for the division of Europe, nor was it for the domination of our continent by two arrogant superpowers.

The need of the moment was to return to the ideals of 1944, "before Europe was struck into two halves," and to heal that division. "If the Convention at Perugia did something to help this healing-process on, then will it have done more than place wild flowers on those distant anti-Fascist graves. It will have liberated the intentions of the dead." [10]

Thompson's essay echoes several themes sounded by Tolstoy and Tolkien. The disgust for war — a disgust derived from experience — is common to all three. So are the antipathy to authority, whether represented by the Great Leader or the jack-in-office, and the respect for the rank-and-file soldier. The criticism of the media's fondness for the myth of heroic agency brings to mind not only Tolstoy's contempt for the notion of the Great Man, supposed maker of history, but also one of his heroes, the photogenic Prince Andrei, risking his life at Austerlitz for a gesture which turns back the French for a matter of minutes and then later, at Borodino, mortally wounded at long range while simply standing and waiting. All three writers celebrate the heroism of doing one's duty at the risk of one's life. However futile on the day, Andrei's bravery at Austerlitz, like Frank Thompson's in Bulgaria, was necessary in that moment and has its counterpart in the valour of the tank crew who embraced necessity by leading Thompson's squadron along the road to Perugia. And Thompson's fellow soldiers, doing what must be done with a minimum of bravado while hoping to get home in one piece, have counterparts in Sam Gamgee and Nikolai Rostov. They saw themselves as having a duty to perform rather than a mission or destiny to fulfil. But was their sense of duty really inspired by the political values that Thompson ascribes to them, rather than ordinary patriotism?

Frank certainly believed in those ideals, and they inspired both him and Edward as undergraduates to join the Communist Party of Great Britain. But the brothers were no slaves to the Party line. Frank joined in 1939 in the conviction that it was the only

---

[10] Thompson, *Heavy Dancers*, 199-201.

organization that could be trusted to resist Fascism effectively. Sideswiped almost at once by the Nazi-Soviet pact of August 1939, he chose to resist Fascism anyway and volunteered for military service. Edward stayed in the Party after the war partly out of admiration for the Communist-led fight against Nazism in the Soviet Union and Nazi-occupied Europe. In 1947 he and his future wife worked as volunteers on the construction of a railway in Yugoslavia before he and his mother went to Bulgaria to be feted by the country's leader as the kin of the heroic Major Thompson, by then commemorated in the name of a village and a railway station. He would quit the Party in protest against the Soviet invasion of Hungary in 1956. By then he had learned how little there was to choose between the jack-in-office and the Party apparatchik.[11]

By joining the Party in the first place, Thompson expressed his rejection of a political and social system which Marxists blamed for both World Wars and the Great Depression. But he also rejected something else. His father, Edward John Thompson, was the son of a Methodist minister who had died young after missionary service in India, leaving his wife to care for six small children. As the eldest child, Edward John was obliged to leave school early, forgoing the prospect of a scholarship to Cambridge University, and take a job as a bank clerk. After several years' drudgery, and partly in response to his mother's wishes, he entered a Methodist seminary; and in 1910, as an ordained minister, he went to India to teach at a mission-ary college. By then he had taken an external degree at the University of London. A dozen years in India, punctuated by service as an army chaplain in the Middle East during the First World War, left him disillusioned with his vocation, disgusted by British rule in India, and notorious as the drafter of a protest by Christian mission-aries against the Amritsar Massacre of 1919 — the military slaughter of several hundred civilians in a crowd gathered to celebrate a harvest festival. In 1923 he left the country to take up what was at first a part-time teaching position at the University of Oxford. Here he became an outspoken advocate of Indian independence, hosting

---

[11] Michael Bess, *Realism, Utopia, and the Mushroom Cloud: Four Activist Intellectuals and Their Strategies for Peace, 1945-1989* (Chicago and London: University of Chicago Press, 1993), 94-9; *The Guardian*, 28 Sept. 2016 <www.theguardian.com/uk-news/2016/sep/28/historian-ep-thompson-denounced-communist-party-chiefs-files-show?INTCMP=sfl> (accessed 14 Oct. 2016).

nationalist leaders such as Gandhi, Nehru and the poet Rabindranath Tagore, and producing a stream of novels and histories in service to the cause, but his chief love was poetry.[12]

The elder Thompson rose, then, from modest beginnings to considerable success; but he was always something of an outsider. At Oxford he became the friend and neighbour of Robert Bridges and John Masefield (successive Poets Laureate), the young poet Robert Graves, and the eminent classical scholar Sir Gilbert Murray. He acquired a modest influence on India policy but remained a somewhat marginal figure at the university, and his anti-imperialism set him at loggerheads with its Indian Institute, which was dominated by veterans of the Indian Civil Service. This probably cost him an appointment to a senior academic position in Indian history — a matter of personal mortification but also of real practical consequence, since he never had much money. Having not received a proper university education, he was determined that his sons should not suffer the same deprivation; but this required them to perform well enough at school to win scholarships.

Under his anxious urging they did so: Frank was admitted to Oxford and Edward to Cambridge. But after completing his degree, Edward spurned the prospects of advancement within the capitalist system which his father's striving and his own academic success had won him. Instead he exiled himself to the margins of academic life by taking a job in the Department of Extra-Mural Studies of the University of Leeds, which offered courses in conjunction with the Workers' Educational Association, a charity set up to serve working men and women who (like his father) could not afford higher education. From 1948 to 1965 he would deliver lectures and conduct seminars, not in some ivory tower, but in whatever rooms and halls were available in towns throughout west Yorkshire.[13]

There is a curious symmetry between the younger Edward's life and his father's: one might say that the son embraced with enthusiasm what the father had endured with ambivalence. The father had embarked on a less than heartfelt vocation as a missionary to

---

[12] Mary Lago, *"India's Prisoner": A Biography of Edward John Thompson, 1886-1946* (Columbia and London: University of Missouri Press, 2001).

[13] Peter Searby et al., "Edward Thompson as a Teacher: Yorkshire and Warwick," in *Protest and Survival: The Historical Experience. Essays for E. P. Thompson*, ed. John Rule and Robert Malcolmson (London: Merlin Press, 1993), 1-23.

India; the son became an ardent missionary to the working men and women of his own country. The father had sought, at least in theory, to make Christians; the son brazenly declared that his purpose in becoming a teacher was to create revolutionaries.[14] But both father and son identified with their pupils rather than their employers. The father devoted himself to educating rather than converting his pupils. The son was not paid to convert his pupils — the Extra-Mural Department was not in the business of making revolutionaries — but he led a minority of his colleagues in resisting the department's efforts to impose a rigid academic standard that he thought inappropriate for adult part-time students. Despite his professed interest in creating revolutionaries, he did not, apparently, try to impose his political views on his pupils.[15]

"I had then a somewhat reverent view of Marxism as a received orthodoxy," Thompson recalled of his early years in adult education. He wrote this to explain how "some hectoring political moralisms, as well as a few Stalinist pieties," had intruded into his book on William Morris, published in 1955.[16] Apparently, though, he was too humane to be much of an ideologue. Recalling him addressing a peace rally in Leeds in 1953, a participant remembers that "he struck me then as a person devoid of dogma." For much of his adult life he battled for the soul of Marxism with comrades whose efforts to apply Marx's ideas to their own time were, he felt, too rigid and schematic to address the complexity of real life. Dorothy Thompson, his wife and fellow-toiler in the field of working-class history, records that he increasingly hesitated to call himself a Marxist: "He preferred to say that he wrote within a Marxist tradition."[17] He came to see even the book on Morris as a work of "muffled revisionism," and twenty years later he radically revised it to remove the muffler. Purged of pious excrescences, the new edition emphasized the fact that Morris had reached communism by his own route before ever

---

14 Searby et al., "Edward Thompson as a Teacher," 3.

15 Lago, *"India's Prisoner"*, 4, 178-79; Searby et al., "Edward Thompson as a Teacher," 4-7, 13.

16 Thompson, *William Morris* (1977), 769.

17 Thompson, *Morris* (1977), 769; Dorothy Thompson, "Introduction," in *the Essential E. P. Thompson*, ed. Dorothy Thompson (New York: New Press, 2001), viii, ix-x; *Visions of History: Interviews ... by MARHO, the Radical Historians Organization*, ed. Henry Abelove *et al.* (New York: Pantheon, 1984), 16-21.

hearing of Marx and had brought to it — so Thompson maintained — a libertarian idealism which Marxism, as directed by Friedrich Engels after Marx's death, had rejected to its lasting disgrace.[18]

Deep down, Thompson's views were probably always closer to those not just of Morris but of E. M. Forster, who corresponded with his father on Indian and literary matters and whose distaste for Great Men and jacks-in-office is epitomized in "What I Believe," his anti-state manifesto of 1939, with its celebrated declaration: "Two cheers for Democracy: one because it admits variety and two because it permits criticism."[19] Forster, a humanist and civil libertarian, was the first president of the National Council for Civil Liberties, founded in 1934. Ironically, he quit the Council in 1948 owing to suspicions of Communist influence,[20] but he would have appreciated the reverence for freedom of the press and for another "bourgeois" principle, the rule of law, that pervades the mature writing of E. P. Thompson.

In any case, the author of *The Making of the English Working Class*, a book destined to transform the study of history, was far from being a conventional academic. His teaching was devoted as much to English literature as to history, and Dorothy Thompson remarks that literature, especially poetry and drama, was probably always his first love. He had no record of publication in reputable academic journals, and his book on Morris had been published by the Communist party publisher, Lawrence and Wishart, not by a mainstream press. His later career was scarcely more orthodox. He taught for some years at the newly founded University of Warwick before quitting to pursue a less-than-lucrative career as a freelance scholar and political essayist "when the children were old enough for his wife to take a full-time job." His few academic articles tended to appear in the journal *Past and Present*, which he had helped to found in 1952 as a member of the Communist Party Historians Group, or in foreign journals, including some of the periodicals devoted to the "new

---

[18] Thompson, *Morris* (1977), 763-819; quotation p. 810.

[19] E. M. Forster, *Two Cheers for Democracy* (London: Edward Arnold, 1951), 79; Harish Trivedi, *Colonial Transactions: English Literature and India* (Calcutta: Papyrus, 1993), 165-203.

[20] *Encyclopedia of British and Irish Political Organizations* (London: Pinter, 2000), 1330; David Goodway, *Anarchist Seeds Beneath the Snow: Left-Libertarian Thought and British Writers from William Morris to Colin Ward* (Liverpool: Liverpool UP, 2006), 143.

social history" that had proliferated in the wake of *The Making*. And at the end of the 1970s he gave up scholarship entirely for several years, leaving several projects unfinished, in order to campaign for peace in Europe.[21] At the peak of his fame he remained, like his father, an outsider.

Thompson's history: the epic framework

Written between 1959 and 1962, *The Making* celebrates the self-sacrifice of individuals, and the determined endurance of ordinary people, as they confronted an economic and social transformation — "The Industrial Revolution" — which destroyed their way of life. By resisting, they developed self-consciousness as members of a social class: the working class. That consciousness imbued them with a shared understanding of their plight, and with a unity of purpose that would make their resistance more effective as the struggle for a better life continued.

As with its author, the circumstances of *The Making*'s birth and upbringing go far to explain what it became. Victor Gollancz, a commercial publisher of left-wing leanings, invited Thompson to write a textbook on the British labour movement from 1832 to 1945. These dates made sense in conventional terms. In 1832, Britain's essentially medieval electoral system had been reformed after a long struggle, but the reform left most working people still disfranchised. A mass movement — the Chartist Movement of 1837-48 — arose to pursue the much more radical reforms enshrined in a document called the People's Charter. The year 1945, when the Labour party first attained real political power, could be seen as the culminating date of that struggle. But Thompson persuaded Gollancz to accept a book on "Working-Class Politics, 1790-1921,"[22] and finally submitted a massive text that ended more or less where Gollancz had wanted it to begin. The planned book on working-class politics had become a book on the "making" of the working class. Why and how did that happen? And why and how, in the process of

---

[21] Dorothy Thompson, "Introduction" (quotation, p. ix); E. P. Thompson, "Diary," *London Review of Books*, 7 May 1987, 20-21. *See also* Bryan D. Palmer, *E. P. Thompson: Objections and Oppositions* (London and New York: Verso, 1994), and the select bibliographies in *Protest and Survival*, 417-21, and *E. P. Thompson: Critical Perspectives*, ed. Harvey J. Kaye and Keith McClelland (Philadelphia: Temple UP, 1990), 276-80.

[22] Goodway, *Anarchist Seeds*, 275.

transformation, did the projected textbook acquire a scope and tone that evoked *Moby Dick* and *The Lord of the Rings*?

Pondering these questions, we must bear in mind that *The Making* posed a challenge to two rival orthodoxies. One was mainstream British historiography. Primarily focused on the state — its institutions, its wars, its economy, and the political struggles within the elite to control it — this tradition paid little or no regard to the common people, who figured in the story mainly as passive objects of state policy, hapless victims of inevitable economic change, food rioters in times of scarcity, and mobs manipulated by demagogues in times of political instability. Their ideas about their lives and the world they lived in were not worth considering.

This offended the scholar who had chosen to work as an educational missionary to the people rather than a tutor to the elite. He could not expose the people to *their* history, as opposed to that of their rulers, unless he wrote it himself. He determined, therefore, to write "history from below" — a story that would give a voice to "the poor bloody infantry of the Industrial Revolution" and reveal them as articulate and rational, if not always well-informed, fighters against changes which, far from being inevitable, were imposed upon them by political power. "I am seeking to rescue the poor stockinger, the Luddite cropper, the 'obsolete' hand-loom weaver, and even the deluded follower of Joanna Southcott, from the enormous condescension of posterity," he declared in a much-quoted statement. It was a matter, not of advocating a certain view of history, but of "defending history itself."[23]

But these remarks were aimed at Marxists as well as mainstream historians. The *Communist Manifesto*, first published in 1848, includes a bold synopsis of world history based on the idea that all of human history has been the history of class struggles, which have now reached the point where society is increasingly split "into two great hostile camps, into two great classes directly facing each other: bourgeoisie and proletariat."[24] The former, the great manu-

---

23 E. P. Thompson, "History from Below," *Times Literary Supplement*, 7 Apr. 1966, 279-80 (*bis*); Thompson, *The Making of the English Working Class*, rev. ed. (Harmondsworth: Penguin, 1968), 13. Luddites were artisans who combined to destroy industrial machinery that they believed posed an unfair threat to their livelihood. Joanna Southcott was a religious prophet.
24 Karl Marx and Friedrich Engels, "The Communist Manifesto," in *Essential Works of Marxism*, ed. Arthur P. Mendel (New York: Bantam, 1961), 14.

facturers, are steadily concentrating the means of production in their hands, eliminating the smaller rivals who cannot compete with them and forcing them into the proletariat — the masses who, dispossessed of everything but their labour, must sell their labour in a buyer's market. In words that ring true in today's world of globalization and "precarious work," the *Manifesto* describes how the bourgeoisie

> has put an end to all feudal, patriarchal, idyllic relations. It has pitilessly torn asunder the motley feudal ties that bound man to his "natural superiors," and has left remaining no other nexus between man and man than naked self-interest, than callous "cash payment." It has drowned the most heavenly ecstasies of religious fervor, of chivalrous enthusiasm, of philistine sentimentalism, in the icy water of egotistical calculation. It has resolved personal worth into exchange value, and in place of the numberless indefeasible chartered freedoms, has set up that single, unconscionable freedom—Free Trade. In a word, for exploitation veiled by religious and political illusions, it has substituted naked, shameless, direct, brutal exploitation.[25]

Thompson had left the Communist Party by the time he wrote *The Making*, but he still valued the idea of history as class struggle. However, the standard Marxist account tended to see the emergence of the working class, or proletariat, as an inevitable consequence of industrialization — a result of what the Industrial Revolution had *done to* working people. It attached little more importance to their political ideas and deeds than its mainstream rival did. Thompson set out to correct both orthodoxies by constructing a grand narrative of the historical process that had engendered the Marxian vision — an account which, by highlighting the role of working people in their own emancipation, would inject historical realism into themes that the *Manifesto* treats in a couple of paragraphs. In doing so, he produced a work that stands in relation to Marxist prophecy somewhat as *Paradise Lost* stands in relation to Christian prophecy.

In considering *The Making* as an epic, this metahistorical dimension is an obvious starting-point. Like *War and Peace* and *The Lord of the Rings*, Thompson's book tells a story suspended in a wider history. He frames his narrative as an account of a critical moment not just in English but in human history, and he places it in the context of a historical vision almost as comprehensive as that of the Bible. The Marxist story of mankind does not touch on the Creation,

---

[25] "The Communist Manifesto," 15.

but it does encompass the whole of human history. After describing the contemporary situation, the *Communist Manifesto* predicts that the means by which the bourgeoisie has achieved ascendancy will inevitably lead to its downfall and the triumph of the proletariat; whereupon, heaven on earth having been achieved, human history (though not mankind) must presumably come to an end. Much as *Paradise Lost* fleshes out and naturalizes the transactions sketched in the opening chapters of the Book of Genesis, *The Making* recounts the actual history underlying the *Manifesto*'s secular version of the birth of the Messiah — a version in which humanity, collectively embodied as the working class, is to save itself. To Thompson, as a Marxist historian, the making of the English working class was as much a fact as the Creation and the Fall were facts to Milton. Both writers were inspired to imagine the story behind the facts, and each titled his story for the historical turning-point it recounts.

Like Milton, then, Thompson took on an epic subject: a founding moment, albeit of a social class, not the entire human race. And the two subjects were alike in their epistemological status: like the Bible story of the Fall, Marx's notion of a self-conscious working class was truth to those who believed, but a myth to those who did not. That was precisely why Thompson had to write his book: in order to prove that, "when every caution has been made, the outstanding fact of the period between 1790 and 1830 is the formation of 'the working class'" (212).[26] But because his subject was relatively recent history, his story had to be based on empirical evidence. No fictional treatment, no matter how closely attuned to reality, could serve his purpose.

Of course, one might suppose that *The Making* is history because Thompson was a historian. But he was no conventional historian, as we have seen; indeed, according to one commentator, *The Making* "was not written by a historian."[27] That is going too far, but no ordinary historian could have written it — it required the epic temperament, a rare attribute among academics of any discipline. We may wonder why so gifted a writer devoted so much of his life to academic history. Leaving aside temperamental causes, one

---

[26] Page references in both the text and the footnotes are to E. P. Thompson, *The Making of the English Working Class*, rev. ed. (Harmondsworth, UK: Penguin Books, 1968).
[27] Michael Merrill, E. P. Thompson's *Capital*: Political Economy in *The Making*," *Labour/Le Travail*, 71 (2013), 151.

reason may be the prestige that "scientific" history enjoyed in mid-twentieth century Marxist thought as a key to understanding the human condition. No more a conventional Marxist than a conventional historian, Thompson was not content with that history as he found it, but his response was to try to improve it. The result is a humanized history which reflects the influence of William Morris.

One source of Thompson's affinity with Morris was the dream of a more equitable — perhaps even utopian — state of social existence to be achieved by eradicating capitalism, a future which Morris had dared to imagine in his dream-fantasy *News from Nowhere* and in speculative essays. Another is to be found in another Morris dream-fantasy, *The Dream of John Ball*, which concerns the Peasants' Revolt of 1381 and one of its leaders, the reputed author of a famous rhyme which crystallizes popular resentment of social oppression: *"When Adam delved and Eve span / Who then was the gentleman?"* It is, perhaps, this second influence, with its evocation of Eden, which bears more directly on *The Making*. In accordance with Northrop Frye's formula, Thompson's story of the making of the working class is set in the context of a larger narrative or "total action"; but in the case of *The Making* there are two such stories. In addition to the Marxist narrative, and ultimately more important, there is the story — much older than the Industrial Revolution — of the people's struggle for liberty. By shifting the starting-point of his book back to the 1790s, the era of the French Revolution, Thompson was able to set the making of the English working class in the context of the age-old struggle of the Free-born Englishman, a figure redolent of vaguely historical notions of Anglo-Saxon liberty and of mythic incarnations such as that avatar of resistance to aristocratic repression and the Norman Yoke, Robin Hood.

Rather than springing fully armed from the soil of the factory system as the outcome of an inevitable historical process, Thompson's battling workers are children of catastrophe, formed in the crucible of despair.[28] He dwells on the traditional way of life that was overwhelmed by the advance of capitalism. As with the Rostov domain and Tolkien's elf havens, a world is conjured up only to be destroyed. In this case, it is one of small industrial producers

---

[28] "We can now see something of the truly catastrophic nature of the Industrial Revolution; as well as some of the reasons why the English working class took form in these years": Thompson, *The Making*, 217; and see generally 207-22. On *Despair*, see below, 221-22.

working to their own rhythm in family units or small workshops, protected by statute and custom from employment practices and machinery that would undermine their way of life; or one of rural cottagers enjoying customary rights to augment their earnings as farm labourers by cultivating small plots or grazing a beast or two on the common: in short, a real-life version of Tolkien's Shire. Like *The Lord of the Rings* and *War and Peace*, *The Making* tells a story of epochal conflict. And it is not only a conflict of "classes" — the working class versus the bourgeoisie — but one of good against evil: the struggle of mutuality, cooperation and fairness against the exploitative onslaught of *laissez-faire*, or "free-market", capitalism.

Paradise Lost: Thompson's Golden Age

In Thompson's story, as the eighteenth century advances, the traditional order is increasingly assailed by the aristocracy and gentry (the so-called *landed interest*, which controls the British Parliament) and the rising class of industrialists. In parish after parish, during more than half a century, the common lands are divided among the landowners by the so-called Enclosure Acts: legislation that wipes out the time-honoured, but generally unwritten, customary rights of the cottagers. Traditional defences for skilled trades such as weaving and framework-knitting (the production of hosiery) — safeguards against competition from cheap machine-made products and unskilled labour — are nullified by legislation or judicial fiat; old laws that prohibit profiteering in staple foodstuffs during times of scarcity are no longer enforced. Once-thriving communities are reduced to penury, the traditional family is destroyed, and employment disappears into a new world of work — the factory — where the "hand" (often a child) is subject to the discipline of the overseer and obliged to work at a pace set by the machinery. Stringent penalties are enacted against workers who try to protect their standard of living by forming trade unions. Finally, a system of poor relief (welfare) which succours the poor in their own homes, supplementing inadequate wages from public funds, is replaced by one which forces the indigent to seek relief in the parish workhouses made infamous by Charles Dickens in *Oliver Twist*.

That is the story in outline, but Thompson told it with an amplitude calculated to bring home to his readers the reality of those ravaged lives and communities. He built the world of his narrative out of thousands of details, many gathered from previously disregarded sources in the libraries of the towns where he taught; and he told his story as much as possible in the words of those who lived through it.

This method served both of his purposes in writing the book. On one hand, he was challenging a conventional wisdom that had sanitized the Industrial Revolution as an "inevitable" process of "modernization" and dismissed the stories of brutality and suffering associated with it as exaggerated or exceptional. That consensus relied heavily on generalizations from economic statistics relating to wages and prices and tended to discount specific accounts of impoverishment and abuse as anecdotal and unusual. In order to undermine those generalizations, and so discredit the complacent attitude towards the Industrial Revolution that was founded on them, Thompson recorded in painstaking detail the degradation in working conditions and quality of life that befell the victims of industrialization. On the other hand, he confronted a historically naive Marxism which ascribed the formation of the working class to the rise of the factory system. Factory workers, he pointed out, were a small minority of the industrial workforce as late as the early 1830s, when "the cotton hand-loom weavers alone still out-numbered all the men and women in spinning and weaving mills of cotton, wool, and silk combined" (219). In the first third of the century, the hand-loom weavers as a whole constituted the largest occupational group in British industry (only farm labourers and domestic servants were more numerous). Thompson set out to shift the focus from the factory workers to this much larger group, conventionally dismissed as hapless and benighted opponents of industrialization.

Accordingly, the chapter on the weavers is crucial to his story. Cotton and woollen weaving, the main branches of the craft, were concentrated in the villages of the Pennine Hills, the range that divides the county of Lancashire, on the west side of northern England, from Yorkshire on the east. Wool-weaving was concentrated on the Yorkshire side, with its ample moorland sheep-grazing; cotton-weaving throve on the Lancashire side, in the uplands surrounding the mushrooming cotton-spinning metropolis of Manchester, which acquired that status through its proximity to the great Atlantic port of Liverpool. At the beginning of the nineteenth century, weavers were skilled craft workers who plied their trade in their own homes, often as a family enterprise, or in small village workshops. By mid-century, however, the industry was almost entirely factory-based and domestic manufacture virtually extinct.

The social catastrophe produced by this sudden occupational obsolescence became a focus of humanitarian concern in the 1830s, when it was investigated by several parliamentary committees. The evidence was published, and histories based on it tended to portray the hand-loom weavers as wretched victims of technological change, pitiably clinging to an occupation that had lost its economic value. Thompson told a different story, one in which the weavers and their families were victims not just of technological change but of *exploitation* (that charged term from the *Communist Manifesto*) by capitalists applying a ruthless ideology with the connivance of the state. It is a story, too, in which the weavers figure not merely as wretched but, more importantly, as heroic combatants in resistance movements from Luddism to Chartism.

Observing that "the history of the weavers in the nineteenth century is haunted by the legend of better days" (297), Thompson notes the conventional wisdom that the legend was in general a myth — that is, that the weavers' memories of a "golden age" had no basis in historical reality. Asserting that so pervasive a memory was unlikely to be totally false, he unfolds a story of tragic irony: there was indeed a golden age, but in it were sowed the seeds of the weavers' ruin. The mechanization of spinning in the cotton and wool industries produced a great increase in the output of yarn and consequently in the demand for weaving. The boom brought prosperity to the weaving trade, but it allowed the merchants who put out the yarn for weaving to subvert the traditional relationship between master-weavers and journeymen by employing the latter directly. "This was, in wool as in cotton, the 'golden age' of the journeyman weaver" (302).

However, the prosperity that liberated the journeyman also attracted many new hands to the trade — including, in Lancashire particularly, Irish immigrants — whom the putters-out were happy to employ without regard for traditional apprenticeship restrictions. When the weavers tried to enforce those restrictions in the courts, they found the judiciary increasingly loath to act on them even before Parliament finally repealed the centuries-old laws that enshrined them. On the other hand, attempts to combat their impoverishment by industrial action — for instance, by striking in support of a minimum wage, as the cotton-weavers did in 1808 — were hampered by new legislation which outlawed trade unions as criminal conspiracies. Wages were screwed lower and lower, yet even so "the number of weavers continued to increase over the first three decades of the nineteenth century; for weaving, next to general labouring, was the grand resource of the northern unemployed ... Agricultural workers, demobilized soldiers, Irish immigrants — all continued to swell the labour force." A strike in 1818 won short-lived concessions at the cost of the imprisonment of several of the strike leaders, but "thereafter wages continued to be beaten down ... until the 1830s."[29]

After a few pages illustrating the misery inflicted on once-thriving communities, Thompson points out "the sheer scale of the tragedy that was enacted. Weaving communities, some ... with 300 or 400 years of continuous existence, some of much more recent date but with, none the less, their own cultural patterns and traditions — were literally being extinguished" (321). He sketches this culture — "Every weaving district had its weaver-poets, biologists, mathematicians, musicians, geologists, botanists" (322) — and calls the roll of half-a-dozen labour leaders who came out of it, before ending the section with what can only be called a peroration.

> The *making* of these later leaders was in communities of this kind ...They had, like the city artisan, a sense of lost status, as memories of their "golden age" lingered; and, with this, they set a high premium on the values of independence ... But they had, more than the city artisan, a deep social egalitarianism. As their way of life, in the better years, had been shared by the community, so their sufferings were those of the whole community ... This gave a particular moral resonance to their protest, whether voiced in Owenite or biblical language; they appealed to essential rights and elementary notions of human fellowship and conduct rather than to sectional interests. It was as a whole community that they demanded betterment, and utopian notions of redesigning society at a stroke ... swept through them like fire on the common. But essentially the dream which arose in many different forms was the same — a community of independent small producers, exchanging their products without the distortions of masters and middlemen. As late as 1848 a Barnsley linen-weaver ... declared at the Chartist National Convention that when the Charter was won "They would divide the land into small farms, and give every man an opportunity of getting a living by the sweat of his brow."[30]

---

[29] *Making*, 307, 308-9. Here Thompson is describing the plight of the cotton weavers, but the woollen and worsted weavers underwent a similar decline with a fifteen to twenty-year lag.

[30] *Making*, 326; italics in original. The word *Owenite* refers to the contemporary socialist Robert Owen.

We ran across this Chartist ideal when talking about Tolkien, and we noted the egalitarianism that distinguishes it from paternalist critiques of industrialism. It is a dream of the Shire without its gentry — a Shire in which Frodo Baggins will have the opportunity to dig his own potatoes.[31]

Thompson's sensitivity to the moral sensibilities underlying the workers' protest, and to the culture that gave rise to those sensibilities, epitomizes the revolutionary quality of his work. No earlier historian had distinguished the peculiar moral resonance of the weavers' protest from that of the city artisans, because none had paid much attention to what either group thought. The close-up focus reaches beyond the wage and price statistics, which conventional wisdom touts as a truer guide to the social effects of the Industrial Revolution, to yield a poignant story, which tells not just of a tragedy but of a crime — a crime in which the state is an accomplice.

The state's complicity is a constant theme in Thompson's story. In the chapter on the hand-loom weavers, he emphasizes it in order to challenge the conventional view that their suffering was an inevitable consequence of technological change — that the power-loom was simply a more efficient producer of textiles than the most adept hand-loom weaver, and so their craft, ancient and honourable as it was, was doomed. Thompson points out that by the 1830s, when steam power actually began to displace them, the weavers — especially in cotton — had already been subjected to decades of wage-cutting and of degradation in their working conditions. They did not see their suffering as inevitable; they saw it as a consequence of the state's refusal to protect them from exploitation by the employers while at the same time criminalizing their efforts to protect themselves by collective action. They were the victims of wicked men, and of a political system in which they had no voice.

But why were the capitalists so privileged in a system in which, even after the epochal Reform Act of 1832, the landed interest was still more powerful than the *Communist Manifesto*'s rampant bourgeoisie? The answer first appears in a pivotal chapter, aptly entitled "Exploitation," which introduces Thompson's discussion of industrialization and the rise of the ideology of *laissez-faire*:

> Throughout this time there are three, and not two, great influences simultaneously at work. There is the tremendous increase in population ...

---

[31] See above, 59, 96.

> There is the Industrial Revolution, in its technological aspects. And
> there is the political *counter*-revolution, from 1792-1832 (216).

It was the workers' misfortune that the Industrial Revolution coincided with the French Revolution and the answering upsurge of
political radicalism in Britain. As a result, the politically dominant
landed interest and the industrial bourgeoisie put aside their
mutual antipathy and joined forces to repress the masses. The
landed interest supported the bourgeoisie in its exploitation of the
workers, while the bourgeoisie supported the landed interest in its
opposition to political reform. In Thompson's view, this political
conjuncture played as large a part as the water-wheel and the
steam-engine in shaping the consciousness and institutions of the
working class. That is why his story had to begin in the 1790s.

Epic scale

Our initial exploration of *The Making* has revealed the outline of a
saga of conflict between good and evil, featuring a vanished golden
age and set in a total action of vast temporal extent. These are three
defining features of the epic of disaffection. Besides this, the structure and sheer scale of the narrative enhance its epic character. The
story of the workers' struggle for political power, and of their resistance to the abuses that industrialism brought, is told in abundant
detail and with a wealth of allusion to events peripheral to the main
narrative. It unfolds in three successively longer parts, each with its
own title and title-page adorned with art and thematic epigraphs.

In classic epic fashion, the narrative commences *in medias res*
with the founding meeting in 1792 of the London Corresponding
Society (LCS), a body set up to promote parliamentary reform in
collaboration with similar societies throughout the land. At a tavern
off The Strand, nine men enjoy a bread-and-cheese supper, washed
down with porter and followed by a pipe — Tillyard's simple
sensualities indeed — before settling down to adopt a constitution.
The prime mover and first secretary of the society, a forty-year-old
journeyman shoemaker named Thomas Hardy, walks home with
the members' weekly subscriptions — a penny each — in his
pocket. Six months later the Society will claim more than two
thousand members, all committed to the pursuit of manhood
suffrage: the right of every adult male not disqualified by insanity,
criminality, or nobility to vote in parliamentary elections (19).

All this and more in just over a page; then we jump ahead two years. Sundry dignitaries appear at the shoemaker's home with two police officers to arrest him for high treason. They ransack the place for evidence and carry off, along with their prisoner, four large silk handkerchiefs filled with letters and a corn-sack full of pamphlets, books and manuscripts. Mrs. Hardy is pregnant and stays in bed. On to Whitehall, where Hardy and some fellow-prisoners are interrogated by His Majesty's Privy Council, including Prime Minister William Pitt, the Home Secretary (the cabinet minister in charge of homeland security), and England's top judge.

Here our witness is the poet John Thelwall, friend of the greater poets Wordsworth and Coleridge, reporting from prison to a newspaper called the *Morning Post*. Quoting Thelwall, Thompson recounts how the prisoner, after refusing to answer questions,

> turned his back on the august company and "began to contemplate a drawing in water-colours." The Prime Minister dismissed him and summoned for interrogation a fourteen-year-old lad, Henry Eaton, who had been living with the Thelwalls. But the boy stood his ground and "entered into a political harangue against Mr. Pitt; upbraiding him with having taxed the people to an enormous extent" (21).

A dozen prisoners go to the Tower, and then to Newgate Prison, to await trial. Mrs. Hardy dies in childbirth from shock sustained when their home is besieged by a loyalist mob. Brought to trial after several months in prison, the widower is acquitted by a jury of London citizens and drawn in triumph through the streets. Other acquittals follow, and the remaining prosecutions are abandoned. But the repression continues; the LCS — now a mass organization — is outlawed; public meetings are banned. The agitation for parliamentary reform collapses under the pressure. "It seemed, after all, that 'tradesmen, shopkeepers, and mechanics' had no right to obtain a Parliamentary Reform" (22).

Thompson pauses to ponder these events. As a political initiative of the disenfranchised masses, and an organization with "unlimited" membership dedicated to the pursuit of manhood suffrage, the LCS posed a fundamental challenge to a political order based on landownership. "Such a challenge was bound to lead on to the charge of high treason." Yet it was not unprecedented. The narrative plunges nearly 150 years into the past, to an earlier time when manhood suffrage was on the agenda: the Putney Debates of 1647, during the English Revolution, when members of the New Model Army, finally victorious over the forces of King Charles I, disputed over the future constitution of England. On that occasion the Levellers (whose leading voice was John Lilburne, an exponent of the myth of the Free-born Englishman[32]) had been defeated by the Grandees (the most prominent of whom was Oliver Cromwell). The Grandees' victory had preserved the oligarchy of landed and commercial property, the restoration of the monarchy in 1660 had confirmed it, and the "Glorious Revolution" of 1688 — which secured a constitutional monarchy against the threat of Stuart absolutism — had entrenched it. To Thompson, the movement headed by the LCS was no new phenomenon but a resurrection of the Leveller challenge in a new world of paper money, government debt, rapid industrialization, and — above all — the French Revolution, with Thomas Paine taking up Lilburne's role. Significantly, an organization founded later in 1792 to combat the Jacobin threat epitomized by the LCS was called the Association for Preserving Liberty and Property Against Republicans and Levellers (22-27).

Having set the scene with this sprightly introduction, Thompson does not press ahead with his tale. Instead, he dives into the past again with three chapters on the popular culture that nourished the radical resurgence of the 1790s. First he reviews the religious developments that fuelled the revolutionary politics of that decade and the subsequent growth of working-class consciousness. Protestant Dissent, epitomized by John Bunyan's *Pilgrim's Progress* (1678), nurtured in its antipathy to Church and State a slumbering radicalism that might awaken when conditions were propitious. Bunyan's book and Paine's *Rights of Man* were "the two foundation texts of the English working-class movement," and nearly all the movement's theorists emerged from the London Dissenting tradition. The upsurge of Methodist revivalism within the Church of England also fostered radical politics, despite the political conservatism of its leader, John Wesley.[33]

A popular political culture also fostered the resurgent radicalism. One typical form of collective popular action was resistance to merchants who tried to stockpile foodstuffs and force up prices in times of scarcity. A traditional behaviour marked by special rituals, such as carrying aloft a loaf decked with black ribbon and an appro-

---

[32] Rachel Foxley, "John Lilburne and the Citizenship of 'Free-Born Englishmen,'" *Historical Journal*, 47:4 (2004), 849-74.
[33] *Making*, 28-58 (quotation p. 34).

priate slogan, the food riot might entail seizing stocks of the scarce commodity (usually wheat, flour or bread) or taking control of a market and forcing the sale of foodstuffs at what was held to be the fair or customary price. Thompson details several instances, including one when "a great many Women" prevented London-bound grain ships from leaving a south-western port. Such actions were legitimized by the old paternalist "moral economy," a system enshrined in a long-established body of law which prohibited profiteering but which, in the later eighteenth century, judges were no readier to enforce against the supposed "laws" of supply and demand than they were to uphold apprenticeship regulations.[34]

In the large cities, especially London, a more common form of collective action was political violence against an unpopular group, institution or individual, be it the government, or a religious minority such as Methodists or Catholics, or (as with the "Church and King" riot that resulted in the death of Thomas Hardy's wife) some political group that Establishment propaganda had demonized as an enemy of the people. Even the most reactionary rioters generally "felt themselves, in some obscure way, to be defending the 'Constitution' against alien elements who threatened their 'birthright'" — a birthright of freedom, as they fondly imagined it. "Patriotism, nationalism, even bigotry and repression, were all clothed in the rhetoric of liberty" (85).

This "liberty" did not politically enfranchise the common man or preclude the severe repression of persons and ideas that the authorities saw as a danger to political stability. However, it entailed certain "notions which Old Corruption felt bound to flatter and yet which were to prove dangerous to it in the long run." (*Old Corruption* was the populist journalist William Cobbett's term for the political and social elite.) Those notions included constitutional (as opposed to absolute) monarchy; equality before the law; elements of due process such as trial by jury (Hardy and Thelwall were, after all, acquitted) and freedom from arbitrary arrest, search and seizure; some limited liberty of thought, speech and conscience; and the freedom even of people who had no vote to express themselves tumultuously at election time. The Glorious Revolution had, after all, been a revolution and could therefore be construed as legitimizing violent resistance to oppression.

---

[34] *Making*, 59-73 (quotation p. 72).

But the Glorious Revolution had also entrenched the rule of Big Property, so manhood suffrage advocates tended to reach back beyond 1688. The silversmith John Baxter, who was arraigned for high treason in 1794 along with Thomas Hardy, published two years later a long history of England which supposed that "originally the constitution must have been free" and that all history was the history of its corruption. With its premise of a political Garden of Eden, this is the Bible story of the Fall of Man translated into politics. Other reformers advanced the theory of the Norman Yoke — the idea that a "free" constitution based on manhood suffrage had been suppressed by William the Conqueror, Duke of Normandy, after ousting the Anglo-Saxon King Harold in 1066 (94-95).

Most radical of all, however, were those who relied not on historical precedent — the so-called Ancient Constitution — but on natural right, thereby arguing not just for the rights of Englishmen but for the Rights of Man. Thomas Paine's book of that name appeared in 1791 and sold briskly. Paine did away with monarchy, the hereditary principle, and the traditional rights of the great landowners and the Established Church. His thoroughgoing egalitarianism extended to social innovations such as a graduated income tax (at a time when Britain had no income tax at all), family allowances, public education, old-age pensions, and maternity benefit (99).

Only now, after this long review of a back-story reaching back in myth to the Creation has established an epic temporal depth, does Thompson "return to Thomas Hardy and his friends who met in 'The Bell' in Exeter Street in January 1792" (111). With that, the main story begins at last. A chapter entitled "Planting the Liberty Tree," nearly a hundred pages long — nearly as long as all that has gone before — tells of the Corresponding Societies and their struggle in the 1790s for political rights for all men. We read of the sensational impact of Paine's *Rights of Man*; the rise of a popular movement for manhood suffrage; Prime Minister Pitt's long-delayed decision to prosecute Paine for sedition *in absentia* (the author had fled to France and got himself elected to the Revolutionary legislature); the intensifying repression in 1793 after the guillotining of the king and queen of France; the resilience and continued growth of the reform movement; its tactical retreat from Paine's natural-rights egalitarianism back to the less radical ground of the "original constitution."

The scene shifts to Scotland, where judges are less scrupulous, juries more malleable, and the letter of the law friendlier to repression. Two reformers are sentenced to long terms of transportation.

The LCS sends two delegates north to show solidarity. They suffer the same fate. Then we re-visit the arrest of Hardy and his confrères; a newspaper jeers at Mrs. Hardy's death; the acquittal of the London prisoners revives the movement. And so it goes: a succession of mass demonstrations, riot, and repression punctuated by external events — a dialectic of challenge and response — until the final collapse of the reform movement late in the decade. By the end of Part One ("The Liberty Tree"), the Corresponding Societies have been suppressed and nearly all the radical leaders are either exiled or in prison.

Thompson's argument against the historians

In *The Making* there is always an argument thrusting through the surface of the narrative. If *War and Peace* is a story distended by an argument, Thompson's book is essentially an argument in the shape of a story, or perhaps several arguments adding up to one big one. In both cases, of course, it is an argument against "the historians."

Thompson makes one argument simply by noticing the political thought of people whom orthodox history dismissed as insignificant. His insistence on the seminal importance of Paine's ideas challenges a received wisdom that rates Paine as a marginal figure next to Edmund Burke, the theorist whose diatribe against the new French republic *Rights of Man* was written to rebut. But Paine is only the beginning of the story:

> These artisans took the doctrines of Paine to their extreme — absolute democracy, root-and-branch opposition to monarchy and aristocracy, to the State and to taxation. In times of enthusiasm, they were the hard centre of a movement which drew the support of thousands of small shopkeepers, of printers and booksellers, medical men, schoolmasters, engravers, small masters, and Dissenting clergy at one end; and of porters, coal-heavers, labourers, soldiers and sailors at the other (172).

Likewise, when Thompson goes on to say that "the movement produced only two considerable theorists," the very suggestion that it produced theorists at all is a challenge to received wisdom. And who are those theorists? One is the poet Thelwall, who, even after his trial for high treason in 1794, courageously presses a cogent and uncompromising Jacobinism upon his audience in the teeth of the gathering repression; who insists that the French Terror was a consequence, not of Jacobinism, but of "the old leaven of revenge, corruption and suspicion which was generated by the systematic cruelties of the old despotism" (174); who advocates the right of working people to trade unions, education, and an eight-hour working day. Emphasizing social and economic issues more than Paine did, Thelwall "took Jacobinism to the borders of Socialism" (175). The other theorist is the schoolteacher Thomas Spence, also arrested in 1794, who proclaims the rights of women and children as well as men and calls for the abolition of private property in land.

By the end of Part One, Thompson has done a fair job of rescuing the plebeian radicalism of the 1790s, and the political and social traditions that nourished it, from "the enormous condescension of posterity." But dwelling on the dignity and importance of British Jacobin thought is not enough: what matters most is its continuity with both earlier and later radicalism. Thompson rejects the idea that manifestations of popular discontent throughout this period are just a mindless response to hard times. Far from it — they express a tradition of popular resistance traceable back to the Levellers. And although historians have scoffed at the idea, it is in part a *revolutionary* tradition (183). Both Thelwall and Spence are bridges to the post-war movement for parliamentary reform. The former is politically active, though in a less revolutionary vein, into the 1830s. Spence dies in 1814; but he and his disciples are the only Jacobin group to maintain a continuous existence throughout the wars against Revolutionary and Napoleonic France, and his chief disciple, Thomas Evans, had been a secretary of the LCS in the 1790s. Two other Jacobins — John Gale Jones, a surgeon and author, and John Frost, an attorney — also link the LCS and the post-war movement, but the Spencean Philanthropists above all are a manifestation of something to which historical orthodoxy is blind: an English revolutionary underground.

Thompson's insistence on the existence of a revolutionary underground was deeply subversive of conventional wisdom. The orthodox interpretation of English history celebrated a national character marked by an instinctive moderation and a genius for compromise. Alone among nations, it rejoiced, Britain had achieved a free and democratic society without bloody revolution. An ascendant middle class had peacefully loosened the aristocracy's grasp on power and then drawn the working classes into political citizenship as the latter became "respectable," and the working classes were willing partners in this process of co-option. Thus J. D. Chambers warned of "ideological element that verges on sheer fantasy ... a fixation on revolution as a political method, and an inextinguishable thirst for bourgeois blood, both of which are foreign, I should have thought, to the genius of the English working-class movement." This mattered because students were not just reading the book — they were buying it, even at the high price of three and a half guineas. Chambers feared they might read nothing else.[35]

To Thompson, this image of a working class compliant in its own co-option was the fantasy. As we have seen, he told a different story — one in which the middle-class reformers, frightened of the working people but too weak to break the aristocratic monopoly on their own, had first combined with the landed interest to suppress the popular reformers and later, when stronger, had exploited the menace of the popular movement to coerce the ruling class into a reform that empowered the middle class while excluding the people. It was prolonged oppression in this specific form, not some native moderation and genius for compromise, that had made the English working class what it was.

That is one of Thompson's arguments against the historians, but there is another, no less important. In Thompson's telling, even as Jacobin ideas are driven from the city streets, they take root in the weaving villages, in the workshops of the Nottingham framework knitters and Yorkshire croppers, and in the Lancashire cotton-mills.

> Isolated from the other classes, radical mechanics, artisans and labourers had perforce to nourish traditions and forms of organization of their own. So that, while the years 1791-5 provided the democratic impulse, it was in the repression years that we can speak of a distinct 'working-class consciousness' maturing ... By 1811 we can witness the simultaneous emergence of a new popular Radicalism and of a newly-militant trade unionism (199).

It is from the exposure of distressed artisans and factory workers to Jacobin ideas that the English working class emerges. Part One ends with a statement by John Thelwall that seems prophetic:

> Monopoly, and the hideous accumulation of capital in a few hands ... carry in their own enormity, the seeds of cure ... Whatever presses men together ... is favourable to the diffusion of knowledge, and ultimately promotive of human liberty. Hence every large workshop and

---

35 J. D. Chambers, "The Making of the English Working Class," *History*, 51 (1966), 188. Thompson answered his critics in a Postscript to the revised edition.

> manufactory is a sort of political society, which no act of parliament can silence, and no magistrate disperse (203).

And in a segue worthy of Tolstoy's discussed earlier,[36] Part Two begins with a series of remarks in the same vein by observers as various as the nobleman Viscount Torrington in 1792 and the German manufacturer's son Friedrich Engels, Karl Marx's collaborator, in 1844. Evidently, the idea that capitalism contains the seeds of its own downfall anticipates the *Communist Manifesto* by more than half a century.

Strikingly, it is only now, at the beginning of Part Two, that Thompson fully states his grand themes. He comments:

> However different their judgements of value, conservative, radical and socialist observers suggested the same equation: steam power and the cotton-mill = new working class ... It is as if the English nation entered a crucible in the 1790s and emerged after the Wars in a different form. Between 1811 and 1813, the Luddite crisis; in 1817 the Pentridge Rising; in 1819, Peterloo; throughout the next decade the proliferation of trade union activity, Owenite propaganda, Radical journalism, the Ten Hours Movement, the revolutionary crisis of 1831-32; and, beyond that, the multitude of movements which made up Chartism. It is, perhaps, the scale and intensity of this multiform popular agitation which has, more than anything else, given rise ... to the sense of some catastrophic change (209).

As it happens, this list of events and developments is to be the main subject of Thompson's story; but the story is postponed until Part Three. Thompson must first set the scene by sketching the sufferings inflicted on working people by the economic tyranny of "market forces." Hence the title of the chapter that opens Part Two: "Exploitation". Hence, too, the title of Part Two as a whole — "The Curse of Adam" — and the bleak Bible verse that is its epigraph.[37]

And of course, he has set up the equation *steam power + cotton-mill = new working class* only to dismiss it for ignoring the artisans of the industrial villages, whose traditions made them so receptive to Jacobin egalitarianism. This idea is crucial to his story, because it places the myth of the Free-born Englishman at the heart of the making of the English working class.

------

[36] See above, 147.

[37] *Genesis* 3:19: "In the sweat of thy face shalt thou eat bread, till thou return unto the ground; for out of it wast thou taken: for dust thou art, and unto dust shalt thou return."

The changing productive relations and working conditions of the Industrial Revolution were imposed, not upon raw material, but upon the free-born Englishman — and the free-born Englishman as Paine had left him or as the Methodists had moulded him. The factory hand or stockinger was also the inheritor of Bunyan, of remembered village rights, of notions of equality before the law, of craft traditions. He was the object of massive religious indoctrination and the creator of political traditions. The working class made itself as much as it was made (213).

And in factories and blighted industrial villages alike, it was shaped as much by politics as by the water-wheel and the steam-engine — in particular, by the repressive alliance of the large landowners and the industrial bourgeoisie.

Thompson pursues these ideas through three chapters on the experiences of different parts of the labour force (including the weavers, reviewed above), one chapter on different aspects of the standard-of-living controversy, and then one on the counter-revolutionary force of Methodism, to which Thompson ascribes a sublimating effect that he provocatively calls "psychic masturbation" (the very word sent a shudder through the ivory towers). The variety of topics makes Part Two diffuse in structure compared to the others, but it is unified by its themes, of which there are three main ones: Community, Exploitation, and Despair. "Community" is the title of the final chapter of the section, but the theme pervades the whole as an integral feature of the traditional world that Exploitation destroys. Despair, of course, arises from that destruction. The word figures in the title of a long section of a chapter on Methodism: "The Chiliasm of Despair." Along with "psychic masturbation," the term encapsulates Thompson's controversial thesis that working people oscillated between a rebellious determination to build a good life in this world and a hyper-religious sublimation of their daily misery which dwelt on the reward awaiting the submissive sufferer in the world to come. The final chapter addresses not only the broad theme of Community, meaning the ties that bound traditional society as a whole, but also the so-called friendly societies and other mutual aid institutions of the nascent working class — shelters which, in the social wasteland wrought by Exploitation, "the working people, in antagonism to their labour and to their masters, built for themselves."

This phrase rounds off the tiny four-page section that sums up Part Two as a whole. The section is titled "Myriads of Eternity," a phrase borrowed from William Blake. *The Making* is dotted with literary allusions, mainly to Thompson's favourite romantic poets. Wordsworth is cited to illustrate the disillusionment of the middle-class intelligentsia with the revolutionary moment — an alienation lapsing first into quietism and then into reconciliation with the status quo. Byron, Coleridge, Shelley and Southey all make appearances. To illustrate Despair, Thompson turns to Blake — an engraver (and thus an artisan) as well as a poet, and a radical Dissenter very much in the cultural line of descent from the Levellers. Thompson's account of the crushing of the Jacobins — with whom Blake, though not personally militant, sympathized sufficiently to come within a hair's breadth of being prosecuted for seditious libel — is accompanied by these lines from *The Four Zoas*, Blake's Bible-based mythopoeic history:

> What is the price of Experience? do men buy it for a song?
> Or wisdom for a dance in the street? No, it is bought with the price
> Of all that a man hath, his house, his wife, his children.
> Wisdom is sold in the desolate market where none come to buy,
> And in the wither'd field, where the farmer plows for bread in vain.

And at the end of Part Two, from the same source, Thompson gives us Blake's lament for the crushing of Community, and the craft industry that sustained it, by the emergent industrialism:

> ... all the arts of Life they changed into the arts of death.
> The hourglass contemn'd because its simple workmanship
> Was as the workmanship of the plowman and the water wheel
> That raises water into Cisterns, broken & burn'd in fire
> Because its workmanship was like the workmanship of the
> shepherds
> And in their stead intricate wheels invented, Wheel without wheel,
> To perplex youth in their outgoings & to bind to labours
> Of day & night the myriads of Eternity, that they might file
> And polish brass & iron hour after hour, laborious workmanship,
> Kept ignorant of the use that they might spend the days of wisdom
> In sorrowful drudgery to obtain a scanty pittance of bread,
> In ignorance to view a small portion & think that All,
> And call it demonstration, blind to the simple rules of life.

Thompson comments: "These 'myriads of eternity' seem at times to have been sealed in their work like a tomb."[38] And there they languish, under the Curse of Adam, at the end of Part Two.

---

[38] *Making*, 192, 488. Both extracts are given as they appear in the book.

"Secret History"

Thus the *story* of the making of the working class, when it finally gets under way in Part Three, is a story of resistance, a march against Despair. This Part is nearly as long as its two predecessors combined, creating a structure that consigns all that has gone before to the status of a prologue, somewhat as Tolstoy's expanded treatment of 1812 does to the first half of *War and Peace*. It also brings us to the source of the book's character as an epic of disaffection and a dissenting history.

Yet even now the main story is deferred, since Part Three begins by picking up the account of popular radicalism commenced in Part One. Thompson relates how the radicals adapted to the anti-Jacobin repression by rallying behind respectable figureheads of Radical sympathies in a series of electoral contests in the London-area constituencies of Middlesex and Westminster. In Westminster in particular, an urban constituency with a large electorate, the Radicals could exercise a decisive influence through a political organization, the Westminster Committee. But the heartland of the Industrial Revolution was in the north, where the mushrooming factory towns had not yet, for the most part, acquired municipal government or parliamentary representation. The chapter ends: "The Westminster Committee had no message for the Luddites. North of the [River] Trent we find the illegal tradition" (514).

Only now does Thompson commence the story of this "illegal tradition," the heart of the book. It unfolds in two massive chapters, each well over a hundred pages long. They recount what at first sight is an odd mix of events, starting with the execution in London of Colonel Despard and others for high treason in 1803, ending with the execution of Arthur Thistlewood and several other Spencean Philanthropists in the same place and for the same offence in 1820, and taking in the Luddite risings of 1811-12 and the Pentridge rising of 1817, both of which occurred hundreds of miles to the north. These and other, apparently disparate, incidents are forged into a single story by Thompson's thesis of an underground revolutionary tradition that historians have overlooked.

Thompson suggests three reasons for its neglect. Firstly, the main evidence comes from a government notorious at the time for its use of informers, spies, and even *agents provocateurs*. Historians have therefore dismissed it as a concocted or exaggerated excuse to suppress peaceable reform agitation. Secondly, historians have relied too much on the memoirs of Francis Place, the organizing genius of the Westminster Committee. As a young journeyman tailor, Place had been active in the LCS; but later, as a prosperous master tailor, he gravitated towards the moderate political opposition and fell out with the more extreme radicals. Place's memoirs play up his own role and belittle his rivals' contribution; and besides, mutual suspicion meant that much went on without his knowledge. Finally, there is the simple fact that the organized resistance was necessarily covert and took pains to cover its traces, although not always successfully (508-14).

For these reasons, earlier historians simply dismissed the reports of spies and informers as fabrications by scoundrels who depended for their bread and butter on giving the government what it wanted, and they discounted the panicked reports of provincial magistrates as groundless hysteria. Thompson sees something else: far from being duped by a series of impostors, the government showed extraordinary skill in forestalling serious revolutionary developments and acquiring intelligence on insurrectionary conspiracies that were very real. Accordingly, the "secret political tradition" figures in history as a series of pitiful or contemptible fiascos: Despard, Pentridge, Thistlewood's conspiracy. But the authorities were much less successful in penetrating labour organizations, and where the secret political tradition effected a junction with the secret *industrial* tradition it has been largely invisible to history. As a result, "From Despard to Thistlewood and beyond there is a tract of secret history, buried like the Great Plain of Gwaelod beneath the sea."[39] This "secret history" brings us to the conjuncture foreshadowed at the end of Part One: the simultaneous emergence by 1811 of a new popular radicalism and a newly militant trade unionism. For what is foreshadowed is Luddism, mistaken by historians for a purely industrial movement with no political goals but in fact a "quasi-insurrectionary movement, which continually trembled on the edge of ulterior revolutionary objectives" (604).

In Thompson's story, the destruction of time-honoured legal safeguards for skilled labour, sharpened in 1799 and 1800 by legislation outlawing collective bargaining, alienates the victimized workers from the state. Unionism is driven underground, where the Jacobins lurk. Luddism, the recourse of men who have been denied justice in court and in Parliament, is the result. To the croppers, skilled workers in the woollen manufacture, "Ned Ludd was the

---

[39] *Making*, 529-42 (quotation, p. 542).

defender of ancient right, the upholder of a lost constitution" (578-79) — that is, a *political* hero. A song from Nottinghamshire, the site of Sherwood Forest, projects Ludd as a modern Robin Hood, a champion of "Custom and Law," anxious for peace but driven by official corruption to fight for justice as an outlaw. Thompson portrays the Luddites as upholders of a moral economy enshrined in a social compact against the anti-social innovations of an insurgent capitalism. The machines and industrial practices they oppose are *wicked*, not just because they threaten livelihoods but because they mock a complex and arduous craft and de-humanize its adepts. (One thinks of Tolkien's orcs, created by the Enemy as an impious parody of elves.) The stockingers, or framework-knitters, destroy only machines that are used to make cheap shoddy goods or are operated by unqualified labour.

Throughout the story, Thompson insists that the Luddite movement is both politically aware and linked to the underground political tradition. The campaign to uphold "the customs of the trade" is conducted in the courts, and in the lobbies and committee-rooms of Parliament, as well as by night-time raids on workshops. The workers enjoy the backing of public opinion; their political efforts are financially supported by a cross-section of the community, including a "handsome" contribution from Lord Byron, whose maiden speech in the House of Lords is a scathing attack on the government's heavy-handed yet ineffectual response to the upsurge of machine-breaking. Above all, their resistance to "market forces" is underpinned by a coherent social theory:

> What was at issue was the "freedom" of the capitalist to destroy the customs of the trade, whether by new machinery, by the factory-system, or by unrestricted competition, beating down wages, undercutting his rivals, and undermining standards of craftsmanship. We are so accustomed to the notion that it was both inevitable and "progressive" that trade should have been freed ... from "restrictive practices", that it requires an effort of imagination to understand that the "free" factory-owner or large hosier or cotton-manufacturer, who built his fortune by these means, was regarded not only with jealousy but as a man engaging in *immoral* and *illegal* practices. The notion of the just price and the fair wage lived longer among the "lower orders" than is sometimes supposed ... They could see no natural law by which one man, or a few men, could engage in practices which brought manifest injury to their fellows (600-1).

As for the links between Luddism and the political underground, Thompson does not need to unearth evidence of them: his task, rather, is to discredit the conventional wisdom which dismisses that evidence as fabrications by spies and informers. Bringing the Free-born Englishman into play, he is able to argue that the politicization of Luddism was only natural, and that historians have discounted the possibility out of a mixture of ignorance and sheer prejudice.

In 1815, with Napoleon finally defeated and machine-breaking in temporary remission, a new chapter begins. "The Wars ended amidst riots. They had lasted, with one interval, for twenty-three years ... Thousands of disbanded soldiers and sailors returned to find unemployment in their villages. The next four years are the heroic age of popular Radicalism" (660). This radicalism is not the minority propaganda of the 1790s, identified with a few organizations and writers. By now the claims of Paine's *Rights of Man* are taken for granted, so the rhetoric of resistance concentrates on the many different ways in which the state is organized for the benefit of "a venal, self-interested clique of landowners, courtiers and placemen" (660) — William Cobbett's Old Corruption. It blames corruption for high taxes and high taxes for unemployment. The London crowd retains its radical temper, and the capital becomes again, as in the 1790s, a base for nation-wide political proselytizing. What is novel is the upsurge of popular political consciousness in the Midlands and the north, including the heartlands of the Industrial Revolution. The new chapter is largely about the interplay between London and the emergent northern radicalism.

This phase of the story starts with Major John Cartwright, a country gentleman and former naval and militia officer, who is also a veteran democrat and staunch believer in the Ancient Constitution. In 1812 and 1813, and again in 1815, the septuagenarian Radical tours the centres of Luddite disaffection, hoping to channel the popular discontent into a campaign for manhood suffrage. To this end he sets up Hampden Clubs (named after John Hampden, a seventeenth-century tax resister and revolutionary leader) in the cities and towns he visits. These gather strength with the onset of the post-war economic recession in 1816, and a meeting of delegates is convened in London in January 1817.

In London the Spencean Jacobins emerge from the wartime shadows and hold three mass demonstrations at the end of 1816, the last of which spawns the Spa Fields Riots, a semi-spontaneous, booze-fuelled attack on the Tower of London. The disorder prompts a government crackdown and frightens middle-class reformers away from the Radical movement. Cobbett decamps to the United States for a year and a half. Cartwright soldiers on, "daring the authorities to imprison him, issuing Addresses, looking up antique constitutional precedents ... and expedients half a shade on the right side of the law" (698-99). In the old Luddite areas, economic distress keeps the reform pot bubbling. In the spring of 1817, Joseph Mitchell and William Oliver set out from London to talk up insurrection in the provinces. Mitchell is arrested, but Oliver carries on. "Thereafter an extraordinary situation existed, in which insurrectionary preparations were going forward in several districts, but in which the only London contact-man who can be identified was a Government agent" (717). We are in the lethal company of Oliver the Spy.

The Pentridge Rising of June 9, 1817, is "one of the first attempts in history to mount a wholly proletarian insurrection, without any middle-class support." It is a fiasco — an abortive uprising involving a few villages in Luddite country. Thompson disposes of it in a couple of pages, folding it into another story that he calls "one of the great stories of English history which came to partake almost of the quality of myth. Oliver was the archetype of the Radical Judas, and his legendary rôle was to carry influence throughout nineteenth-century history." Granted that Oliver was not just a spy but a provocateur, who urged his hosts on to insurrection while reporting their plans to his paymasters, how far was the government responsible for his actions? Thompson does not accuse it of complicity in the provocation; however, he concludes that it could have forestalled the rising but chose to let it go ahead: it "wanted blood — not a holocaust, but enough to make an example." However, the exposure of Oliver, which occurs on the eve of the revolt but not in time to abort it, turns the event into a propaganda coup for the reformers. Dozens of insurrectionists (though not the Pentridge contingent, who had killed a man) are subsequently acquitted at trial. In the longer term, though, it discredits the pursuit of reform by violence.[40]

And so to Peterloo — not a battle like Waterloo, after which it is sarcastically named, but a massacre, since only one side is armed and bent on violence. The event, a huge open-air political meeting in August 1819, constitutes the early apogee of the new tactics of orderly demonstration based on the marching ceremonial of trade

---

[40] *Making*, 711-34 (quotations, 733, 726).

unions and friendly societies. Disciplined bands of working people dressed in their Sunday best converge by tens of thousands on St. Peter's Field in Manchester to hear an address by a leading Radical, Henry Hunt. The demonstration is conspicuously peaceful, even festive; but the local magistrates have made up their mind to arrest Hunt and disperse the meeting, and — perhaps dismayed by the very discipline and decorum of people they like to think of as a rabble — they stick to their plan. The task of arresting Hunt falls to the local Yeomanry, a mounted militia of ill-trained volunteers who ride into the dense crowd, get stuck, and start lashing out with their sabres. More than a dozen men and women are killed; hundreds are injured.[41] Peterloo is the instant and lasting label attached to the event — a savage mockery both of the perpetrators of the massacre and of the Duke of Wellington, victor of Waterloo and a leading cabinet minister. Public opinion is scandalized. For weeks the country trembles on the verge of insurrection, but the government masters the situation by means of repressive legislation and the arrest of leading reformers (734-69).

Thompson's account of the heroic age of popular radicalism ends with a doleful coda: the so-called Cato Street Conspiracy, named after the location where Arthur Thistlewood and his fellow Spenceans plotted at the beginning of 1820 to assassinate the entire British Cabinet. Thwarted by a spy in its midst, the conspiracy is the last gasp of the old Jacobin-linked Radicalism. Thistlewood and his accomplices go bravely to the gallows, like Jeremiah Brandreth (leader of the Pentridge rising), Despard, and their accomplices before them, not to mention a score or more or unnamed Luddite machine-breakers. But it is Peterloo that points the way ahead:

> Even Old Corruption knew, in its heart, that it dare not do this again. Since the moral consensus of the nation outlawed the riding down and sabreing of an unarmed crowd, the corollary followed — that the right of public meeting had been gained. Henceforward strikers and agricultural workers might be ridden down or dispersed with violence. But never since Peterloo has authority dared to use equal force against a peaceful British crowd (779-80).

The chapter ends by quoting the recollection of Samuel Bamford, the Radical weaver, of how he rallied a contingent nearly a thousand

---

[41] Modern scholarship puts the death toll at 17 and the number of injured at more than 650: Robert Poole, "'By the Law or the Sword': Peterloo Revisited," *History*, 91 (2006), 254-76.

strong after the massacre and marched them home with fife and drum playing and their only remaining banner waving.

Peterloo may show the way ahead, but the end of the "heroic age" deprives *The Making* of much of its narrative drive. The final chapter is very different in tone from its two predecessors. It has its heroes but, instead of focusing on places and events, resembles Part Two in being predominantly thematic in nature, and its main theme is the development of the plebeian political culture in the 1820s and early thirties. The narrative resumes briefly in the final section, which recounts the political crisis that finally led to the enactment to a measure of parliamentary reform in 1832. However, the drama is gone. There are no conspiracies to relate; no secret gatherings and drilling on the moors; no nocturnal manoeuvres by bands of machine-breakers. The mass meetings are larger than Peterloo, but no massacres ensue. The drama takes place in the palaces of the metropolis, and the working people are on the outside looking in; but they do not break into the palaces like the Paris mobs of the 1790s and 1830, and Thompson stays outside with them. What keeps them out is a political compromise that is specifically designed to exclude them from power while including the middle class. The narrative ends amid a cloud of allusions to events occurring in the few years following the passage of the Reform Act before shading into a conclusion that is surprisingly brief for so long a work.

Epic Transformation

It is possible to imagine a very different treatment of these years in a book on the making of the English working class, and a very different ending to such a book. An account of the 1820s might focus on events such as the epochal woolcombers' strike of 1825 and the cotton-spinners' strike of 1829. The former lasted nearly six months, and supporters throughout the land contributed up to £20,000 to support the strikers. It ended in total defeat, and "the woolcomber was translated almost overnight from a privileged artisan to a defenceless outworker" (312). Thompson's main mention of it is brief and occurs 500 pages earlier in his chapter on the weavers in Part Two. The cotton-spinners' strike, comparably long and almost as disastrous, receives even less notice, although Thompson calls its leader, John Doherty, "one of the three truly impressive trade union leaders who emerged in these early years" (851). Since Doherty had also played a leading part in a strike in 1818, when he was barely twenty, and served two years in prison for it, one might think him tailor-made for stardom in *The Making*, but he receives only a few brief mentions.

Does Thompson neglect Doherty in order not to overstate the role of the factory workers in the making of the English working class? That cannot explain his neglect of the woolcombers' strike, since they were outworkers; and besides, a glance at the other two leaders in his pantheon suggests otherwise. John Gast of the shipwrights' union gets a bit more attention, but only because he founded a newspaper. The only one who figures as a hero in Thompson's story is Gravener Henson, the framework-knitters' leader at the time of the Luddite outbreaks. Henson's skilful leadership of the stockingers' parliamentary lobbying in 1811-12, the unsolved mystery of his relationship to Luddism, his imprisonment without trial in 1817, and his leading role in the campaign in 1823-24 to repeal the ban on collective bargaining: all these combine to place him at the centre of Thompson's story of the "illegal tradition." But why should an account of the making of the English working class devote so much space to the illegal tradition, Westminster radicalism, and the travails of certain printers jailed for publishing Thomas Paine, and so little to instances of actual collective action by the nascent working class?

These questions go to the heart of the book's transformation from the textbook commissioned by Gollancz into an epic tale of resistance to evil. By Thompson's own account, he accepted the commission because he needed the money and wrote the book while engaged in a variety of political activities, ranging from the Campaign for Nuclear Disarmament to a running debate on theoretical issues with Marxists of less humane temper. A book composed under such circumstances was bound to rely heavily on the author's prior research. Thompson's research was focused on the history of the West Riding of Yorkshire, a wool-spinning and weaving centre from 1750 to the present, and he was planning — perhaps even writing — a book aimed at his own adult education students. That project was itself a distillation of his three-year course on the social and industrial history of England from 1750, each section of which included special "Yorkshire Topics."[42] No doubt this was the source of much of the material in Part 2.

---

[42] David Goodway, "E. P. Thompson and the Making of *The Making of the English Working Class*," in Richard Taylor, ed., *Beyond the Walls: 50 Years of*

What gave the book its epic narrative drive, however, was his encounter with two major archival collections that brought him face to face with the illegal tradition: the government archives, rich with reports from spies and informers and correspondence with local officials, and the papers of Earl Fitzwilliam, the government's chief representative in the West Riding. Confronted by this trove, his epic temperament took over; or, in his own words, "the material took command of me, far more than I ever expected."[43] The projected book on "working-class politics, 1790-1921" emerged after three years as an epic account of "the making of the English working class." But it remained a book on working-class *politics*, because Thompson held that the English working class had been made by the Free-Born Englishman as much as by implacable historical forces.

Even more than its structure, this insistence on the heroic agency of ordinary men and women inspired by a myth and culture of liberty imbues *The Making* with an epic essence; and it marks it as an epic of disaffection in particular. In this respect, as in others, the paradigm is *Paradise Lost*. Milton's poem is almost an anti-epic, in which the author expressly mocks the traditional subject-matter of the epic and assigns the conventional heroic role to an anti-hero, Satan. But a story of the beginning of human history must also be a story of the beginning of human heroism, for who needed heroism in Eden? Heroism begins at the end of *Paradise Lost*, when Adam and Eve, newly apprised of their mortality and the suffering it must entail, "hand in hand with wandring steps and slow," embark on their long exile. But "When Adam delv'd and Eve span / Who was then the gentleman?" The heroism of Adam and Eve is not, Milton tells us, the valour of "fabled Knights / In Battels feignd" but "the better fortitude / Of Patience and Heroic Martyrdom / Unsung."[44] Like Tolstoy and Tolkien, Thompson sings the heroism of Everyman.

Heroes without gods

Like Tolkien, Thompson appropriated a publisher's commission to the purpose of writing expansively from the heart. I have compared the outcome to *Paradise Lost*, and another historian, Michael Mer-

---

Adult and Continuing Education at the University of Leeds, 1946-1996 (Leeds: University of Leeds, 1996), 134-37.

[43] *Visions of History*, 14.

[44] Bk. XII, l. 648; bk. IX, ll. 30-33. On the politics of *Paradise Lost*, and Milton's up-ending of epic norms, see Quint, *Epic and Empire*, 248-324.

rill, has declared that *The Making* "can be read as a great historical novel — as great, certainly, as *Moby Dick*, which it structurally resembles. I say this not to diminish Thompson's scholarship, but to exalt his style."[45]

I am not sure about Merrill's first proposition. A historian may well be captivated by certain novelistic notes in the structure and language of *The Making* — even J. D. Chambers enthused over its "moving account of the handloom weavers ... written in such a way as to read like a freshly told tale."[46] However, if you open it hoping to encounter a great historical novel, you are in danger of finding it about as rewarding as reading the Prologue and appendices of *The Lord of the Rings*, or the didactic passages of *War and Peace*, while skipping the actual story; nor, I suspect, are non-historians likely to feel it merging with Tolkien's story in their mind as Meredith Veldman did. On the other hand, a reader who does not approach it with that expectation may be taken by surprise. In any case, both Tolkien's and Tolstoy's narratives show how the multigeneric character typical of the epic is expressed partly in the intrusion of historical modes of discourse. In *The Making*, generic diversity is manifest partly in the intermingling of narrative and discursive sections; but the observations of Merrill and Veldman alert us to the possibility that it also appears in devices typical of fiction, and the comparison with *Moby Dick* opens a space for pursuing this idea.

Considered as a novel, Melville's masterpiece is a curious specimen. Its plot and characterization are skeletal, and its long disquisitions on whales and whaling make it as much documentary as fictional — more so, even, than *War and Peace*, in which the didactic passages are counterbalanced by an abundance of character development and interaction. The *Pequod* sails the ocean, chasing whales and sometimes catching them. Finally, Captain Ahab realizes his private obsession by tracking down his nemesis, the White Whale, which gets fed up with being chased and harpooned and summarily fixes the problem by annihilating boat and crew. End of story. And the story, such as it is, offers little account of the crew as individuals or of the relationships that must develop in the course of a long and close association. The result is a sense of temporal stasis, which brief encounters with other vessels do little to dispel.

---

[45] Michael Merrill, "E. P. Thompson: In Solidarity," *Radical History Review*, 58 (1993), 155.
[46] Chambers, "Making of the English Working Class," 183.

How does Melville's story rate as an epic, then? It is loaded with the simple sensualities and intimations of the numinous prescribed by Tillyard; but what is the pattern of history that it illustrates, and what the larger action (to quote Northrop Frye) in which it is suspended? There is no great story of the rise and fall of nations, no overarching theme of a grand alignment of opposing forces moving towards a climactic battle, nor even the heroism of the common man doing his duty. Far from it: the one character with an inkling of impending doom, the first mate Starbuck, shrinks from what he must do to avert it (kill Ahab); it is as though Winston Smith in *Nineteen Eighty-Four* had forgone Julia and rebellion in favour of the quiet life. Nor, finally, is there any hint of a grand march of human history from beginning to predestined end as in *Paradise Lost*. Ahab most resembles the classic tragic hero brought low by hubris, and the story seems to end as sharply on his downfall as any Shakespearean tragedy.

But does it? *Moby Dick* deviates from the tragic model in two ways that bring it close to epic. First of all, the tragic action is deferred until the very end of the story, and the overall shape of the plot is that of a quest — the hunt for the White Whale. It is Sauron's quest rather than Frodo's, but a quest nonetheless. Secondly, if you take the *Pequod* — that snug little barque tossing or gliding on a vast ocean — as a microcosm, a context opens up for the tragedy that is cosmic rather than human, thus giving rise to that prophetic song, identified by E. M. Forster, which is so unexpectedly in harmony with Tolkien's.[47] There is little suggestion of movement in that context — on the contrary: once fate, embodied in the White Whale, has slapped down Ahab's impious challenge, the sea rolls on "as it rolled five thousand years ago" — that is, as it has done since the Creation. The effect is not of a story taking place in time but of one taking place in timelessness. But the reason is not that the story is devoid of temporal context: it is that the context is so vast, and the story occupies such a tiny moment in it, that no movement in time is perceptible.

Perhaps, then, we can adapt Henry Fielding's humorous description of his novel *Joseph Andrews* as a comic epic poem in prose and define Melville's story, somewhat more seriously, as a tragic epic docudrama in prose. In this respect it is another epic of disaffection, the politics of which is even more completely reduced to symbolism

---

[47] See above, 81-82.

than those of *War and Peace*: a story of a charismatic leader leading his people to ruin in pursuit of an insane quest. (Sauron's quest is Napoleon's too.) However, the detailed account of the work and life of whalers makes it a social history epic, a fictional counterpart of *The Making*. The alternating passages of narrative and documentary exposition may make for a structural resemblance, but it is more significantly one of content.

In Thompson's book, the novelistic notes commence with something to be expected in a fictional narrative: the author's passionate engagement with his story and its actors. Thompson, says Merrill, "took the condescension of posterity ... absolutely personally,"[48] and this can be felt in his approach both to his characters and to their twentieth-century detractors. His story tells of heroes, sometimes armed heroes. "Men must be judged in their own context, and in this light we may see such men as George Mellor, Jem Towle and Jeremiah Brandreth as men of heroic stature" (648). This is said of three hanged men, two of them convicted murderers, in defiance of historians who celebrated the legacy of Francis Place but ignored or belittled those who actually tried to strike a blow against injustice:

> [T]he hundreds of men and women executed or transported for oath-taking, Jacobin conspiracy, Luddism, the Pentridge and Grange Moor risings, food and enclosure and turnpike riots, the Ely riots and the Labourers' Revolt of 1830, and a score of minor affrays have been forgotten by all but a few specialists, or, if they are remembered, they are thought to be simpletons or men tainted with criminal folly (648).

Again:

> Who *was* Jeremiah Brandreth? The Hammonds, characteristically, describe him as "a half-starved, illiterate, and unemployed framework-knitter", "ready to ... forward any proposal, however wild". This is pejorative writing. We know that Brandreth was not illiterate. If he was half-starved and unemployed, so were many hundreds of his fellow stockingers (731).

Nor was Brandreth's wife illiterate. Thompson quotes her poignant letter to Brandreth in jail ("Oh that I could atone for all and save your life"), which he never received because the jailer withheld it, and Brandreth's last letter to her ("My beloved ..."). He rehabilitates Arthur Thistlewood and celebrates the heroism of his followers (abused by another historian as "ruffianly guttersnipes"). They

---

48 Merrill, "Thompson," 154.

weren't all illiterate either: "Now, my dear, I hope you will bear in mind that the cause of my being consigned to the scaffold was a pure motive. I thought I should have rendered my starving fellow-men, women, and children, a service ..."[49]

In two cases Thompson's sense of identification with his heroes seems peculiarly personal. One is that of Maurice Margarot and Joseph Gerrald, who headed north in 1794 as delegates of the London Corresponding Society to succour the beleaguered Scottish democrats. As Thompson tells it, the two men "knew perfectly well the danger they were running. They were rushing 'supplies' of moral solidarity to their Scottish comrades which — if withheld at that moment — would have resulted in the demoralization of the Scottish and English movements." He records Margarot's comment in a letter asking for extra funds so that they can visit reform societies outside Edinburgh: "No excuse for recal [*sic*] can be valid, unless founded on *fear*; and that we must remind you is our concern, not yours." More poignantly still, Gerrald, after being bailed so that he could go back to England and wind up his affairs, rejects his friends' appeals to jump bail and, embracing his fate, returns north to face his trial. Sentenced to transportation for fourteen years, he is dead within a year of landing in Australia.[50] One thinks of Frank Thompson rushing supplies of moral solidarity to the Bulgarian partisans at the cost of his life.

The other case is less tragic but not without pathos, and the author's sense of identification may be even more immediate. It is that of John Thelwall, second-rate poet, first-rate orator, supple political tactician, and political theorist, who took Jacobinism to the borders of Socialism and revolutionism. Acquitted of high treason in 1794, he did not lie low but boldly resumed his political lectures and, when a law was passed to ban them, evaded it by lightly disguising them as lectures on Roman history. Such bravado

> required, perhaps, a dash of the actor in his temperament; the vice of the English Jacobins (except for Hardy) was self-dramatization, and in their histrionic postures they sometimes seem ridiculous. But it was an age of rhetoric, and the rhetoric of a *parvenu* is bound to be less composed than the rhetoric of a Burke. The flourishes of the Tribunes of Liberty (who really were tribunes of real liberty) can surely be forgiven if they served to give them courage (173).

---

[49] *Making*, 770-75.
[50] *Making*, 135-41 (quotation, p. 138).

As Merrill recalls, "No one ever caressed a podium as lovingly as E. P. Thompson."[51]

But lecturers are nothing without listeners, and there are no leaders without followers. As befits the memoirist of the road to Perugia, Thompson reaches even beyond the Captain Tushins of his tale to salute those who suffered under their command.

> It was the heroic age of popular Radicalism, but, on the national scene, its leaders rarely looked heroic and sometimes looked ridiculous ... Its true heroes were the local booksellers and news-vendors, trade union organizers, secretaries and local speakers for the Hampden Clubs and Political Unions ... who, in many cases, were too obscure to do more than leave a few records of their political activity in the local Press or the Home Office papers. These men provided the platform without which their ... leaders would have been impotent ... (691).

And so Thompson tells us not just about Richard Carlile, the deist-turned-atheist journalist and printer who was jailed for reprinting the works of Tom Paine, but about the 150 volunteers — shopmen, printers and news-vendors — who rallied to his appeal to keep his press running and themselves went to prison for their hardiness. "The men and women who came forward were, in nearly every case, entirely unknown to Carlile. They simply came out of London; or arrived on the coach from Lincolnshire, Dorset, Liverpool and Leeds. They came out of a culture" (717). It was a culture of the radical intelligentsia, derived partly from the Jacobinism of the 1790s and nourished by the radical romanticism of Byron and Shelley; but Thompson winds up by hailing the industrial workers too. "The working people should not be seen only as the lost myriads of eternity. They had also nourished, for fifty years, and with incomparable fortitude, the Liberty Tree. We may thank them for these years of heroic culture" (915).

With these words, reaching back across more than 400 pages to the bleak close of Part Two, and then back further still to the very start of the story, the narrator falls silent. He has recited a saga of heroic resistance to evil with a cast of thousands; the tale of a turning-point in history set against the backdrop of a world destroyed — a lost past, partly mythic, linked to a future which is, ultimately, the reader's own time. These are some of the features that mark *The Making* as epic. But where are the gods? Where can

---

51 Merrill, "Thompson," 152.

they be? Even *War and Peace* gives us little more by way of the numinous than a fairyland of the mind and a sky that is a source of ambiguous revelation. But that doesn't matter: we are not looking for stock literary tropes belonging to an essentially pre-modern genre. We are looking for the source of an effect — one that marks off Thompson's story from the common run of modern narrative histories by imbuing it with a hint of the numinous. I find it in the space created by his setting of the narrative in time.

This temporal positioning has two aspects. First, the past is not just the past — it is a world that is lost; yet, though lost, it lives in the recollection of its posterity like Paradise Lost: "The history of the weavers in the nineteenth century is *haunted* by the *legend* of better days."[52] This theme of loss pervades the book, especially Part Two, where the section entitled "Myriads of Eternity" (a phrase vibrant with temporal resonance) sums it up:

> The experience of immiseration came upon them in a hundred different forms; for the field labourer, the loss of his common rights and the vestiges of village democracy; for the artisan, the loss of his craftsman's status; for the weaver, the loss of livelihood and independence; for the child, the loss of work and play in the home; for many groups of workers whose real earnings improved, the loss of security, leisure, and the deterioration of the urban environment ... (487).

What exactly is lost varies with place of residence and means of livelihood, but it all adds up to widespread dispossession and exile resulting from the destructive onslaught of the "free market," empowered by the state, on traditional communities and the moral economy.

Thompson refuses to sentimentalize what was lost: "While many contemporary writers, from Cobbett to Engels, lamented the passing of old English customs, it is foolish to see the matter only in idyllic terms ... The passing of Gin Lane, Tyburn Fair, orgiastic drunkenness, animal sexuality, and mortal combat for prize-money in iron-studded clogs, calls for no lament" (451). He allows that the lost world may have been idealized — "suffused with nostalgic light" (595) — by those who invoked it against the present. Still, his tale is founded on songs and testimonies of loss, not of deliverance. To the croppers, as we have seen, Ned Ludd was the defender of ancient

---

[52] See above, 209. My italics.

right, the upholder of a lost constitution; to the framework-knitters he was a modern Robin Hood.

Ned Ludd and Robin Hood: such allusions make Thompson's beleaguered craft workers the functional equivalent of Tolkien's elves, Tolstoy's Rostovs and Walter Scott's MacIvors: it invests them with doomed glamour. As we saw with *War and Peace*, a realist narrative needs only a barebones Middle-earth to evoke the numinous, and like the Rostovs, Thompson's doomed artisans can stand in for both hobbits and elves.[53] But the reference to a lost constitution brings up the second aspect of the narrative's temporal positioning. The lost world is not just a world of relative ease and plenty. More explicitly than Tolstoy's epic zone, it is a political Eden, too. The story of the making of the *English* working class does not just slot into the Marxist narrative embracing the whole of human history. It also fits into the story of the Free-born Englishman, with its own mythology reaching back past Anglo-Saxon times to an original constitution which must, thought the silversmith John Baxter, have been free. Thompson does not endorse the myth but, by allowing it to colour his narrative and weaving it into a tale that continues in our own day, he produces a romantic intensity and a glint of the numinous.

The Making sings of heroic resistance to insurgent evil, and not just of heroism but of loss. The main narrative covers a period of only forty years, but its temporal context is developed with a depth which, like the spatial immensity of *War and Peace*, strikes great chords. Whence came the passion that imbued Thompson's history with notes so compelling, yet so alien to the spirit of academic discourse? I described earlier how both Tolkien and Tolstoy, bent on transmuting troubling experiences into art, found it necessary to transpose their experience to a different milieu. So did Thompson. Like Tolkien, he had first tried to render his war experience in a realist mode: what he called in retrospect "a 'war novel' which mercifully the world was spared."[54] And, like Tolkien, he recouped by "transforming experience into another form and symbol"; but where Tolkien did so by writing imaginary history, Thompson did so by writing history that was scholarly in form but projected the spirit of 1944.

---

[53] See above, 171.
[54] Thompson, *Heavy Dancers*, x.

However, academic norms pose a limit to how far even genius can go in the processing of personal experience. *The Making* is epic in structure, mood and amplitude, but it feels like an unfinished epic. Thompson's reason for bringing his story to an end in 1832 is clearly stated:

> At this point the limits of this study have been reached; for there is a sense in which the working class is no longer in the making, but has been made. To step over the threshold, from 1832 to 1833, is to step into a world in which the working-class presence can be felt in every county in England, and in most fields of life (887).

But while Thompson tells us this, he does not make us feel it. And he does not make us feel it because he does not tell the story of the surge of trade union activity in the 1830s and the Chartist struggle for manhood suffrage from 1837 to 1848. The general theme of Part Two is the destruction of the traditional communities by insurgent capitalism, and Part Three is an account of the political resistance to that destructive onslaught. But the destruction recorded in Part Two goes on into the 1840s, and the tale of resistance stops abruptly in 1832. Chartism, repeatedly alluded to, looms over the story as its impending climax;[55] but when we get to the end that climax is missing. It is as though Tolstoy had led us to expect that his story would culminate in the Decembrist rising.

Maybe it was simply time to call a halt. Treating the Chartist years on the same scale as the rest of the book would have taken another two or three hundred pages; and anyway, the history of Chartism was to be the professional domain of his wife, Dorothy. What he had already written was enough to revolutionize thinking not only about English history but about the study of history in general, and not just history but several other branches of social science. Like *The Lord of the Rings*, it would inspire a flood of emulation.[56] Besides, Thompson's subject was — or had become — the *making* of the working class, not its struggles once made.

This point is important for what it implies about the character of *The Making* as an epic of disaffection. Earlier I described the advent of the working class, as announced in *The Communist Manifesto*, as the Marxist counterpart of the birth of the Messiah. Bearing in mind

---

55 See, *e.g.*, the quotation on p. 220 above.
56 Paul Buhle, "E. P. Thompson: A Revolutionary and a Scholar," *Tikkun*, 8 (Nov.-Dec. 1993) <www.tikkun.org/article.php?story=nov-1993_buhle>. Accessed Oct. 15, 2012.

David Quint's distinction between epics which tell of victory and those which recount defeat, how can we call a narrative that ends on so positive a note an epic of disaffection? Moreover, Quint points out the propensity of the "losers' epic" to ascribe the tragic outcome to accident and misfortune as opposed to predestination. In both *The Lord of the Rings* and *War and Peace*, the narrative undermines the triumphalism of the great victory by carrying the story far enough beyond it to reduce it to a moment in history. Thompson, however, stops at the moment of triumph, and in doing so seems to leave the triumphal teleology of *The Communist Manifesto* intact.

There are two arguments against this. Firstly, the making of the working class and the birth of Christ are not final victories over anything; they are way stations on the road to a promised final victory that may be attained only after an immeasurable period of further struggle. The example of *Paradise Lost* suggests that this narrative structure, in which final victory is deferred to an indefinite future, is quite compatible with the epic of disaffection. Secondly, the advent of the working class owes its triumphal promise to its embedding in a deterministic ideology which proclaims that victory is inevitable, but Thompson explicitly framed his book as a challenge to that determinism. The working class of *The Communist Manifesto* arises from inexorable socioeconomic processes culminating in the factory system of industrial production, which makes working people conscious of their common identity and interest as cogs in the capitalist machine. In Thompson's history, working-class consciousness is the outcome of two convergent struggles, and its final emergence is in fact a consequence of defeat and betrayal. One struggle is that of working people to defend their way of life against the onslaught of free-market capitalism; the other is the campaign for manhood suffrage inaugurated in the 1790s. The defeat of manhood suffrage, owing to its desertion by the middle-class opponents of Old Corruption, notifies working-class suffragists that they are on their own. The realization leads in short order to Chartism and further defeat.

Final victory is out of the question, anyway. Guided by William Morris on one hand, and on the other by his own perception of the spirit of 1944 and its subsequent betrayal on both sides of the Iron Curtain, Thompson overlaid the Marxist narrative with the myth of the Free-born Englishman, a narrative that is cyclical rather than linear in shape and therefore inherently subversive of teleology. It is a tale of recurrent struggle against oppression, which may achieve temporary success but is never finally won. Its keynote is not victory, let alone predestined victory, but resistance with no warrant of success. In this respect, *The Making* is closer in tenor to Tolkien's long defeat than to any tale of triumph.

7

The End of History: *The Sykaos Papers*

Each of Thompson's epics corresponds to a crisis in his life. *The Making* reflects the disillusion caused by the Soviet invasion of Hungary, which to Thompson epitomized the betrayal of the spirit of 1944. *The Sykaos Papers* projects the angst arising from his break with contemporary Marxism at the end of the 1970s. Like most of Thompson's writing, it is deeply historical; but it is fiction, not academic history, and is set not, like *War and Peace*, amid actual historical events but, like *The Lord of the Rings*, in an imagined history.

Thompson's science-fiction fantasy relates the adventures, mainly on Earth, or Sykaos, of a humanoid creature called Oi Paz, a voyager from the planet Oitar in a distant galaxy. It is a protean work. The first quarter is largely devoted to Oi Paz's experiences and observations of an alien and alienating culture, which at first is a complete mystery to him. The central portion — some 300 pages — records his three-year sojourn on a country estate in southern England, where he continues to investigate human culture while himself being a research subject for the humans who hold him. He becomes sufficiently humanized and acculturated to commence a sexual liaison with one of his "keepers", as he calls them — a cultural anthropologist called Helena Sage. Their relationship develops against the backdrop of a growing crisis in international and interplanetary relations as Earth's two superpowers, aware that Oitar has built a base on the moon with a view to colonizing Earth, compete to recruit the extraterrestrial power as an ally. This sets up an apocalyptic climax.

The plot is coherent enough, but it unfolds in stages that differ greatly from each other in tone and style. This diversity perplexed even readers who esteemed Thompson as a historian and public intellectual. Characterization, plot and structure all came under attack. One reviewer praised the interplay of characters but disparaged the "ramshackle" sequence of events by which Thompson engineers his dénouement. Another, enthusiastic about the story as a whole, complained that it shared the structural flaws of Thompson's historical work. Michael Merrill, who compared *The Making* to *Moby Dick*, dismissed *The Sykaos Papers* on the ground that Thompson was not "engaged, as fiction writers have to be, by the effort to invent others through whom he could speak." (I will suggest, on the contrary, that Oi Paz's distinctive voice is one of the supreme achievements of the novel.) The historian Perry Anderson noted "a striking contrast between the minor opening sections of the novel, heavy-handed burlesque of the popular press and urban scene of the Eighties, whose humour can make one wince, and the energy and wit of the major plot development that follows." However, Anderson recognized it as "the most complete single statement of [Thompson's] thought, giving imaginative form to ideas that find comparable expression nowhere else in his work."[1] It is also the fullest expression of Thompson's epic temperament.

I have presented the epic of disaffection as an expression of the writer's engagement with history and politics. I discussed *The Lord of the Rings* as an account of what Tolkien called an "imaginary historical moment," which is set in an encyclopaedic imaginary history and exemplifies Tolkien's idea of the pattern of history. Although imaginary, the history was imagined in response both to the events of Tolkien's own time and to human history as a whole, perceived as "the long defeat." We saw how Tolstoy, in a fictional rendering of an actual historical event, shaped his account of Russia's fight against

---

[1] Michael Irwin, ""Final Jam," *London Review of Books*, 2 June 1988 <http://www.lrb.co.uk/v10/n11/michael-irwin/final-jam> (viewed 27 Sept. 2012); Benjamin DeMott, "The Poet Who Fell to Earth," *New York Times*, 25 Sept. 1988 <http://www.nytimes.com/1988/09/25/-books/the-poet-who-fell-to-earth.html?pagewanted=all&src=pm> (viewed 27 Sept. 2012); Michael Merrill, "E. P. Thompson: In Solidarity," *Radical History Review*, 58 (1993), 155; Perry Anderson, "Diary," *London Review of Books,* 21 Oct. 1993, 24.

Napoleon to fit his own conception of history, and how Thompson, attempting to inject historical reality into a theoretical construct, imagined the unfolding of a critical moment in the Marxist scheme of history. *The Sykaos Papers* represents yet another variant of the epic temperament's encounter with history: a historian's fictional imagining of its final outcome. Like Tolkien's fantasy, Thompson's changed and grew in response to contemporary events.

Thompson's satirical intent makes *The Sykaos Papers* a very different sort of fantasy from *The Lord of the Rings*, but less different than one might suppose. Satire is criticism by caricature. It typically proceeds by exaggerating the salient characteristics of its target, often to the point of ridicule; thus Northrop Frye observes that it "demands at least a token fantasy, a content which the reader recognizes as grotesque."[2] He cites Jonathan Swift's *A Modest Proposal*, an essay which proposes to aid the Irish poor by selling their children as food for the rich. Frye's association of satire and fantasy is supported by the congruence between Viktor Shklovsky's notion of defamiliarization, which we discussed in connection with Tolstoy's satirical comedy, and Tolkien's idea that one of the functions of fantasy is to beguile the reader into viewing the familiar in a fresh light.[3] Both Shklovsky and Tolkien are talking about distorted representation of the actual designed to induce the reader to see reality with fresh eyes.

There is a difference, of course, as Frye recognizes when he distinguishes between satire and what he calls *pure* fantasy. He does not elaborate, but we may distinguish the two as follows. "Pure" fantasy, as envisaged and practised by Tolkien, is oriented away from the transitory present and towards the eternal. It is lyrical and elegiac, and what it presents, no matter how strange, is to be taken at face value. The fantasy of satire, on the other hand, is trained on the present; but more importantly, no matter how gentle or savage it is, it has a whimsical quality which is essential to its function of attacking through ridicule. Fantasy in its Forsterian sense can, of course, be whimsical without being satirical; but in satire the element of whimsy, signalling that what is presented should not be taken at face value, helps to render the fantasy compatible with realism. Tolkien and Forster go to show that defamiliarization

---

[2] Frye, *Anatomy of Criticism*, 224.
[3] See above, 121, 74.

pertains to fantasy in general rather than satire in particular. All satire, however, entails defamiliarization.

The Sykaos Papers is a mixture of pure and satirical fantasy, and I will argue that its epic transformation can be seen as a shift from satirical towards pure fantasy. The key to the transition is the story's initial incarnation as an inversion of *Gulliver's Travels*, which Thompson identified as the chief influence on his story.[4] Swift's satirical fiction places an ordinary Englishman in a series of fantastic milieux designed to mock English politics, institutions and manners. *The Sykaos Papers* inverts this situation by recounting a bemused alien's encounter with contemporary English manners, institutions and politics, and the hero's identity as a traveller from a distant galaxy favours expansive spatial and temporal development of the narrative. Deliberately prophetic in a way that Tolkien is not, Thompson never loses his focus on the present; but as the narrative proceeds, the perspective broadens and the initial satirical purpose dwindles in importance. To understand this progression, we must first explore the personal experiences and political developments that combined to engender Thompson's apocalyptic vision.

Lear on the heath

The Making was a work of profound originality — very much the first rather than the last word on many of the issues it raised. A host of historians followed Thompson, amplifying and modifying, challenging and vindicating, his many suggestions and contentions. Most of his own later historical research and writing was devoted to developing essential points of his argument, particularly about the traditional world that capitalism had destroyed. This pursuit led him further back into the eighteenth century, to the age of Jonathan Swift, where he exposed a surprising unruliness among the common people in an era which orthodox scholarship celebrated as an age of political and social stability between the political turmoil of the seventeenth-century revolutions and the social turmoil of the Industrial Revolution.

His next history book — *Whigs and Hunters: The Origin of the Black Act* — was no untidy epic but an even untidier exercise in

---

4   http://archive.tribunemagazine.co.uk/article/17th-june-1988/8/e-p-thompson-on-his-new-novel (viewed 29 June 2012).

close historical investigation in obscure sources.[5] Enacted in 1723, the Black Act imposed the death penalty for many offences against landed property (poaching, destroying fish ponds, etc.) committed by persons armed and in disguise, colloquially called Blacks. Originally it was to expire after three years; but it was continually extended and broadened, both by legislation and by judicial interpretation, until it became a bloody penal code adapted to subdue the common people by terror in the absence of an effective police force.

Puzzled by the sudden enactment of this draconian statute at a time when there was no obvious reason for it, Thompson dug deep and discovered unexpected links between poaching and politics. The poaching targeted by the Black Act was a response by the population of certain forested areas to the efforts of some great landowners and royal officials to curb established common rights for their own benefit. The officials were largely newcomers, as was the King himself — George I, a German prince, had recently been installed in preference to the heir of James II, the monarch ousted by the Glorious Revolution of 1688. The landowners were mainly men who had made or magnified their fortunes by supporting the winning side. They were grabby folk, who had done well out of a new style of government which featured a standing army, a National Debt, paper money, and close ties to large, newly created financial monopolies including the Bank of England and the South Sea Company. Keen advocates of the rights of Property, they were hostile to customary use-rights which hampered their enjoyment of their domains.

Their political arm was the Whig party, which had consolidated its hold on power in 1715 by defeating an uprising by supporters of James II's son; but five years later their ascendancy was shaken by a huge financial scandal involving one of their friendly financial monopolies and featuring the bribery of influential politicians. The infamous South Sea Bubble enriched some speculators — mainly insiders — and ruined many more, and the Whigs had to clean house. In this emergency, the Black Act served the interests of leading Whigs and of men whose support they needed. More broadly, it signalled the rise of the landed elite whose heirs would unite a century later with the industrial bourgeoisie against popular radicalism and labour militancy.

---

[5] E. P. Thompson, *Whigs and Hunters: The Origin of the Black Act* (New York: Pantheon, 1975).

Like *The Making*, Thompson's new book took aim at both right and left. On one hand it exposed the seamy underpinnings of the social stability that historical orthodoxy celebrated as the chief achievement of the Whig ascendancy. On the other it condemned "a certain contemporary fashion of romanticizing crime," which excused the offences of persons subject to social and economic oppression no matter what their crimes. In a closing section entitled "The Rule of Law" (apparently included on his wife's advice), Thompson took issue with Marxists who dismissed the ideal of the rule of law as merely a mask for class oppression. In a state that based its claim to legitimacy on an ideology of personal freedom and legal equity, there were limits to how far its officers, no matter how brutal and venal, could transgress those principles without undermining that claim. Even the Black Act required trial by jury, and where the proceedings seemed oppressive a jury would sometimes acquit, just as, later in the century, juries would acquit Thomas Hardy and John Thelwall. The superiority of such a system to the exercise of arbitrary extra-legal power was something that the twentieth century should have made clear (Thompson tartly remarked) even to the most exalted thinker.[6]

By the time *Whigs and Hunters* appeared, the success of *The Making* had wrought large changes in Thompson's life. In 1965 he had quit the draughty classrooms of adult education for the brand-new University of Warwick, where he became the founding director of its Centre for the Study of Social History. Having lost his battle for the soul of the New Left, as earlier for that of the Communist Party, he gained a new arena of activity as a public intellectual in the pages of mainstream periodicals such as *New Society* and the *Times Literary Supplement*. An international reputation yielded invitations from overseas, and he became a regular visitor to North America. In both the Old World and the New he became something of a guru, but he kept his distance from the student radicals of those turbulent years, suspecting that their revolutionary fervour had something of a recreational aspect.

Then, in February 1970, students occupying administrative offices at the University of Warwick found a letter to the vice-chancellor (the administrative head of the university) which

---

[6] *Whigs and Hunters*, 193, 258-69; Penelope Corfield, Review of Scott Hamilton, *The Crisis of Theory: E. P. Thompson, The New Left, and Postwar British Politics* <www.history.ac.uk/reviews/review/1137> (viewed 5 Feb. 2012).

touched Thompson in an official capacity. Its subject was David Montgomery, an American labour historian who was then a visiting lecturer at the Centre. Its author was the managing director and CEO of Rootes Motors (a British subsidiary of Chrysler International), who was much involved in university affairs. A former factory worker and union organizer in the US, Montgomery had made contact with British trade unionists, and the CEO had sent an agent to one of his talks to gather evidence for prosecuting him as an alien fomenting industrial unrest. Montgomery had said nothing to warrant prosecution, but Thompson at once raised the alarm within the university at this threat to academic freedom and published a piece in *New Society* exposing the university's subjugation to big business. It scorned the academic staff for knuckling under to the Philistines and applauded the student demonstrators for standing firm at risk to their academic careers. A few months later he edited a book in which he, along with several colleagues and students, developed these themes. Then he quit the university to write as a freelance.[7]

It was a difficult time for Thompson, both as an Englishman and as a socialist. The British industrial economy was suffering from foreign competition and poor labour relations. British foreign policy was defined by subservience to the United States, which successive governments seconded as loyal subalterns in the Cold War. The Campaign for Nuclear Disarmament had lost steam after failing to capture the Labour Party in the early 1960s. The bright promise of 1968, when the radical youth of several countries had staged militant and momentarily effective demonstrations against the status quo, soon faded. In Northern Ireland, the campaign for Catholics' civil rights evolved into a low-level civil war between militant Irish nationalists on one hand and Loyalists and the British Army on the other. The state security apparatus and the police responded to these exigencies, real and perceived, by instituting

---

[7] E. P. Thompson, "The Business University," in Thompson, *Writing by Candlelight* (London: Merlin, 1980), 13-27, first pub. in *New Society*, 19 Feb. 1970; *Warwick University Ltd: Industry, Management and the Universities*, ed. E. P. Thompson (Harmondsworth: Penguin, 1970); Merfyn Jones, "The Point is to Change It", *International Socialism*, no. 44 (July/Aug. 1970), 42-44; Ivor Gaber, "Middle-Class Posturing or a Victorious Fight for Real Changes?" *Times Higher Education Supplement*, 18 Apr. 2003; Bryan D. Palmer, *E. P. Thompson: Objections and Oppositions* (London and New York: Verso, 1994), 108-13.

practices and promoting legislation designed to weaken traditional constraints on their freedom of action. In a series of judicial reforms disguised as "modernization", and an assortment of policies designed to suppress whistle-blowing, Thompson detected a trend towards authoritarianism, all the more alarming because public opinion, lulled by official PR and the mainstream media, seemed all but oblivious to it. "We are living now through a contemptible decade of British history," he wrote.[8] For this the Left was almost as much to blame as the Right.

Thompson's rise to authority as a public intellectual had not softened opposition to him among Marxists who did not share his sensitivity to history and its lessons. In a reminiscence evoked by Thompson's death, the journalist Christopher Hitchens would think back across a quarter of a century to an occasion during his own undergraduate days at Oxford, when he and a clutch of demonstrators against racism, jammed into a police cell, discovered that they had something else in common.

> All had heard Edward Thompson's bravura talk on the Enclosure Acts a few weeks previously, and once this had been established there was no other topic of conversation. He had finished a tremendous account of the lost world of the common land and the common people with a recitation of the poetry of John Clare. And all the clichés about bringing history to life had become ... vividly and properly true.

Yet even so, Hitchens now recalled with pain, he had been inclined at the time to regard Thompson as a bit of an eccentric, who, in his unrelenting fight for the soul of Marxism, "often seemed like the crusty old provincial rebuking the young city slickers."[9]

That was in 1969, when Thompson was a crusty 45-year-old and the motto of what he called "the revolting sons and daughters of the bourgeoisie" was Don't Trust Anyone Over 30.[10] During the ensuing *contemptible* decade, what he dismissed as a phoney Marxism remained ascendant among the left-wing intelligentsia — a highly theoretical discourse, which sneered at civil liberties and democratic practices as mere masks for bourgeois hegemony. Under its influence, the "unofficial Left" (i.e., that which was independent of the Labour and Communist parties) had responded with apathy to

---

[8] In general, *see* Thompson, *Writing by Candlelight* (quotation, 254).

[9] Christopher Hitchens, "Minority Report," *The Nation*, 27 Sept. 1993, 306.

[10] Thompson quoted in Michael Kenny, "Socialism and the Romantic 'Self': The Case of Edward Thompson," *Journal of Political Ideologies*, 5:1 (2000), 115.

successive encroachments on the time-honoured liberties of the nation — hence Thompson's defiant paean to the rule of law in *Whigs and Hunters*. When trial by jury, which he esteemed as the cornerstone of British liberty, came under attack in its turn, his efforts to raise the alarm had been met with scorn in the purlieus of the New Left. Exasperated by this dismissive response, he remarked: "The trouble with all such arguments is that they presume to contrast sordid reality with some pure alternative which exists only in an intellectual's abstracted utopian noddle ... I can imagine better laws, and I can imagine better jurors, but I cannot imagine a better system."[11]

An article from 1978 reveals why the struggle mattered so much to him. It was prompted by a concatenation of events. Two years previously the British government had ordered the deportation of two Americans as threats to national security. Philip Agee was a former CIA agent who had published a whistle-blowing book on the Agency, and Mark Hosenball a journalist who had published an article on Anglo-American electronic intelligence operations. A defence committee was set up to support the two men, and Thompson was a member. Then, a year later, three other men were arrested for national security offences: one, an ex-soldier, for passing highly classified information, and the others, both journalists, for receiving it. These two events epitomized the abuse of state power in the name of national security, and the scandal ballooned when the two cases turned out to be related. The ex-soldier had been passing information that he thought might help Agee and Hosenball, and the arrests occurred because the police were spying on their defence committee.[12]

The three men's trial coincided with the publication of a memoir by Chapman Pincher, a veteran right-wing journalist with privileged access to defence and security circles. The book detailed Pincher's career as a favoured recipient of official leaks, and its contents prompted Thompson to heavily ironic reflections on how the state sought to control the flow of information in order to manipulate

---

[11] Thompson, *Writing by Candlelight*, 164-70 (quotations, 166, 169).

[12] Duncan Campbell, "Official Secrecy and British Libertarianism," *Socialist Register*, 16 (1979), 75-88; Crispin Aubrey, *Who's Watching You? Britain's Security Services & the Official Secrets Act* (Harmondsworth: Penguin, 1981). Aubrey and Campbell were the two journalists accused in the so-called ABC Trial. (Their accused informant was John Berry.)

public opinion. Besides its broad importance, the topic had deep personal significance for him. Firstly, it was likely that he too had been spied on as a member of the Agee-Hosenball defence committee. Secondly, the issue of official secrecy rankled because of his failure, over more than thirty years, to screw convincing information out of the government about the circumstances of his brother's death in 1944. Pincher's patriotic preening, as one dedicated to exposing "the machinations of the extreme Left against the interests of the country I love," was the last straw.

The dust-jacket of Pincher's book puffed his war service in the 6th Armoured Division and then at the Military College of Science, where he had done research on anti-tank weapons, but it made no mention of combat experience. Writing as a veteran of the 6th Armoured whose research into anti-tank weapons had been conducted (as he put it) at the receiving end, Thompson embarked upon a train of reflection about "the betrayal of the past and the calumny of the dead." He recalled what was now forgotten:

> a resolute and ingenious civilian army, increasingly hostile to the conventional military virtues, which became — far more than any of my younger friends will begin to credit — an anti-fascist and consciously anti-imperialist army. Its members voted Labour in 1945: knowing why, as did the civilian workers at home. Many were infused with socialist ideas and expectations wildly in advance of the tepid rhetoric of today's Labour leaders ... Our expectations may have been shallow, but that is because we were overly utopian, and ill-prepared for the betrayals at our backs.

It pained Thompson that one could no longer speak of these things to the young without encountering scorn and disbelief. And the reason was in part that Pincher and his kind had made "an uncontested take-over of all the moral assets of that period," appropriating the war to their own right-wing, authoritarian political mythology and expunging all recollection of the spirit of 1944.

In a poignant coda, Thompson mused on how memories affect one in middle life.

> For months the past stretches out behind one, as an inert record of events. Then, without forewarning, the past seems suddenly to open itself up inside one — with a more palpable emotional force than the dead present — in the gesture of a long-dead friend, or in the recall of some "spot of time" imbued with incommunicable significance. One is astonished to find oneself, while working in the garden or pottering about in the kitchen, with tears on one's cheeks.

> I have found myself like this more than once since reading Mr. Pincher's book. I have no notion what the tears are about. They are certainly not those of self-pity. There may be something in them of shame, that we should have let that world be degraded into this. There is also fury — that younger people, and among them some whom I most approve or admire, should have had this foul historical con imposed upon them — should suppose that this is all that that generation was ... Pincher's sort of people!
>
> I can now see what was wrong with that generation. It was too bloody innocent by half, and some of them were too open to the world, and too loyal to each other to live.[13]

Thompson closed with an ironic self-reference: a line from King Lear raving on the heath. It is, of course, in his raving that Lear finally achieves self-understanding.

The article was a performance, but it was a performance of the truth as Thompson saw it.[14] As such it throws light on another performance of his, which was then to be found in select bookstores. *The Poverty of Theory* takes its title from a very long essay, highly rhetorical in style, which savages the thought of the French structuralist philosopher Louis Althusser. It is an abstruse and difficult rebuttal of a highly theoretical discourse, but at one point Thompson ascribes his belief in the *historical* importance of personal heroism to the experience of growing up during a "decade of heroes" (1936-46), when there were Guevaras in every street and wood (a dig at the cult of the glamorous Argentinian guerrilla leader, whose posterized photo then adorned many walls) and a sense of the *historical* importance of individual action had momentarily imbued Marxist discourse with notes resonant of liberalism ("the choices of the autonomous individual") and Romanticism ("the rebellion of spirit against the rules of fact"). In celebrating the fight against fascism, and lamenting the subsequent polarization of

---

[13] Thompson, *Writing by Candlelight*, 132-33 (ellipsis in original); and see generally 113-33.

[14] One thinks of Thompson's remarks on the theatricality of John Thelwall. For an interesting reflection on Thompson as a performer, see Jonathan Rée, "E. P. Thompson and the Drama of Authority," *History Workshop Journal*, 47 (1999), 211-21.

the Cold War, the passage echoes the diatribe against Pincher; but in this case Thompson's target is Stalin's "sort of people."[15]

Hence the traumatic outcome of the controversy, in November 1979, at a conference of the History Workshop, a fraternity of socialist historians dedicated to the Thompsonian practice of "history from below" (its founder, Raphael Samuel, had shared Christopher Hitchens's police cell a decade previously). On a dark and stormy night, in a large derelict Oxford church, a plenary session convened to discuss Thompson's essay. The three panellists were seated at the altar before an audience of hundreds, some perched on scaffolding around the walls. Bright spotlights (reported *New Society*) increased the sense that a theatrical performance — not a closely knit discussion — was demanded. The chairman "called for a high level of 'co-operative discourse' ... but in the circumstances, such a thing was unimaginable." After presentations by fellow-panellists Stuart Hall and Richard Johnson, Thompson took the stage and

> proceeded on a demolition job on his critics which caused evident personal pain and discomfort to many of those present. At one point he dismissed the theoreticists for performing "a psycho-drama within the enclosed ghetto of the theoretical left," for "entrapping" generations of socialists into internal disputes, for offering "ideological justifications of stalinism." The Althusserians, he said, had captured philosophy, and art criticism, had invaded literary criticism and were now "massing on the frontiers of history itself."
>
> All this was delivered with maximum theatrical force. The result was that subsequent discussion was almost impossible. The aftermath of the Saturday night's fusillade hung like a pall of smoke over the rest of the conference.[16]

Our business here is to establish the intellectual and emotional sources of *The Sykaos Papers*. The details of Thompson's quarrel with "the theoreticists" are irrelevant; what matter are his state of mind and perception of the issues. Richard Johnson took the brunt of his ire, above all for an ivory-tower academicism which had little

---

[15] E. P. Thompson, *The Poverty of Theory and Other Essays* (London: Merlin, 1978), 264. I sometimes wonder if Thompson meant to write "rule of facts." But would it make a difference?

[16] Martin Kettle, "The Experience of History," *New Society*, 6 Dec. 1979, 542-43; *People's History and Socialist Theory*, ed. Raphael Samuel (London: Routledge & Kegan Paul, 1981), 376; Richard Johnson, "Edward Thompson, Eugene Genovese, and Socialist-Humanist History," *History Workshop Journal*, 6 (1978), 80-100.

bearing on the real world. Thompson pointed out that, while Marx had written texts that could be classed as economics or philosophy, neither had been Marx's primary concern. "It was to understand *power* in society that he entered that lifelong detour into economic theory." And power, of course, meant politics.

> Richard Johnson will not have us inflating differences: our discourse must be "careful and respectful" and be conducted in a "brotherly and sisterly way". It is easy to be respectful, sisterly and brotherly, if one's theory can never do so much as bend a pin in the real political world: if one never has to be called to account for one's theories, since the gap between theory and actuality is so rarely crossed: or if theory is reduced ... into little more than a psycho-drama within the enclosed ghetto of the theoretical left.[17]

When important matters were at stake it was necessary to be blunt.

The historian Robert Gray suggests that, just as 1956 was crucial for Thompson's political and intellectual project, 1968 was crucial for the Marxisms against which he was reacting.[18] What matters, though, is that Thompson's view of both crises was shaped by his memory of the spirit of 1944, for which his own brother and so many brothers-in-arms had died, and the betrayal of that promise by Pincher's and Stalin's "sort of people." Still too young to vote, Thompson himself had been obliged not just to risk his own life but to send others to their death. In 1956 he was moved by the sight of men and women again resisting tyranny at the cost of their lives. 1968, by contrast, presented a spectacle of acting-out by a generation that in Britain had never known military service, let alone war, against an authority that might be unfair and repressive but was not tyrannical in a fascist or Stalinist sense — hence his gibe, not against Guevara, but against the *cult* of Guevara. And as the ensuing contemptible decade neared its end, he perceived that the reluctant heroes of 1944 had been betrayed again — desecrated by a perversion of memory as atrocious as that which the enormous condescension of posterity had inflicted on the Luddites. In the 1980s

---

[17] E. P. Thompson, "The Politics of Theory," in *People's History and Socialist Theory*, 400. There is a lucid summary of the issues in Scott Hamilton, *The Crisis of Theory: E. P. Thompson, the New Left and Postwar British Politics* (Manchester: Manchester UP, 2011), 155-216.

[18] Robert Gray, "History, Marxism and Theory," in *E. P. Thompson: Critical Perspectives*, ed. Harvey J. Kaye and Keith McClelland (Philadelphia: Temple, 1990), 159.

he would try to revive the promise of 1944 by dedicating himself to European Nuclear Disarmament, a movement that sought to unite peoples on both sides of the Iron Curtain against governments seemingly bent on making Europe the battleground of the Third World War.

His manifesto appeared a few months after the History Workshop dust-up. Ominously entitled "Notes on Exterminism, the Last Stage of Civilisation," it rejected the logic of mutual deterrence by challenging the notion that relations between the rival power-blocs were amenable to rational control. *Exterminism* signified the inertial force of the nuclear arms race, with its constant generation of new weaponry which, once brought into existence, exacted reciprocal escalation from the other side regardless of reason. The process had reached a crisis because the advent of new, more accurate missiles had fostered the delusion that limited, controllable nuclear conflict might now be possible. The only hope of stopping this vicious circle of mutual challenge and response lay in mobilizing the peoples of both blocs against political establishments that were in thrall to the demented logic of "mutual assured destruction." The likely price of failure was the extermination, not necessarily of all life, but of human civilization. *The Sykaos Papers* imagines the outcome of exterminism.[19]

Swiftian satire

By Thompson's own account, parts of *The Sykaos Papers* date back to the 1960s, suggesting a gestation of some twenty years. The story's development from "minor opening" (Perry Anderson's words) to apocalyptic climax reflects this — the tell-tale sign of a narrative that, like the others discussed here, began as one thing and grew into something very different. Oi Paz's early comic misadventures are hardly more promising as a matrix of epic fantasy than the opening pages of Tolkien's *Hobbit*-sequel; but as with *The Lord of the Rings*, the transformation was stimulated by world events: in this case the deployment of Cruise missiles and the

---

[19] Thompson, "Notes on Exterminism, the Last Stage of Civilization," *New Left Review*, 121 (May-June 1980), reprinted in Thompson, *Zero Option* (London: Merlin Press, 1982), pub. in US as *Beyond the Cold War: A New Approach to the Arms Race and Nuclear Annihilation* (New York: Pantheon 1982). See also Karen Sayer, "History, Politics and Imagination in E. P. Thompson's *The Sykaos Papers*," *Foundation*, no.93 (Spring 2005), 107-15.

advent of the Strategic Defence Initiative under Ronald Reagan. Accordingly, the Swiftian satire of the early pages is focused mainly on issues that preoccupied Thompson in the 1970s, while the subsequent deepening and darkening reflects the superimposition upon those concerns of a revived threat of nuclear war. The interweaving of apocalyptic drama and burlesque in the later chapters expresses the ironic sensibility of a prophet who could imagine himself as King Lear on the heath. There is a moment in one of Dostoyevsky's novels when a girl has hanged herself, leaving a note in which she apologizes for cutting short her debut into life, and two characters discuss how it is possible to joke in a suicide note.[20] *The Sykaos Papers* is not a suicide note, but it does seriously contemplate the species-suicide of a nuclear holocaust and many of its jokes smack of gallows-humour.

There is, then, a valid rationale for the unusual range of style and tone in the narrative; but what sort of narrative is it? Like Tolstoy more than a century earlier, Thompson had to confront the assumption that his long fictional narrative was a novel. In an interview headlined "E. P. Thompson on his new novel," his very first remark questioned whether it was a novel "in any recognised sense." It was certainly not science fiction, and certainly not a realist novel. Maybe it was three things: "one part is entertainment or fable the reader is supposed to laugh [at]; another part is satire; and a third part is imaginative exploration, in which differing modes of consciousness interrogate each other and, in the course of this, explore how human culture and even personality is constructed."[21] This is more helpful than Tolstoy's remark that *War and Peace* was "that which the author wished and was able to express in the form in which it has been expressed"; but it is not necessarily the whole truth. *War and Peace*, while "not a novel," is still more a novel than anything else, and a long fictional narrative which explores how human culture and personality are constructed must be at least partly a novel. And a plot that depends on the operations of imaginary technology must be at least partly science fiction.

Like *The Lord of the Rings*, however, *The Sykaos Papers* is a fantasy written by a scholar; and like Tolkien, Thompson applies his expertise to the invention of faux-scholarly texts as a means of

---

[20] *A Raw Youth* (trans. Constance Garnett, New York: Dell, 1961), 208. The title is sometimes translated as *The Adolescent*.
[21] Cited above, 245, n.4.

realizing his imaginary universe. But he applies this device much more comprehensively than Tolkien, since the entire story takes the form of a scholarly compilation of documents. The subtitle describes it (in typographic layout appropriate to a title-page) as:

> An Account of the Voyages of the Poet Oi Paz to the System of Strim in the Seventeenth Galaxy; of his Mission to the Planet Sykaos; of his First Cruel Captivity; of his Travels about its Surface; of the Manners and Customs of its Beastly People; of his Second Captivity; and of his Return to Oitar. To which are added many passages from the Poet's Journal, documents in Sykotic script, and other curious matters. Selected and Edited by Q, Vice-Provost of the College of Adjusters. Transmitted by Timewarp to E. P. THOMPSON.

The "Account" is wrapped in metafictional packaging, starting with a Preface by "E. P. Thompson" which relates how the documents in question were somehow transmitted to his "word-processor" (meaning — in those days before the World-Wide Web — a personal computer used to type and edit text). "Thompson" points out that the events described in the documents take place a decade or so in the future and notes that backward transmission in time would present no problems for Oitarian technology. He concludes: "We will have to wait with what patience we can command to discover whether the Gracious Goodnesses sent us this input as an admonition or as a programmed doom."

The Preface is followed by an official Oitarian document entitled "Judgement of the Sublime Couch of Oitar," which declares in part, in a ceremonious yet quirky idiom, "That these records contain obtuse expressions which blaspheme against the Sacred Wheel" and might therefore "do injury to the ratios of youth." They are to be placed on the Sublime Index; but, in view of their intrinsic interest, ten copies are to be held by the College of Adjusters and the College of Stellanthropology — any reader, however, must seek instant absolution in the Bumple of the Wheel. Only now comes a Contents page with a list of the chapters, or "Segments", which make up the Account. These Segments, except for the first and last, are compilations of documents in many forms and voices (some, for instance, are transcriptions of electronic media). Each segment is prefaced with an explanatory Editor's Note by "Q" and is dotted with occasional footnotes, which typically show absolute incomprehension of the subject-matter and a marked hostility to Oi Paz.

Of course, Thompson's fictional universe is not quite as imaginary as Tolkien's, and many of the documents are satirical parodies of contemporary media or bureaucratic discourse; but as the story becomes more novelistic, this digressive material gives way to more plot-bearing forms of document such as diaries and memoranda — mainly those of Oi Paz and his human lover, Helena Sage. As with the narratives I have already discussed, this metamorphosis is the key to the story's epic essence. However, unlike those stories, the transformation is holometabolous: that is, the unity of the finished narrative is analogous to that of an organism such as a butterfly or moth, which goes through several distinct forms on its way to maturity. In this respect, the course of the narrative parallels the metamorphosis undergone by its unusual hero. Oi Paz is no more poorly integrated than comparably pivotal characters such as Aragorn or Prince Andrei, and *The Sykaos Papers* is no worse constructed than the epics of Tolkien and Tolstoy.

The short first chapter comprises the most conventional narrative in the entire story, but only because it is based on a single document that is narrative in form. Oi Paz's account of his arrival on Earth is a virtuoso blend of lyricism and farce-tinged satire, which immediately sets the main action in a vast temporal and spatial frame. The lyricism resounds in Oi Paz's vibrant account of the planet's beauty. Oitar is a dying planet owing to the waning of its sun — that is why its inhabitants are interested in Sykaos, which they have discovered only after millennia of interstellar exploration. Several thousand years previously they had retreated within vast climate-controlled enclosures, and now the entire surface of Oitar is covered with ice that partially melts only at the height of summer. Within their translucent domes they lead a highly programmed and sensually deprived existence, deriving sustenance from nutritional pellets which they supplement with small quantities of vegetable roughage for biological reasons. Apart from a few crops essential for nutrition — milkstem, egflour and bredstik are named — they grow a limited range of flora for the sake of their medicinal virtue, harmonious pigment, or trance-inducing qualities, and their livestock is limited to the Sentient Seven and the Sacred Three.

When his scouting expedition from the Oitarian moon base terminates in a crash-landing in a tall tree somewhere, apparently, in the west Midlands of England (where Thompson himself lived), Oi Paz is entranced by his surroundings. He climbs down to the "crust" to find himself amidst an immense variety of flora, including "many varieties of small-leaved plants, of no evident function but the leaves of which seemed to come from the hand of a most choice designer."

> The warmth and the varying lights of sunset induced in me a melodious mood of well-being. The clouds made me reflect upon the extraordinary, unprogrammed cycle of this world, the sun drawing up the vapours from the seas and lakes which cover much of the planet's surface, and these clouds in turn releasing water in a fountain of drops on to the land ... And (as I was to find out) this same cycle induces the continual motion of air, so that these winds move clouds of vapour across the sky, like white water-sledges across a blue lake, and so give to the quietest day a sense of motion, as if the sky were a living being, or as if some unseen hand were moving this planet towards some agreeable end (18-19).

Oi Paz begins to feel that he has "passed through a time-warp into the Eu Topaz of our earliest legends" (20).

Obviously Oi Paz is a person of feeling, and of good feeling. He is in fact a poet by "roll", or vocation, even more than he is an astronaut, and he is on the Earth expedition because the Gracious Goodnesses of Oitar ordained that the first landfalls should be made by poets and philosophers.

> For if the planet should prove habitable, then there would be many generations which could learn the secrets of its soil and plants; but a record must be preserved through all time of the thoughts who first came to land. And if Sykaos were inhabited by harmonious beings, then the first meeting of the worlds would be a moment of unexampled beauty (5).

But, though cast as observer and recorder, he is not a blank slate. On the contrary, he is fully inscribed with a set of unquestioning values and prejudices, including a well-developed species-chauvinism. As he goes on to explain,

> A record should be made of the ecstasy of the Sykaans when they were first admitted to the privilege of Oitarian discourse, and of their delight at learning that they were not to be left unvisited and unregarded on the very margin of the cosmos, but were to receive the benefit of our colonisation. And a record might also be made of the first Articles of Agreement entered into between our ambassadors and these creatures, by which they should be offered the choice of remaining encamped at a little distance from our cities, where they could perform certain services for us alongside our butlers and discards (such as the quarrying of stone, the clearing of tundra), in return for instruction in Oitarian mysteries; or ... of withdrawing to some private portion of their globe, where we could establish a reservation within which they might

> continue to practise undisturbed their own untutored and bestial culture (5-6).

At a stroke Oi Paz is cast as a missionary type all too common in the history of Western imperialism, and he will bring to his encounter with *Homo sapiens* a matching set of values. Even before he encounters Sykaans, he is as much offended as enchanted by the disorderly profusion of their planet:

> At the last oxygen-count I had thrown open a hatch, and there came now into the craft a flow of raw air, a carrier of unknown intoxicants — the scents of strange organic matters and seductive oils and waters ... While the sense-receptors were thrown into a state of alert, the organs of reason, aesthetics and duty were dulled, as if — once caught within the magnetic lusts of this planet — the intellect must submit to the thrall of blood, and the spirit must endure within the dim light filtered through the shrouds of flesh (14).

Once recovered from his first rapture at his surroundings, he notices something that makes him doubt his first belief in an intelligent designer. "For all this beauty in each part, there was neither order nor regularity of cultivation in the whole. This was an archaic land, wastefully bearing unselected vegetation in its promiscuous disorder ... I began to suppose that this planet's crust had become carpeted with vegetation by some random spillage of undirected life." (18-19).

Oi Paz, in fact, is being set up as a puritanical version of the innocent abroad on the model of Voltaire's Candide or the virtuous protagonists of Henry Fielding's "comic epic poem in prose," *Joseph Andrews*. His coming humiliation is foreshadowed by his account of his first moments on Earth following his landfall in the tree — or, as he perceives it, "a gigantic multi-brachiate creature," whose "ceaseless nodding motions" persuade him that it might be a sentient and intelligent creature. "I therefore enacted the primary rituals for encounters with astro-feral civilisations. Throwing open the main hatch, I stood in the doorway, threw apart my robe to disclose that I wore no weapons, and extended both arms in a gesture of welcome" (15-16). Apparently the Oitarian gesture of greeting to strangers is identical to the Sykaan gesture of flashing — here surely is a Don Quixote in the making. The chapter ends when, having identified the actual intelligent denizens of Sykaos, he steps out onto a highway and flashes a speeding car. Between these events comes another quixotic episode in which he attempts diplomacy with a herd of cows and observes a bull advancing with palpably hostile intent. Divining that it is their Chief, he stands his ground and unfurls an illuminated scroll of Condescending Accost which just happens to be crimson in colour.

By the end of the first chapter, it seems that Oi Paz is in for a rough time at the hands of an unfeeling world, but also that we are not to take his sufferings too seriously. The next two chapters confirm this surmise. Segment Two records the "first cruel captivity" advertised in the subtitle, and not surprisingly it is in a hospital. Here certain physical oddities (including a remarkable resistance to high-speed impact), his claim to be an emissary from the planet Oitar, and his complete anonymity earn him the nickname Freddy the Freak. The "cruelty" of his captivity is in part a by-product of the difficulties attendant on treating a conspicuously weird foreigner who appears to be a harmlessly psychotic drug addict; but it is also a correlative of Oitarian cultural chauvinism and taboos, which include touching and public eating. Oi Paz is disgusted both by the routines of his medical treatment and by the gustatory routines of a public hospital ward, with its mealtimes and daily parade of visitors bearing gifts of fruit and confectionery. At first he needs no hospital food, since he has his supply of nutritional pellets; but these are discovered and confiscated in the belief that they are drugs, leading him to conclude that his "warders" (as they must be, since they keep him in a ward) intend to starve him to death. For their part, the staff can only understand his continuing refusal to eat as a protest against the loss of his drugs.

Fittingly, it is a gross obscenity that saves him from starvation: a fellow-patient thinks to cheer him up by sharing his private supply of "the Real McCoy."

> It bared its teeth and waved the flask before my face; and as I sought to turn away from this new assault, it held it within a finger's breadth of my nose, whereat the most powerful trance-inducing gases invaded my nostrils and took possession in a moment of my saporific organs, weakened by my long starvation. Whereupon this creature forced open the vulva of my mouth and inverted the flask, thrusting it into the orifice, and a great quantity of liquor passed, without any mediate tube, directly into my throat (47).

The resulting sense of ease weakens his inhibitions, and he "falls into mortal sin" by consuming some food placed before him. The sin quickly becomes habitual, and soon he gets impatient if kept waiting for his "tea" (a hot brown liquid) and "toast" (fired bredstik). But he shuns the "slabs of red or brown substance called by these creatures 'meat'" (49).

The ease with which Oi Paz acquires a taste for fired bredstik and the "real McCoy" is more significant than first appears: given time and opportunity, he will adapt more fully to Sykaan ways than at first seems possible. Before that, though, he must overcome the obstacle of his warders' language. His explorer's outfit includes a Translator, which can simultaneously translate speech even in languages unknown to its designers. However, its efficacy is limited by its inability to process the many homonyms in the English language and the profusion of metaphors and other idiomatic usages in colloquial speech, with its "gross fractures of logic" and "hideous grammatic lesions." (32). The difficulty is illustrated by the Editor's Note to the chapter, which egregiously misinterprets a newspaper report of Oi Paz's highway accident. The car driver is quoted as saying: "It was some kind of Jesus freak in fancy dress. He seemed to drop out of the sky ... I don't know what he was made of ... Any ordinary mortal would have been knocked to the moon and back." The Editor, Q, interprets this as affording

> definitive proof that they were instantly aware that they were being visited by an extra-terrestrial ambassador — as thus: the description "freak" (a term of distinction reserved for those who do not conform to mortal norms); the comparison to "Jesus", their most celebrated ghost who in myth came to "Earth" as an inter-stellar visitor; and (conclusively) "Any ordinary mortal would have been knocked to the moon and back." Hence our Messenger, who had "dropped out of the sky", was never mistaken for a Sykaan (35).

No less confusing are the gendered pronouns (sometimes also compromised by metaphor, as when the driver refers to his vehicle as "she"). Q is driven to exclaim at the "extraordinary profusion of gender terminology, as if the gender of a mortal specimen was always to be signalled and pushed forward into notice and was, indeed, more important than its role-kit or Collegiate attachments" (32).

Helena Sage, the anthropologist, and David Nettler, the linguist, will later conclude that Oitarian culture is designed to repress the destabilizing potentialities still lurking in the individual, and that the main Oitarian language, a rigidly logical system purged of any capacity for metaphor or other sources of ambiguity, is the primary means of repression (233-4, 319). Oi Paz himself, relieved of repressive programming, will assimilate to human culture more fully than these early passages forebode. But one of his crucial early lessons is that he can use the Translator only for vocabulary. To construe his warders' linguistic deformities, he must rely on observation and intuition.

The police, of course, are interested in Oi Paz because of his complete anonymity, his personal peculiarity, and above all his curious paraphernalia, which happens to include a fortune in gold and gemstones. Their early investigations are stymied by the unbridgeable language and culture-gaps, but their interest only increases when the autumn leaf-fall exposes Oi Paz's spacecraft in the tree where it crashed. Finally the Oitarian emissary receives the attention he has been demanding, and he is whisked off to London. However, when close examination of his spacecraft reveals no means of propulsion, the police conclude he is a hoaxer and, finding no crime that they can reliably charge him with, strip him of his valuables and eject him into the streets (65-76).

An ensuing series of ludicrous misadventures climaxes when, starving, he falls into the clutches of an Australian impresario, Nigel Harmer, who sees his entertainment potential and has the wit to exploit it by first getting him hooked on the Real McCoy in all its magnificent variety. Harmer makes him the star of a TV reality show featuring abrasive encounters with panels of celebrities and prophetic calls to repentance. The show is banned from British television, but Oi Paz is now an international cult-figure and Harmer takes him on a world tour with stops in the Soviet Union (now liberalized by Mikhail Gorbachev) and the United States. By now the shooting down of a larger Oitarian spacecraft has given new credibility to Oi Paz's outlandish claims. During a chaotic appearance at Pasadena's Rose Bowl, he is kidnapped by British agents and spirited backed to England, where he is incarcerated as an Official Secret on a country estate.

In this phase of the narrative, the widening of Oi Paz's field of vision produces a widening in the field of satire. By having his hero resume the narrative that broke off with his road accident, Thompson enables him to embellish his day-by-day account of events with insights gained only after long reflection. This device yields incisive mini-essays on Sykaan concepts of Law, Property and Money. For the most part, though, the satire continues to emerge in the course of events. Thus a newspaper report of a political demonstration mentions a mealy-mouthed but draconian new statute, the *Public Obedience and Suppression of Disaffection Act,* which provides that any gathering designated as illegal may immediately be attacked by the Forces of Law, although "authorised organisations" may demonstrate if they apply for a license at least three weeks in advance and the demonstration takes place on waste ground at least three miles from any government building or defence installation (90). Another article, a knowingly up-market account of Sapio the Spaceman's world tour, deprecates "a kind of Apocalypse ground-base [*sic*] which is getting heavier each time and drowning the wit. Maybe a hangover from the boring Eighties, when the anti-nuclear trip became a culture trap?" (119).

By this time, a transcription of Sapio's TV show has allowed us to sample his act — a crazy ranting word-salad with Shakespearean echoes:

> Howl, howl, ye crawlies, and go guilty to your undergrounds, whose holes the Gracious Goodnesses will stop with traffic wax! Aha, I see thee belch and whinge. Is there no sucker to be found? Not in thy kinky profits, no, nor in thy gigs and balls. Repent and pulp thy ill-begotten tapes and tracks! (108)[22]

It sounds a bit like Lear on the heath. It is now that Oi Paz's Translator (which has a fail-safe mechanism that causes it to "choke" when it encounters obscene input) proves to have a mind of its own and protests at being made to process the smug remarks of a politician named Dr Charon on nuclear deterrence and proliferation. Oi Paz and the Translator get into a row, he smashes it, and from then on is truly alone (113-15).

Satirical novel

A lot of this is both funny and pointed, but it hardly amounts to a novel in any conventional sense, still less an epic. In keeping with the admitted influence of Swift on the narrative, we can easily see Oi Paz, in his physical and moral repugnance towards the species among which he finds himself, as a Gulliver-shaped (i.e., humanoid) Houyhnhnm, revolted by mankind just as Swift's Houyhnhnms are revolted by Gulliver's account of mankind and as Gulliver himself is revolted by the Brobdingnagians and Yahoos. With Oi Paz's incarceration at Martagon Hall, however, the story turns into something different and more complex. It acquires a heroine, in the form of

---

[22] "Undergrounds" refers to London's subterranean railway system and "tapes and tracks" to then-current modes of video and audio recording.

Helena Sage, and a cast of supporting characters. Oi Paz remains the focus of the narrative; but his voice, although still important, ceases to be dominant. Having observed him mainly from inside his own head, we finally get a sustained external perspective. He continues to explore Sykaos and its culture, but the Sykaans now embark on a systematic reciprocal investigation — one that is reported, and in part conducted, by Sage, whose voice becomes the main conduit of the narrative. Even as their investigation proceeds, however, its subject steadily becomes less Oitarian and more Sykaan.

In part, this change is a response to the relationship he forms with Sage and Nettler, the linguist. It is a slow process, because Oi Paz needs "drying out" and at first interprets the withholding of the Real McCoy as torture. Fortunately, the medical establishment of Martagon Hall is comprised in the sympathetic person of Rani Satpathy, a young Indian woman who, as his ward nurse in hospital, had been the only member of the medical staff to achieve any rapport with him. Finally he realizes that booze is poison and Satpathy has been trying to cure him. He begins to find his "coop" agreeable — especially the grounds, with their noble trees and spring flowers, and the stables, where "an officer named an Equerry ... minds a club of noble horses, with whom in the early hours of morning Oi Paz may exchange vibes. And we vibe together about the harmonies of this blue-green planet, which, were it not for the wastes committed by mortals, resembles the Eu Topaz of archaic myth" (143). (With Swiftian nicety, Oi Paz refers to *Homo sapiens* collectively as "mortals" to repudiate the absurd idea that they resemble his own species, "humans".) Still, rapport is slow to form. Months pass before Nettler and Sage get close enough to Oi Paz to discover that he is as interested in Earth and its cultures and they are in him and Oitar. Then they realize that they can "trade" information with him: Sage on customs and social structure, and Nettler on poetry.

About now it comes to light that Oi Paz has been developing physiologically. Oitarians, it appears, have developed an artificial system of procreation and reproduction, designed for the eugenic production of offspring to perform particular social roles, which does not involve sexual intercourse or uterine gestation, let alone familial nurturing. Each year only a handful of males are born that can generate sperm, and this is viewed as a sort of holy affliction — the "sper-malady" — which determines their lives like any genetic "role-kit". The vast majority of Oitarians are virtually asexual, and gender is not part of their identity. Tactile sensuality is rigidly repressed, and interpersonal touching is taboo (hence Oi Paz's disgust at it), but there is no taboo against physical exposure (hence the Oitarian gesture of greeting). However, after more than a year of Sykaan sunlight and nutrition, Oi Paz begins to develop secondary sexual characteristics — somewhat to the embarrassment of the virginal Satpathy, who is his regular bath attendant. She takes Sage along to inspect him, and he demands reciprocity. To his own surprise and Satpathy's consternation, his inspection of the naked Sage triggers an erection.

The parade of human characters presented realistically, if not necessarily objectively, through Sage's eyes makes the narrative more novelistic in nature. So does the confinement of the action to a single, ostensibly mundane, milieu. Still, a strong tincture of farcical satire continues to pervade it: for the sake of disinformation, the top-secret establishment to which Oi Paz and his investigators are confined is called, the Foundation for Advanced Research into Climate and Eco-Systems (FARCES), though internally it is designated by the code-word LUNATIC. Much of the early plot business relates to Sage's annoyance with the pompous males who run the place — Pincher's sort of people — and their female enablers, but as the months pass she starts to find allies in unexpected places. One is Ann the Equerry, who got the job by a ludicrous bureaucratic bungle and turns out to be a free spirit, happy to accommodate Oi Paz's desire to ride the stallion Macho against the anticipated objections of the powers that be. However, Sage's most important and unexpected ally is Major Sorley, the signals officer who turns up some nine months into the game to set up and command a Lunar Communications Unit.

Nine months at Martagon have not increased Sage's fondness for military males, and her instinctive antipathy to Sorley is only aggravated by his assumption that they are both at Martagon to "defend Earth." The outer man is personable ("mid-thirties, blondish hair, very blue eyes," the latter slightly sad), but she dismisses his modesty as "simulated" and puts down his apparent rapport with Oi Paz and Satpathy to deviousness: he "pretends to be shy" (179-80, 206). So far he is a romance archetype along the lines of Prince Andrei in *War and Peace* (he even turns out to be recently widowed — hence the sad eyes). But just as Sage at her advent was a different type of character from any (except perhaps Satpathy) that had appeared previously, so is Sorley. He turns out to be not just a hero but a Hero, and not just a man of action but something of a sage — far more so than Sage herself, who for all her intelligence and sophistication is essentially a clueless *ingénue*. Aragorn (with a strong dash of Gandalf) to her hobbit, he quickly deflates her pride by revealing how little she knows about what is going on. She learns that her and Nettler's rooms are bugged, that Oi Paz himself has been bugging everyone, and that the non-executive staff have regular contact with the outside world through a secret tunnel, and some even frequent the local pub. The Americans are listening in from outside; the Russians aren't bothering because they have moles inside.

Sorley, of course, is doing his own bugging, and so can come to the rescue when the FARCES directorate discovers that Sage and Nettler, having begun to empathize with Oi Paz, have been withholding information about him and Oitar which they believe the authorities would misuse. This is a possible breach of the Public Obedience and Suppression of Disaffection Act, which makes it a criminal offence to withhold information relating to the national interest from the authorities. Sorley's eavesdropping enables him to sweep into Sage's room and scoop up most of her tapes and notes before Martagon security gets there. That night the head of Martagon security, Jack Mayhem, and his accomplice, cryptography expert Jane Crostic, defect to the USSR with whatever Sorley did not get first. Crostic makes it over the wall, but Mayhem is fatally savaged and snacked on by the guard dogs. These and other shenanigans give Sorley the chance to zoom about in a Land-Rover, looking macho and generally taking charge. And just as Prince Andrei is revealed as one of the best dancers of his day, Sorley (who is named after a very minor character in *A Passage to India*, a Christian missionary of liberal bent) turns out to cook a dynamite curry.

In this phase of the story, Swiftian satire has ceded dominance to a burlesque of British middle-class manners and values faintly echoing the early novels of Michael Frayn — in particular, perhaps, *The Tin Men*, which is also set in a research institution. Against this backdrop of farce-tinged satire, however, a big picture with a distinctly apocalyptic tint begins to take shape. Its focus is the largest of existential questions: can *Homo sapiens* co-operate effectively against a threat to life on Earth as we know it? The issue is posed in two passages: one a paper by Oi Paz on the prospects for Oitarian colonization of Sykaos, the other a discussion between Sage and Nettler on Oitarian social structure. With these revelations, arising from the information-trading between Oi Paz and the two scholars, the narrative definitively resumes the expansive spatial and temporal perspective first adumbrated in Oi Paz's account of his arrival on Sykaos.

Oi Paz's paper on colonization prospects is a wide-ranging conspectus of the planet's condition with a startling and pessimistic conclusion. Among the thousands of planets that Oitar has explored, Sykaos is a world of unique perfection, but its perfection is unimaginably fragile. The atmosphere is a thin filament lying upon the oceans and land, to be torn away by any natural event, such as the impact of an asteroid or a flux in the solar wind. The highest of the planet's little mountains rise into zones where the oxygen count is too rare to support human life. Even in the temperate zones the smallest hills are swept with winds and may be covered with snow although the plains beneath them bask in radiant sun (196).

After rehearsing the nine great extinction events that have already occurred, Oi Paz comes to the fly in the ointment.

> All of the mammalian species are of very recent evolution, and in the history of life of this planet they may be seen as trials or brief experiments, soon to be extinct and to give way to fresh trials. And the most recent in evolution is the species "man", which bears a likeness to the physical constitution of humans [*i.e.*, his own species], although deprived of human spiritual faculties. It must be evident to any human observer that this species also is a botched experiment, whose deadline for extinction may indeed hap at any moment.
>
> The failure of the species 'man' arises from this paradox: evolving within a hospitable and bountiful environment ... they have supposed that the resources of life-support were provided for them effortlessly, as if from the decree of some benign Goodness who would bestow upon them water, sunlight, air and foodstuffs throughout eternity (197).

Thus the very bounty of the planet has fostered an unbridled egoism in the species. "Mortal culture ... is fragmented into as many identities as there are living specimens, and each one of these many millions posits its own need as an 'I'." Consequently,

> wherever one goes ... this odious species is at work, hacking down trees, killing beasts more sentient than they, burning up oils, casting open the rocks and soils, planting their hideous swarming nests upon the genial fields, polluting air and water, and devising new disasters. So that this hospitable ecosphere is now threatened with destruction, not from some natural cause ... but from the restless and self-centred appetites of its own dominant species.

Oi Paz concludes that Sykaos is perfectly adapted to Oitarian colonization if only the destructive activities of its dominant species can be brought to an end. "Since the species is self-programmed to extinction, no scruple need concern us if we should find it advisable to advance by a little the species' dead-line. (In doing so, we would undoubtedly save from extinction a number of more noble and serviceable species.)" (198).

Alas, the Oitarians have arrived a generation too late. Mortals have discovered the secrets of primitive nuclear fission and, as they do with every force, are busy turning it into engines of destruction. "In several great regions of the planet segments of the species are already preparing 'wars' against other segments, and plan to detonate huge nuclear explosions on the other parties." (A footnote explains what "war" is.) "This will fulfil the logic of the evolution of the species, and will perhaps be the apt terminus of its self-extinction." Unfortunately, the holocaust would render the planet uninhabitable for humans (*i.e.*, Oitarians), as in some places the pollution from nuclear power stations has done already (199).

Oi Paz, of course, belongs to a civilization shaped by just such an existential crisis as he predicts for *Homo sapiens.* As Sage and Nettler proceed with their research on Oitarian culture, they come to realize that the imperative of survival on a dying planet has enforced the centralization of power in an engineering elite which enjoys total command of all available resources. Oi Paz is the product of an advanced computer culture, which is devoid of any concept of kin or family or even elementary feelings such as love, fate, fear, and need. Its very rulers or deities — the Gracious Goodnesses that Oi Paz invokes from time to time — may in fact be mythical personifications of the artificial intelligence residing in banks of very advanced computers.

There are several Oitarian languages, including the archaic tongue of the ancient myths, the ceremonial Bumple Utter, and the expository Fact Utter. The everyday language, however, is Neuter Utter, a language so much like a computer programme that Nettler finds himself trapped within its de-humanizing algorithms and suffers a brief nervous breakdown. Its machine-generated logic-paths constrain thought from straying from the straight and narrow into antisocial by-ways. "If the Oitarians do come here in *that* phase of their consciousness," he tells Sage, "they will be quite merciless. That's not quite right, since Neuter Utter won't have any concept of mercy. It will simply be a compulsion, to compel Planet Earth to conform to the GGs' programme" (319). On this reading, the Oitarians sound disturbingly like the Khmer Rouge in nation-building mode.

The cultural antithesis between Oitarians and Sykaans crystallizes around their idea of history. Oi Paz can scarcely conceive of *Homo sapiens* as having a history. Its advent is so recent, its appointed life-span is so brief, and its record amounts to nothing more than a series of random, unintended occurrences. "In very recent times they have by such happenstance settled, cultivated the soil, built houses and cities, invented writing, and made their tools out of metals. This latest phase of their history they term 'civilisation'" (220). To Sage, on the other hand, Oitarians scarcely have a concept of history as she, as an anthropologist, understands it: to them, history is the patterned reiteration of their life-cycle as ordered by the Rule that governs every aspect of their existence. Early Oitarian myth is "vigorous with history" in the form of epic encounters with natural forces, and hazardous space explorations; but while these stories excite Oi Paz, he has (unlike J. R. R. Tolkien and the silversmith John Baxter) no sense of continuity between then and now. History begins with the advent of the Rule (227-29).

However, Oi Paz is more open to new ideas than Sage imagines. Certain striking similarities between Oitar and Sykaos, which are reflected in their languages, prompt him to startling speculations on ancient Oitarian myth. He cites an ancient epic, dating back to the onslaught of the first great glaciations, which tells that the intrepid explorers Hō Mā, In Kā, Bōd Hā, and Krish Nā set forth in two great armadas which ventured into unknown regions and dwelt on an uncharted planet for seventy of that planet's years; and only one ship, captained by Bōd Hā, returned.

> Although Bōd Hā was immeasurably weary, with memory banks nulled, yet from the halting tales of the far-travelled missioners amongst the crew was fashioned the great 'Energising and Summoning Myth' handed down to us from archaic times — the myth of the Planet Bathed in Yellow Sun, or Eu Topaz, with blue skies and green gardens which has inspired so many generations of our explorers — together with those darker tales of how our colonists were surrounded by hostile humanoid creatures, with horned helmets and with sickles in their hands, and were driven back to the fires of their encampments, which were overrun, one after the other, by white horsemen, until from the last encampment, at a place named Apo Kalyps, Bōd Hā and the depleted crew escaped (223-4).

Oi Paz speculates that miscegenation occurred, citing the "repeated motif within the mythology of every Sykotic nation, where it is often rehearsed that mortals are the product of both angels and devils; or where they imagine gods who descend from the heavens and inseminate their species." If so, "the whole history of the species, since the time of our colonisation, has been a degeneration from this origin" (226).

This passage is spoofy in several respects: Oi Paz the scholar letting his imagination run away with him; the Editor Q pedantically tracing Oi Paz's account of ancient myth to "'Arch. Myth (Misc.)', Tom. XXIII, cap. 7" and "Hō Mā, 'Argodyssey', Book I"; the same Q rejecting the very idea of miscegenation as absurd and offensive but also making the empirical point that prehistoric armadas could never have reached the Seventeenth Galaxy; and finally, perhaps, the idea of the history of mankind as a story of decline from an original state of grace. The spoof comes close to facetiousness at the point where Oi Paz identifies Stonehenge as an Oitarian structure and speculates that it is the place where Bōd Hā's lieutenant, Droo Id, came to a violent dead-line. However, the satirical playfulness stands as a counterpoint to the argument, not a negation of it. The names may be flippant, but Oi Paz's rehearsal of the myth is no less ardent than Aragorn's telling of the story of Beren and Lúthien on Weathertop, and his identification of the Blue Planet as the Eu Topaz of archaic myth is essential to Thompson's poetic argument. The next Segment is set in, and named after, the Zone of Eden.

Idyll, epic, apocalypse

"Zone of Eden": the very title turns out to be a double entendre, and the chapter brings the multiple tonalities of Thompson's story to full intensity — but not at once. It starts on the darkly humorous note on which its predecessor ended. NATO — i.e., the Americans, also known as the Cousins (as they literally were to Thompson, whose mother was American) — takes over Martagon Hall in the form of a horde of gum-chewing, computer-savvy young men in flowered shirts and sneakers. Neo-conservative luminary Lowell Himmelfarb, Jr.,[23] assumes effective control of the Hall as Associate

---

[23] Thompson borrowed the surname from Gertrude Himmelfarb, an American neo-conservative ideologue and specialist in British history who was one of his critics.

Director; the library, its books crated and stored, is converted into an open-plan office; a Coke machine and an ice-cream freezer, both huge, are installed in the Officers' Mess/Senior Common Room. Sorley, promoted to the rank of lieutenant-colonel and named Assistant Director, assumes control of the estate grounds and outbuildings, including a dower house where he arranges for Oi Paz, Sage, Nettler and Satpathy to take up residence along with Ann the Equerry.

A committee of academic experts arrives from the U.S. to check out Oi Paz's bona fides and usefulness. After enduring a polygraph test, during which the gauges are inert while he speaks but flail madly whenever his interrogators open their mouths, he declares a strike and demands to join the staff union; this allows Thompson to unveil the *Total Industrial Peace Act*, a labour-relations counterpart to the Public Obedience Act. A brief work-to-rule causes the ice-cream to melt, and the Presidential panel flees to more congenial climes (Florida), having reported recommendations that include keeping their panel in existence ("with credible honoraria"), the training of "achievement-oriented, fully adjusted space missionaries, with a view to converting Oitarians to the Freeworld Way of Life," and a mission to the moon to capture more "specimens" for lab testing (331-33).

Meanwhile, Thompson starts to ramp up the apocalypse by a heavier emphasis on the Oitarian threat. In a Gandalfian sketch of the big picture, Sorley reveals that the Oitarians are rapidly expanding their moon-base and clearly possess a capacity to generate electro-magnetic energy that is light-years ahead of human technology. It is now that we hear the full story of David Nettler's nervous breakdown and his foreboding reflections on Oitarian mercilessness. Sage finally begins to face up to the reality of the extraterrestrial menace and decides that she can best meet it by pursuing her investigation of Oitarian culture.

From this grafting of the apocalyptic onto the satirical, the idyllic emerges. As in *War and Peace* and *The Lord of the Rings*, its setting is a refuge beset by evil; and as in Tolstoy's story, its idyllic essence is at first obscure — and for the same reason. As with the Rostov domain, the evil that besets Thompson's Zone of Eden is mundane and rendered satirically, making a careful, gradual transition to the idyllic essential. In *The Sykaos Papers* the transitional mechanism is twofold. Firstly, the shift from Martagon Hall to the dower house segregates Oi Paz and his Sykaan sympathizers from the increasingly alienating milieu of the larger institution; but in the early days that segregation is incomplete because both Oi Paz and Sage remain bound to the Hall, he by his involvement with the Presidential panel of experts and she by her acquaintance with one of the panel, a former lover. Secondly, the idyllic emerges in two phases. The first, which arises out of the satirical strain, is mainly comic. The second, predominantly lyrical, phase arises out of the apocalyptic strain.

The milieu in which the idyll unfolds is that of the dower-house, its garden and the surrounding park. As spring turns to summer, Sage finds herself leading a not-quite-Hippie communal life with Oi Paz, Nettler, Satpathy and Ann, while Sorley pops in and out of view like Gandalf on a mission. Suddenly the nurse and the linguist, who have been thrown together by the latter's nervous breakdown, are courting madly, and Sage, who has just turned 39, is left feeling frumpy, washed up and teased with unappeasable desire. Stymied in her yearnings for Sorley, who has hooked up with Ann, she throws herself into the investigation of Oitarian culture, a project which involves her in reciprocal interpretation of Sykaan culture to Oi Paz. The love-relationship developing before their eyes has captured his interest, and the project of explaining how two "I's" can bond into a "We" seems to require that he become aware of his own "I" — a property which to him, as we have seen, is one of the deformities that distinguish *Homo sapiens* from the "humans" of Oitar. Sage instructs him to commence a diary, in which he can explore his feelings — another concept that is alien to him.

The comedy in this phase flows mainly from the tensions in the lovers' relationship. Nettler wants sex. So does Satpathy, but her values demand not only pre-marital chastity but a sort of wedding that is quite impossible under Martagon's high-security regime, which precludes importing either family or officiating clergy. Ann resolves the impasse by suggesting that they make up their own ceremony, and Oi Paz undertakes to preside over it, since it is to be held in the Temple of Flora, an eighteenth-century architectural folly that he has adopted as his "bumple". The ceremony combines Hindu, Christian and Oitarian rituals and features a leading role for Tigger the cat, another refugee from the Hall. (Oitarians revere cats even more than horses.) The wedding is a great success, and the newly-weds retreat into a private idyll of sexual bonding.

By focusing Oi Paz's anthropological curiosity on Sykaan sexual customs, juicing up Sage's frustrated sexuality, and thrusting them into each other's company, this comic business serves as a lead-up to their sexual union. Thompson hardly bothers to camouflage the destined event, but two things save it from triteness. One is the protagonists' ongoing investigation of each other's culture, which generates an intriguing clash of ideas and personalities, so that the sexual tussle seems to arise partly out of the intellectual tussle. As Oi Paz mocks her sentimental belief in freedom and the intrinsic worth of the individual, Sage feels as if entangled in an argument about determinism with a post-Marxist French structuralist; but Thompson allows the reader to feel that Oi Paz has had the better of the argument. Secondly, when the relationship reaches the crucial point, the burden of narration shifts to Oi Paz, who is still pretty clueless as to the connection between mind and body. This enables Thompson, in a textbook example of defamiliarization, to portray the climactic encounter through the eyes of an innocent who has no prior understanding or expectations of the event. It also lets him hint at Sage's inner turmoil without getting bogged down in it in an unhelpfully novelistic way.

The switch of narrative perspective from Sage to Oi Paz is crucial because it is Sage's voice that projects the realist element in the narrative. As soon as she begins to speak, we are in the presence of a well-defined human character from a world with which even some non-British readers will have some rapport. Functionally speaking, her character is the "true" lens through which the quiddities of Martagon Hall are refracted: she is a mature, sensible observer of the follies of FARCES — although also, just perceptibly, an ingénue through whom things come to light of which she is not herself aware until events or other characters reveal them. As long as we see through her eyes, the narrative must project itself as a novel, and that aspect reaches its highest intensity as her personal encounter with Oi Paz becomes more intense.

The shift to Oi Paz's perspective helps achieve that intensity. Perceptive and sensible as she is, Sage as narrator is no more a blank slate than Oi Paz and has been a flawed interpreter of the unfolding tale: over-confident in her opinions, sometimes misled by her prejudices, blind to much that is happening. We have observed her in moments of unhappiness arising from her unfulfilled personal life. But she has always been consciously pursuing a program — the discovery of Oitarian culture by interrogating Oi Paz — and this underlying sense of purpose projects an aura of control — or self-control at any rate. Now, however, under the defamiliarizing scrutiny of an intelligence at once penetrating and naive, she is revealed as confused and vulnerable. Oi Paz records the signs in his new diary, and does so without any attempt at interpretation because he is an innocent. Whereas previously her vibes were "not hostile, but distanced, like a sun behind white clouds," suddenly they are "like a cyclone ... sparkling now like hot rays upon my sensors, now withdrawing into a chill of distance" — especially when he unabashedly throws off his robes in the hot sun and proposes that she do likewise. And observing himself with equal detachment, he notes how his own vibes "open and close like valves" in response to hers and his "corpse also quickens in its pump and corporeal senses as if it were a mortal body" (363). This is more than Sage is aware of, apparently, since she notes her discomfort at Oi Paz's nude sunbathing but seems to have no idea of what she is communicating to him.

In short, Sage is much less in control either of herself or of their relationship than she seems to think; and Oi Paz's innocence is one reason. When goatish, goateed Professor Sir James Pepper, jet-setting Director of FARCES (a Saruman figure) tries to soften her up for sexual conquest by pointing out an elementary blunder in her report on Oitarian culture, and when Presidential expert John Blossom, a professional colleague and former lover of West Indian origin, does so by playing the race card, she twigs their game at once. But Oi Paz pummels away at her intellectual self-confidence with no ulterior motive, and when he demands to be enlightened concerning human sexual practices, to him it's just research. When Sage does finally enlighten him, it is with a strong sense of ambivalence. Teachers really should not have sex with their pupils, or anthropologists with their subjects, but the subject of this tutorial is the autonomy of the body. How can Oi Paz understand human nature and culture without experiencing the compulsions of the flesh?

But while subjecting Sage to external observation at this crisis serves to intensify the encounter, that is not its main effect. To Oi Paz, Sage is not just a woman: she is Woman, the female of the species *Homo sapiens*. As a result, even as it heightens her humanity, the peculiarly objective nature of his scrutiny has the effect of turning her into an archetype. The climactic encounter occurs in a beautiful walled garden planted with fruit trees, including a fig tree; Sage is tipped into complying with Oi Paz's demands by the apparition of a snake in an apple tree; she plucks an apple and tells her companion to take a bite, saying that it will give him knowledge of all mortal customs. The prototypal sexual tutorial of modern English literature, given by D. H. Lawrence in *Lady Chatterley's*

Lover, is also dotted with allusions to the Garden of Eden, and Thompson's treatment of the theme would be a bit heavy-handed for a realist novel. But he is not batting on that wicket. To him, unlike Lawrence, the Edenic allusions matter as much as the relationship between the characters, because they serve to position his story in relation to *Paradise Lost*.

This brings us to the epic essence of *The Sykaos Papers*. Beside *War and Peace* and *The Lord of the Rings*, it may look like an unlikely candidate for epic status. It is relatively short (less than five hundred pages) and has only a handful of characters. Instead of multiple interlaced plot-lines, it has a single main plot, which recounts the adventures of Oi Paz and his encounter with Sage. The action is mostly confined to an English country house and its park, and, as a function of the story's Protean character, the overarching theme of a grand alignment of opposed forces moving towards a climactic battle emerges only slowly.

Still, the story is quite long, and length is only a secondary characteristic of epic in any case — a consequence of its vast subject-matter. In the present case, Thompson's "documentary" narrative technique permits a quasi-theatrical compression of time and space. The temporal compression is most conspicuous in "Zone of Eden", where two years pass in a few pages without affecting the narrative flow. The spatial effect is that of the microcosm: the documentary narrative technique achieves an epic effect with a mere handful of characters by presenting them against a multitude of individual voices reporting or commenting on events that are playing out off-stage, thereby linking the little world of Martagon Hall to the unfolding drama that is its *raison d'être*.

That drama, of course, is not merely global but cosmic in scope, the crucial decisions being made not just in Washington and Moscow but on the moon and distant Oitar. This epic spatial perspective emerges right at the start, when Editor Q identifies Sykaos as just one of thirty thousand planets inspected in a patient exploration of galaxy after galaxy; and an epic temporal perspective appears with the reason for the exploration: Oitar's dying sun. The idea remains latent while Thompson schools his hero in salient aspects of Sykaan fecklessness and depravity, but it resurfaces as Oi Paz, in his Second Captivity, begins to generalize what he has learned into a grand synthesis. As he does so, Martagon transforms from a country estate into a microcosm with a symbolic geography not unlike that of *War and Peace* and *The Lord of the Rings*, although it does not constitute the stage for a quest or any travel that doubles as a journey in time.

The geography of Martagon, with its lake, common, copse, and assorted architectural curiosities, starts to take shape with the move from the Hall to the dower house. It is more complex than Tolstoy's west-east and Petersburg-Ryazan polarities, but less so than Tolkien's elaborately mapped Middle-earth. Since Thompson does not map it, it remains impressionistic; yet it is palpable — the Zone of Eden, after all, is a *zone* — and it emerges in stages. The first sign is the divided jurisdiction that accompanies the NATO take-over: Sorley's Astrosigint lunar communications station, situated at the point furthest from the Hall, becomes a locus of countervailing power. The new boundaries are tested almost at once as the Hall regime, goaded by Oi Paz's strike and the union work-to-rule, sends a gang of goons in battle fatigues to invade Eden and kidnap Oi Paz. They are foiled by Sorley, who has hastily set up a laser cordon around the dower house. The goons spray the house with gunfire but cannot penetrate the cordon, and they flee when Ann charges them on Macho. It is farce — but epic farce, with Sorley figuring as Gandalf in pyrotechnic mode.

The second, more sombre, phase occurs with the replacement of Associate Director Himmelfarb by a military "Co-Director" and the corresponding militarization of Martagon. The Hall ("Zone One") is to be out-of-bounds to all but U.S. military personnel; the Astrozone, comprising the Astrosigint station, will continue to be manned by British personnel under Sorley's command, "with NATO advisers on attachment subject to the Assistant Director's requirements" — evidently the Americans mean to keep an eye on him. The dower house unit is to be designated a "Zone of Eden" under the secret *Articles of Abrogation (Sovereignty, UK)* signed in 1955 by the British Prime Minister, Sir Anthony Eden, in the presence of President Eisenhower, which "designated certain zones as reservations for the sole use of the native inhabitants (Windsor Castle, Balmoral, Chequers, the House of Lords and such others as may from time to time be agreed)." Evidently the walled garden is not part of this demi-paradise: soon afterwards, Sage pays a sentimental visit and finds that it has been bulldozed to make a baseball field. Or maybe it was part of it. One can hardly expect such quixotic arrangements to withstand the exigencies of NATO.

The symbolic geography of Martagon points up Sorley's nature as an epic hero, a combination of Aragorn in his earnest heroism and Gandalf in his strategic savvy and techno-wizardry. Like the Tolkienian parallels in *War and Peace*, it reflects the fact that *The Sykaos Papers* is a saga of heroic resistance to rampant Evil. Of course, each story works out the problem of heroism differently according to its mode and its author's viewpoint. Tolkien the romancer allows Aragorn to fulfil his kingly destiny and Gandalf, Galadriel and Frodo to quit Middle-earth for a better place after a job well done. Tolstoy the realist grants his genuine heroes no earthly glory, and his wizard and elf-prince turn out to be duds. In Thompson's prophetic fantasy, his hero-wizard has to be the genuine article in order to serve his tragic purpose, which is to dramatize the feebleness of individual virtue in confrontation with systemic evil. One thinks again of Frank.

Besides Sorley, Thompson's story offers an even more striking parallel to *The Lord of the Rings*. A preternaturally handsome poet, gorgeously robed, whose people dwell in communities insulated from the intractable realities of physical decay; an androgynously (at first) charismatic aesthete possessing superhuman attributes; on Middle-earth but not of it; a keen-eyed commentator on the follies and foibles of the mortals who fondly think the Shire is theirs for ever — surely Oi Paz is an elf. He even, like Tolkien's elves, speaks a language of his own — not the Oitarian "utters" (although Thompson does give us a few lines of Neuter Utter here and there) but a unique idiom, rendered in English, which is perfectly suited to the projection of his thought, personality and culture and is especially vital to sustaining the energy of those long early passages where his is the main or only voice. Painstakingly sustained across hundreds of pages, it is one of the imaginative highlights of the narrative.[24] And like Tolkien's elves, Oi Paz gives voice to the vast cosmic context in both space and time. Unlike Tolkien's omniscient elves, however, he is newly arrived in Middle-earth. Like Lemuel Gulliver, he must learn as he goes.

The character of Oi Paz is a tour de force in its unexpected, but plausibly executed, transition from satirical butt to tragic hero. Something similar happens to Pierre in *War and Peace*, but the feat is more dramatic in *The Sykaos Papers* because the modal shift from satire to epic tragedy is starker: Pierre, after all, is a comic hero in

---

[24] A momentary lapse gives the measure of this achievement. Unlike everything else Oi Paz says or writes, "Must much remain obscure" (352) is pure Thompson: cf. "Much will always remain obscure" (*The Making*, 176).

Tolstoy's novel, whatever the future may hold. In any case, Thompson's story ends with Oi Paz in an even bleaker exile than the Decembrists'. The triumph of systemic evil demands no less.

To achieve this outcome, Thompson must show his heroes striving diligently, but in the end ineffectually, in the righteous cause; and this is the main point of the last part of the book. Two years pass in a few pages — something Thompson contrives through editor Q's mention of torn or obliterated pages in the protagonists' diaries. The gap is bridged by a handful of surviving documents, most of which speak to the failure of U.S.-Soviet cooperation in the face of the Oitarian threat. When Sage, now the mother of one-year-old Adam, resumes her diary, it is to record (though we do not know it) the few weeks of her life. American paranoia has reached such a pitch that the U.S. government is spoiling for a pre-emptive strike, either against the now massive Oitarian moon base or (if that is impossible) against the Soviet Union in collaboration with Oitar. Sorley has finally managed to establish effective two-way communication with the moon, and his unique insight into Oitarian culture, based on the otherwise neglected discoveries of Sage and Nettler, has earned him sufficient influence in NATO spheres to block this madness for a time. He teams up with Oi Paz to present Oitar with a proposal that might possibly forestall Armageddon.

Deftly phrased to appeal to Oitarian logic, the proposal identifies *Homo sapiens* as the great obstacle to Oitarian colonization and explains why the obvious solution — extermination — won't work: even if it does not provoke a retaliatory nuclear holocaust, it will leave hundreds of nuclear power plants in a potentially dangerous state. Colonization must therefore be achieved in cooperation with *Homo sapiens*, but this requires careful attention to the psychology of a species whose "principal botch" is that "no part can bond without Threat of Other, and Others must be furnished from among themselves." If Oitar can take on the role of Other, it may possibly induce the mortals to cooperate with each other in response to the perceived external threat; but the Oitarian threat must be carefully calibrated to avoid a crazed and destructive reaction.

Thompson works this plot out adroitly. Sorley dispatches Oi Paz and Sage to the moon in a European spacecraft along with Adam, whose presence Oi Paz demands in the hope that it will help him resist attempts at de-programming. Sage is plunged into a bleak environment among beings with little apparent capacity for empathy with each other, let alone for an alien whom they would scarcely class as human. When they find that she and Adam eat solid food, Oi Paz has to intervene to save his family from being housed with the "butlers" — long-haired ape-like creatures who perform much of the menial work. She notes distinctly hostile vibes in the Chief Lunar Adjuster, one of the two directors of the base along with the Base Commander. Half of Adam's food vanishes, whisked off to Oitar for analysis.

Sage seeks sanctuary from the culture shock in work. In a new notebook, she records her first glimpses of Oitarian society as reflected in the atypical environment of the moon base. Her jottings on the base, its inhabitants, and the arid lunar landscape that surrounds them conjure up a vivid sense of place. Earth, huge and blue, going through its phases in the lunar sky, is a recurrent image that takes us back to the very beginning of the narrative, when it so impressed Oi Paz on the eve of his fateful solo expedition. Thompson deftly connects Earth and moon, and sustains the narrative continuity, by having Astrosigint and the moon base establish an audio-visual link by which Sage is able to talk to Sorley and Ann as they appear on a large TV screen. More importantly, the a/v link allows Sorley to communicate directly with Oi Paz.

At first, things go well enough. The Oitarians may be merciless, but they are not irrational and they agree to accept a lightly populated area of sub-Arctic Canada as a colonization zone. It is *Homo sapiens* that proves unequal to the challenge. At first it seems that the pressure of international opinion has compelled the superpowers to surrender their powers to the United Nations, but then two weeks of jamming and cacophony ensue. When contact is restored, it emerges that both superpowers have made competing proposals to Oitar, the Americans offering them Russia and the Soviet government counter-offering North America. Another heroic intervention by Oi Paz persuades the gods in the Oitarian machine to reject both proposals and stick with Plan A, but it is all in vain. Sage and Oi Paz are looking on when Sorley, having received an urgent message off-screen, is gunned down by US Security hoods just as he is requesting a massive electro-magnetic jamming attack on nuclear weapons installations worldwide to prevent Armageddon. Then they watch from the Command Observatory as, a quarter of a million miles away, Armageddon unfolds.

The Oitarians lose all interest in Earth and prepare to leave the moon at once. Sage may or may not be the last Sykaan (not counting

Adam) left alive, but she will not be going home to find out. Her diary records the sudden disintegration of her life. First her ailing son, whom the Oitarians have renamed Hō Mō, is torn from her arms and whisked off to Oitar for medical treatment; then her husband, whose hard-won English is rapidly succumbing to intensive de-programming, is sent home for analysis and maybe "cure & re-rolling". Sage herself, surplus to requirements, her body degrading from malnutrition, is sentenced to "instant dead-line." Before she pre-empts her liquidation with a lethal dose providently acquired from Satpathy, one of her final reflections is: "O. was right, pro-gramme was botched from Genesis. Original sin = primordial bug. Just took a few millennia to work out. Wld have terminated sooner if mortals had had the means" (458). For Thompson, as for Tolkien, systemic evil = human nature.

We have come far since Oi Paz began the story of his solo journey to Sykaos, some four years since, and the narrative metamorphosis enhances the sense of an epic passage. The reason is this. The trans-formation of Oi Paz from a cog in the Oitarian machine to a feeling, autonomous being is the central thread of the story, and the changes in narrative form parallel that metamorphosis. By the end he has become both an epic and a domestic hero, the devoted protector of his wife and child in a world which is completely alien to them and hostile to him in its incapacity to empathize with the person he has become. The disintegration of the bond between him and Sage, like that between Winston and Julia in *Nineteen Eighty-Four*, symbolizes the impossibility of love in that world; Thompson's rendering is more poignant, however, because the relationship is more substan-tially and plausibly developed. At the end, Oi Paz struggles, through the growing language barrier, to convey his continuing affection for her. Their private agony crystallizes the pathos of the tragedy that is unfolding a quarter of a million miles away.

The end of human history

The story ends with a sheaf of Oitarian documents explaining why the papers have been placed on the Sublime Index. They record the sad career of Hō Mō: his obstreperous childhood, his affliction by the "sper-malady", his skipping of religious exercises to study the inputs of Oi Paz and Helena in the databank of the College of Stel-lanthropology. A Decree of the Sublime Couch, judging him to be irredeemable, condemns him to an immediate dead-line. But there is all too much of the old Adam in the new Adam — or perhaps just enough. Instead of going quietly as expected, he delivers a subversive harangue to the crowd and, flouting Oitarian taboos to evade capture, heads off for Sykaos in a space ferry designed for Earth colonization, which is on display at the College. With him goes a young female named Vev, whose remarks reveal that he has been secretly instructing her in the Custom of the Apple. After assuring the Gracious Goodnesses that the expedition is doomed to failure, the report ends by noting rumours that the craft landed that evening near Oi Paz's hermit-prison, and alternatively that it crashed in flames.

Adam and Vev: the Edenic, or more strictly Miltonic, allusions expose the essence of *The Sykaos Papers* as an epic of disaffection. *Paradise Lost* recounts the crucial events that culminated in the beginning of human history, and it sets those events in the context of a universal history extending from the Creation to the Day of Judgment. Thompson's story sets the end of human history in a version of universal history that is geophysical rather than eschatological. It presents the whole of human history as a fleeting moment in the history not only of Sykaos but of Oitar, and it presents the geophysical history of both planets as fleeting moments in the history of the universe. Oitar's encounter with the Sykaans is framed in Oitarian myth and history, and that narrative is dominated by the geophysical evolution of their planet and solar system, which is framed in the larger story of the evolution of the universe as a whole. Yet Thompson's epic vision is also evocative of *Moby Dick*. Viewed from outer space, what is Sykaos but another *Pequod*, a ship of fools doomed by human (indeed, American) hubris? But Ahab's barque sails on a turbulent but fundamentally unchanging ocean, a microcosm in an essentially timeless cosmic context. Thompson projects the opposite image: that of a world afloat in a cosmos that is serene on its surface but seething in its depths, a cauldron of geo- and astrophysical processes in which nothing is for ever but time itself.

I noted how Thompson muffles the triumphal teleology of Marxism by overlaying it with the myth of the Free-born Englishman, a narrative that conforms, rather, to the cyclical structure that David Quint ascribes to the epic of defeat. But while *The Making* is devoted to the rehabilitation of history's losers, at least it leaves us with a sense of a struggle in progress, and Thompson justifies his subject-matter by invoking the prospect that "causes which were lost in

England might, in Asia or Africa, yet be won."[25] In *The Sykaos Papers*, any glint of a Marxian temporal framework, hinting at a secular counterpart to salvation for the righteous, is obliterated in a total human history that promises no survivors and is itself diminished by a cosmic context in which it occupies but a fleeting moment. The brief metafictional coda precludes our calling *The Sykaos Papers* a leap into the abyss, but it certainly takes a long hard look into it. Thompson's epic history is a poignant evocation of history's losers and a suggestion that they were not quite such hopeless losers as the orthodox narrative ordains. In his fictional epic, with its imaginary history and mythology, no one is a winner.

The four narratives discussed here are all very different in nature, a reflection of the generic differences that make their common character as epics of disaffection so striking. As a parable of human self-destruction, Thompson's story is more conventionally prophetic than the rest, and that accounts for some of its distinctive features. It may also help to explain its low profile. The story dramatizes Thompson's preoccupation with nuclear weapons in the context of the Cold War, but within a year of its publication the Cold War was over, eradicating its topical urgency, and the end came under circumstances inimical to the intellectual tradition that Thompson had inhabited throughout his life. Understandably, if illogically, the collapse of the Soviet Union cast a shadow of inconsequence, if not discredit, over all things Marxist, making Thompson's lifelong engagement with that doctrine suddenly seem trivial — and not just his engagement with Marxism but with "history itself." A very different idea of the End of History from that of *The Sykaos Papers* came into fashion: a foretelling of mankind's entry into a political paradise of liberal democracy.[26]

In a longer view, though, Thompson's prognostications begin to look more prescient than the fleeting euphoria of the post-Cold War moment, especially if you allow for technological innovations since the 1980s. (The Oitarians cripple Sykaan infrastructure with electro-

---

[25] Thompson, *The Making*, 13.

[26] Francis Fukuyama, "The End of History?", *The National Interest*, No. 16 (Summer 1989), 3-18; *After History? Francis Fukuyama and His Critics*, ed. Timothy Burns (Lanham, MD: Rowman, Littlefield, 1994); Howard Williams, E. Gwynn Matthews, and David Sullivan, *Francis Fukuyama and the End of History* (Cardiff: University of Wales Press, 1997); Francis Fukuyama, *The End of History and the Last Man* (New York: Perennial, 2002).

magnetic surges rather than cyber-attacks.) The "generals' coup" against Gorbachev may have been little more than a fifty-fifty guess, but the idea of an upsurge of right-wing nationalism in the United States, leading to the disintegration of civil cohesion there, strikes an all-too-timely note, as does the renewal of strategic rivalry between Washington and Moscow. But above all, there is the primordial bug, manifest in a casual obliviousness to the fragility of the human ecosystem and our inability to co-operate to preserve it. In the end, whether the human capacity for self-destruction is realized through a nuclear or a climatic holocaust is just a detail.

8

Conclusion: Prophecy, Myth and the Numinous

A heroic romance, a novel, a history book and a satirical fantasy — four narratives that became infected with what E. M. W. Tillyard calls the epic strain and turned into something far removed from the original idea. I conclude with further thoughts about features of the epic transformation that are common to all four narratives: the underlying prophetic impulse, the expression of that impulse by means of numinous imagery, and the temporal placement of the main narrative as an episode in a total history.

Prophecy

In chapter 1, I linked the intrusion of the epic strain to the author's urge to prophesy. What, looking back, might that mean? One thinks of prophecy as some sort of apocalyptic prediction or admonition inspired by immediate personal revelation. That idea may fit *War and Peace* and Thompson's books, since Tolstoy first imagined his project as an exploration of a national crisis and Thompson too was emphatically a man with a message. But Tolkien set out to write a children's story, not the optimal vehicle for prophetic admonition, and as it became less child-focused it did not turn towards didacticism or propaganda. It is full of foretelling, but the prescience refers to Tolkien's fantasy-world rather than our own. Besides, Tolkien expressly disowned what he called "the conscious purpose ... of preaching, or of delivering myself of a vision of truth specially revealed to me." The notion that his story had somehow captured the zeitgeist, let alone helped to define it, was "an alarming conclusion for an old philologist to draw concerning his private amusement."[1] Tolkien's denial of an intention to propagate a "message" challenges the notion of an urge to prophesy in his case at least.

Yet it was our discovery of certain mystical yearnings in his thought and personality that brought prophecy into the discussion, albeit in the curious form of E. M. Forster's musings on prophecy as an aspect of the novel. Forster's idea emphasizes evocation of the numinous rather than foretelling or a call to righteousness, and our exploration revealed an unexpected affinity with Tolkien's personal perception of a world of spirit existing beyond the bounds of common consciousness. Noting Tolkien's emotional hunger for what I called the *possibility* of revelation, I visualized *The Lord of the Rings* as an attempt to evoke the sensation of that experience in art. In a sense, Tolkien fabricated prophecy just as he fabricated history, so perhaps in his case one should talk not of an urge to prophesy but of a craving for prophecy.

There is an interesting resonance here with Thompson's idea of psychic masturbation.[2] Thompson applied the term to the emotional and physical paroxysms associated with evangelical Methodism, interpreting them as the sublimation of spiritual impulses that were potentially revolutionary. These collective "orgasms of feeling" may seem very different from Tolkien's "private amusement," but in both instances the behaviour may be rooted in existential angst, engendered in Thompson's Methodist artisans by the undermining of their way of life by insurgent free-market capitalism and in Tolkien by the experiences of early childhood. At any rate, the metaphor seems no less apt to Tolkien and may help to explain the cult-like intensity of his popularity and the quasi-prophetic impact of his writing.

The distinction between an urge to prophesy and a craving for prophecy may not matter anyway. As we noted, Forster's idea does not depend on the novelist's intention: "His theme is the universe, or something universal, but he is not necessarily going to 'say' anything about the universe; he proposes to sing ..."

---

[1] See above, 68, 79.
[2] See above, 221.

Prophecy in this sense is not an outright affirmation of some transcendent reality, or a description of that reality, or even a description of a character's experience of it. It is something that happens when the writer contrives — not necessarily on purpose — to kindle a flicker of it in the reader's mind. Tolkien's denial of an intention to prophesy cannot, therefore, disqualify his writing as prophecy in Forster's sense. What matters is how his "song" is received.

If prophecy is in the eye of the beholder, it takes more than just mounting a soapbox and inveighing against current evils to make you a prophet: at best, that makes you a crank, at worst a bore. You don't become a prophet until your crankiness finds a receptive audience: in Forster's words, unless we approach the prophet with humility, our eyes will behold a figure of fun instead of his glory.[3] Thompson was a crank who achieved glory by appropriating a commission to write on working-class politics to the posthumous rehabilitation of a bunch of cranks; but he became a prophet only when undergraduates began buying his work at three-and-a-half guineas a time, a Penguin paperback ensued, and he had to swap his soapbox, first for a podium, then for a public address system. Not that he ceased to be a crank: who is crankier than Lear on the heath? As a reader in distant British Columbia wrote in not un-cranky response to one of Thompson's shapely diatribes against the "security state": "Oh E. P. Thompson what crap! (but) what superb crap!!"[4]

One might have said the same of Tolstoy, a famously cranky prophet. He mounted the soapbox for Christian anarchism only after the mid-life crisis that issued in his embrace of Christian asceticism. but he was already thoroughly disaffected some twenty years earlier, when he embarked on the quirky hybrid narrative which he would characterize in a series of negatives and that clearly, if symbolically, expresses the essence of his pacifist anarchism. It is no coincidence that Prince Andrei, the secondary character who forced his way to the front of Tolstoy's imagination and became pivotal to the epic transformation of the narrative, is a drop-out with pacifist leanings.

Perhaps, then, *The Lord of the Rings* expresses an alienation too profound for the idea of propagating a message even to have

---

[3] See above, 80.

[4] *New Society*, 10 Jan. 1980 (vol. 51, no. 901, p. 80); parentheses in original.

crossed Tolkien's mind. Perhaps, in conjuring up the numinous to satisfy his craving for revelation, he distilled the quintessence of Forsterian prophecy — the *song* — and so created the conditions for becoming a prophet despite himself. Perhaps, by charging the text of his *Hobbit*-sequel with intimations of transcendence uncoupled to any explicit message, he gave his readers the opportunity to fill in the blank. However, in chapter 3 we saw that Tolkien was not just a story-teller but a believer in the explanatory power of story, and that his theory of myth and fantasy closely resembled Forster's idea of prophecy as an aspect of the novel. That convergence of ideas suggests a different conclusion.

Forster differentiated the effect that he called prophecy from foretelling and from a call to righteousness. It was manifest in "a tone of voice," in "implication" rather than direct expression, not in speech but in "song." But he did not deny that prophecy might accompany those other things, and he mentioned D. H. Lawrence in particular as a preacher as well as a prophet, observing that "it is this minor aspect of him which makes him so difficult and misleading."[5] Forster's remark suggests that he saw no necessary connection between Lawrence's preaching and his prophecy, but he did not pursue the matter. Our study of epics of disaffection implies that there is a connection, since it ascribes the epic transformation to an urge to prophesy that was triggered by the author's alienation from modernity, and this is just as true of *The Lord of the Rings* as of the rest.

Indeed, Tolkien did not deny that his writing contained a message; he denied only the "conscious purpose" of delivering one. He admitted his story was infused with his "tastes, ideas, and beliefs," and that is true of all the narratives under discussion here.[6] Each was coloured by a worldview that embraced the gamut of epic attributes specified by Tillyard and so was primed with prophetic potential, but Tolkien's worldview was no less comprehensive than those of Tolstoy and Thompson, and we have noted his sympathy for those prime soapbox orators, William Morris and the philosophical anarchists. The *young* philologist may have started composing his legendarium as a private amusement, but it was an amusement that poetically expressed his deepest convictions, and the middle-aged philolo-

---

[5] Forster, *Aspects of the Novel*, 146.
[6] See above, 68.

gist was trying to reach a wide audience even before he had completed *The Hobbit.*

Significantly, his first push to publish, by means of the quickly abandoned "The Lost Road," entailed linking the modern world and the imaginary kingdom of Númenor, which he had just begun to incorporate into his mythology. The advent of Númenor was a striking departure, since it entailed a shift in focus from Elves to Men and to a new Age of the world in which Men had risen to world power, and the themes associated with its advent are also new. One is the theme of rebellion against the divine order, since the island kingdom is cast down like Atlantis when its people rebel against their mortality by attempting to invade the Undying Lands. But Númenor is not only a land in which the majority are estranged from the gods and from ancient verities, but one in which the righteous minority, who adhere to the old truths, are persecuted.

Contemplating critical dismissal of *The Lord of the Rings* as an exercise in escapism, we noted Tolkien's characterization of his unpublished legendarium as escapism and his qualifying definition of the term as meaning "transforming experience into another form and symbol." The themes associated with Númenor are certainly not escapist in the conventional sense; indeed, the theme of ideological persecution is political. Their appearance at the moment when Tolkien decided to publish his legendarium is unlikely to be a coincidence; at any rate, they could almost be a message. Númenor was a long haul from Bag End, and getting there by means of his *Hobbit*-sequel proved to be possible only with the help of a World War. It was with some surprise that he discovered that his long trek through Power and Domination had only been a detour en route to Death and Immortality, necessitating an addition to his appendices to round out a theme that he could not fit into a hobbit-centric narrative. The point is, however, that Tolkien's story was from its inception not just a retreat from modernity but an attack on it.

The nature of the message is worth emphasizing, because Tolkien never stated it in so many words but did describe *The Lord of the Rings* as "a fundamentally religious and Catholic work," going on to explain that he had left out practically all overt reference to religion because it was "absorbed into the story and the symbolism." This statement has licensed an abundant literature, some of it lightly disguised as critical analysis, which trawls

Tolkien's opus for Christian, or specifically Catholic, themes and symbols.[7] Yet, while Catholic belief formed the core of Tolkien's worldview from a very early age, it does not constitute the main message of Tolkien's masterpiece. We noted in chapter 3 that many versions of Christian doctrine were quite compatible with modernity, and that even the Catholic church was coming to terms with it by the time of Tolkien's birth, but Tolkien's was a peculiarly oppositional faith, its antipathy to modernity manifest in its symbiosis with his scholarly devotion to Old English and Middle English literature. One commentator has suggested that, while *The Lord of the Rings* contains Christian symbolism, its message is a syncretic celebration of community and nature.[8] If so, it is a trait that Tolkien's story shares with the others discussed here.

Often the prophetic voice cries for a return to ancient values, or what it figures as such. Finding enduring value in the past, Tolkien, Tolstoy and Thompson all assert the continuity of past and present against a modernity which they perceive as turning its back on the past, and they celebrate nature and community above all else. *The Lord of the Rings* is a paean to both and a lament for their destruction. Thompson summons William Blake to lament their loss. Treating the making of the working class as an episode in the age-old struggle of the Free-born Englishman, his history traces fraternity back to its source in community, while his fiction laments the progressive degradation of our ecosphere and foretells catastrophe. Tolkien and Thompson were

---

[7] *Letters*, 172. There are several books, and an abundance of articles, essays and online papers. Some examples are Joseph Pearce, *Tolkien: Man and Myth* (London: HarperCollins, 1998); Michael W. Maher, S.J., "A Land Without Stain: Medieval Images of Mary and Their Use in the Characterization of Galadriel," in *Tolkien the Medievalist*, ed. Jane Chance (London and New York: Routledge, 2003) 225-36; Matthew Dickerson and Jonathan Evans, *Ents, Elves, and Eriador: The Environmental Vision of J. R. R. Tolkien* (Lexington, KY: UP of Kentucky, 2006), and Theresa Freda Nicolay, *Tolkien and the Modernists: literary responses to the dark new days of the 20th century* (Jefferson, NC: Macfarland, 2014); Ralph C. Wood, "Tolkien and Postmodernism," in *Tolkien Among the Moderns*, ed. Ralph C. Wood (Notre Dame, IN: University of Notre Dame, 2015).

[8] Patrick Curry, *Defending Middle-Earth. Tolkien: Myth and Modernity* (Boston: Houghton Mifflin, 2004), 96-111.

reacting to the impact of industrialism and the ascendancy of the cash nexus. Tolstoy, writing in an era when his vast country had suffered little from the destructive effects of industrialization, detested what he saw of it,[9] but nature itself is not under threat in *War and Peace*. Whether as sky above, earth below, or ancient oak tree, it symbolizes an eternal order which is indifferent to human hopes and follies and largely unaffected by them. Tolstoy's alienation is directed against political innovations disruptive of the traditional rural social order, and he celebrates a small-scale, organic community similar to Tolkien's nostalgic ideal.

In each of these very different stories, the author's alienation is expressed in imagery or rhetoric that evokes the irreparable loss of primal happiness and innocence: the depiction of an Edenic haven, or allusions to a vanished golden age. Even in Tolkien's myth-drenched Middle-earth, it is the golden garden called Lothlórien that represents the farthest distance from the mundane reality of the "suburban" Shire. Its counterpart in *War and Peace* is Otradnoye and its environs, and in *The Sykaos Papers* the Zone of Eden and its walled garden. In a scholarly narrative, of course, an imagined evocation of the idyllic would be out of place, but *The Making* comes close by rescuing, from the oblivion to which they had been consigned by the enormous condescension of posterity, an insurgent people's recollections of a world of idealized labour and a political Garden of Eden where Englishmen walked free.

Since we are evermore sundered from Eden, its appearance in a tale of the night world or the everyday can imply a voyage through or out of time. This is true even of a fantasy, but one can be franker about such things when describing an imaginary world. Since *The Sykaos Papers* is already set in the future, Thompson can get where he wants merely by coining the ironic *double entendre* "Zone of Eden" and employing imagery that evokes the book of Genesis and *Paradise Lost*, dispensing with the need for time travel altogether. Tolkien, likewise, separates Lothlórien from the rest of Middle-earth simply by inserting the sensation of a time-shift into Frodo's thoughts as he sets foot in it. But in the realist mode, evocation of the Edenic demands more circumspection. Tolstoy contrived to insinuate a time-journey

---

[9] Wilson, *Tolstoy*, 334.

into *War and Peace* by disguising it as an expedition over land; by investing Andrei's visit to Otradnoye with an aura of enchantment, he set the story on the path to fairyland.

Perhaps, from a realist perspective, the safest course is to be found in Thompson's history, where Eden has already been lost and survives only in memory. But if Eden is already lost, leaving the myriads of eternity sealed in their work like a tomb,[10] what is it that makes *The Making* an epic of disaffection as distinct from a post-cataclysmic dystopia — that is, a depiction of the degraded state of mankind after some catastrophe? The comparison draws attention to two features of the epic of disaffection that are peculiarly expressive of what Tolkien called the epic temperament. One is its numinous effects, which constitute, if not the medium of prophecy, at least the tip of the prophetic iceberg. The other is the temporal positioning of the narrative within a metahistorical structure.

Locating the numinous in space and time

We have encountered the numinous as a verbal effect which exposes the reader to the unearthly, be it angelic, demonic, or simply uncanny. Like the prophecy that E. M. Forster discerned in it, it exists in the eye of the beholder. The poet Coleridge captured the relationship in a comment on the concept of the Sublime — the shape, or cluster of shapes, which the idea of the numinous took in his day. He wrote: "No object of Sense is sublime in itself; but only as far as I make it a symbol of some Idea."[11] This idea of the sublime is epitomized in Tolkien's account of perceiving a mote gleaming in light and recognizing it as a symbol of his own relationship to God as mediated by his personal guardian angel.[12] The gleaming mote becomes sublime when Tolkien identifies it with an idea that is already in his mind.

The numinous, then, is not something that is "out there," to be located in space or time. However, it is typically experienced as an effect external to oneself, prompting the subject to locate the numinous "out there". This externalizing of the numinous speaks to the sense of not being masters of our fate. The traditional notion of mankind as the creature of one or more gods, beings

---

[10] See above, 222.
[11] Quoted in Philip Shaw, *The Sublime* (London: Routledge, 2007), 95.
[12] See above, 75.

conceived anthropomorphically and thus as possessing abodes — perhaps on a mountain-top, or in some zone beyond human reach — is an idea that enfolds the world of everyday experience in something bigger and necessarily mysterious.

In evoking the numinous for a secular audience, however, it is vital to the suspension of disbelief that God does not leak into the narrative. Curiously enough, my three writers all found ways of ensuring this that reflect Forster's distinction between prophecy and fantasy, which assigns the former to the upper air and the latter to the lower air. Our four prophetic histories, the fictional ones in particular, show a distinct tendency to bring the celestial down to earth by transposing its manifestations from the upper to the lower air.

Even Tolkien is very sparing with hints of active divinity or with effects that tend to locate the numinous in the upper air, where the Christian deity was traditionally thought to reside. He was well aware of Forster's "small" gods, as we have seen; and although he acknowledged that the word "fairy" had long been consecrated to imbecility,[13] he himself was still inclined to take fairies seriously. In *The Lord of the Rings* they figure in two principal forms, both strongly attached to place. Tom Bombadil and Goldberry are one form: pure examples of the *numen*, local deities with no pretensions to divine majesty themselves and no evident connection to any higher power. The other form is the elves. Unlike Tom and Goldberry, and also unlike the elves of folklore on which Tolkien based them, Tolkien's elves stand in an undoubted, if mysterious, relationship to the higher deities that live beyond mortal ken, and their domains are not just touched with magic but are facsimiles of Eden. They cannot be angels, the Biblical deity's messengers to mankind, since that would completely discredit the narrative. However, they are the nearest thing to angels in Tolkien's story: quasi-autonomous intermediaries, whose aid is crucial to the triumph of righteousness if no guarantee of its triumph.[14] They proclaim a hope, not a promise, and even the hope is muted by the aura of melancholy that invests them.

Tolkien had to make his fantasy-world plausible to readers who lacked his belief in angels. Tolstoy took on the challenge of

---

[13] Tolkien, *Tree and Leaf*, 11-15.
[14] *Cf.* Friedman, "Fabricating History," 140.

infusing a world of mundane experience with a hint of transcendence. In *War and Peace*, intimations of the numinous take two main forms: the celestial visions of Andrei and Pierre, and the glamorous aura of the Rostov domain and its enchanted environs. George Steiner rightly disparaged the former for their flatness, and Tolstoy himself seems to have felt that something stronger was needed as a catalyst for the redemption of Andrei, not to mention the other symbolic purposes pertaining to the Rostov family. He found the answer in the magic of place; hence his transformation of the Rostov domain into an idyllic zone beset by fairies and of Uncle into a *numen*. Tolstoy takes care to keep his upper air unpopulated, and the two possible instances of heavenly manifestation in his story are both severely displaced. One is the angelic chorus that manifests itself inside Petya's head without being named as such and without the ghost of a message attached to it. The other is Platon Karatayev. I have called him, too, a *numen*, but conceivably he is something more: not the saviour of mankind, but Pierre's guardian angel or personal saviour. This might have become clear had Tolstoy written a sequel.

However, the numinous can abide in any intimation of existential terror or serenity: no inkling of divinity, either of the upper or the lower air, is needed to evoke it. Leaving the gods aside, it emerges in our sense of the contrast between the immensity of time and space and our own minuteness and mortality. In the case of Tolkien's elves, much of their numinous quality derives from a wisdom rooted in their knowledge of a past unknown to mortals — they are not quite messengers from the past, for the reasons I have stated, but they are visitors from it. Tom Bombadil is rooted in a corner of Middle-earth, but he too has knowledge of ancient things, being himself more ancient than most. And we have seen how, in *War and Peace*, Tolstoy imbues the Rostov domain with a timeless aura reminiscent of Tolkien's elf-havens.

So it is with Thompson, whose world-view was avowedly secular even if touched in subtle ways by his parents' somewhat threadbare Methodism. Thompson shares Tolstoy's handicap of a "real-world" setting even in *The Sykaos Papers*; but here his futuristic theme and science-fiction treatment give him some freedom from mundane reality, and his didactic purpose is highly conducive to the evocation of the numinous. His theme is the peril that human egoism poses to mankind and the planet, and so he sets up his story to emphasize the preciousness and fragility of what is in peril. The hero is a poet from a distant galaxy, whose unfamiliarity with Earth equips him to perceive both its beauty and its frailty with sharp urgency.

Like Tolkien's elves, Oi Paz gives voice to the vast cosmic context in both space and time, revealing both the transience of the human moment and the breath-taking beauty, complexity and fragility of the minute ecosphere within which that moment has transpired. In doing so he conjures up those vast outer spaces of Forsterian prophecy in which divinity might reside. But he also records in highly charged language his rapturous discovery and enjoyment of the planet at close quarters, thus evoking the intimate spaces that belong to Forster's lesser gods. And as to the role of "Gracious Goodnesses" in creating this miraculous beauty, he is never quite convinced by Sage's insistence that it is all due to chance — and why should Sage know better than he?

The Making of the English Working Class, as non-fiction, offers little scope for projection of the numinous in any shape; but in the context of academic discourse a little goes a long way. There is the strong sense of place that imbues the story, deriving from an apparently intimate knowledge of the lives lived in those places and from hints of dark doings on the moors at night. There is also the temporal grounding of an epochal event — the advent of the English working class as announced by Marx and Engels — not just in history but in the never-ending struggle of the Free-born Englishman, a struggle dating back in myth to Anglo-Saxon times and ultimately to the very Creation. Spatial and temporal elements combine most powerfully in the tale of the Luddites' doomed defence of their craft and way of life. A striking feature of Thompson's narratives is the way myths that are not of his own time and place operate to broaden the temporal context — the myths of the Free-born Englishman and a lost golden age in his academic history, the myths of Oitar in his imaginary history.

Positioning the narrative

In all four narratives, the imagery of Eden positions the action in time as well as space, implicitly setting it in a history of decline from a primeval state of innocence and bliss into one of suffering, death, and constant struggle between good and evil. In doing so, it imparts a numinous resonance without the explicit evocation of divinity. But does such imagery *necessarily* have that effect?

One might think that the vivid depiction of a bucolic refuge has numinous resonance almost by definition, but arguably it does have to be a refuge and — just as important — a station on a journey, a place to which there is no going back. There is no going back to Lothlórien, and the point is driven home by the story of the death of Arwen. There is also, I have suggested, no realistic prospect of a return to Otradnoye, however hard Nikolai may be striving for it at the end of *War and Peace*: even if he does buy it back, the magic will be gone or something awful will happen. And Sage learns by bitter experience that there is no going back to the walled garden. In all three fictional narratives, the refuge is under threat from encroaching evil even while we are there; and there is no going back, even if the narrative climaxes in the defeat of evil, because the very struggle has changed the world for the worse. Even in *The Making*, which contains the barest allusions to an Edenic past, that past is a world we have lost, and we are condemned to the endless slog towards a notional Paradise.

An instructive counter-case, in which Edenic imagery and mythic allusion do not achieve this effect, is presented by *Lady Chatterley's Lover*. D. H. Lawrence was only six years older than Tolkien, and his novel, like Tolkien's fiction, expresses revulsion at the condition of Britain between the wars. It is also set in virtually the same part of England as some of the key episodes of *The Making*, and as a result there is one point where all three works come together. And just as *War and Peace* and *The Lord of the Rings* feature climactic victories that prove to have a sting in the tail, so the cataclysm that defines Lawrence's novel is an event that culminated in what looked like victory to Lawrence's compatriots, although the Germanophile Lawrence never saw it as such: the First World War.

Lawrence is one of the four novelists whom Forster recognized as achieving prophetic expression, and we have stressed the importance of spatial representation in the evocation of the numinous, which Forster identifies as the essence of the prophetic effect. But in *Lady Chatterley's Lover*, which appeared the year after *Aspects of the Novel*, Lawrence treats space in a way that sabotages any hint of the numinous. Wragby Wood, the novel's Eden — or perhaps anti-Eden — is decked with spring flowers for Constance Chatterley's redemptive encounters with the gamekeeper Oliver Mellors. Sunlit bluebells make "sheets of bright blue color ... sheering off into lilac and purple," amid bracken that "lifted its brown curled heads, like legions of young snakes with a new secret to whisper to Eve." Lawrence glances back at deep time by mentioning a plant known locally as Robin Hood's Rhubarb and identifying the wood itself as a remnant of the great forest where the legendary hero hunted. He even nods towards Tolkien's beloved Anglo-Saxon heptarchy, describing a pheasant chick as "the most alive little spark of a creature in seven kingdoms at that moment."[15] But the great chords, as E. M. Forster called them, do not sound — instead there is the tolling of a bell.

Lawrence makes clear that the wood is no refuge. "He knew that the seclusion of the wood was illusory. The industrial noises broke the solitude, the sharp lights, though unseen, mocked it. A man could no longer be private and withdrawn. The world allows no hermits" (133). The problem is not just that the wood lies next to coal mines and a modern chemical works — after all, Otradnoye, Lothlórien and the Edenic grounds of Martagon Hall are also beset in different ways. In this case, however, the chemical works are not just adjacent to the wood but are visible from a clear-cut knoll within it.

> It was half past two. But even in its sleep it was an uneasy, cruel world, stirring with the noise of a train or some great lorry on the road, and flashing with some rosy lightning-flash from the furnaces. It was a world of iron and coal, the cruelty of iron and the smoke of coal, and the endless, endless greed that drove it all (161-62).

It is as though Frodo could see and smell Mordor from the crown of Cerin Amroth in Lothlórien; but this wood actually belongs to the Enemy in the person of Connie's husband, himself a colliery owner, who is on hand and acting his most Bad-Baronetish even as we eye the bluebells and bracken. Other annoying people also turn up there at inopportune moments. Even the "secret" clearing, with its hut where Connie and Mellors first make love, is not all that secret. When Connie mentions the hut to her

---

15 D. H. Lawrence, *Lady Chatterley's Lover*, 2nd ed., intr. Mark Schorer (Modern Library: New York, 1983), 208 (*bis*), 209, 46, 127. Subsequent citations in text.

husband, he seems to know all about it — and why not, since Mellors is his gamekeeper, the hut is his hut, and the clearing is the place where Mellors is raising pheasant chicks at his behest?

Like the wood he lives in, Connie's lover is too bound up in the world — that world which allows no hermits. Initially he appears to her in a faun-like aspect (73), which hints at the numinous, but he is not confined to the wood as Tom Bombadil is confined to the vicinity of the Old Forest and Uncle to the Rostov domain. As Sir Clifford Chatterley's servant, he is in regular contact with his employer — Connie even finds him in the latter's room on one occasion. He is burdened with an uncouth wife, from whom he is estranged but who lives nearby and knows the way to his cottage all too well, and he also has a mother and a daughter in the neighbourhood. And just as the wood figures in the narrative not as a way station on a quest but as a main scene of the action, Lawrence conclusively subverts any hint of numinal status by making Mellors a primary character and opening his mind to the reader. The end-result is that there is no differentiation between light world and night world, as there is with Lothlórien and the Rostov domain — no sense of Wragby Wood as a special place, sequestered from the outside world and accessible only by some special grace. This quality of Lawrence's novel corresponds to the positioning of the narrative in history.

The essential elements of the epic of disaffection, considered as history, are the over-arching conflict between the forces of good and evil, the climactic encounter of the opposing forces, and the coda that exposes the outcome of that encounter in a broader, and essentially tragic, perspective. The four narratives discussed in this book each underwent a transformation that culminated in such a structure. Fantasy imposes fewer constraints than strict realism, and in the case of the two imagined histories the structural transformation was simple enough in essence: a broadening of spatial and temporal perspective, and where necessary of character (as in the progressive "rounding" of Oi Paz). Both *War and Peace* and *The Making*, however, exhibit a more complicated process — one that combines conceptual expansion with chronological regression and contraction.

Tolstoy's initial idea of a novel with an essentially contemporary focus extended back in time until it became a grand historical chronicle covering half a century; then it contracted into a novel which covered just seven years at the very beginning of that expanded time-period. Finally, this novel, when largely complete, underwent a seismic change into a form that could express Tolstoy's vision of the human condition. That change included an epilogue which carried the narrative several years beyond its climax. With *The Making*, too, the original time-frame shrank and the chronological focus moved back in time as Thompson first insisted on pushing back the starting-point back some forty years and then produced a narrative covering just those four decades, turning what was to have been a book about the English working class into a book about its making. Since the focus on a historic crisis is a hallmark of the epic, it is significant that in both cases the chronological contraction re-focused the narrative on such a moment: in *War and Peace* the defeat of Napoleon, and in *The Making* the crystallization of working-class consciousness in response to the onslaught of laissez-faire capitalism.

The occurrence of this process of chronological contraction and re-positioning in two such dissimilar works affords a striking example of the epic temperament at work, and the outcome of the process illuminates the difference between the epic of disaffection and the post-cataclysmic dystopia. Both types of narrative tell of defeat, but in the former the narrative is positioned on the cusp of epochal change — a change that may even look like victory. In the latter, the change has already occurred — the second sentence of *Lady Chatterley's Lover* declares: "The cataclysm has happened, we are among the ruins." In hindsight, any sense of the war as a victory is entirely lost in its consequences; Clifford Chatterley's disabling wound has its counterpart in Wragby Wood, where the chemical works and the colliery railway are visible from the knoll because the knoll was clear-cut to aid the war effort. Clifford asserts that the wood is "the old England, the heart of it; and I intend to keep it intact," but the colliery hooters blare, Mordor-like, even as he speaks (47). In short, at the beginning of the novel the night world has already engulfed the light world. In this respect, despite its "happy" ending, it is more like *Nineteen Eighty-Four*, another tale of post-cataclysmic dystopia featuring redemptive sex in a secret glade.

If the narrative positioning of *The Making* on the cusp of change is determinative, it answers the question as to whether its imagery of a vanished and irretrievable golden age smacks of the post-cataclysmic dystopia rather than the epic of disaffection. The Edenic havens we visit in the other stories are no less doomed than the lost world of Thompson's artisans, and to that extent their serenity is an illusion, but in fiction it is possible to depict the lost or doomed haven through the eyes of the characters. In a scholarly treatise, there is no other way of evoking the Edenic than by reporting the beliefs of those men and women to whom, as memory, it was real. What matters is that, being remembered, it was a spur to collective action. It is no coincidence that the hero of Orwell's post-cataclysmic dystopia works in a government department dedicated to the destruction of the memories that make resistance possible. He himself has vague recollections of a past that was less horrible, but they are private memories, not the shared myth of a community; and when the prospect of collaborative resistance does arise, it turns out to be a delusion and a trap.

But *Lady Chatterley's Lover*, too, is about the destruction of collective memory. The domestic drama is set against an England blighted by industrialism and maimed by the Great War, an England in which "stately homes" are giving way to a "terrifying" and "gruesome" suburban mediocrity (177). The theme of incurable decline, personified by the war-crippled Clifford Chatterley, is omnipresent and occasionally strident:

> This is history. One England blots out another. The mines had made the halls wealthy. Now they were blotting them out, as they had already blotted out the cottages. The industrial England blots out the agricultural England. One meaning blots out another. The new England blots out the old England. And the continuity is not Organic, but mechanical (176-77).

Because Lawrence's novel is set in the same part of England as much of *The Making*, Robin Hood turns up as a cultural marker in both books, but with a difference of resonance which reflects the authors' opposed perspectives on their common topic. Thompson is concerned to emphasize the underlying continuity between past and present, as manifest in the enduring struggle of the Free-born Englishman. In *The Making*, therefore, the allusions to Robin Hood and the Anglo-Saxons belong to the culture that Thompson is bent on rescuing from the enormous condescension of posterity. Along with the memories of an irrecoverable golden age, they live in the minds of the people as symbols of resistance to the Norman Yoke and hence as an inspiration to action. In Lawrence's story, those allusions belong to the narratorial voice and are extrinsic to the action, the difference reflecting the fact that he sees not what he calls organic continuity but the blotting-out of the past.

These opposed perspectives come together in a striking conjunction of images and ideas that embraces Tolkien as well. In chapter 6, I suggested a symmetry between Tolkien's idea of orcs, created by the Enemy as an impious parody of elves, and the Luddites' condemnation of certain machinery and industrial practices as a de-humanizing mockery of their craft. In Lawrence's landscape the Luddites have vanished like Tolkien's elves, leaving only colliers of distinctly orc-like aspect,

> trailing from the pits, grey-black, distorted, one shoulder higher than the other, slurring their heavy ironshod boots. Underground grey faces, whites of eyes rolling, necks cringing from the pit roof, shoulders out of shape ... Something that men *should* have was bred and killed out of them ... [T]hey were "good". But even that was the goodness of their halfness. Supposing the dead in them ever rose up! But no, it was too terrible to think of (180).

Observing these proto-orcs from the shelter of her chauffeured car, Connie imagines them as:

> weird fauna of the coal-seams. Creatures of another reality, they were elementals, serving the elements of coal, as the metal-workers were elementals, serving the element of iron. Men not men, but animas of coal and iron and clay. Fauna of the elements, carbon, iron, silicon: elementals (180).

Lady Chatterley's Lover offers a bleak version of the end of a story of which *The Making* tells a version of the beginning. To that end, Lawrence adopts an aggressively mundane perspective and applies mythic imagery in a way that negates the numinous both in space and time.

Prophecy and history

In chapter 1, I noted E. M. W. Tillyard's statement that the epic poet "must express the feelings of a large group of people living in or near his own time" and "must seem to know everything."[16] Tillyard's words capture the connection between prophecy, as we have come to understand it, and the epic; but how does the

---

[16] See above, 16.

prophecy become imbued with epic resonance? My three writers were driven towards epic expression by the urge to prophesy the values of a lost, doomed, or threatened world, but in each case the epic strain entered because the prophecy was couched in a historical narrative. The historical impulse seems to express the feeling of being caught up in a course of events over which one had little, if any, control.

Tolkien felt this so strongly that he spent most of his life inventing an imaginary history originating with the Creation, but his distress finds its most dramatic expression in that epiphenomenal story of a journey in time — an account of ordinary folk swept away on a flood-tide of history — which gives *The Lord of the Rings* its initial impetus. In Tolstoy's account of ordinary (if aristocratic) folk swept away on a flood-tide of history, a similar distress assumes two quite different forms. One is the Rostov brothers' encounter with fairyland. The other is the didactic passages that burst through the surface of his fiction to deny that the course of human events is subject to human control, least of all by anyone who sets out to control it. As for Thompson, the activist who made it his mission to "defend history itself" against schematic approaches that obscured the reality and belittled the importance of actual human experience, even *The Making* projects the disillusion of battles lost. A quarter of a century later, *The Sykaos Papers* expresses the anguish of one who fears he has lost, not just one more political battle, but the battle for "history itself."[17]

Thompson's distress brings us back to David Quint's distinction between epics of the victorious, which celebrate the hero's triumph as predestined and the ascendancy of his illustrious progeny as the fulfilment of an immanent design, and epics of the defeated, which tend to ascribe the dénouement to historical contingency rather than predestination. Even the three stories that seem to climax in epochal victory employ narrative strategies that undercut the triumphal force of the victory, thereby imparting an aura of imminent, if not actual, defeat. The prolonging of the narrative in *The Lord of the Rings* reduces the conquest of Sauron to a moment in the "long defeat." A similar device in *War and Peace* leaves the survivors of 1812 heading towards new disaster. In *The Making*, Thompson muffles the triumphal Marx-

---

17 See above, 203, 253.

ist teleology implicit in the title by reducing the making of the working class to an episode in the Sisyphean struggle of the Free-Born Englishman.

The history for which Thompson fought was "history from below," and a recent historical essay on *War and Peace* calls Tolstoy "an early exponent of history from below" on account of his elevation of the common people and scorn for the Great Man as historical agents.[18] This is a surprising characterization of a nobleman who unabashedly chose to write about his own class because they were the only sort of people he understood, and his story certainly contains no hint of that painstaking unearthing of common lives and popular values which made *The Making* such a revolutionary work of historical scholarship. There is, nevertheless, a tincture of "history from below" in all the stories discussed here, arising from something all three writers have in common. For all of them, their feeling of powerlessness in the face of history was amplified by, if not rooted in, their personal experience of warfare.

We have seen how both *The Making* and *The Sykaos Papers* express Thompson's war experience: in this context, his description of his working-class protagonists as "the poor bloody infantry of the Industrial Revolution" is a stock phrase but a significant one. The heroism he celebrates, like the spirit of 1944, is not just individual but collective.[19] *The Lord of the Rings*, written by a man who endured the mud and blood of the Somme, gives us the horror of the Dead Marshes, with their battle-dead staring up from the bottom of brackish pools, but also the workaday courage of Sam Gamgee and the valour of the Rohirrim, both asserted in the face of probable defeat. In *War and Peace*, Tolstoy takes us inside the minds of individuals grappling with their personal demons, but the story comes closest to his war experience

---

[18] Dominic Lieven, "Tolstoy on War, Russia, and Empire," in *Tolstoy on War: Narrative Art and Historical Truth in "War and Peace"*, ed. Rick McPeak and Donna Tussing Orwin (Ithaca and London: Cornell UP, 2012), 18.

[19] Michael Merrill captures this aspect in his comment (quoting Thompson) that *The Making* recounts "a 'real historical process,' in which people struggle to improve and maintain their conditions of life, *as members of specific communities and cultures*, in the midst of changes they can affect but not control." Merrill, "E. P. Thompson's *Capital*: Political Economy in *The Making*," *Labour/Le Travail*, 71 (2013), 155; my italics.

in the two brief set-pieces, one involving Prince Andrei and the other Pierre, of artillerymen working cheerfully as a team in the face of death. All four stories, in their different ways, celebrate the heroism of doing your duty in the face of adversity — the heroism of *soldiering on*, of fighting the long defeat. It is a workmanlike heroism, which does not stand on its dignity.

In *The Making*, as we have seen, Thompson remarks of the "heroic age" of popular Radicalism in the early nineteenth century that its national leaders "rarely looked heroic and sometimes looked ridiculous."[20] But he also recognizes that heroism and looking ridiculous could go together, as in the case of the Jacobin leaders such as Thelwall, whose histrionic excesses he excuses as the equivalent of whistling in the dark. It is the hero who is unassuming, or unsung, or possibly a bit ridiculous, or perhaps all three, that represents the bottom-up perspective in the three fictional narratives. Sam Gamgee's development from a knockabout comedy type to "chief hero" of *The Lord of the Rings* is matched by the transformation of Oi Paz from satirical butt to tragic hero and by Nikolai Rostov's growth from the pistol-hurling novice of 1805 to the cool but disenchanted professional of 1812. But Tolstoy in particular also shows us that heroism can go hand-in-hand with appearing ridiculous, or that perhaps there is a fine line between the two. Captain Tushin imagines the French guns as giant tobacco pipes while puffing madly on his own. Prince Andrei's voice breaks into adolescent shrillness as he leads the charge at Austerlitz, and at Borodino he disdains to save himself at the cost of his dignity. Andrei symbolizes history from below, despite his noble rank, because he dies an unsung hero, having cast aside his callow dreams of glory to throw in his lot with a regiment of poor bloody infantry, and his observation of Tushin at Schoengrabern helps to set him on that path. A similar experience at Borodino does the same for Pierre, although his subsequent journey is only hinted at.

Our four stories are epics because they recount episodes of epochal struggle set in a broader total action (Northrop Frye's term), and they are epics of disaffection because they are redolent of defeat. Another crucial trait, which constitutes a further point of resemblance with Quint's epics of the defeated, is the characteristically romantic note of nostalgia. Extending his

---

[20] See above, 236.

study into the nineteenth century, Quint detects such a note, often attached to a narrative of heroic resistance culminating in defeat, in several of the national epics recovered, or freely concocted, from folk materials by folklorists of the period. In chapter 2 I noted the influence of these materials on Tolkien, whose heroic romance is steeped in such nostalgia; but finding it in the work of such an apparently anti-romantic writer as Tolstoy may seem more surprising — although less so, perhaps, now that we have seen that his repertoire of devices for undermining the triumphal teleology of the great victory includes a quest romance.

This affinity arises from the fact that each writer is contemplating the victory through the lens of subsequent defeat. The nineteenth-century folklore movement was influenced by the fabrications of the Scottish fabulist James Macpherson, which he published in the 1760s as the work of the pseudo-mythic folk poet Ossian. His chief work, *Fingal*, is bathed in the bitterness and shame of defeat even though it culminates in total victory, a paradox which Quint ascribes to the fact that Macpherson was writing under the inspiration of the Jacobite defeat of 1745 and the subsequent suppression of the Gaelic language and culture by the conqueror.[21] Similarly, Tolstoy views the victory of 1812 through the lens of the defeat in the Crimea and the accelerating Europeanization of Russia, and Tolkien views the triumph over Sauron through the lens of the long defeat. As for Thompson, whose world-view was shaped by his youthful exposure to the spirit of 1944 and the spectacle of its subsequent betrayal, the romanticism underlying *The Making* is made explicit in his later evocation of a "decade of heroes," when the historical importance of individual action had momentarily imbued Marxist discourse with something akin to Romanticism, which he defines as "the rebellion of spirit against the rules of fact."[22]

This nostalgia is crucial, because it distinguishes the epic of disaffection from post-cataclysmic dystopias such as *Lady Chatterley's Lover* and *Nineteen Eighty-Four*. It does so partly because of the temporal positioning it dictates. Tales of a dystopian world that has already undergone catastrophe can at best tell of private resistance to triumphant evil, as offered by Connie and Mellors

---

[21] Quint, *Epic and Empire*, 347, and generally 343-60.
[22] See above, 253.

in Lawrence's novel or Winston and Julia in Orwell's. The four narratives discussed here offer something else: a heroic story of collective resistance to evil insurgent but not yet triumphant.

Tolkien positioned himself to imagine such a story by forsaking contemporary England for an imaginary past — a position he took up when he began writing his legendarium. Thompson did so in *The Making* by commencing his study of working-class politics at the moment when the Free-born Englishman, already under assault by *laissez-faire* political economy, encounters the inspiring example of the French Revolution; indeed, to the extent that Thompson's history tells the beginning of the tale of which *Lady Chatterley's Lover* tells the end, we can indeed think of *The Lord of the Rings* as its fictional counterpart. Tolstoy, having set out to write a novel with a contemporary focus, found in the recent past a vantage-point from which to contemplate a world that was vanishing, if not quite lost. In *The Sykaos Papers*, an essentially contemporary setting achieves the same effect by positioning the artist to imagine a future cataclysm. In all four cases the epic imagination, bent on capturing the moment of cataclysm rather than contemplating it as a *fait accompli*, sets the narrative in the imagined space of the world on the brink of crisis.

INDEX

(Titles are abbreviated as follows: *The Lord of the Rings*: LR; *The Making of the English Working Class*: MEWC; *The Sykaos Papers*: SP; *War and Peace*: WP.)

www.ingramcontent.com/pod-product-compliance
Lightning Source LLC
Chambersburg PA
CBHW060902140726
47996CB00001B/81